DO-IT-YOURSELF MANUAL

Better Homes and Gardens®

DO-IT-YOURSELF MANUAL

Dennis M.Smith

CONTENTS

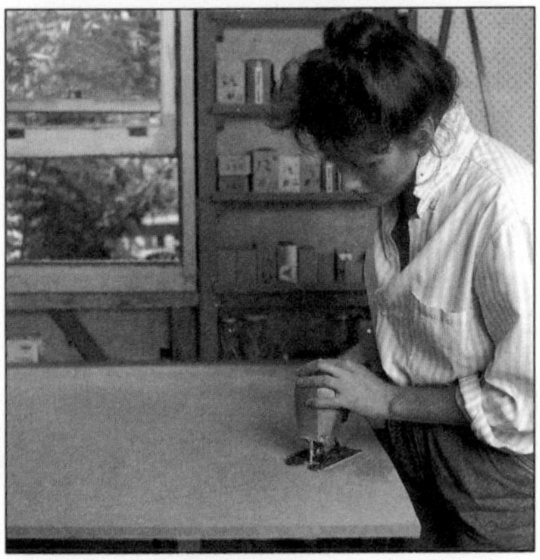

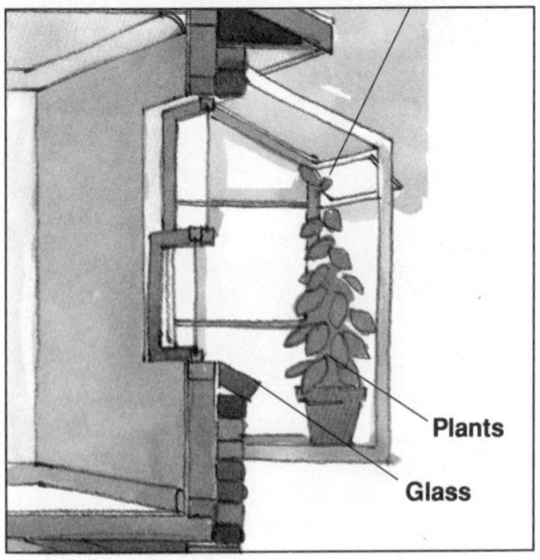

CONTENTS

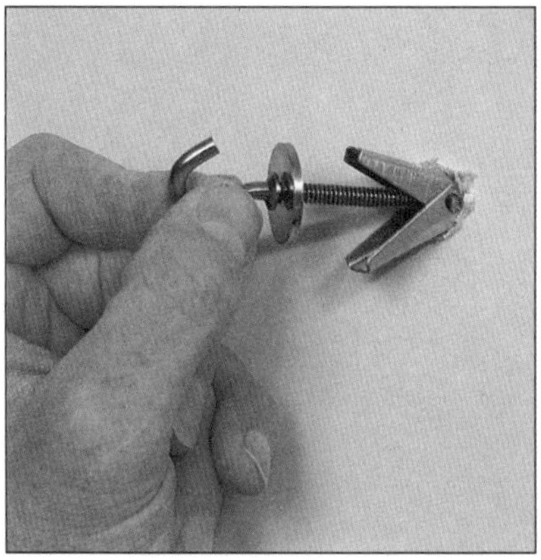

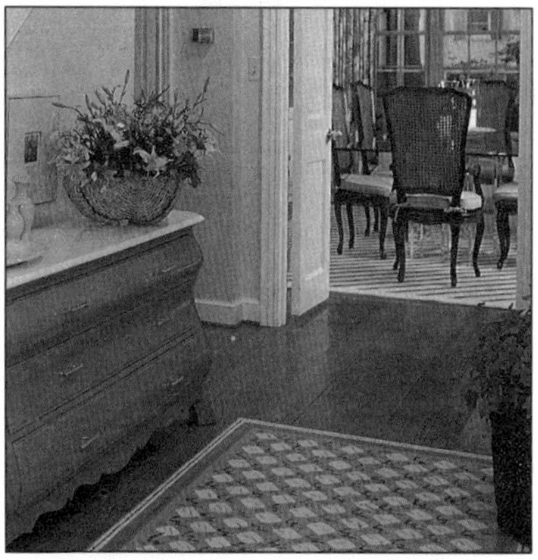

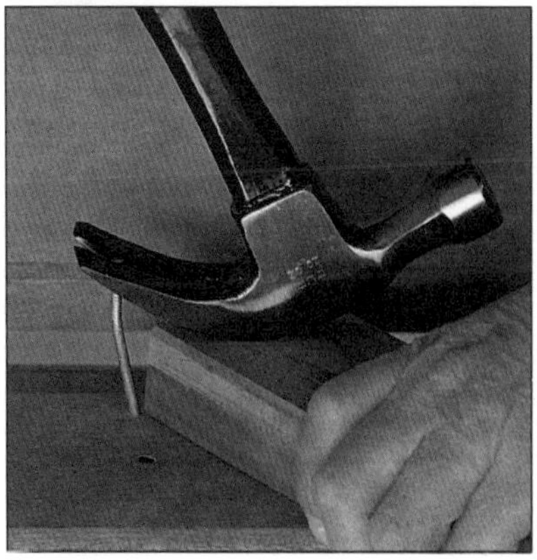

CONTENTS

INTRODUCTION

Have you ever wished you could put up a shelf, install a skylight or hang a door? Have you ever wished you didn't have to call a plumber every time the sink becomes blocked? Have you ever wished you could turn your backyard into a work of art? Well you can! Even if you have never attempted anything of this kind before, *The Essential Do-It-Yourself Manual* will enable you to carry out jobs like these with confidence. It is brimful of ideas for projects to enhance both your home and your garden, and it explains in clear language how to do simple household repairs.

For your first project, pick one of your good days when you're not tired or distracted and no friends are likely to call. Wear old clothes but don't be sloppy – loose clothing can be dangerous. Wear thin gloves if you are worried about your hands and put long hair up out of the way. If you are using electric tools make sure someone is around just in case something goes wrong, and always keep leads away from water.

Arrange the tools and all the materials required neatly in the work area. If there is going to be a mess, lay down some old sheets. Cover all surfaces that could be damaged by metal tools, etc. with an old blanket and remove all Ming vases! Read the instructions before you begin, several times if necessary, so you know the general procedures beforehand.

When you've finished, don't forget to tidy up and put your tools away neatly. Check you've cleaned off any excess glue or paint runs that might set and that there aren't any suspicious bits and pieces left on the bench (like a washer that should be in a tap). Then, stand back, admire your handiwork and go out and celebrate a job well done!

HOME IMPROVEMENT PROJECTS

CHAPTER 1

APPROACHING HOME IMPROVEMENT

Before undertaking anything in life, you should have a clear idea of what you want to achieve. It is one of the requirements for success. The following points, although brief, will assist you in considering the home improvements you propose to make from the correct perspective. If you ask yourself a few basic questions before you begin the tasks that need doing around your home, you'll save yourself a lot of time, expense and trouble.

Home improvement. What needs doing in your house?

Any physical change you make which adds value to your home or increases its amenities can be considered a home improvement. This can range from doing a minor task such as fixing a picture hook, to a decidedly major undertaking such as adding a second storey. A gradual progression (with plenty of intermediary stages for learning and the mastering of techniques) should typify your do-it-yourself ambitions.

Should there be a theme?

Yes, yes, yes! This important factor is too often overlooked by the home owner. When effecting any series of changes it is important to make sure they harmonise; otherwise, the result will probably resemble the house that Jack built.

The logic is simple. To be shown off to advantage, a new blouse or shirt should complement the other items you're wearing. If not, the result can be a curious mismatch at best; a disaster at worst. Similarly, you should have a definite idea of what you want to achieve with your home so that each new change you make adds to a co-ordinated, simple, overall theme.

Keep in mind commonsense parameters such as preserving the style of the home (unless you're very clever, don't mix traditional and contemporary architecture, for example), choosing materials that complement those used in the basic construction of your house and selecting harmonising colours.

Can you over-capitalise?

Again the answer is: yes! You must be very careful to relate the overall cost of home improvement to the value of the property, both present and expected. In other words, if it appears that you won't get your money back, don't go ahead. It's a

The positioning of windows plays a large part in controlling energy costs.

simple enough dictum. But, unfortunately, trying to establish what a property may be worth five or 10 years down the road is a haphazard undertaking even for the experts. Suburbs can be taken over by commercial interests, thus reducing residential values; interest rates change, greatly affecting supply and demand and, therefore, price; industries sometimes relocate or become outdated leaving an area to die; new airports, freeways and gaols may be built. Informed guessing is the best that anyone can do.

However, this dictum has to be matched against the potential usefulness and enjoyment that each improvement may bring. That is sometimes difficult to evaluate. For example, installing an expensive combustion fire may not add to the property's value (for some buyers it may actually detract from it), but who can put a monetary value on the happy, warm hours spent dreaming in front of the glowing coals? The same thinking applies to items such as pools and billiard rooms.

The best you can do is to work out the total cost of the improvement, and then try to assess the probable increase in the value of your home. With expensive improvements, if in doubt, ask a reliable real estate agent. If there is no probable increase in value, try to put a satisfaction value on the improvement and relate that to the cost.

Establish an overall plan

Smart people plan everything well so that success is assured. With home improvement, the same logic applies. Some items may have to be attended to immediately; others, fortunately, speak in softer voices.

Once you've settled properly into your home (experience a summer and winter first, if you can), draw up a list of all the minor improvements that you feel should be done. Next,

Garden furniture adds to the usefulness of a backyard.

mark the five or 10 most pressing ones and attend to them first. Once they're out of the way, plan the rest by arranging them in geographical or generic groupings.

The geographical approach necessitates doing all the kitchen improvements, for example, first. When the kitchen is complete, move to another room. Once the inside of the home is done, go outside.

The generic approach could involve using something like the headings in this book. For example, following a burglary, you may want to upgrade your home security. So, you should immediately install keyed window locks and dead bolts to the doors and, if you can afford it, follow that up with an alarm system, wall safes, and outside lighting that switches on if a sensor is activated. In other words, you do all the security items before moving to something else.

Either of these approaches will work but if a bit of overlap should happen, no-one but you will ever know, so don't worry.

Approaching the first job

The success of any job depends on several factors. Generally they fit into the following progression:

1. PLANNING

Before you do anything, sit down and do a bit of thinking about the proposed project. Inevitably, you will need tools, materials and equipment. The essential requirements for most of the jobs have been listed.

The materials include not only the purchase of the new item itself (or the things from which the item is to be made), but the necessary bits and pieces to fix it in position and finish it off. Make a list of all the materials and equipment that come to mind. Don't forget things such as paint thinners, glue, sandpaper, and similar small, but vital, articles.

The tools required depend on the job itself. If you don't have all of them, you may be able to borrow the missing ones. Sometimes a bit of improvisation may be required. Equipment includes things such as ladders, extension leads, stools, drop sheets, cleaning rags, brooms, dust shovels and brushes.

Additional information on tools and materials is provided in Chapter 11.

2. PREPARATION

Once the materials and tools are to hand, look at the job procedure carefully and try to imagine yourself doing each step. If something is unclear, it's essential that you seek advice before starting the job. Ask yourself whether or not the area should be cleared of furniture, shrubs, or some other obstacle. Very importantly, are there plumbing or electrical pipes or cables that have to be moved, avoided, or cut off? Remember that doing electrical or plumbing work without an licence is illegal. Will the project affect the structural strength of other components of your home? If so, check with a builder or your council inspector. Are there tools with which you are unfamiliar? Allow some time to practise in case you ruin expensive materials. Does cleaning or sanding need to be done to ensure good adhesion or paint quality?

Carry out all the preparation thoroughly beforehand, otherwise frustration can result on the day the project begins, or later when the finished project doesn't live up to your expectations.

Innovative lighting need not be expensive.

3. BEGINNING THE PROJECT

Choose a day when you're at peace with the world and there is little likelihood of interruption. Assemble the materials, items and equipment in neat clusters. Sharpen your pencil and begin to lay the job out. Proceed slowly if the job is totally unfamiliar, stopping frequently to check your work. If a problem develops, keep calm. Getting angry won't fix it. Sit down and try to figure out what is wrong. Have you left out a step or misread an instruction? If this doesn't overcome the problem, ring your local builder's hardware shop, a supplier, or a knowledgeable friend, and ask questions.

Open up your house with French doors.

4. FINISHING THE PROJECT

This may seem a strange heading but it's remarkable how many people get most of the way through a project, then leave it unfinished. The job is not finished until everything is done, including the painting, cleaning up, and the putting away of all the gear. If you don't finish as you go, you'll end up with a houseful of annoying, incomplete projects. Should you ever want to sell the property, it will cost you dearly.

With these few words of wisdom tucked away in the back of your mind, it's time to get started.

The direction in which a room faces will affect energy costs.

Decks are great places for entertaining and relaxing.

CHAPTER 2

SPACE CREATORS, IMPROVERS AND STORAGE

Space and storage are limited in nearly all homes. But, there are clever ways to make space, to improve on space usage, and to create storage areas. In the following chapter you'll be amazed at the diversity of ideas and projects that are presented. Study them carefully. You may find that they have to be modified slightly to suit your exact circumstances, but that shouldn't create any real problems other than altering the quantity of the materials you require and perhaps a few measurements.

BUILT-IN STORAGE

As the name implies, building-in involves the erection of a permanent cupboard structure, one that is usually hidden behind doors. Unlike a piece of furniture, this construction can't be moved because it becomes part of the fabric of the room. When you are designing such a unit there are a few things to keep in mind:

1. List the important items you want to store (television, books, stereo, clothes, for instance). Measure each item or group of items and apportion a section of the built-in unit to it. Draw the unit to scale to make sure everything will fit. A scale of 1:10 is ideal. Any leftover space can be used for shelving (open or enclosed) and storage of little-used items, or kept free for those things you'll acquire sooner or later.
2. If possible, extend the unit from floor to ceiling. This minimises its obtrusiveness and does away with the dust-collecting platform on the top of traditional wardrobes.
3. To make sure the unit blends with its surroundings, try to design it so that skirtings, picture rails and cornices extend across it.
4. If mantelpieces and windows are involved, make part of your unit line up with them so that it appears to become an integral part of them.
5. If you want to minimise its visual impact, completely enclose the unit with doors and paint the built-in the same colours as the walls and trims.
6. If moisture is present, you must use materials that will not be affected by it.

The photographs featured here show two built-ins. The first is of a cupboard recessed to allow for the door opening. The second shows a window incorporated into the unit. Both involve a combination of open and enclosed shelves and doors.

The successful integration of the storage unit with the window creates the impression that the built-in is part of the wall.

Building-in principles

Because every house is different, it's impossible to give anything other than general advice on the building of each of the major components of a built-in cupboard.

The base platform

As the diagrams overleaf show, the base of the cupboard is usually formed upon 100 mm or 75 x 25 mm dressed timbers fixed on edge. Then, shelving made from ply or particle board (either plain or melamine-covered) is fixed to them. It can project past the front edge to form a kickboard (see Diagram 2) or it can be made flush and the skirting run flush along it (see Diagram 1).

The carcass

The cupboard can be made in a number of ways. Diagram 1 shows the cupboard comprising particle board shelves and dividers. The top extension and hanging space shelf is supported by 50 x 25 mm battens which are nailed or plugged to the wall. Use edged particle board if possible for the best finish.

By making a step in the cupboard, the space behind the door can be utilised while still creating hanging space.

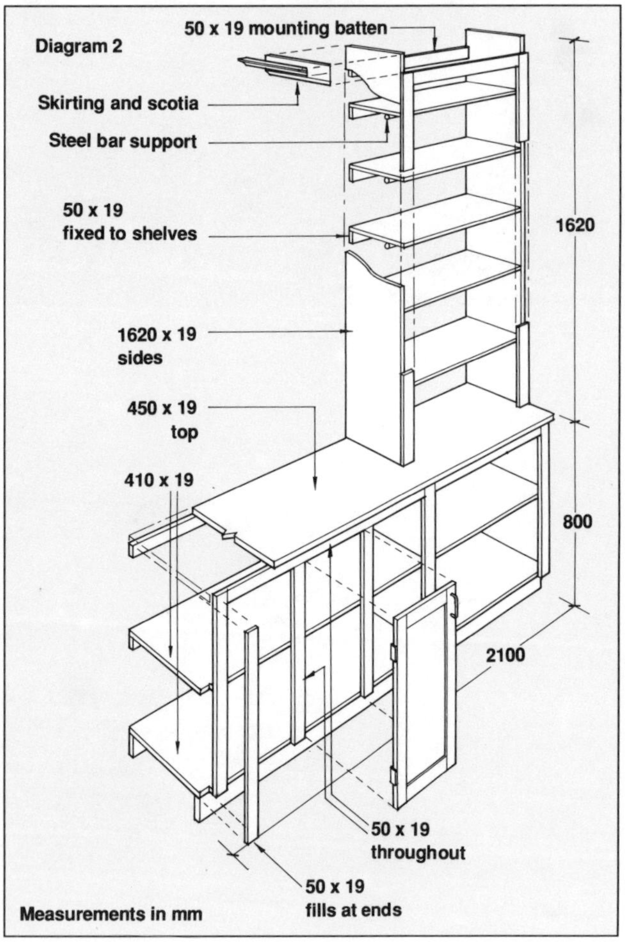

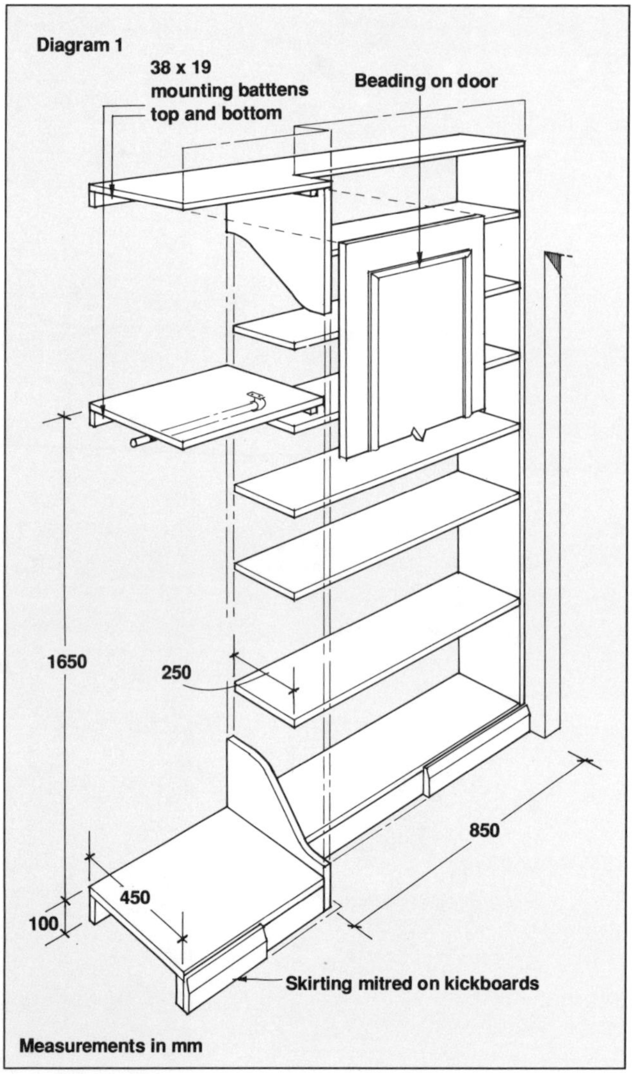

The doors

As Diagram 1 shows, the left-hand side of the cupboard is covered by the doors, so the unit ideally should be designed with standard door sizes in mind. Diagram 2 shows the front of the cupboard faced with 50 x 25 mm DAR (dressed all round) battens. In both cases, stock-size doors are used for the enclosed sections. Full-size doors require butt hinges. Smaller doors can be hung on concealed hinges.

TOOLS

Circular saw; square; tape; pencil; spirit level; screwdrivers; hammer; nail punch; plane; sandpaper and cork block; electric drill and drill set; chisel.

OPEN SHELVING

A unit of open shelves can look attractive in a kitchen and provides a fantastic amount of storage space. The only obvious drawback is that, being open, it tends to attract dust and other air-carried pollution often found in kitchens.

This unit has a narrow bottom shelf so that use of the bench and sink is not restricted in any way. This small shelf is great for cups and similar items. The curved shaping which bridges the gap between the first narrow and second wider shelf is achieved by means of a sabre saw. Stick-on edging will give it a neat finish. The vertical structural divisions are made not more that 800 mm apart so that the adjustable shelves will support the surprisingly heavy weight of crockery and other paraphernalia. Nail and glue the joints together, spacing the 50 mm spiral nails at 100 mm centres.

The mounting battens (second and top shelves) should be made full-length so that they will support the weight. To do this you'll need to recess them into the vertical members (see diagram, right). The best way to build these open shelves is to make them up as a complete unit on the kitchen floor. Purchase a piece of 50 x 25 mm batten and use it as a rod to mark the distance between the walls less 5 mm. Then you will be sure that the unit will fit.

When lifting the unit to mark the fastening positions, you'll need to commandeer a couple of friends into giving you assistance. If they're unavailable, you must build a temporary support off the top of the lower cupboards. When fixing to the wall, ensure that the screw fasteners bite into the stud (or plug) at least 50 mm and are spaced no further apart than 450 mm.

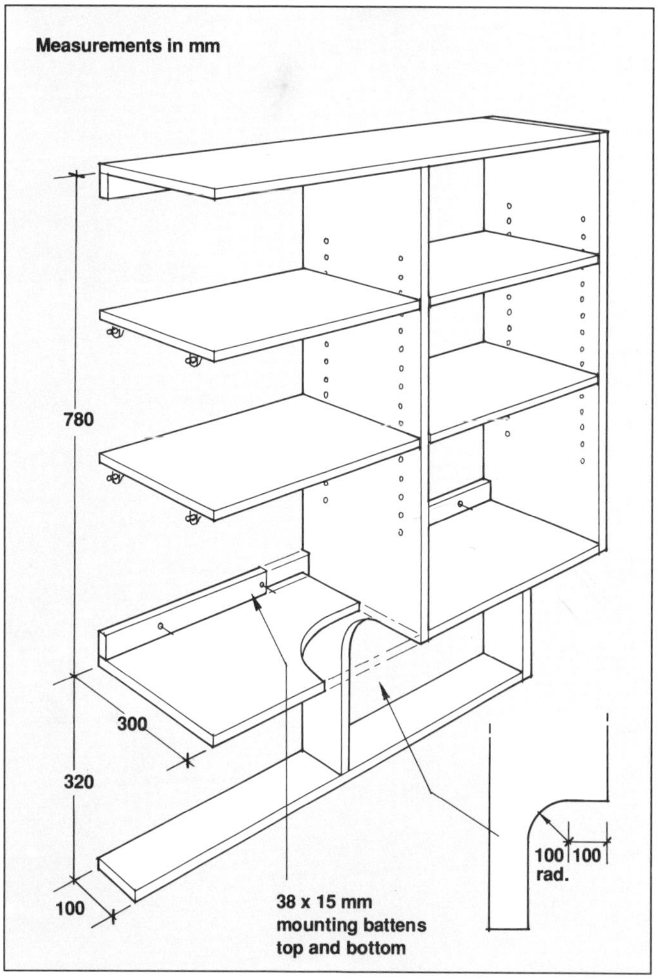

This cleverly designed set of open shelves makes full use of a blank wall behind the kitchen sink. The shelf positions have been carefully considered in order to cater for items of different size.

A BATHROOM BUILT-IN

Here is a smaller version of a built-in, but one that still employs the basic principles previously discussed. The bottom of the cupboard lines up with the basin while the top can align with the tiling line or the top of the architrave, or be as high as the adult users can reach. The diagram shows that the doors are swung on spring-loaded concealed hinges; holes must be bored in the back in this instance. The bottom is left open for knick-knacks, a hairdryer, shaver and so forth. The whole unit can be put together in the garage, then fixed to the bathroom wall through the mounting battens which are fitted under the second and top shelf. The back of this unit is covered with thin, white, moisture-resistant, melamine-faced sheeting (although it could be omitted as the wall is painted) while the carcass and shelving can be made from similarly faced 16 mm thick particle board. This eliminates the necessity for painting. The shelf spacing and number of shelves will be determined by the height and quantity of the items you wish to store. When making this unit, ensure it is square. **Note:** When plugging the wall for the screws or nailing, always take care that you don't hit the water pipes or electrical wires.

This neat unit, which incorporates both concealed and open shelving, will solve bathroom storage problems.

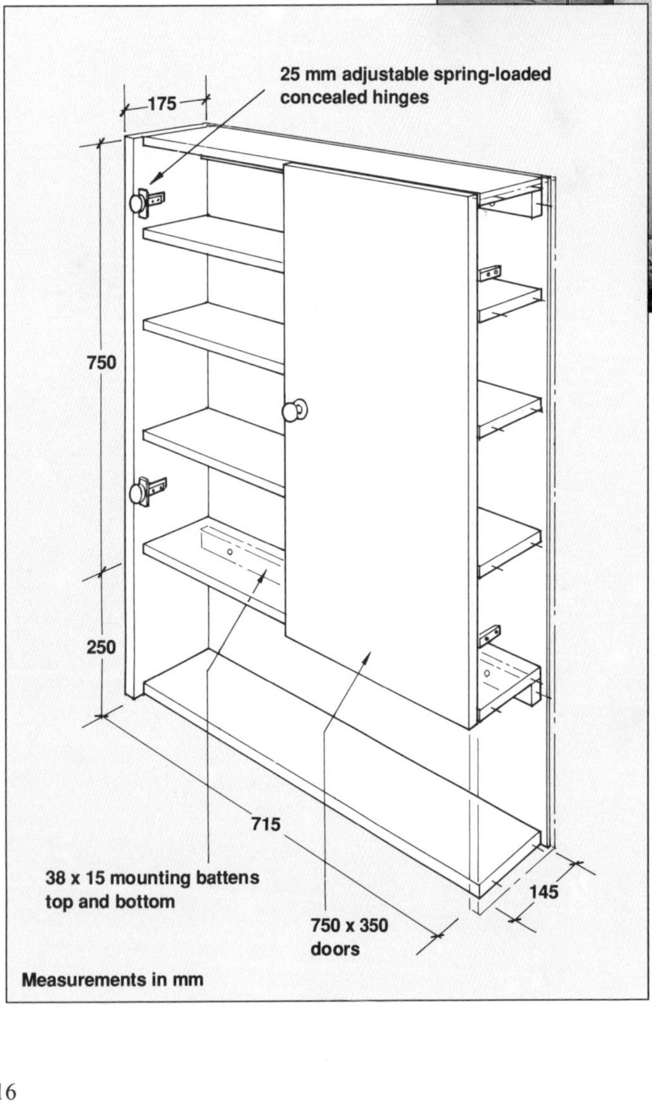

A BATHROOM SHELF UNIT

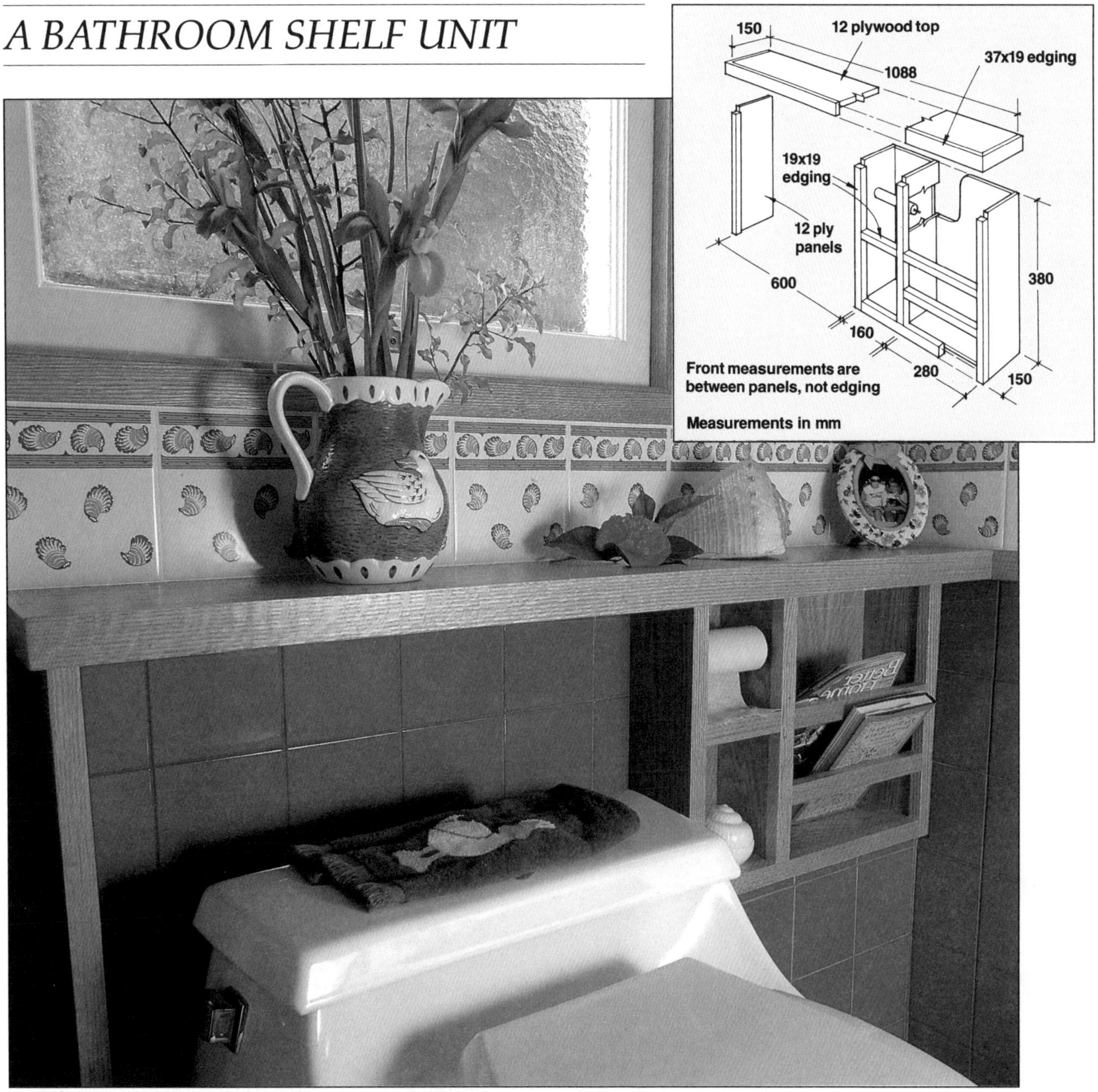

No room? Don't overlook the space above the cistern for installing a handy shelf.

In a bathroom, the available space in this typically small area is often irregular. This calls for a bit of creative thinking.

One solution is a unit made from a sheet of 12 mm thick plywood (solid timber could be used as an alternative). Use a three-ply or tempered hardboard backing. The unit is faced on the top with 50 x 25 mm batten (finished size 37 x 19 mm) and with 25 x 25 mm batten (19 x 19 mm finished size) elsewhere. Plywood should be of a moisture-resistant type or it could delaminate in the steamy environment. The vertical on the right-hand side could be deleted if preferred.

The unit incorporates a magazine rack and a toilet-roll holder but, if the toilet is not the place where you indulge your literary interests, this could be modified to provide more towel and toiletry storage.

The unit is nailed and glued together and fixed to the wall by screws and plugs (once again, watch out for the plumbing and wiring). The unit shown is finished in clear polyurethane, and its edging is of Tasmanian oak.

It could also look most attractive if made with different materials such as melamine-covered, moisture-resistant particle board with stained or painted timber edging.

BATHROOM BENCH

Do you wish you had a bench you could sit on while you dry your feet or put your socks on? Here's a simple solution which could be fitted into a bathroom as well as a cabana or swimming-pool change room. It's ideal when space is at a premium.

This bench consists of nothing more than two angle brackets fixed to the wall, and a slatted seat which is fixed to the top. Simply enlarge the dimensions if you have sufficient room. The timber should be oregon or Tasmanian oak. Both are strong and ideal for withstanding the moisture that builds up in bathrooms.

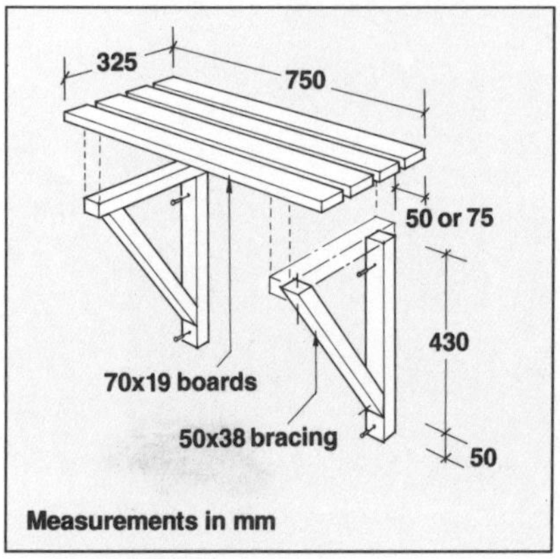

The basic bench can be enlivened with a colourful cushion made from easy to launder towelling material.

PROCEDURE

1 On a scrap piece of ply or particle board, draw the shape of the brackets full-size. Using the diagram, mark out the pieces and cut them to length. Be especially careful when cutting the bracing ends. If they are slightly out, it's important to plane them carefully with a sharp plane.

2 Once the parts are fitted, chamfer the visible ends with the plane and smooth them with sandpaper and a block. Fix them together, again using the drawing to make sure they are square. Epoxy glue and fine 75 mm nails will do the job efficiently. If you are using PVA glue, two 60 mm screws in each joint are a safer bet than nails.

3 Drawing a level line along the wall, fix the two brackets to it making sure they are vertical. If the wall is masonry, use two expanding masonry bolts. If it is a timber-studded framed wall, use 100 mm coach screws. In either case, do take care, once again, that you don't hit any plumbing or wiring.

4 Once the brackets are secure, fix the slats, using 38 mm countersunk screws. Before you do, chamfer all the edges to minimise splinters. After a quick sanding of the exposed surfaces, all that's required is an application of clear or opaque paint.

A SUNKEN SHELF UNIT

If shelf units projecting into your bathroom (or laundry) are not to your taste and the bathroom walls are timber frame, you may be able to sink a unit into them – a neat little one that projects only a few millimetres from the wall surface. Of course, if there were a cupboard behind the wall, you could steal a little of this space and make the shelves even wider to accommodate a few bulkier items.

The spacing between the studs and their dimensions restricts the width of the unit but, if the studs are 100 x 50 mm and spaced at 450 mm centres, you should end up with about 360 mm of clear space. Studs in modern houses are now often spaced at 600 mm centres and studs 100 x 38 mm are frequently used, giving even greater shelf length.

PROCEDURE

1 Using a fine nail and hammer, locate the edges of both studs. Mark this down the wall with a level. Then, establish the height of the unit. Keep in mind that a nogging may run across between the studs. This can again be located with the nail. It can either be used for the base of the unit or removed.

2 Once the space is marked out, cut the gypsum plaster away with an old saw, watching out for electrical wiring. The unit, made from 150 mm (make it 200 mm wide for towels) x 25 mm timber, Customwood or melamine-covered particle board, can be constructed with either fixed or adjustable shelves. It should be 5 mm smaller all around than the opening width to allow for levelling up. Use tempered and primed hardboard for the backing, although the back of the gypsum plaster on the other side of the of the wall could also be used.

3 Install the unit using timber packing for adjusting; nail into the studs on either side. A quad around the unit would hide the joint between it and the gyprock. Alternatively, it could be filled (as shown) although this is not ideal as, inevitably, it will crack. Once the unit is complete, give the paint a few days to cure before storing belongings. If steam is present, watch out for cans with bottoms that rust.

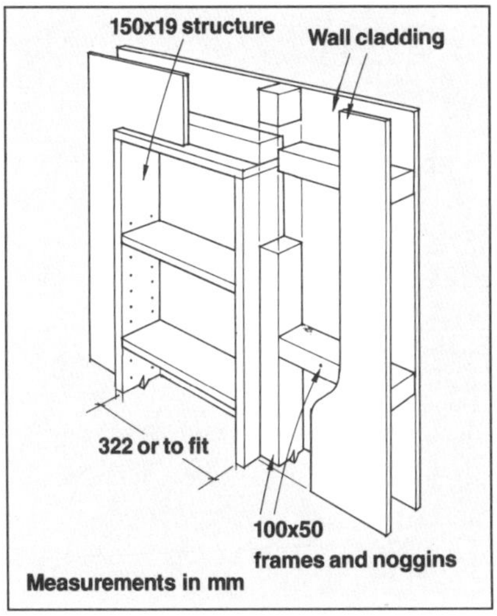

Vary the depth of shelving in this unit. 150 mm is ideal for bottles, while you'll need at least 200 mm to accommodate towels.

A TOWEL RAIL

A very good way to make a kitchen (or bathroom) door more useful, is to install a towel rail on the back of it. You will find that most internal doors are hollow, preventing you from screwing things properly to their thin facing. So, the method of fixing requires a bit of ingenuity. The answer is the hollow wall anchor or the spring toggle. These devices are natty little fellows which you poke through a hole in the door. When they are tightened, part of them folds back securely against the back of the door facing. This results in immense holding power.

MATERIALS
Purchase suitable brackets and a rail. You can use heavy chrome brackets like the one shown here plus a chrome rail, or a lighter, prefabricated type that comes in one unit and is suitable for tea-towels. You also need to purchase toggles or anchors to suit the brackets.

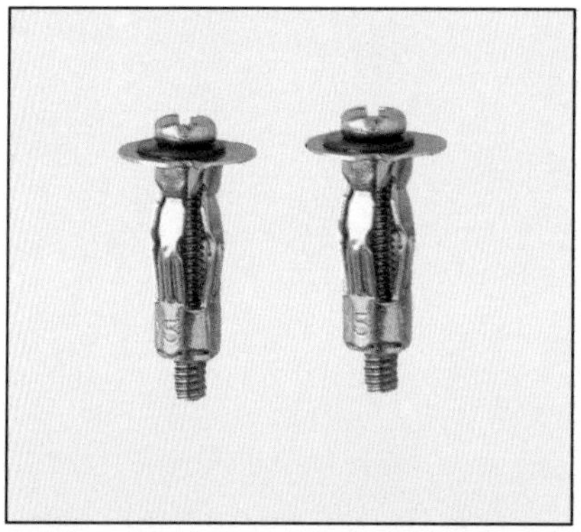

Hollow Wall Anchor. These work on the principle that as the screw is tightened, the body collapses and forms a backing which rests against the back of the door facing. The tighter you screw, the firmer it gets.

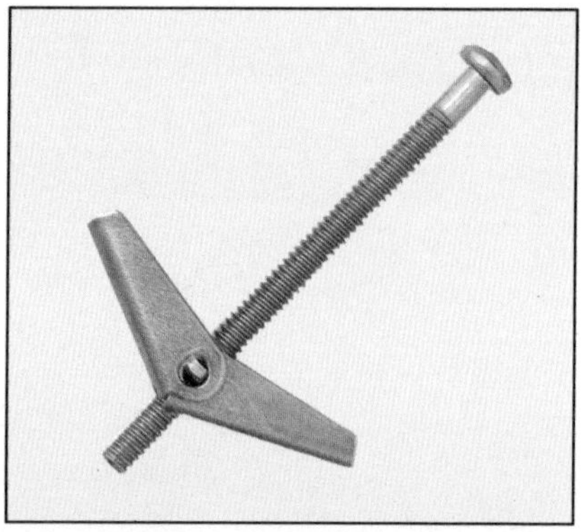

Spring Toggle. The arms are either spring activated or rely on gravity. Once the fastening is inserted in the opening, the toggles spring or fall open and, as the screw is tightened, they grip the back of the material.

TOOLS
Hand or power drill; level; drill bit to suit fastener; tape and pencil; screwdriver (the correct size is important, see step e); a fine nail punch or a 50 mm nail; a hammer.

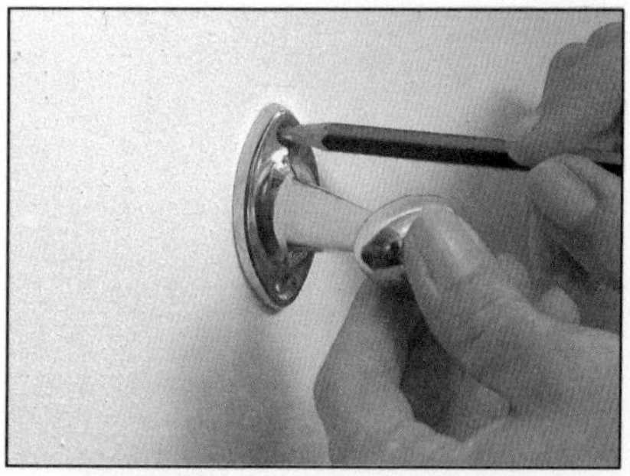

a. *Check the size of the towels and cut the rail to suit. Position brackets at a convenient height and mark the position of the holes.*

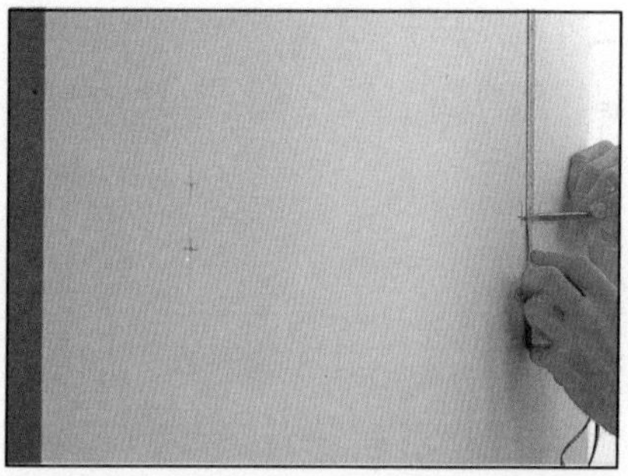

b. *Make sure you come in the same distance from both edges of the door. Check that the brackets won't hit anything when the door is opened.*

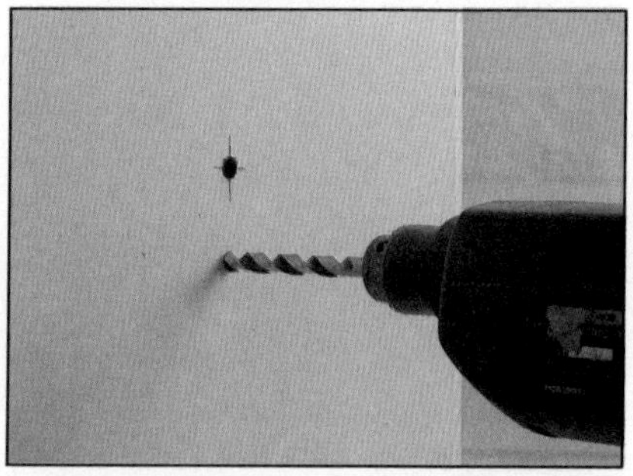

c. *Drill the holes to a size that allows the toggle or anchor to pass through. Take care that you don't go through to the other side.*

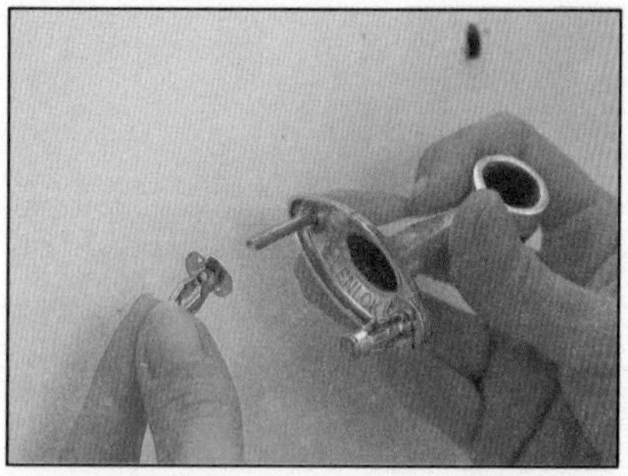

d. *You must now remove the fastener screws and push them through the bracket. Then, screw them back into the fasteners.*

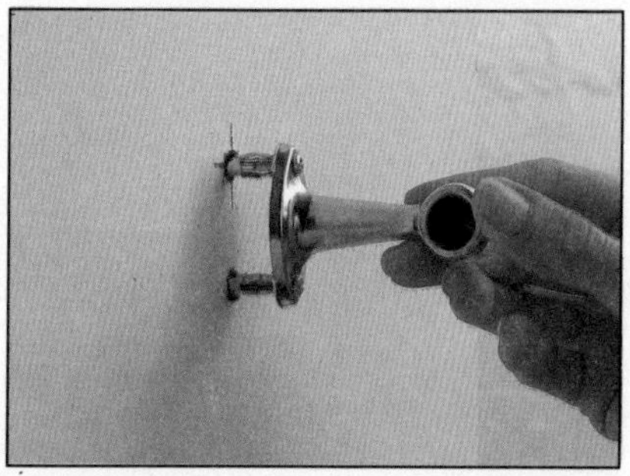

e. *Push the fasteners into the holes, then tighten the screws. It is important to select the correct size of screwdriver for the job.*

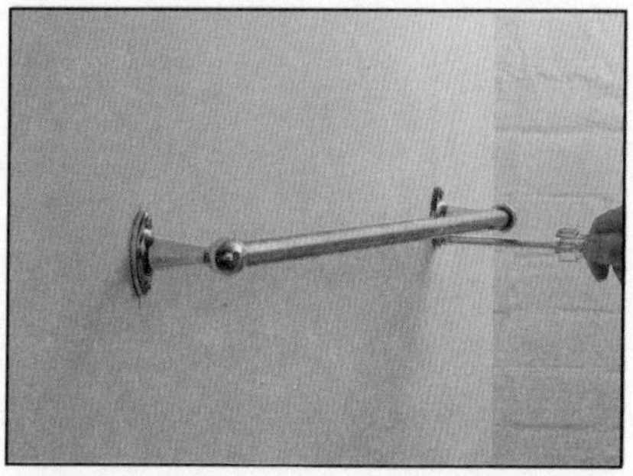

f. *Once one bracket is tight, push the towel rail into place, put the bracket on the other end and repeat the instructions in step d.*

BEHIND-THE-DOOR STORAGE

Apart from the convenience of creating more storage space, making a unit such as this forces you to be tidy, and helps you find what you want.

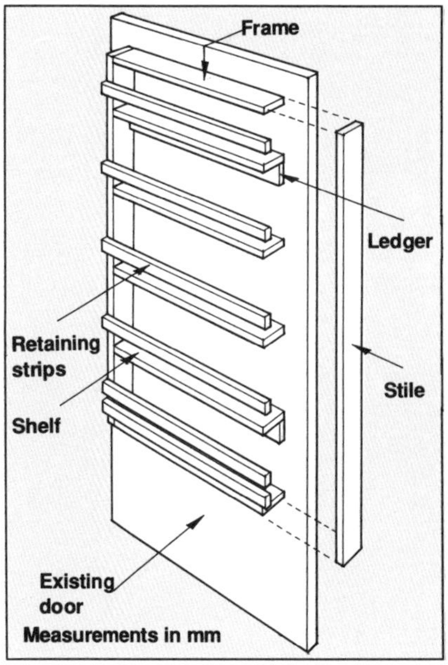

Kitchens are places where storage, no matter how plentiful, never seems to be enough. But more storage space does lurk, frequently unused, in a pantry or a broom cupboard, behind an entry door or in many other convenient, out-of-the-way spots.

Here, a shelf unit 90 x 19 mm (finished size) comprising frame, shelves and ledgers with 42 x 12 mm retaining strips, is fixed easily and unobtrusively behind a pantry door. The size of the unit and the spacing of the shelves can be modified to suit your particular needs. Keep in mind that you could use 142 x 19 mm material for greater storage if there is sufficient room.

PROCEDURE

1 Cut the shelves, ledgers and stiles to length and sand each of them thoroughly. Then nail and glue them together. Check carefully that the unit is square by measuring the diagonals. Bore two holes in the centre of the ledgers; come in 50 mm from either end.

2 Sand the unit and finish it in your favourite colour. To hang the unit on a solid door, you need four 50 mm countersunk wood screws. Position the unit and use a nail punch to mark the hole positions. Pre-drill the holes and screw the unit to the door.

If the door is hollow core (which is most likely) use spring or gravity toggles. To install these, bore a hole in both the ledger and door to the recommended diameter. Take the metal screw out of the toggle, push it through the ledger, and refix it to the body of the toggle. Position the unit and push the body of the toggle into the holes in the door. Then, simply tighten the metal screw. The wings on the back of the toggle will tighten against the back of the door facing, suspending the unit solidly and permanently.

Now fill the shelves with those essential items and forget about your storage problems. Cover the shelves with plastic sheeting. This will help stop paintwork being damaged.

KITCHEN SHELF UNIT

Here's a handsome storage unit that would enhance any kitchen. If you intend to paint it, use medium-density fibre board (Craftwood) or meranti. If staining it, match the timber in the kitchen, if any, or use radiata pine, Tasmanian oak or whatever seems most appropriate in your setting.

The diagrams show the set-out. This may need to be adjusted to suit special items you wish to feature.

MATERIALS LIST			
Item	**Materials in mm**	**Length in mm**	**No.**
Sides	160 x 12	763	2
Backboard	160 x 12	450	1
Bottom shelves	160 x 12	450	2
Second shelf	135 x 12	450	1
Top shelf	110 x 12	450	1
Bottom shelf front	42 x 12	450	1

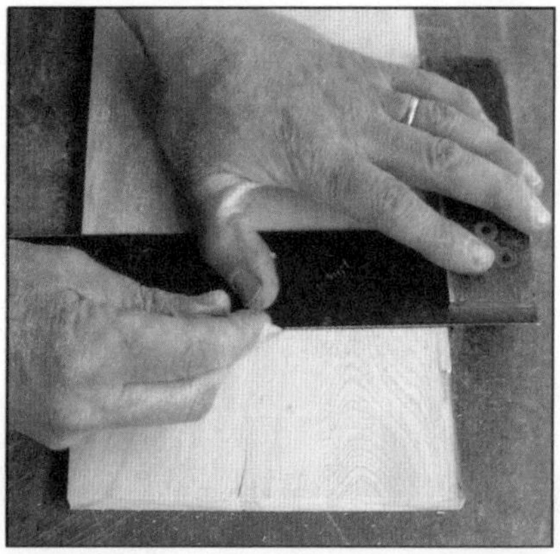

a. Mark out all the pieces and cut them to the sizes indicated. Use a sharp pencil and make sure the square is held tight against the edge.

The Materials List indicates the timber sizes which can be cut from a 12 mm thick sheet 800 x 800 mm. You'll need 25 mm brads and 25 mm countersunk screws. Why not make a feature of the screws by using brass roundhead screws? The glue can be PVA if you are intending to paint. If staining or applying a clear finish, use epoxy glue.

TOOLS

Jigsaw; panel saw; hammer; square; nail punch; tape and pencil; plane; fine rasp; sandpaper and cork block; screwdriver.

PROCEDURE

1 Mark out all the pieces and cut them to the sizes indicated. See how the backboard and bottom shelf front shapes are arrived at by using a 20 mm grid section which is drawn on the timber. Pick off the intersections and draw the curves using a French curve or flexible straight-edge (which you can get from a draughting supply store). Cut out the curved sections with the jigsaw, smooth them off with the rasp, then finish off with sandpaper wrapped around a dowel. Any straight edges can be finished off with a plane. When sanding or planing, if you put similarly sized pieces

b. Clamping the piece to the edge of your bench, carefully cut out the shape with the jigsaw keeping a little clear of the line to allow for sanding.

c. Pre-drilling the screw holes and countersinking them will make assembly of the unit easy. Allow plenty of material for the thread to bite into.

d. After screwing the unit together, allow the glue to dry and then fill the screw holes with a suitable filler. After it cures, sand smooth.

together this will ensure that they end up the same size.

2 Mark the shelf positions on the insides of the two sides and check they are opposite one another. Tack the unit together to make sure everything fits and then pre-drill the screw holes. If countersunk screws are being used, the heads should be sunk below the surface so they can be filled.

3 After nailing and gluing the backboard and bottom shelf front to the respective shelves, apply the glue and, with the shelves standing vertically, nail or screw them on one side. Carefully turn the unit over and, after gluing, secure the other side of the shelves.

At this stage you should check the unit quickly for square by measuring the diagonals as shown in the diagram. If it is square, they should be the same. If they're not, you will have to pull the unit until they are.

4 Wipe off all excess glue and allow time to dry. A quick sandpaper (with the grain) will remove any raised fibres or other matter. Apply the desired finish and fix the unit to the wall using two holes in the backboard in the position shown. If you like the idea of a continental touch, use some attractive stencilled motifs.

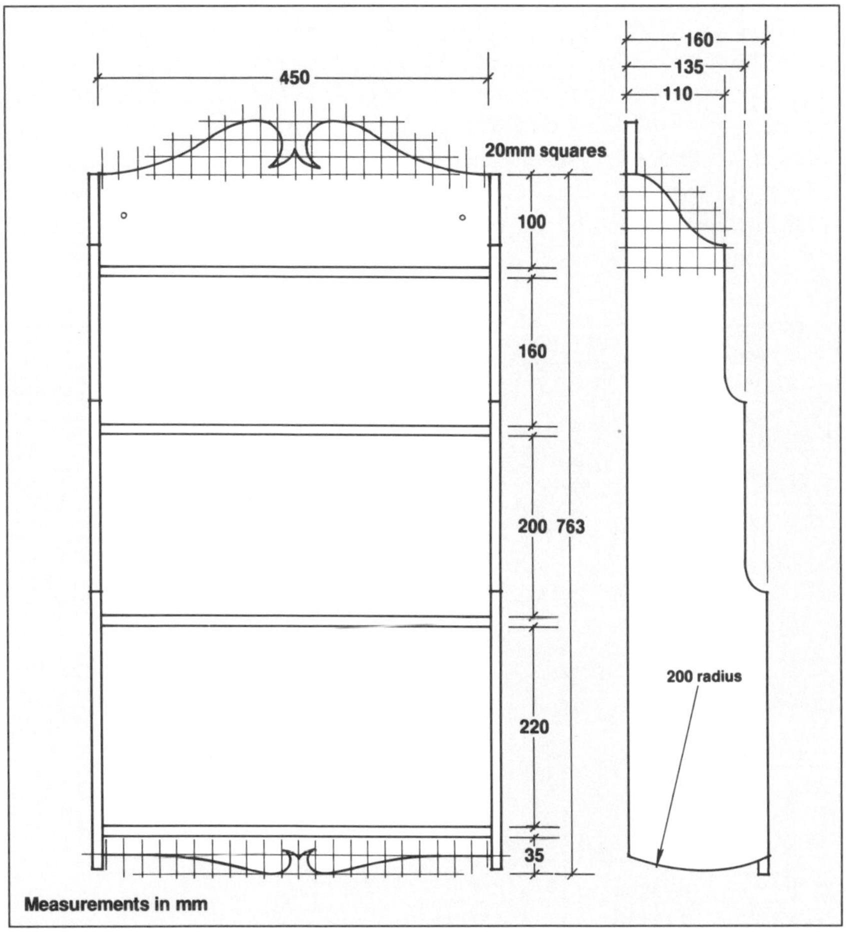

PRACTICAL POINTER

To stop sandpaper cracking while you are working with it, pull it diagonally across the edge of a table or some other sharp corner, first in one direction, then in the opposite. This simple action breaks up the glue on the paper, making it more flexible and much easier for working.

WALL-HUNG DISH RACK

For a drying and storage facility in one, this wall-hung dish rack provides the answer. The drying aspect dispenses with the need for a tea-towel or the expense of the electricity-gobbling drying cycle in your dishwasher. The rack relies on there being a sink directly underneath it, one with a wide shelf behind the bowls so that the draining water is caught.

The unit illustrated utilises hollow stainless-steel rods but, depending on the style of your kitchen, wooden dowels may appeal to you more. (Unfortunately, they are not as durable.) Painted Tasmanian oak has been used to keep the timber members to a relatively small dimension, but polyurethaned radiata pine would be equally suitable providing it were made a little bigger (for instance, 50 mm wide). Although expensive, teak would be the ultimate choice as it could be left in its natural state.

TOOLS

Electric drills and drill set; hacksaw; tape and pencil; square; dowelling jig; gauge; tenon saw; chisel; hammer; nail punch; sandpaper and cork block.

PROCEDURE

1 Draw out, full-size, the shape of the two angled ends. The front joints used are half-lap joints; that is, half is cut out of one piece and half out of the other. Success with making this joint relies on accurate marking out and careful sawing and chiselling. The rear joints are let in (they could be half-lapped, too).

MATERIALS LIST

Item	Materials in mm	Length in mm	No.
End frame front	32 x 19 Tasmanian oak	322	2
End frame back	32 x 19 Tasmanian oak	830	2
End diagonal	32 x 19 Tasmanian oak	425	4
Front rail	32 x 19 Tasmanian oak	1200	3
Back rail	32 x 32 Tasmanian oak	1200	3
Back spacer	32 x 19 Tasmanian oak	1200	3
Top side rail	32 x 19 Tasmanian oak	175	2
Middle side rail	32 x 19 Tasmanian oak	145	2
Bottom side rail	32 x 19 Tasmanian oak	105	2
Top rod	13 timber or steel	200	28
Middle rod	13 timber or steel	170	28
Bottom rod	13 timber or steel	130	28
Back rod	13 timber or steel	750	28
Top capping	32 x 19 Tasmanian oak	1200	1

Other: 100 mm expanding bolts; 35 and 50 mm countersunk screws; wood filler; nails for pinning.

a. *When assembling the frames, be careful to lay them on a flat surface to ensure they're not twisted. Clean off excess glue with a rag. Don't get epoxy glue on your skin.*

b. *When drilling, wrap several layers of masking tape around the drill to establish the depth. Make sure you clear the drill bit periodically, otherwise it could clog.*

2 Lay the timbers on the drawing, mark off the lengths and angles, gauge the depths, then carefully cut them. Once you've fitted the joints, nail and glue or nail and screw them. Use epoxy glue because it is water-resistant. Fastenings should be galvanised or brass.

3 While the glue is drying, begin to make the three shelves. Cut the three front and three back rails to length, then the side rails. Lay the front and back rails opposite each other. Label them top, middle, and so on, and mark out for the 28 dowel holes. This will make sure they are

Hardwood such as Tasmanian oak is suitable for the framework because it has the strength necessary to support the weight of the china without being too bulky.

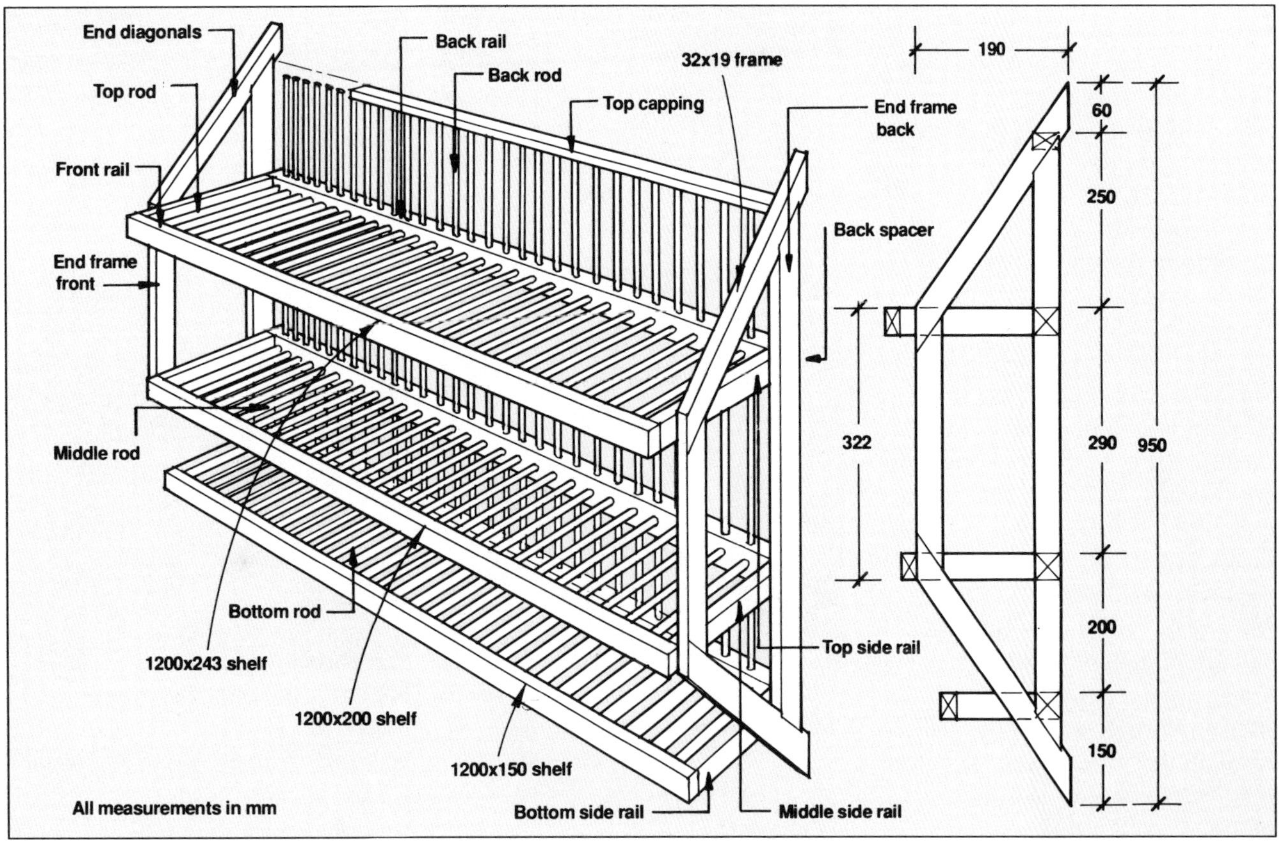

in pairs and the holes are exactly opposite one another.

Keep in mind that if there are 28 dowels there must be 29 spaces. So, if you find the centre of the front rail and go either side half a spacing, this will give you the first two dowel positions. To mark the rest of them it's a good idea to use a compass or pair of dividers to step them off because, when marking a lot of small measurements, it's all too easy to creep a little on each one and then find yourself in trouble.

4 Using a dowelling jig, bore the holes to a depth of 10 mm. Again using epoxy glue, nail and glue the shelves together with the rods (or dowels) in place. Work from one end to facilitate lining the holes up (see photo d).

5 Drill the holes for the back rods in each shelf, making them opposite the horizontal rods. As the diagram shows, the holes pass right through the back rail of the top and middle shelf and are sunk 10 mm into the bottom shelf and the capping piece. Lay the three shelves and the capping piece together and mark the centre points of the holes to ensure they line up. If you don't you'll discover putting the rack together can become a nightmare.

6 Tap and glue the rods into the bottom shelf (photo g), push on the middle and top shelves and finish with the capping piece which is again glued on. Screw and glue the two end frames into position. Fix the three spacers to each of the three shelf backs to throw the unit out from the wall. This will allow the plates and dishes to fit perfectly in the divisions.

7 Fix the unit to the wall by nailing into studs or use expanding bolts; two to the back rail of each shelf and two diagonally through the tops of the end frames. Paint the unit with gloss enamel or leave it natural, if you prefer.

c. *Once the holes are drilled, nail the shelf frames together. When nailing near the end of the timber, pre-drill nail holes or the timber may split.*

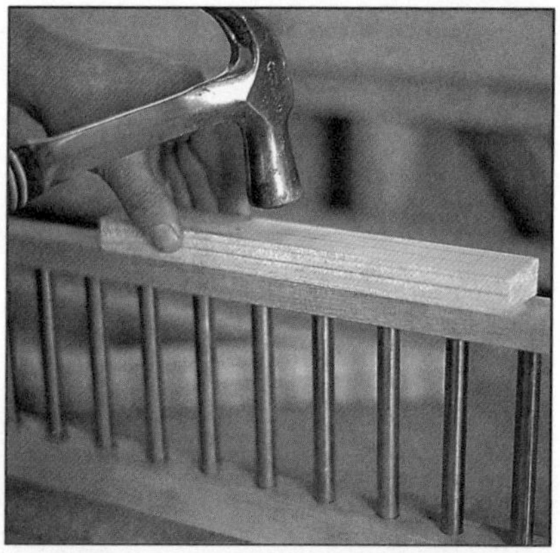

d. *When assembling the shelves, you must line up the rods or dowels with the holes before hammering them together. If not, the rail may split.*

e. *Drilling and pinning the rods to the rails is an alternative to epoxy gluing them and may appeal to the purist. In the case of stainless steel rods, you'll need to use a very sharp drill.*

f. *The spacers, which fit behind the back rails, can be either screwed or glued and nailed. Instead of making them full-length, try using blocks, one at each end and one in the middle.*

g. *Once you've put epoxy glue in each hole and driven the back rods into the bottom shelf, get a friend to help you with threading the other two shelves over the rods.*

h. *Once the end frames are fixed, secure the finished rack to the wall but watch out for the plumbing and wiring or the money you've saved could be lost in an instant.*

KITCHEN SHELVES

Do you have some wasted space between two top cupboards or between a top cupboard and a corner? Why not put up some shelves? A great effect can be achieved for little cost.

Materials for shelving may be solid timber, glass, plywood, timber veneered or plastic-laminate-covered particle board, among other things. Each product comes in a variety of widths, thicknesses and lengths. Standard lengths start from 600 mm and generally go up to 3600 mm in 300 mm increments. Common widths are 150, 200, 250, 300, 450 and 600 mm.

The width and thickness you require have to relate to the size and weight of objects which the shelf has to carry and the spacing of the supports. Be realistic about the probable loading; it is best always to err on the side of safety.

Support systems

There are many types and designs. Basically, they involve installing battens, brackets or track systems. This project involves putting up three short shelves between some top cupboards using 25 x 25 mm battens. If you are extending from a cupboard into a corner, replace the 25 x 25 mm battens with 50 x 25 mm ones at the wall end and use screws and plugs (for brickwork) or toggle bolts (for hollow walls) as fastenings.

Check for those little unused nooks where shelves could be constructed.

MATERIALS

Purchase shelving to suit the opening size (as a general rule, the longer the shelf, the thicker it must be) and sufficient 25 x 25 mm dressed softwood batten (or quad) to go across both ends of each shelf. Radiata pine shelving has been used here; when stained it will provide a pleasing contrast to the painted cupboards on either side. Use 38 mm nails and sandpaper (use epoxy glue as well if the shelves are to carry a particularly heavy load).

TOOLS

Saw; hammer; square; nail punch; cork block; measuring tape and pencil.

PROCEDURE

1 Clearly mark the position of the top and bottom of each shelf on both ends of the cupboards. Square these lines across the cupboard ends.

2 Cut enough pieces of the square batten to fit neatly across the end of each shelf. Make a large chamfer (a 45° angle) on one edge and across two corners of one end using the sandpaper and cork block. Alternatively, make a bevel on one edge and one end (for this you must have a plane). Either way will lessen the squared effect and create a professional finish.

3 After sandpapering each piece smooth (pay attention to the visible end), fix them to the cupboards using 38 mm nails at 75 mm centres. Keep the battens for the bottom shelf level with the top line, and the middle and upper one level with the bottom line. Don't nail any closer to the ends than 50 mm and flatten the points on the nails so that you lessen the chance of the timber splitting. Punch the nail heads.

4 Measure the length of each shelf on the back and front (the cupboards may not be parallel or square to the wall) and cut them to length making sure each one will be a tight fit. After sanding them smooth and taking the sharp corners off, skew nail into position; punch the heads.

5 Finish the shelves with acrylic or polyurethane paint. When dry, load them up with all those items that once cluttered the bench tops.

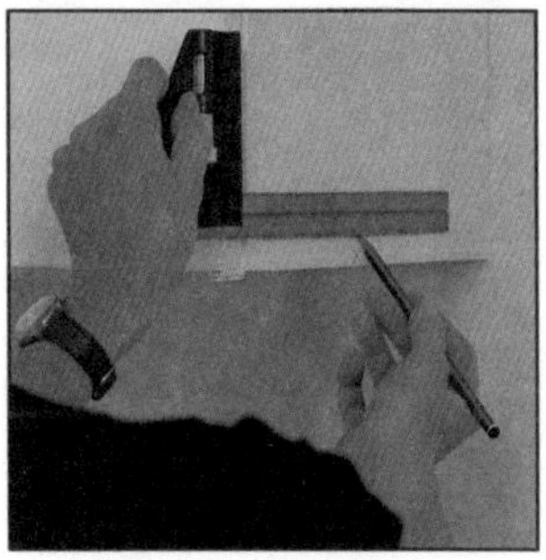

***a.** Clearly mark position of the bottom of each shelf.*

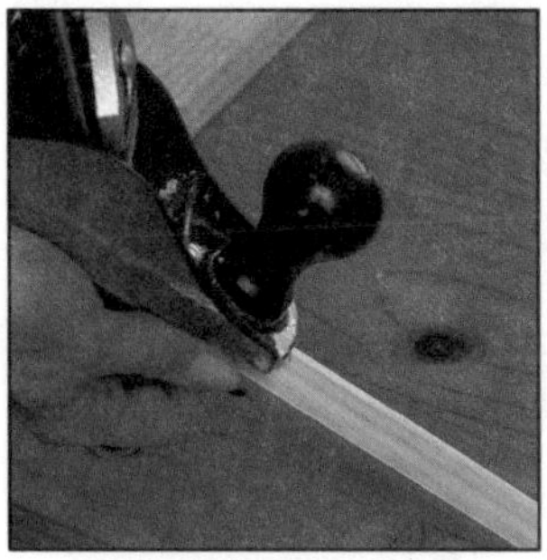

***b.** A bevelled edge looks most professional.*

***c.** Fit battens from inside if cupboard material is thin.*

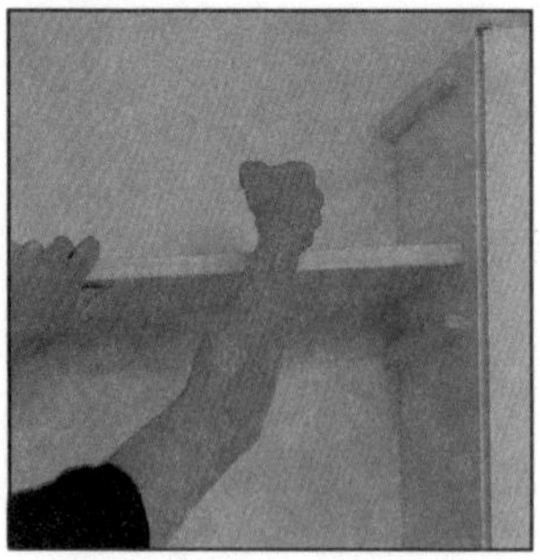

***d.** Shelves must be cut so that they are a tight fit.*

CIRCULAR DINING TABLE

The round table of the Court of King Arthur became a symbol of egalitarianism and convenience, the latter virtue being much appreciated today. Everyone is equidistant from the person sitting opposite them and close enough to those sitting next to them for ease of conversation.

The table featured here has a diameter of 1200 mm because this suits a standard sheet size. The legs are of metal and can generally be bought from furniture stores.

MATERIALS

Sheet of 16 mm thick particle board (or Customwood) 2400 x 1200 mm; a 3000 x 1300 mm piece of plastic laminate; PVA glue; contact glue; two dozen 25 mm countersunk particle board screws; legs; fastenings.

TOOLS

Tape and pencil; screwdriver; electric drill and drills; jigsaw; belt sander; laminate trimmer and cutter; sandpaper and cork block; hammer.
Note: If you've never used a laminate trimmer, it would pay you to make a small cutting board out of scraps of particle board and laminate. Set the trimmer up and try it out on this before you attack the table!

If space is limited and you like to entertain, this circular table could be the answer because it will comfortably accommodate up to nine people.

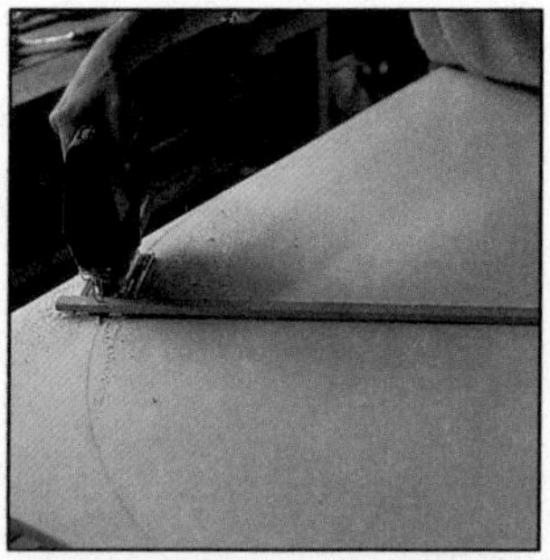

a. The space beneath the fibre board must be clear or you will break the blade.

f. Ensure that you get the laminate correctly lined up before removing spacers.

PROCEDURE

1 Cut the particle board sheet in halves to make it more manageable. Set out the two circles; use a scrap piece of timber with a nail in one end and a pencil at the other as a compass. Cut the circles out freehand or, as (a) shows, screw the batten to the base of the jigsaw and, after boring a hole to get the blade started, let it follow the line for you.

2 Lay the two sheets together and, working from underneath, pre-drill the screws (see photo b).

3 Apply a liberal coat of PVA glue, screw the two sheets together and allow glue to dry (photo c).

4 The edges can be sanded (photo d) but only if can hold the sander exactly square to the face. It's better to fix the sander on its side to a bench, then feed the top against it.

5 Lay the top on the laminate. Clamping it in position, mark around the shape of the top with the pencil. Make sure you leave sufficient along one edge to cut out the edge strips. Score deeply 5 mm clear of the line and carefully snap off the waste. Using a straight-edge, cut the edge strips, making them 2 mm wider than the top plus one thickness of laminate.

6 Carefully vacuum both surfaces, apply the contact glue to them (very liberally to the particle board), and allow to touch dry (photo e).

7 Lay several strips of timber on the table top, place the top in position and slide the battens out. Work from the middle out to avoid air pockets and press the laminate down as you proceed. Go over it, tapping with a smooth timber block and hammer to ensure it is stuck.

8 After you have checked it for adjustment on a scrap piece of timber, use the laminate trimmer to trim around the edge (photo g).

9 Repeat the gluing operation and secure the edge strips, keeping them flush with the bottom. Get someone to help you line these up, because, if you position them incorrectly, you'll have the devil's own job getting them off again (photo h).

10 Make the edge strip flush with the top using the bevelled cutter on the laminate trimmer. This is probably the most critical part of the operation because, if the trimmer is not set exactly as it should be, it could eat into your table top.

Once the top is finished, mark and fit the table legs. One way to find their positions is to draw a line across the bottom of the table top through its centre. Draw a line at right angles to this line, making sure it also passes through the centre. If you come in 150 mm, that should give you suitable leg positions.

Your brilliant new table will seat up to nine (average-sized) people. Bear in mind that, because the top is made up in two pieces, it could be made larger to suit any room.

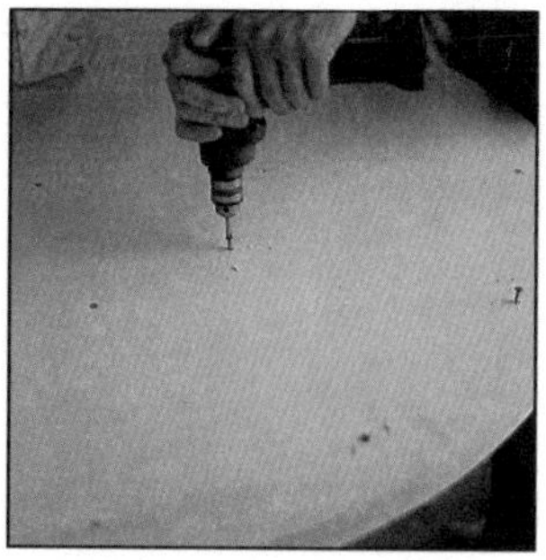

***b.** When screwing, always pre-drill the holes to ensure the screws go in easily.*

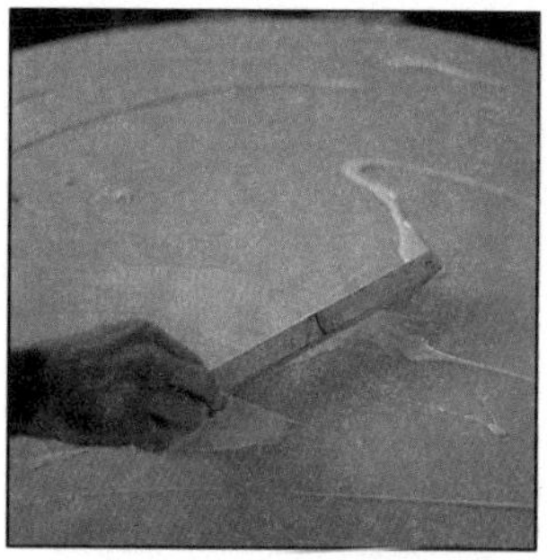

***c.** Spreading the glue with a scrap piece of timber ensures an even glue joint.*

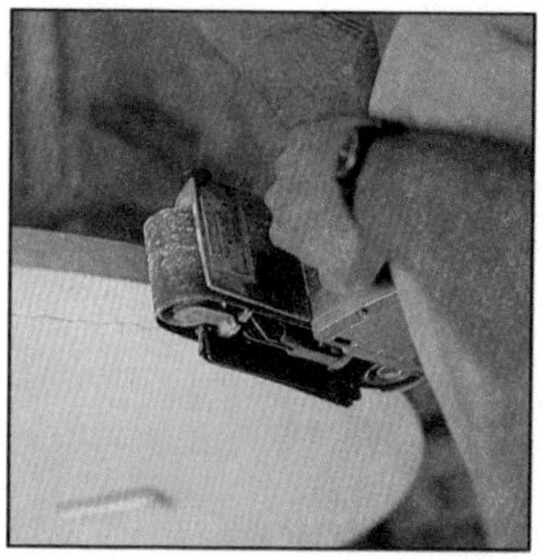

***d.** When using power tools such as this, check clothing cannot get caught in them.*

***e.** You may have to apply two coats of glue to the porous particle board.*

***g.** Make sure all the adjustments on the router are tight before beginning.*

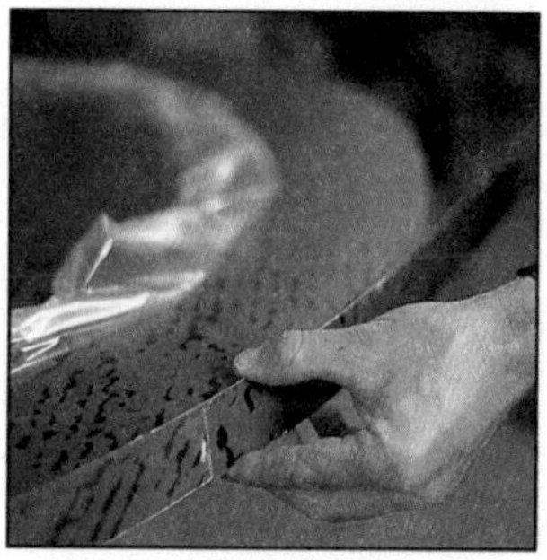

***h.** The edge strips should be 1.5 mm wider than the table to allow for trimming.*

***i.** Wear safety goggles when trimming excess to avoid getting an eyeful.*

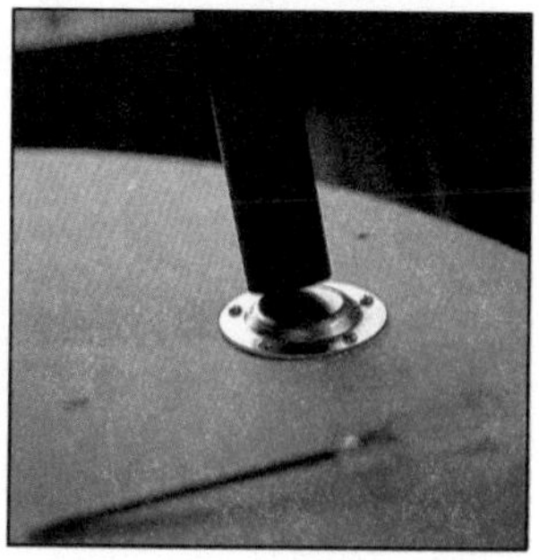

***j.** When pre-drilling for leg socket screws, take care; don't go through table top.*

GATELEG TABLE

Is your kitchen sometimes short on bench space? Do you wish you had somewhere to eat a quick breakfast? If so, a table that just pops up when required could be a boon. A gateleg table, as the name implies, incorporates a support which opens like a gate, and a table top which hangs vertically from a handy bench when not in use.

TOOLS

Tape and pencil; jigsaw; hammer; plane; saw; circular saw; screwdriver; drill; square; glue; sandpaper and cork block.

PROCEDURE

1 Fix the top batten to the wall making sure it's level and the top is 720 mm from the floor. Watch you don't hit wiring or plumbing. After scalloping out the leg batten to provide a finger hold (100 x 18 mm), fix it to the wall in the centre. Check that it is vertical.

2 Fit the leg to the leg batten and floor. Skew nail and glue it into position, keeping it flush with the edge of the leg batten opposite the scallop. Glue and nail the top into position. Mark out and cut the circular top with the jigsaw, and the gateleg with a hand or circular saw. After smoothing them up with a plane and sandpaper and block, screw the piano hinge to the appropriate edge of both the top and the gateleg. When pre-drilling the screws, don't make the holes too big or they won't hold.

3 Screw the gateleg to the centre support, keeping the top down by 2 mm. Fold it out of the way. Screw flap to the top making sure the hinge knuckle is underneath.

4 Paint the whole unit (gloss enamel is best) being careful not to get any paint on the hinges. (Brass hinges look most attractive.) To finish the job, glue a strip of 2 mm felt to the top of the outer end of the gateleg. This will enable it to be opened easily, yet fully support the flap in a level position.

Note: The flap could be made bigger (up to 700 mm) if you prefer. Also, the circular shape can be changed to a rectangular one which gives more bench space but is, perhaps, more run-of-the-mill and lacking in quite the same smart, modern appearance. Why not consider an oval, or even a part hexagon or octagon? These are all most attractive. You are only limited by your imagination and the decorating theme that predominates in your home. The same principles of construction apply in all cases.

MATERIALS LIST

Item	Materials	Size in mm	No.
Top	18 mm medium-density fibre board	1100 x 350	1
Flap	as above	550 radius	1
Leg	as above	720 x 325	1
Gateleg	as above	710 x 325	1
Top batten	38 x 19 mm pine	1100	1
Leg batten	38 x 19 mm pine	700	1

Other: 700 mm and 1100 mm lengths of piano hinging; 25 mm countersunk screws; 35 mm jolt-head nails; glue; paint. Instead of painting, you could cover the top and edges with plastic laminate.

a. A timber batten with a nail in one end and a pencil held at the other makes a great compass.

b. When jigsawing, don't force the blade through the timber. Let it cut its way through for best results.

Folded down, the table becomes a neat bench. Elevated, its attractive, compact design is very practicable.

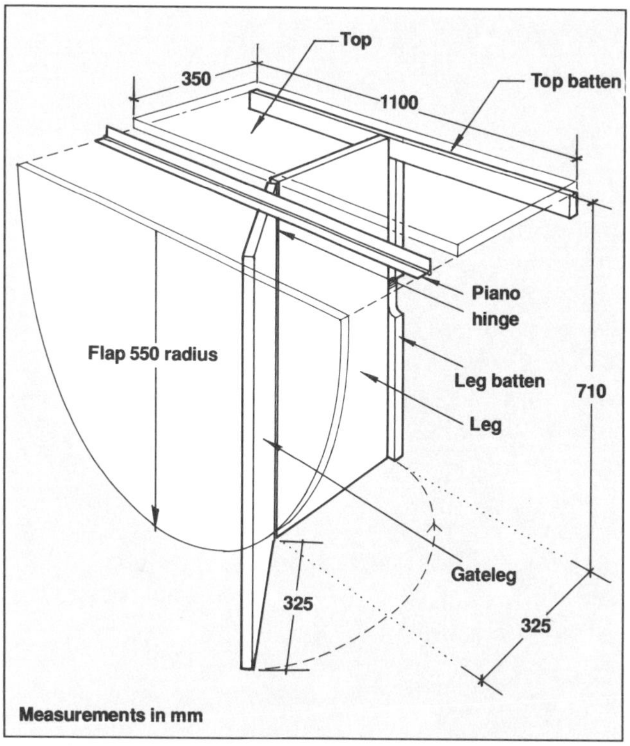

PRACTICAL POINTER

If using particle board instead of medium-density fibre board, you may find when screwing into the edge grain of particle board that some of the screws don't hold. This is because of the way the particle board is made. It is formed in successive layers which, like ply, makes it great for screwing through but is rather difficult to fix into the edge grain.

If this happens, remove the faulty screws and plug the hole with several matches that have glue on them. Wait until the glue has dried, cut the excess material off level with the edge and then re-screw.

c. Clamp the sheet to the workbench, allow the flat section of the hinge to sit on the board edge, then screw.

d. A mitre box (which you can make yourself) and tenon saw will ensure your cuts are perfect every time.

e. Glue and nail (at 150 mm centres) the leg batten to the leg to ensure rigidity in the finished unit.

MOBILE STORAGE

Another way of expanding your do-it-yourself horizons is to try to consider storage as a movable concept. An itinerant kitchen and sewing trolley that can be moved to where you want, when you want, is just such an example. With the simple addition of pegboard, it could easily be converted into a workshop accessory. Use your imagination to adapt it for the laundry or study. The beauty of these units is that they can be hidden away in or under a cupboard when not being used.

Each trolley consists of a base with four castors. The unit comprises two 90 mm deep shelved boxes with ply backs which are mounted on this base in one corner. This forms a right angle which gives rigidity to the trolley. The shelf arrangement can be as intricate or as simple as the items to be stored dictate. The best material to use for this unit is 12 mm Customwood or ply (particle board is a possibility, too, but it requires edging).

MATERIALS

As the diagrams show, six pieces of 326 x 90 mm Customwood or ply specified are used for the box shelves (extra if more than one shelf is required). Four pieces of 620 x 90 mm are needed for the sides. The base (and top, if it is required) measures 445 x 350 mm. If an intermediate shelf is to be included in the back section, it will be 350 x 255 mm and will be supported on 12 x 12 mm timber cleats. The three-ply backing (it could also be hardboard) for the boxes needs to be 620 x 350 mm. To stop things falling off the shelves, use dowels, Perspex or whatever you consider suitable.

Alternatively, you could make a tray 90 mm deep, one that fits neatly into the space behind the boxes and is flush with them (see the kitchen trolley photograph). The fastenings include 18 mm countersunk particle board screws and 38 mm nails. PVA glue and a suitable paint finish complete the requirements.

If you intend making several of these units, it's better to set to and make them all at once, employing a 'production-line' approach.

TOOLS

A circular saw or handsaw; drill and set of drills; screwdriver; plane; tape and pencil; square; sandpaper and cork block.

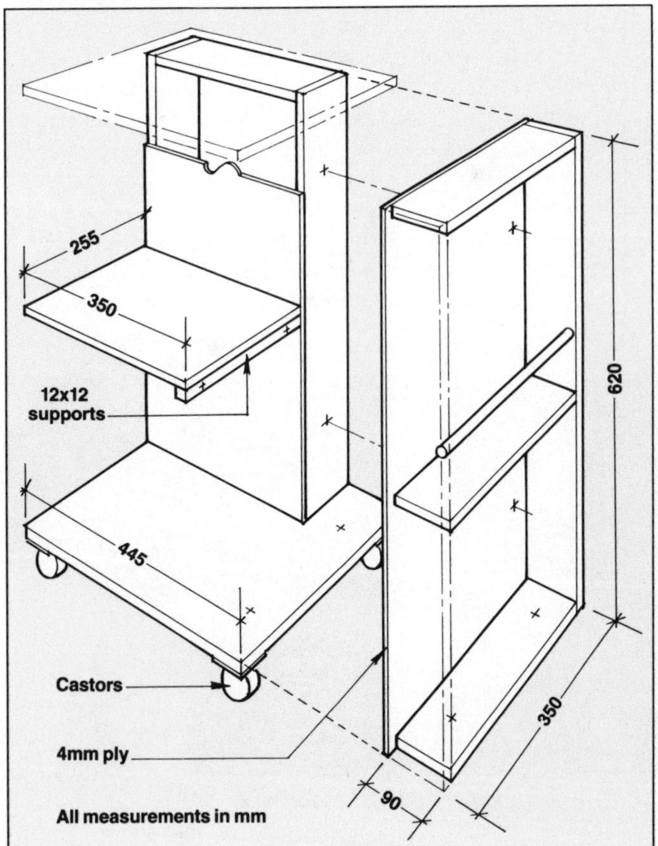

PROCEDURE

1 After checking the box components for square and straightness, assemble them using the screws or nails and glue. While the glue is still wet, nail and glue on the backs to square them up. If you're using dowels, bore holes 6 mm deep in the sides and fit them in place as you're assembling the boxes.

2 Fix the boxes to the base and each other as shown, again using glue and screws. Next fix the top, if any, and/or the intermediate shelf (or shelves) once the cleats are screwed into position. The best way to screw them is to come through the ply into the cleats.

Next fit the castors, but don't secure them in case they get paint on them. Then fill all the holes and apply a suitable gloss or semi-gloss paint system, sanding lightly between coats.

3 When finished, fix the castors, Perspex, elastic cords and whatever other refinements you need, and load up the unit. It will provide years of service.

Ever wished that the things you need could be at hand rather than in some remote place? This little storage unit will follow you around, yet vanish when not required.

A DIVAN BED

In small rooms, every square millimetre of space is important. A multi-purpose divan-bed unit – great for reclining on during the day while you read, and a haven for slumber at night – makes optimum use of limited space.

The unit is basically an open-fronted box. The top of this unit is fixed solidly, but it could be cut along the centre of the back of the bookshelf position, and the rear left loose. A couple of finger holes bored in it and, voilà, you've got a great additional storage space for those little-used items.

MATERIALS

The unit is made from 18 mm particle board which should be edge-stripped to ensure a good finish. You need a top and bottom 900 mm wide x (at least) 1950 mm long, four pieces 900 x 380 mm to make the ends and intermediate divisions, and two pieces the length of the unit x 380 mm for the back and the dividers. The timber plinth is constructed of 75 x 50 mm DAR (you could use sawn timber and plane the face of the front one).

Note: The timber plinth is positioned 50 mm back from the base to form a kick board.

PROCEDURE

1 Clear the floor and, after cutting two of the 75 x 50 mm pieces to length, skew nail them to the floor. Cut in the cross members and lay them in position. You may want to run a straight-edge over them at this stage to make sure the floor doesn't have a dip or a round in it. If there's a problem, you may first have to pack or plane them before fixing.

2 Cut the particle board top and bottom to size and, after making sure the pieces fit in place, lay out the vertical divider positions. Making them 380 mm wide, cut the end and intermediate dividers to length. Note that the intermediate dividers are kept back 50 mm at the front and 18 mm at the back.

3 Using PVA glue and 38 mm nails, stand the ends and dividers on the floor (a friend is handy at this stage) and nail the bottom to them. Fix the back. Turn the unit over, slide it into place on top of the plinth. Cut, nail and glue in the dividers at the back of the bookshelves. The position for these should be set by the size of the books you have. After nailing the unit to the joists, spread a liberal coat of glue on the tops of the dividers and nail on the top.

4 Edge-strip the exposed edges. Paint the unit to tone with the rest of the room.

The curtain rail can be made from metal or timber. Suggested methods of fixing it are shown in the diagram.

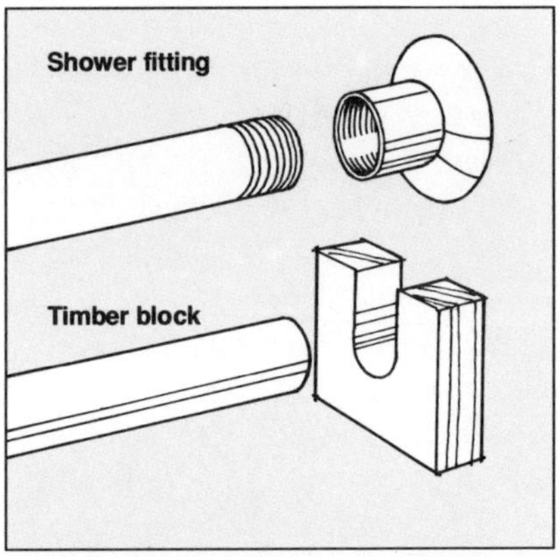

The method of fixing the curtain rail depends on its material. For metal rails, a threaded end such as is used in a shower curtain assembly should work, as long as you can get lengths to suit. For timber dowels, make blocks from plywood, then paint block the colour of the wall.

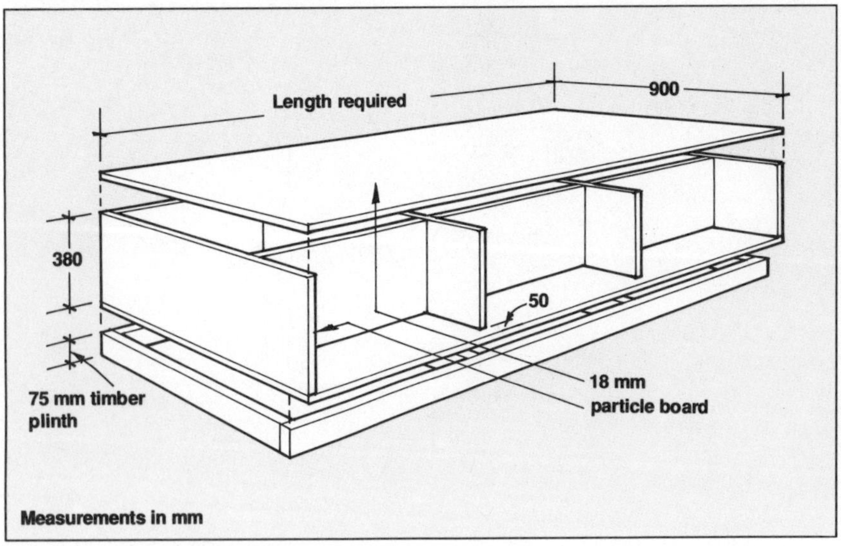

PRACTICAL POINTER

Possibly the most important part of this job is making sure that each of the components is the right length and square. To help you do this as easily as possible, you might find it best to buy a cheap roofing square (you may be lucky and be able to find one in a second-hand tool store).

The roofing square has very long arms and is a particularly good tool for using on those jobs that involve shelving or checking frames for square.

Additional space for books is always worth having. And if you're in bed, it's easy to reach down and select your favourite read.

BLANKET BOX AND WINDOW SEAT

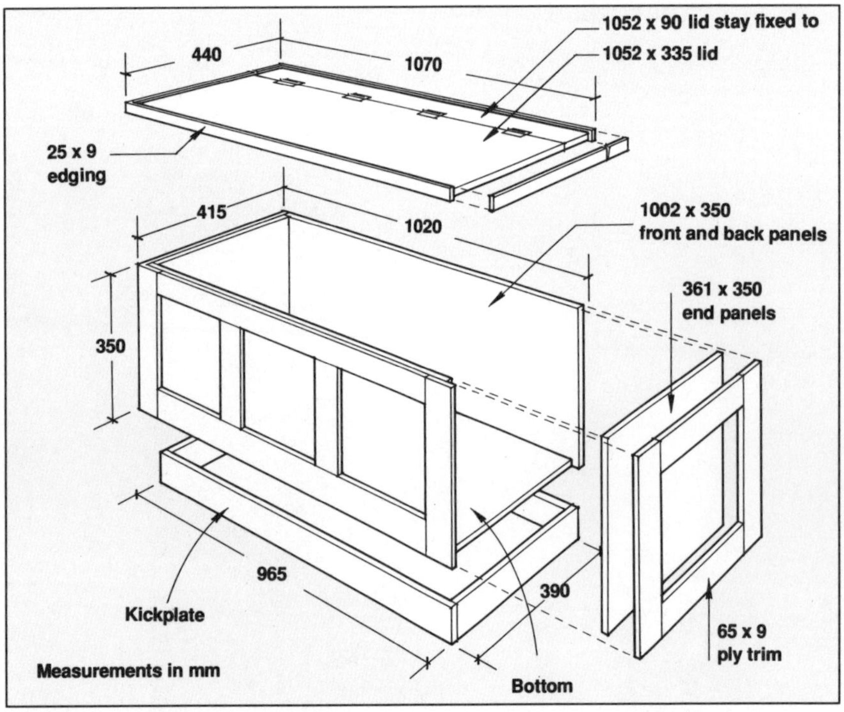

This clever storage and seating unit will look good in any room. If the window gets plenty of sunlight or commands a pleasant view, the unit's usefulness will be further highlighted.

The diagram illustrates that this unit is nothing more than a particle board box which has been given a panelled effect using strips of 9 mm ply (or timber) 65 mm wide. The top of the unit is hinged and edge-stripped with 25 x 9 mm ply. The edge-stripping is kept flush with the bottom to provide a ridge which holds the cushion in place. Instead of the butt hinges shown, you could use piano hinges.

PROCEDURE

1 Cut the particle board to the sizes shown. Plane the edges straight and square, making sure you don't make them undersize. As a variation, you may want to mitre the front joints in the kickboard to do away with the messy end grain. You could also fit the kickboards to the skirting at the back.

2 Nail and glue the kickboards. Begin to make the box, fixing the ends to the bottom. Glue and 38 mm nails should suffice. Glue liberally and nail on the front and back.

3 Cut, plane and fit the panelling strips. Nail and glue them on, doing the ends first. Once the box is finished, screw and glue it into position on the plinth. The lid stay is fixed next. If there is likely to be movement in it when the box is sat on, it could pay to fix a 50 x 25 mm stiffening batten underneath it (on edge).

4 Fix the lid. Complete the project by applying the edging; this can be butt jointed as shown or, better still, mitred. If you want the box to sit flush with the wall, delete the back edging.

5 Take the finished box to the window position, fix it to the wall (and kickboards) by either nailing into the studs or plugging and screwing into the masonry.

Paint the box, and add cushions for luxurious lounging.

MATERIALS LIST

Item	Materials	Size in mm	No.
Kickplate sides	18 mm medium-density particle board	372 x 75	2
Kickplate front	as above	965 x 75	1
Kickplate back	as above	929 x 75	1
Box front/back	as above	1002 x 350	2
Box bottom	as above	966 x 361	1
Box ends	as above	361 x 350	2
Lid	as above	1052 x 335	1
Lid stay	as above	1052 x 90	1

Other: 900 x 600 x 9 mm plywood for panelling strips; 3520 mm of 25 x 9 mm edging; four 35 mm brass butt hinges; 38 mm nails; 25 mm brads.

A BOARD FOR BILLS

The traditional pinboard has its place, but, invariably, you find you've run out of pins or you're treading unsuspectingly on one that's 'escaped' from its moorings. An innovative design that employs elastic strips and bulldog clips in place of pins stylishly eliminates these shortcomings.

To make this board, cut a sheet of 15 mm thick particle board to the size you require (the diagram shows the suggested sizes). Use a plane to smooth off the edges, then run a small chamfer around the top edge to facilitate the stretching of the felt. A piece of green felt (it can be another colour, of course) is glued to the face of the board to keep it rigid, and nailed or stapled to the back.

The board is edged to give it an attractive finish. 19 x 12 mm (finished) timber is suitable. Mitre it on the corners and round off the edges to ensure it is splinter-free. It can be painted to team with the room or the colour of the felt.

Letters, bills and other ephemera are held in place by means of diagonal elasticised strips surmounted by a leather border. Both are held in place by stout drawing pins. Before securing, mark the border shape and strip positions on the felt with a tailor's pencil. Glue may also be used under the elastic for added strength.

Hang the bulldog clips on nails or screw them to the board. The board itself is fixed to the wall using screws and cup washers. Brass ones would harmonise particularly well with the leather. Alternatively, the board could be glued to the wall with epoxy glue. Put blobs of glue on the back of the board, position it, temporarily jam it in place with a timber batten; be sure to put scrap blocks under both ends to avoid damage.

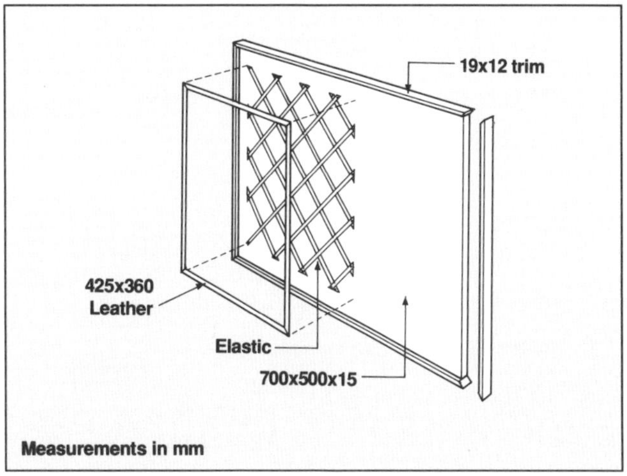

Cover the board in felt in a colour that teams or contrasts with the room scheme. The elasticised strips can be in a different colour for a bold, graphic look.

A BOOK SLIDE

An adjustable book slide is the perfect gadget for keeping your collection of novels and reference books attractively displayed. Its adjustability allows for books to be removed or added, yet the ends can be kept tight and the books will remain upright.

The slide comprises two lengths of tongue-and-grooved boards, one of which is ripped into halves to make the two joints. The tongues are sanded or planed down to give enough clearance to make the slide slip. They are secured to a mitred base frame (although they could also be fixed to a ply or particle board panel). The ends on our slide are hinged, which means the unit can be stacked easily when not in use.

An intriguing design turns the commonplace book shelf into a high-tech, streamlined piece of equipment.

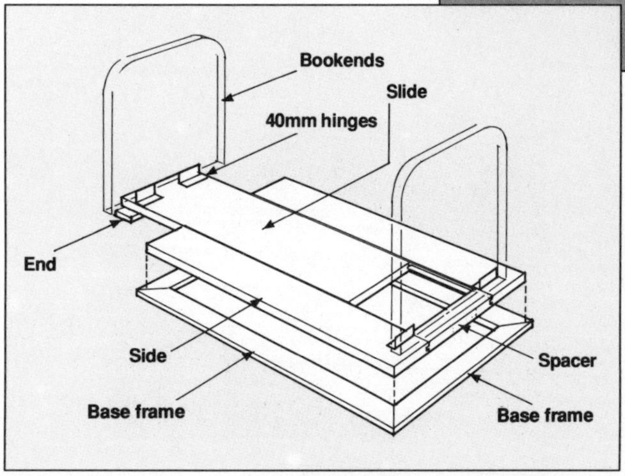

MATERIALS LIST			
Item	**Materials**	**Size in mm**	**No.**
Side	125 x 10 mm Tasmanian oak, tongue and grooved	450	2
Slide	as above	450	1
Spacer	as above	30	1
End	5 mm thick medium-density fibre board	150 x 30	1
Bookends	225 x 12 mm Tasmanian oak	220	2
Base frame	5 mm thick medium-density fibre board	460 x 30	2
Base frame	5 mm thick fibre board	270 x 30	2

PROCEDURE

1 Cut boards to length (450 mm); rip one of them into halves. Plane the roughness and smooth the ends. This is best done by planing but only if the plane is very sharp and set very fine. Stand the pieces in a vice and come in halfway from either side. This is important because, if you plane right through from one side only, you will split off the far edge.

2 Proceed to thin down the tongues until they slide easily. Remember that timber swells in damp conditions so don't make them too tight or you'll have trouble. Once everything works smoothly, make the spacer.

3 Make up the base frame, working from one corner. It must project past the sides and ends by 5 mm. Fit each joint before you proceed to the next; if you have to plane a fair amount off to get it to

fit, the piece won't end up too short. Of course, on the last one you'll have to cut both mitres – but by then you'll be an expert.

4 Nail and glue the base frame together. Nail and glue the sides and spacer in place. Be careful not to nail through the slide. While the glue is drying, make the two ends. Medium-density fibre board (Customwood) is used rather than particle board because the latter must be edge-stripped. If you feel competent, make a fancy design on the ends and cut it out with a jigsaw.

5 Turn the frame over and extend the slide as far as you think practicable. A small block glued to the underside of it will stop it coming right out. Turn it over the right way and fix the 50 mm hinges in position; recess them into the side and end or their projection will damage your books.

6 Fill all holes with coloured putty. Sand the book slide well, dust off. Apply the chosen finish, taking particular care not to get any of it in the tongue and grooving – otherwise you'll find that your slide does not live up to its name. Dust your books. Now you're ready to give them pride of place.

PRACTICAL POINTER

When planing the ends of the timber members to get them smooth, you have two options. The first is to place the timber in a vice, then to plane in from either side to avoid the splitting that will occur should you try to plane from one direction only.

A better solution is to find a scrap piece of timber that is the same size exactly as the piece you're wanting to plane. Put them tightly together, making the ends level with each other. Cramp them in the vice. Then you can plane in one direction without problems.

DESK BOOKCASE

This desk-top bookcase for the home office, den or a child's room keeps those much-used volumes tidy and close to hand. Its tilted shelf locks the books snugly in place even if it's not full.

Timber and ply has been chosen this example, but the bookcase could be made completely from ply or medium density fibre board (Customwood) and painted.

PROCEDURE

1 Mark out the ends to the required shape. While the design shown is simple (basically two quadrants) it can be made more complex or left square with just the corners rounded off. Cut the shape with a jigsaw. With the two pieces tacked together, smooth off the edges with sandpaper and a block.

2 Cut the shelf and back; plane smooth. Make sure the ends are square. Make a small chamfer on the exposed edges. Mark out the shelf and back position on the ends as shown on the diagram.

3 Nail and glue the bookcase together, carefully wiping off any excess glue with a damp rag and punching the nails as you go. When dry, fill the nail heads, sand well and apply paint or varnish.

MATERIALS LIST

Item	Materials	Size in mm	No.
Sides	12 mm ply	350 x 345	2
Shelf	19 mm pine	800 x 262	1
Back	19 mm pine	800 x 240	1
Other: 35 mm jolt-head nails; wood glue; varnish to finish.			

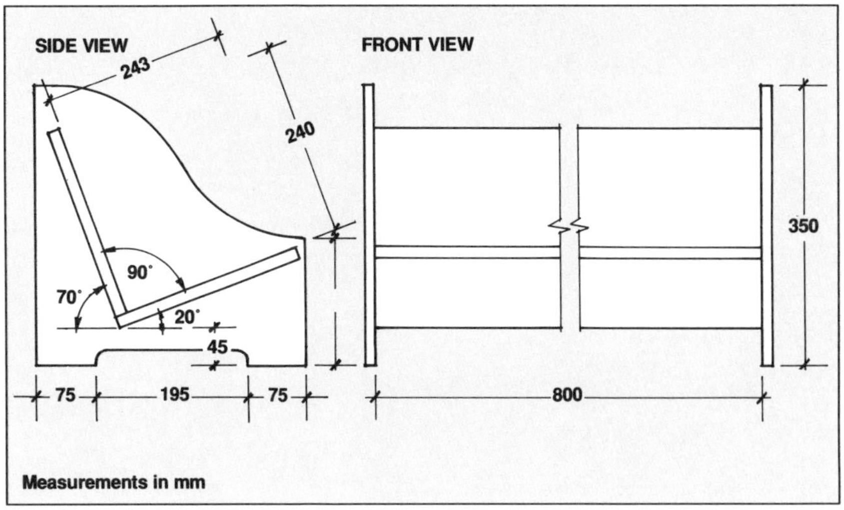

POSTCARD/RECIPE BOXES

You can never have too many boxes for holding the plethora of information and correspondence we all gather about us. Boxes for postcards or recipe cards take up little room, but help keep desk and benchtops under control. Plywood is the basic material for these boxes (three-ply) together with a quad surround to the base.

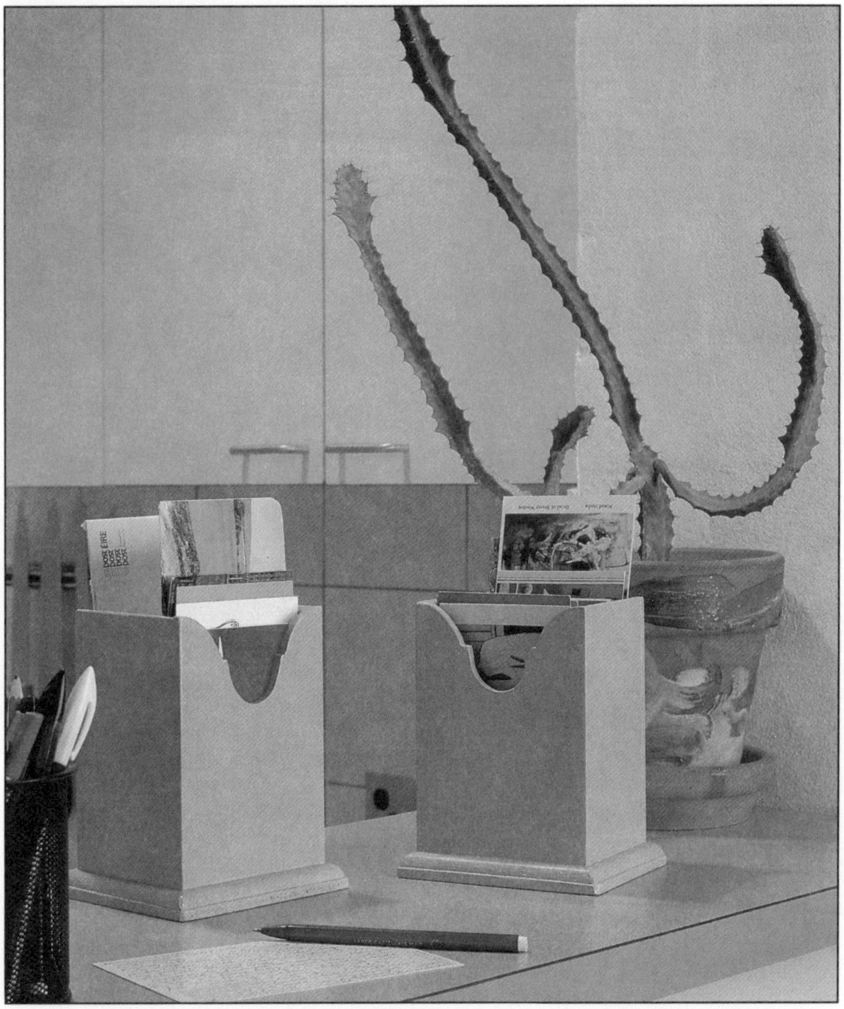

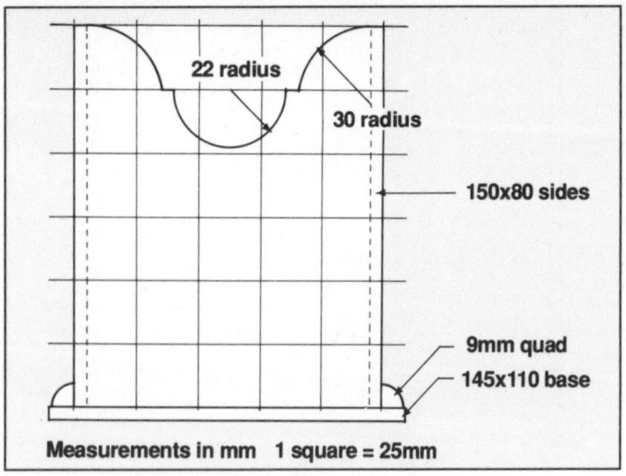

These easily made little boxes will eliminate clutter and give you more bench space. Paint and decorate them in colours to complement their setting.

MATERIALS

You may be able to get some offcuts of three-ply from a joinery shop to make the boxes. The quad can be obtained from a timber yard; you'll need 600 mm per box. You also need a handful of panel pins, glue and some varnish or paint. Then, making it requires only the basic woodworking skills.

PROCEDURE

1 Cut sides to size (150 x 125 mm). Lightly draw a graph of 25 mm squares in pencil on one side, and mark out the top shape, using a compass. Tack the two sides together and carefully cut out the shape with a coping saw or jigsaw. Keep the sides together and use sandpaper wrapped around a broom handle to sand them smooth.

2 Cut ends to size (150 x 80 mm) and the base (145 x 110 mm) and carefully smooth them off, taking care that they are square and straight on their edges. Tack the box together to ensure everything fits. A 10 mm line drawn around the base will make sure you get the projection even. Be careful that you get the nails directly in line with the centre of the ply; otherwise it may split.

3 Knock the boxes apart, apply a liberal quantity of glue (clear if you're varnishing), begin to nail. Fix the box section together. Check for square, nail on the bottom.

4 Once the glue has dried, fit, nail and glue the quad around the base, mitring the corners. A mitre box is handy for this. Again, because the ply is thin, be careful that the nails don't protrude through.

Give the boxes a quick sand and apply several coats of varnish or paint. If you are interested in craft, you could stencil some attractive motifs onto the boxes.

KEY CABINET

Who hasn't suffered the nightmare of trying to find keys? This attractive little cabinet will complement any vestibule and is large enough to provide storage for a multitude of keys. Its panelled-door effect is just pure imitation but when painted, who would know?

It is a simple box-like construction, the top and base extending a little from the sides for added effect. Medium-density fibre board has been used because of the ease of finishing the end grain.

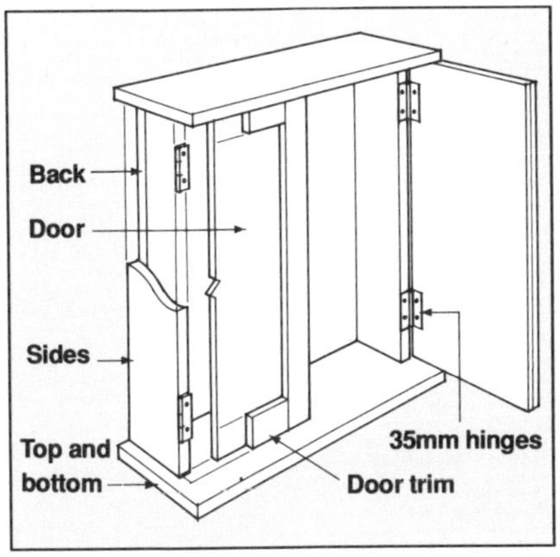

PROCEDURE

1 Cut the sides, top, bottom and back and fit. The back fits between the other members. Tack the cabinet together and check for square. When ready, knock it apart; glue and nail it together.

2 Cut and fit the two doors, making sure you leave 2 mm clearance around each one. Cut the trims and fit. Nail (with panel pins) and glue them to the doors.

3 Position the hinges (brass would look good) 30 mm in from the door ends. Cut out a recess in the front of the sides to take at least one leaf of the hinge. Use a sharp chisel for this. Fix the hinges to the back of the door and then to the sides, using only one screw. If they are slightly out of position, fill the screw holes with a match and glue, then reposition the hinges. When both doors are hanging properly, drive in the other screw, sand the unit, and apply the chosen finish.

4 When complete, screw the cup hooks into place, then screw on the handles and the magnetic catch. Fix the unit to the wall with screws and plugs, or by nailing to studs. Another option you might prefer is to use toggle bolts.

Collect all the keys, check which ones are obsolete and discard them. Use a labelling system that shows which goes where, then heave a sigh of relief. Your key problem is over.

MATERIALS LIST

Item	Materials	Size in mm	No.
Top/bottom	10 mm medium-density fibre board	270 x 95	2
Side	as above	280 x 65	2
Back	as above	280 x 250	1
Door	5 mm medium-density fibre board	278 x 125	2
Door side trim	as above	278 x 25	4
Door top/bottom trim	as above	72 x 25	4

Other: Four 35 mm butt hinges; 50 mm magnetic catch; 12 x 25 mm brass cup hooks; panel pins; wood glue; 25 mm jolt-head nails; two small brass door knobs (or metal of your choice).

CHAPTER 3

ENERGY AND MONEY SAVING IMPROVEMENTS

There is a simple relationship between energy and money: if you save energy, you save money. Lots of it! Take heating, for example. In winter, electricity, gas and timber are consumed in large quantities as we try to warm our homes and beat the winter shivers. In summer, we tend to utilise a similar amount of energy by trying to keep cool. Depending on the extremes of the climate to which we are subjected, the energy costs can be very high. Here is a fund of information and projects that will help reduce your energy consumption and make your home a more comfortable place in which to live.

The theory

Ideally, a home should absorb and store the sun's energy during winter and reflect and shed its surplus in summer. These two ideals appear contradictory. But are they?

Let's discuss the absorption and reflection of the sun's rays – the best source of daytime heating energy we have in winter. But, in the summer (fickle creatures that we are), it's a gift we don't want. If we could somehow design a home to catch the sun in winter and deflect it in summer, we'd have the best of both worlds. Impossible, you say? Think again.

Absorption of the sun's heat is handled efficiently by careful deployment of glassed window areas. In winter, if we have north-facing windows that catch the full benefit of the available sun, then warming comfort is assured.

So, if you are designing a new home, or redesigning an existing one, locate the living areas on the northern side and make sure there are plenty of windows.

Also, the roof of a north-facing room can be constructed of architectural glass, thereby creating a winter solarium (you may need to cover it in summer). Alternatively, roof systems which incorporate adjustable louvres can effectively turn the sun off and on like a tap. If it's impossible or too expensive to change walls or roofs, skylights can be let in or small windows enlarged.

In summer, if the eaves are the correct width, the sun is prevented for much of the day from shining directly on the glass. When it does, it can be 'fielded' with adjustable awnings, shutters or drapes. With west-facing windows – often a nuisance in the hot months – deep pergolas and low screens or dense foliage can be used to create shade.

To store and/or shed energy, insulation methods such as draught stoppers and heavy drapes can assist

An area that allows warmth and light to flood in is inviting and economical.

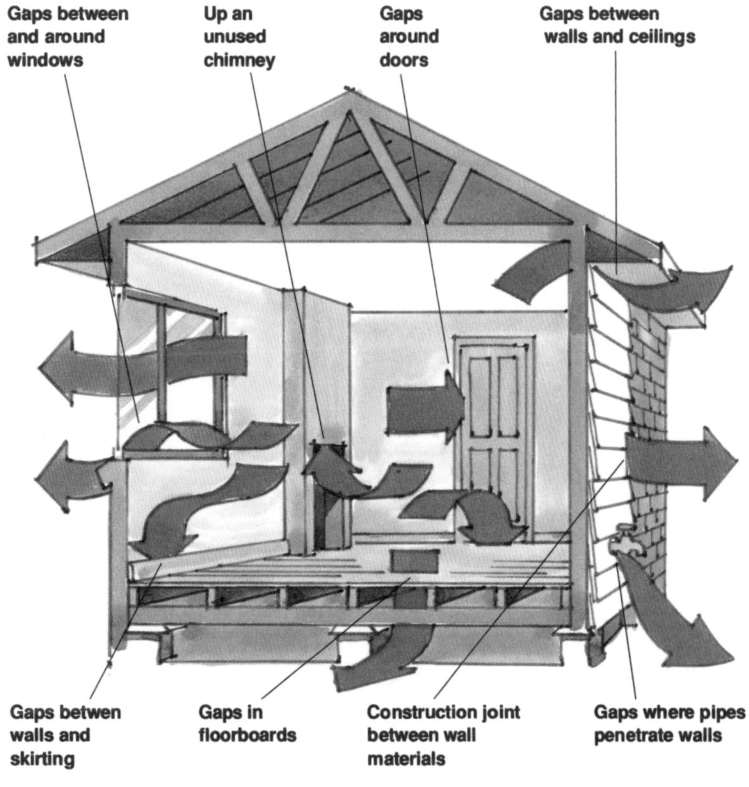

Major sources of heat leaks and draughts

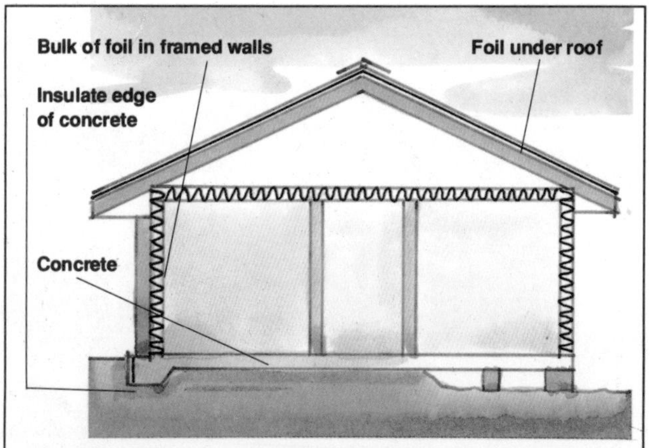

Insulating roof, walls and floor will slow down the movement of heat in summer and winter. Try to do this during construction.

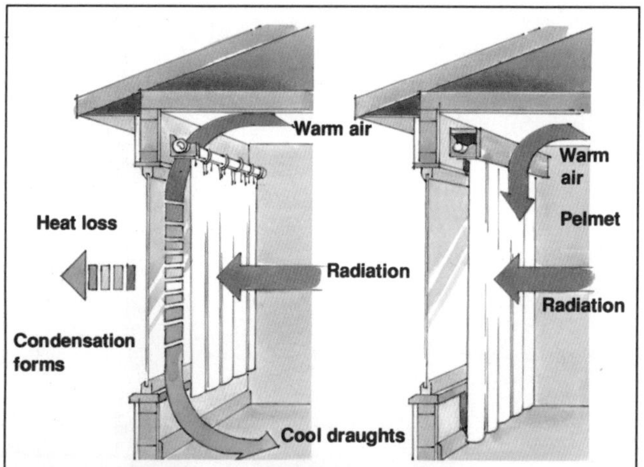

Use a pelmet and curtains to stop winter heat loss.

in holding in heat or blocking it out. Ideally, it should be possible to open up the house in summer to facilitate the movement of cool breezes; casement windows and French doors (see index for project on installing French doors) are but two means which can be used to advantage here. If there are no breezes, the house should be so designed that it can be sealed off to let cooling appliances work at their optimum capacity.

Now that the elementary theory has been covered, it's time for practicalities. Windows will be our first priority because of the important part they play in energy control. It's estimated that they're responsible for up to 90 per cent of heat gain in summer and more than 20 per cent of heat loss in winter.

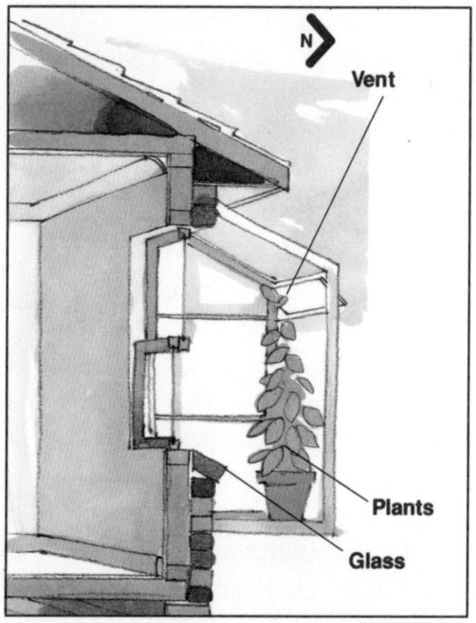

***Left:* The correct width of eave is a controlling agent of the sun's impact. *Above:* A small greenhouse around a window will help regulate the amount of heat you require.**

Window improvement hints

1. Good quality, heavy curtains (it's worth having them lined if they are flimsy) are an effective means of trapping heat, especially if the drapes extend from floor to ceiling and there is a pelmet. Open-weave cloth or slatted blinds are, obviously, less efficient. Use curtaining to shut out the heat on a hot day or to trap the sun's warmth in the room before nightfall.
2. Double glazing, although expensive, is an effective way of locking in heat and shutting out unwanted warmth. Reflective film will also reduce the sun's heat in summer, especially on west-facing windows, but this may not be a plus during winter in colder climes.
3. There are many types of awning on the market. Examine carefully for ease of installation; adjustability; efficient mechanism; longevity (the guarantee will give some indication). Colour and pattern should team well with the style of the house.
4. Pruning or removing trees may provide an unexpected, inexpensive winter suntrap. Conversely, by planting a dense shrub or growing a vine over a screen, you can create an effective natural barrier to a too exuberant summer sun.

HEATING IMPROVEMENTS

Gas and electricity are the cleanest fuels but most people agree there is nothing more comforting than the sight of a blazing open fire.

Heating is typically achieved by either radiant heat – such as comes from an open fire or pot-belly stove – or by convection heat whereby the unit heats air which is often fan-driven to ensure full circulation. Some units incorporate both, which is ideal. When buying a fire, especially a fuel one, check the claims made by the manufacturer about its heating capacity with people who have one. Sadly, some of the claims are greatly exaggerated.

Fuel fires

There are many types of fuel fire. The simplest – an open canopy fireplace – is aesthetically pleasing but, unless designed with some convection capacity, will lose 75 per cent of its heat up the chimney.

Next in line come the ultra-efficient slow combustion stoves. The simplest is the radiant pot-belly stove which, although energy efficient, totally encloses and obscures the comforting sight of the flame. The big brother of the fuel-burning family is the free-standing, glass-fronted, combustion heater (some models of which, like your oven, have a fan-forced option).

Providentially, you can get slow combustion heaters and inserts (see illustration above) that will fit into existing, smoky fireplaces. These reduce the traditional open-fire fuel cost by more than 50 per cent per megajoule unit. As well, if the fire is of large enough capacity, you can duct some of the hot air from one room to another.

Fireplaces and combustion stoves last longer if made from cast iron; guarantees usually range from five to 10 years. Finishes such as vitreous enamel are better than paint. Copper and brass look splendid when new but require great care and effort if their good looks are to be preserved.

Because it creates convective air, a hollow steel insert makes an open fire more efficient.

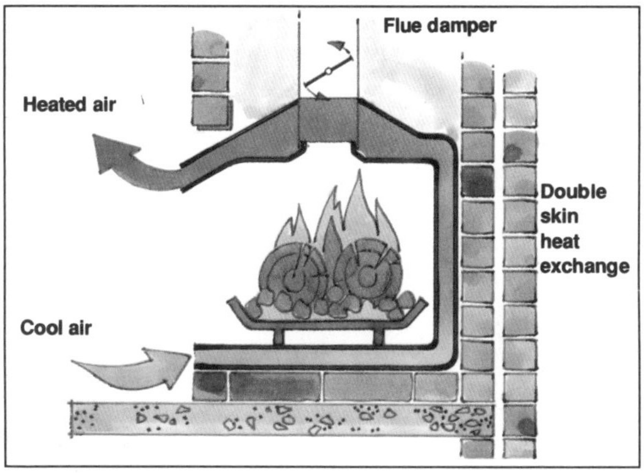

It will probably pay you to have your fire professionally installed. It's a big job that can get tricky, to say nothing of the potential for water leakage or the risk of starting a fire in the wall or ceiling.

Gas and electric fires

Gas and electric fires come in a variety of fixed and mobile types which use both the radiation principle and/or the convection principle.

Gas heaters usually have more heating capacity than electrical ones and are cheaper to run. Installation costs for gas depend on the site, distance from the gas main, the heater location and whether or not a flue is required. Any danger with gas is lessened by the use of electronic ignition. Automatic cut-out switches are activated in the event of the pilot light going out or the heater being knocked over.

Small electric radiators are great for warming your immediate personal space and can be transported where ever you go.

Heating hints

1. Polish the reflecting material behind the radiator element if it has dulled. If you're alone and sedentary, a small radiator is usually sufficient to warm your immediate space – and it's cheap.
2. Line painted brick walls, especially external ones, with insulating materials such as ply or cedar boards (ostensibly as a feature wall) or use heavy wallpaper around the whole room.
3. Use 'warm' materials such as cork or wood underfoot in preference to 'cold' ceramics, stone or vinyl. Or, simply invest in a pair of thick slippers!
4. Have brick chimneys cleaned regularly to ensure efficiency and lessen the risk of fire.
5. Install a ceiling fan in vaulted ceilings. On a very low setting, they help to push warm air down.
6. Create small, cosy areas by using screens, dressers or bookshelves as dividers. Heating these spaces is effectively handled by small radiators.
7. Heating a bedroom can be a costly, wasteful business, especially if you're going to leap straight into bed. An electric blanket costing one cent an hour to run is probably all the heating you need.

PUTTING UP A CURTAIN

It's a simple matter to fix curtains to a brick wall in a home unit or house. The type of curtains you choose will dictate the kind of track required. Brackets will be necessary whether you've selected a thick cornice rod with rings for café curtains, a thinner one for sliding through a pocket in the curtain, or a track with slides for drapes that have a heading or pinch pleating.

The number of brackets is determined by the length and rigidity of the track and the weight of the curtains. There must be one at each end and perhaps several intermediate ones. Typically, brackets will be of either timber or metal and will have to be securely fastened to the wall with screws.

Because bricks and render are too hard to drive a screw into, you must first drill a hole where each screw is to go and fill it with a soft plugging material. Then your screws will hold fast for ever!

Once you've mastered the business of putting up brackets, you'll find that you tackle many jobs involving masonry fixings – putting up shelf supports or picture hooks, for instance – without a qualm.

Curtains in a gauzy fabric soften harsh sunlight and give the necessary privacy without obscuring the view from the window.

MATERIALS

Sufficient wall plugs to fix all the brackets in place; an old sheet; a chair to stand on.

TOOLS

A masonry bit to suit the screw size (take a screw and a bracket with you so your hardware salesperson can advise on the correct drill and plug size); a hand drill to turn it with (if you can borrow or hire an electric drill you'll find it much easier); a rule and a soft pencil; a hammer to tap in the plugs; a sharp knife to make them flush; a screwdriver.

1 Measure the length of track and the width of the window. Mark the point at which the track should start so that it will extend evenly either side of the window. Stand on the chair, holding up one of the curtains on its track, and mark the height the track must be. With full-length curtains, you'll find this too much of a struggle to handle on your own so enlist help.

2 Take one of the brackets and, carefully lining it up with the height mark and start positions, draw around the screws holes. It is essential that you have a sharp pencil for this operation so that the holes will be accurate. Once the holes are marked, take a nail or nail punch and make an indentation in the centre of each circle. This will hold the drill on centre.

3 Repeat the procedure for the other end (and the intermediate brackets, if you are using any), measuring down from the ceiling or up from the window reveal to ensure that all the brackets are in a straight line. The holes should not be placed any closer than 20 mm to the edge of the brickwork (30 mm in the case of rendered) if solidity of the fitment is to be assured.

4 Put an old sheet on the floor to collect the brick dust. Using the hand drill (or electric drill) and masonry bit, drill all the holes, being sure to go at least 5 mm deeper than the point at which the end of the screw will come. If you drill the hole

a. *When measuring, use a sharp pencil and make sure you double-check your measurements for accuracy.*

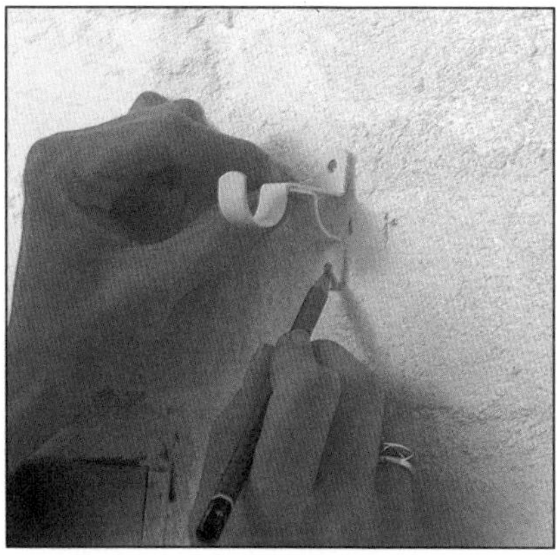

b. *To make sure that the brackets are vertical, mark a plumb line with a spirit level where the holes are to go.*

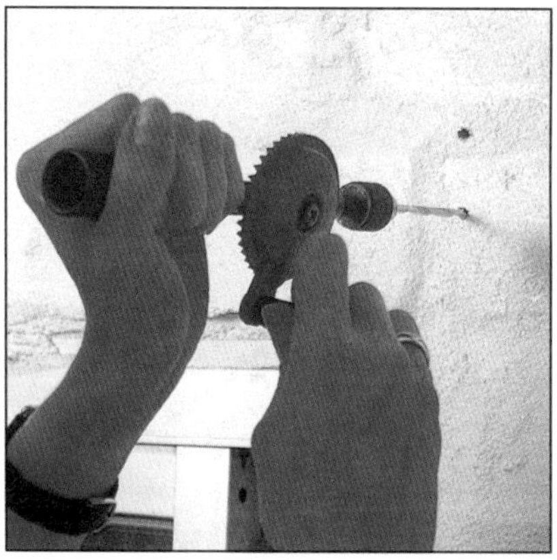

c. *To check whether you are drilling straight, use a square. Watch you don't overbalance or go too deep.*

d. *Make sure the face of the hammer is clean; otherwise it could slip off the plug. Use a piece of fine sandpaper.*

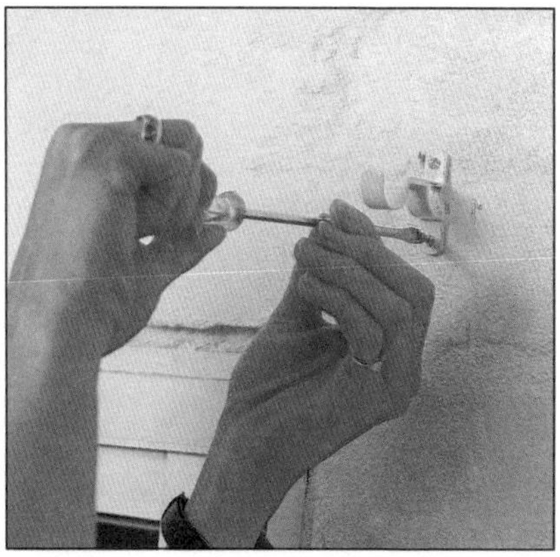

e. *When screwing, the driver and the screen must be in line. The larger the handle, the better the leverage.*

f. *Hanging the curtain and putting on the rod ends is the best part. The curtain should hide the bracket.*

too wide, plug it with a piece of timber dowel cut to size.

5 Tap the plugs lightly into the holes and cut them off flush with the wall surface using a sharp knife. If you don't have the plastic plugs, you can substitute a soft timber such as meranti. Simply cut a small block which is slightly larger than the hole. Drive it in tightly with your hammer.

6 Select the size of screwdriver to suit the screw slot (it should be of almost the same width and fit tightly) and screw the brackets onto the wall. Fix the track and hang the curtains. The skills you have acquired doing this job will stand you in good stead for many other more complex projects.

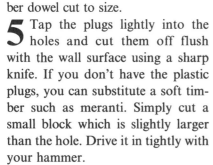

CONTROLLING DRAUGHTS

While there are major things one can do to improve energy storage such as installing fan-boosted combustion stoves or gas heaters, or putting down carpets (all of which involve a fair amount of expense), there are some effective and relatively inexpensive ways to eradicate chilling winter draughts. Some fresh air is essential to good health, of course!

Place sealing strips around all ill-fitting doors (external and internal) and casement window rebates; fit draught (which may also be water) deflectors to the bottom of external doors – those facing south or west particularly will help.

Caulk all draughty external openings such as those that occur under the window sills and around the plumbing pipes as well.

Draught and water deflectors

There are many types. Discuss your particular location with your hardware supplier; take along details such as whether the door opens inwards or outwards, what type of tread you have, and the door width.

TOOLS

A hacksaw (to cut the deflector to length); a hand drill and drills suitable for the screws; screwdriver; tape and pencil.

If you have a terrazzo tread and you purchase a deflector that has a sill, you may find you need a masonry bit and some plugs to fix the sill in position.

a. Measure length of the draught deflector by placing it on the door.

PROCEDURE

1 Measure the door width and cut the strip to length.

2 With the door closed, position the deflector above the tread and mark the screw holes with a punch.

3 Drill a hole of a diameter equal to solid part of thread.

4 Screw the fitting on the door with two screws, check for fit, then complete. The sill, if any, is fitted the same way.

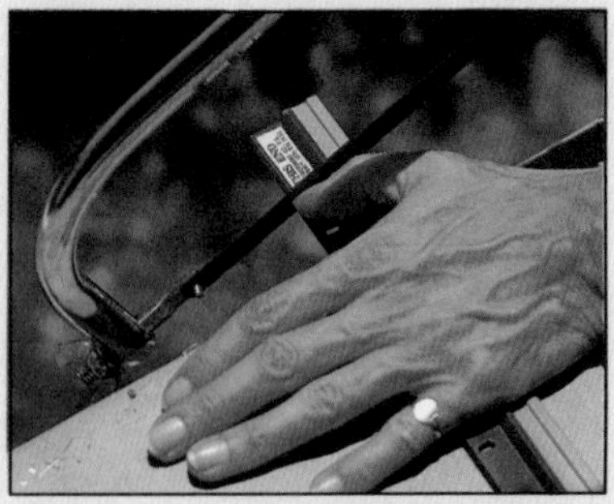

b. When cutting with the hacksaw, take care not to catch your fingers.

c. Once you've marked screw hole positions with punch, pre-drill them.

Gap filling

Silicon caulking is popular for general application, but there are many other products on the market. Select one that is weather resistant, non-drying, non-shrinking, and adheres to most materials. If you want the caulking to be inconspicuous, choose one in a colour that matches its surround or that can be painted. If you have a lot to do, a caulking gun makes the job much easier.

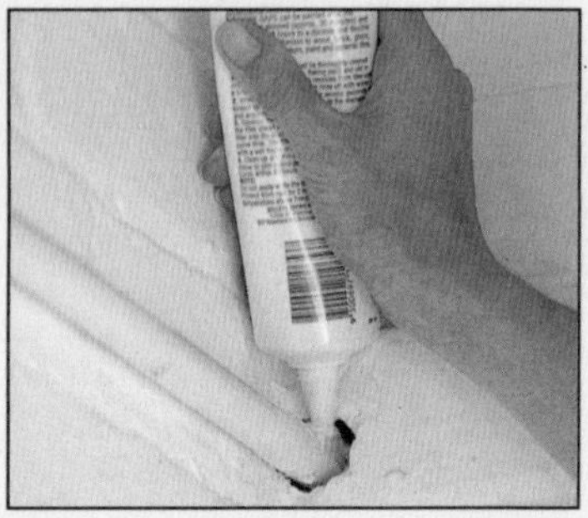

PROCEDURE

1 Check the outside walls and note all positions where gaps occur (around windows, door frames, pipes, etc).

2 Cut the top of the conical cap and squeeze the compound into position. Smooth it off with your thumb. Remove surplus with a rag dipped in a recommended cleaner. To prevent getting caulking where you don't want it, use masking tape around the area. If you intend to paint caulking, first allow the surface to set.

Stick-on sealing strips

These easily installed energy savers are sold by the metre or in rolls. Measure and total the length around each rebate.

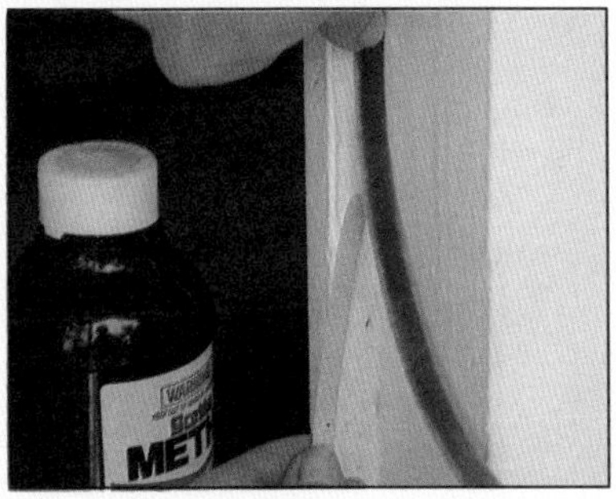

PROCEDURE

1 Open the ill-fitting window or door as wide as possible.

2 Clean the rebate thoroughly; use methylated spirits for the best result.

3 Measure and cut each piece of sealing strip to length; pull off the backing and stick each strip on. There is no need to bother with the side of the casement stays as, if properly fitted, there will be scarcely any gap to worry about.

Other measures

1. Make a habit of closing the doors in all unused rooms.
2. Put draught deflectors on all draughty internal doors especially those facing south and west. Alternatively, use carpet snakes.
3. Block off a unused chimney with ply, hardboard or a painting that you don't mind committing to the task. When a functional chimney is not being used, close the damper.
4. Rugs or carpet will stop the draughts coming through the gaps in the flooring or underneath skirtings, and will insulate you from the cold floor.
5. If the floors are polished, a quad nailed against the skirting will lessen draughts.
6. A door put in a doorless opening could seal in valuable heat. If the idea of hanging a door fills you with horror, install a heavy curtain instead.
7. Install an automatic closer on external doors if the kids or dog can't be trusted to close them.

CEILING INSULATION

Insulation in ceilings places a thick 'blanket' over each room. The cost for an average home of 12 squares is around $750, an investment that could achieve a 30 per cent saving in your heating bills.

If you're handy, agile, sure that the wiring in the roof is safe, and the roof is of high enough pitch, you could insulate the ceilings yourself. This could represent a saving of around $150. Calculate the floor area and get up into the roof to measure the average distance between the ceiling joists. Your insulation supplier will calculate the quantity and size of batts required.

With a lead light and a trimming knife (for cutting the batts to size), begin packing the batts tightly between the joists. Leave no spaces. Take care that you always keep your weight on the joists and not on the ceiling. A short plank will make the procedure more comfortable. Be especially careful around any wiring. For low-pitched roofs, loose-fill material can be sprayed in position.

If you have uncarpeted floors, put batts between the floor joists.

Insulation products

Reflective foil: Foil is laminated to paper with glass fibre reinforcement. Use for ceilings, pitched roofs, metal deck roofs, timber floors and framed walls.

Fibreglass batts: Made of melted glass; excellent fire rating. Wear protective clothing when installing. Use as for reflective foil, above.

Batts with foil facing: Also available in tripolymer which does not shed fibres during installation (unlike fibreglass). Good fire rating. Use in all situations as above, with the exception of timber floors.

Loose fill material: Varying in composition from rockwool cellulose. Ideal in areas in existing houses where access is difficult. Use for ceilings, pitched roofs, cathedral ceilings, metal deck roofs.

Extruded polystyrene boards: Tightly compressed structure gives strength. Also available sandwiched between layers of plaster as an interior liner. Use for cathedral ceilings, metal deck roofs, timber floors, suspended slabs, slab edges, full masonry walls and framed walls.

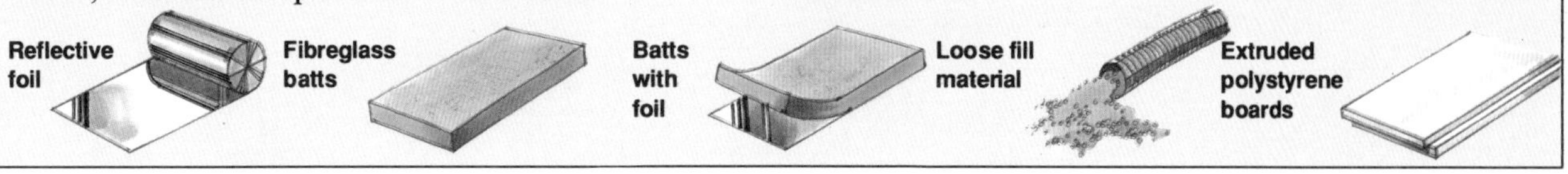

INSTALLING A SKYLIGHT

A skylight is a fantastic way to let light and heat into dreary rooms. It is suitable for a roof with a pitch between 15 and 85°. This is a fixed unit, not to be confused with a roof-mounted window which can be opened.

Putting in a skylight, especially if the ceiling follows the slope of the roof, is not beyond the capability of the average do-it-yourselfer.

PREPARATION

Decide how large a skylight you require; two smaller ones might be better than one large one. Discuss your needs with several manufacturers or suppliers. When it's delivered, carefully read the installation instructions. Keep in mind that you're going to cut a hole in your roof, one which could let in the rain if there is a hold up because you don't know exactly how the unit should be fitted or there's a part missing. Get a small tarpaulin and some ropes, in case.

Assemble the additional materials and tools listed below and get two ladders: one step, one extension.

MATERIALS

75 mm nails; one length of rafter-sized material for trimming; gypsum plaster for filling in around skylight; metal angle; bedding cement; setting cement; paint.

TOOLS

Hand and circular saw; hammer; tape and pencil; screwdriver; level; trimming knife; plane; plasterer's trowel; sandpaper and cork block; tile cutters or a carborundum wheel for cutting the tiles.

***a.** Mark the position of the skylight on the ceiling; make sure that one side of it fits alongside the ceiling joist. Drive a stout nail through its centre.*

***e.** In this instance, an electric cable is running right across the skylight opening. Don't make any attempt to move it yourself! This is definitely a job for an electrician.*

***i.** The flashings are important; they are there to stop leaks developing between the skylight and the roof covering. They must be installed carefully and without damage.*

b. *Once tiles are removed and stacked close by, cut the battens. If you don't have a chain saw (as shown) use a circular saw or handsaw.*

c. *After cutting rafters, until trimmed keep your weight off them. Frame joints must be well nailed – a minimum of four 75 mm nails in each.*

d. *Before sawing the plasterboard, cut deeply into sheet from underneath with a trimming knife. This will lessen the likelihood of paper lining tearing.*

f. *If you've made the opening the correct size, the brackets of the sides of the skylight should stand on the framing members. Make sure the sarking fits the opening.*

g. *Read the manufacturer's instructions carefully, then position the skylight and, after double checking it's correct, temporarily fix it to one of the rafters or trimmers.*

h. *Use your spirit level to check whether or not the skylight is level. If it is not, pack it up on the low side and then, using screws or nails, fasten it securely in place.*

j. *When you are fitting the flashings to the roof tiles, a softwood block can be used for beating the metal gently. Do this until it fits the contours of the tiles exactly.*

k. *When fitting the side and top flashings, proceed slowly. Double-check each step. Imagine the volume of water that runs down the roof in a storm – you don't want a drop inside!*

l. *The final step outside is to replace the tiles. This will involve cutting. Once the job is done, be sure to clear away all the debris that could block the down pipes.*

m. *Measure exposed area between the rebate in the skylight and the ceiling and cut the plasterboard to suit. Then nail the plasterboard in place, using plasterboard nails.*

n. *Metal angles, fixed over corners, strengthen the join and give a straight line to work to when you are plastering. Cut them with a hacksaw and nail them in place.*

o. *Using a trowel, apply the jointing cement in three separate layers, each one getting wider and wider. Make sure that you feather each of the joints away to nothing.*

PROCEDURE

1 Drive a thick nail into the ceiling where the skylight is to go. Wearing non-slip shoes, get up on the roof. Walk on the noses of the tiles, locate the area and remove the tiles. The skylight must not interfere with a ceiling hanger or a purlin.

Cut the tiling battens. Mark out the frame size that will hold the skylight, cut the rafters and put in trimmers in accordance with the manufacturer's instructions (see photo c). Watch carefully for wiring.

2 Cut away the excess plaster with an old saw. Take skylight from its box; remove flashings, trims etc.

3 Stand frame in recommended position and fix it to the rafters and trimmers using the brackets provided (photo g). It must be level across roof at both ends (photo h).

4 Fit the bottom flashing; bend it to follow contours of tiles.

5 Fit the side flashings, the top flashing (see k), and so on. Refit the tiles around the skylight. You could use tile cutters or a carborundum wheel fixed in your circular saw. (If the latter is used, wear goggles and long, protective clothing.) If you've done the steps correctly, your kitchen won't be a swimming pool.

6 Cut and fit the gypsum plaster so it fits into the skylight rebate. Cut and fix the metal angles which strengthen the corners (see n).

7 Plaster the corners. Sand, dry and paint them.

How to cut plasterboard

a. Measure and mark the shapes required. Make sure the face side (unmarked) faces outwards. With a sharp utility knife, cut deeply along the line.

b. Turn the board over and, holding one edge in your hand, give the sheet a bang with your fist. This should cause the sheet to break, creating a 'V'.

c. Using the utility knife, cut along the 'V' on the back of the sheet. This will ensure that the paper does not get ripped. Alternatively, use an old saw to cut sheet.

SOLAR WATER HEATING

When you open the curtains or put in a skylight and allow the sunshine in, you're harnessing solar energy in a passive way (by natural movement). When the sun heats materials such as clay bricks and slate and this stored heat is given off into a room which would otherwise begin to grow cool, you're also making use of solar energy in a passive way.

In fact, if you position a dwelling so that the living areas face north, use building materials that absorb and store heat in the winter (but are shaded in summer) and reduce heat loss by insulation and draught minimisation, what you have done is create the basics of a solar house.

But it needn't end there. You can also use solar panels to generate hot water and make the sun work for you in an active way.

Solar hot water heating

Because hot water heating accounts for 35 per cent of the electricity bills, solar heating could be for you. Whether or not it is a viable option depends on a number of factors:

The climate

Those places that are subject to many cloudy days will have less solar energy available than drier areas. Coastal environs are particularly prone to clouds and rain.

The aspect of your house

If you live in a narrow, south-facing valley, the sun will have difficulty seeking you out. A north-facing aspect is best.

The amount of shade

If your house is lost among non-deciduous trees or high buildings, forget about solar heating (unless it's possible to do any tree lopping).

The slope of your roof

The ideal slope of a roof for our purposes is 25°); the bulk of the surface should face north to ensure there is maximum exposure to the sun. If it faces east or west there is a loss of efficiency. If you have a flat roof, you may have to raise the collector panels. Seek guidance from a solar heating company on this point.

The cost

This will be determined by the amount of heating energy you require, considerations concerning the previous four points, and what amount of gas or electric boosting is required to maintain the temperature during the cooler months.

A quick call to several solar heating companies will soon put you in the picture. It's worth getting in touch with people who have had systems installed and asking them how efficient they find them to be. That way, you are not just basing your evaluation on the possibly generous claims of the manufacturer.

PRACTICAL POINTER

When selecting a solar system, don't forget to look carefully at the material from which the holding tank is made.

Systems that don't rely on water pressure (gravity-fed systems) should have copper tanks which can last a quarter of a century depending on the quality of water in your area.

However, copper is not suitable for mains pressure systems because it is not a strong metal and the tank could burst. Tanks for these systems must be made from mild steel.

To lessen the risk of rusting, the inside of such tanks is lined with glass or vitreous enamel which extends their life to 10 to 15 years. Stainless steel tanks, although expensive, last as long as copper.

Water heating improvements

Water heating accounts for around 35 per cent of your heating bills, so any improvements in the heating or usage of hot water will pay big dividends.

1. Have the hot water system checked periodically. Have leaks fixed and the thermostat checked. Turn the thermostat down in summer. When the heater is due for replacement, consider changing over to an off-peak model.
2. Wrap hot water pipes in insulation wherever possible to minimise the heat loss.
3. Fix dripping hot water taps immediately. This will save on water bills as well as on the heating costs.
4. Install a water-saving shower head (but not the type you find in some motels where the water flow is almost non-existent).
5. Limit baths; they use three to four times the amount of water expended for a quick shower. Use a plug in the handbasin rather than let the water run unheeded.
6. Washing machines: Wait until you have sufficient items to wash to warrant turning the machine on. If possible, make every load a full one; use cold washes; make use of 'sudsaver' and 'soak' cycles.

INSTALLING A NEW SHOWER ROSE

Is the shower rose in your bathroom old-fashioned? Is it too low? Does it leak or use too much water? What about the shower taps – have they almost achieved antique status?

A quick way for you to take years off your bathroom is to replace these ancient fittings with new, good-looking modern ones. They can, in most cases, simply be screwed onto the existing wall outlets.

Shower roses come in a variety of shapes and finishes. Many have specific uses. For example, by varying the number of holes in the shower rose and their diameter, some shower roses cut down water consumption. This is useful if water and heating bills are excessive or if water pressure is low. The bubble-stream shower rose is a clever little innovation worth considering; it mixes air with the water to give the illusion of a fast-running shower.

Other roses are pulsating and, according to the manufacturers, they are therapeutic as well as stimulating! These types metre the water out in spurts of varying intensity and volume, and can also be adjusted to give a normal spray.

Note: Keep in mind that it is illegal to interfere with existing plumbing by cutting into, replacing or extending pipes. There is a real potential for health hazards should foreign substances get into the water supply. A plumber must be employed to handle any such alterations. If in doubt about local regulations, check with your water supply authority.

MATERIALS

Make a quick sketch of your existing shower rose and taps (complete with a few measurements) and make your way to a plumbing supply outlet or large builder's hardware shop. You'll find a huge range to choose from so good luck! Purchase some thread tape as well and, if finances permit, consider replacing the bath and basin taps and spouts so that all the fittings are the same style.

However, bear in mind that where fittings are attached directly to a basin or bath, you may not be able to replace the handles without replacing the plumbing 'body' underneath. This will require the services of a plumber. Your hardware or plumbing supply store will be able to advise you.

TOOLS

A large adjustable spanner and a screwdriver.

PROCEDURE: SHOWER TAPS

1 Choose a day when the plumbing supply stores are open (in case of unforeseen problems). Undo the tap handle by either lifting the hot or cold indicator button and undoing the screw, or, for very old-fashioned taps, by loosening the screw that secures the handle (see diagram opposite).

2 Take off the spring-held cover or threaded flange. Install the new handle and cover.

In the event that the existing spindle and stuffing box assembly (SBA) is different from the new, turn off the water supply at the water metre. In the case of gravity-fed hot water systems, turn it off in the roof as well; if not, the tank may empty and damage the heating unit. Unscrew the SBA and return to the plumbing supply store to buy one that matches your handle and flange. Replace it, using thread tape to seal the joint. Install the new cover and handle. Turn the water supply back on and check for leaks.

***a.** Make sure the spanner fits the collar neatly, otherwise it could slip off causing damage either to your person or the shower recess.*

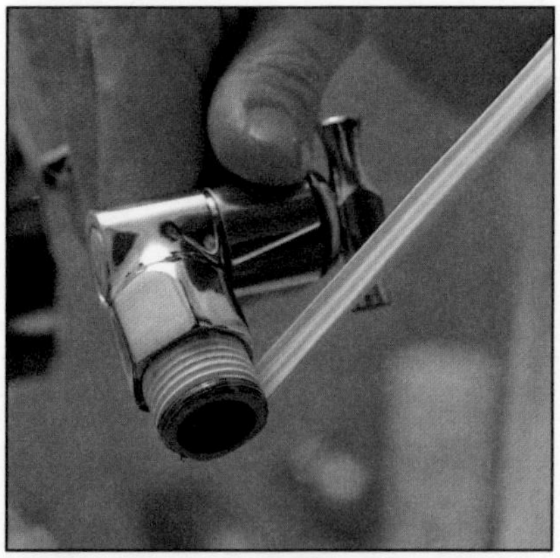

***b.** The tape seals the joint between the threads ensuring that no leaks occur and that the shower rose can be tightly positioned.*

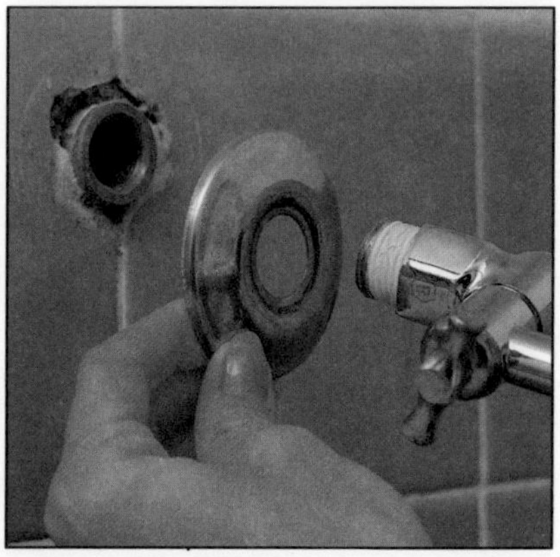

***c.** Be sure that the fitting lines up with the outlet pipe before you start screwing it on, otherwise you could find cross-threading occurring.*

PROCEDURE: SHOWER ROSE
Use the adjustable spanner on the collar at the base of the rose to unscrew it in an anti-clockwise direction. Wrap a layer of thread tape around the thread and screw the new rose into position, taking care you don't cross-thread it.

Cross-threading occurs when the fitting is put on crooked – this then makes it impossible for the threads to mesh correctly. Further tightening ensures they just chew each other to pieces. If the new fitting is initially hard to screw on, take it off, check the thread for damage and start all over again.

Note: If the fitting in the wall does not fit the shower rose (ie, you don't have a proper male/female connection) you may need to buy an hexagonal nipple to effect the join. There are all manner of adaptor fittings from which to choose; check at your plumbing supply store.

PROCEDURE: BATH SPOUTS
Twist the whole spout anti-clockwise using your hand, a screwdriver poked up the spout, a wrench that has its jaws covered with a thick cloth, or an adjustable spanner should the spout have a nut-shaped collar. Using thread tape, screw on the new fitting.

d. The result is most attractive. With this type of fitting, the height of the rose and the angle of water flow can both be adjusted.

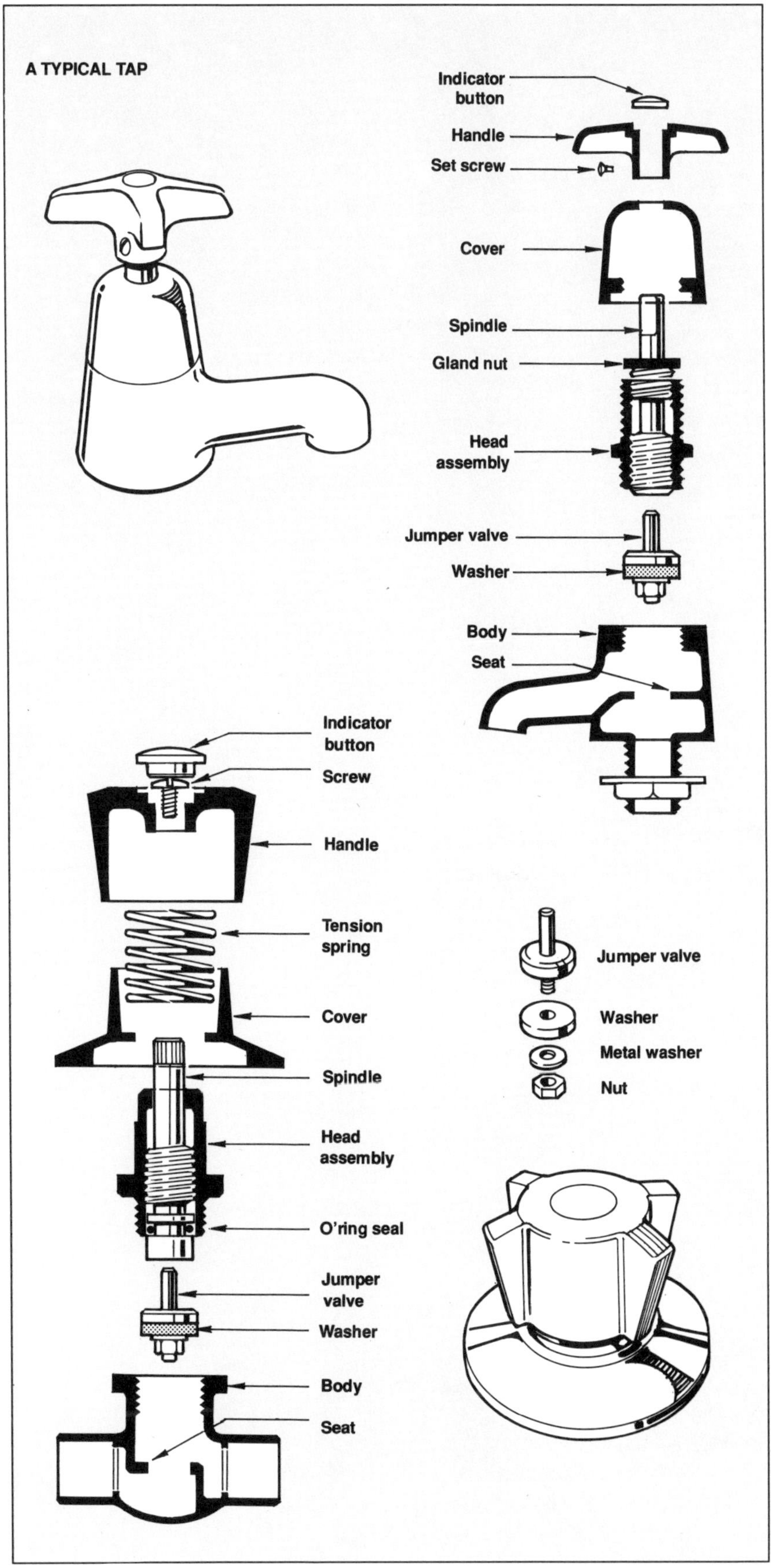

LIGHTING IMPROVEMENTS

Lighting, like heating, consumes energy. A little commonsense can go a long way in helping minimise electricity bills.

1. Dusty and dirty light globes can reduce lighting efficiency by half, to say nothing of the added eyestrain they inflict. Cleaning them regularly will make a remarkable difference

2. Fluorescent lights use a third to a quarter of the power of a conventional bulb. Down lights and spotlights are attractive but fairly inefficient forms of lighting.

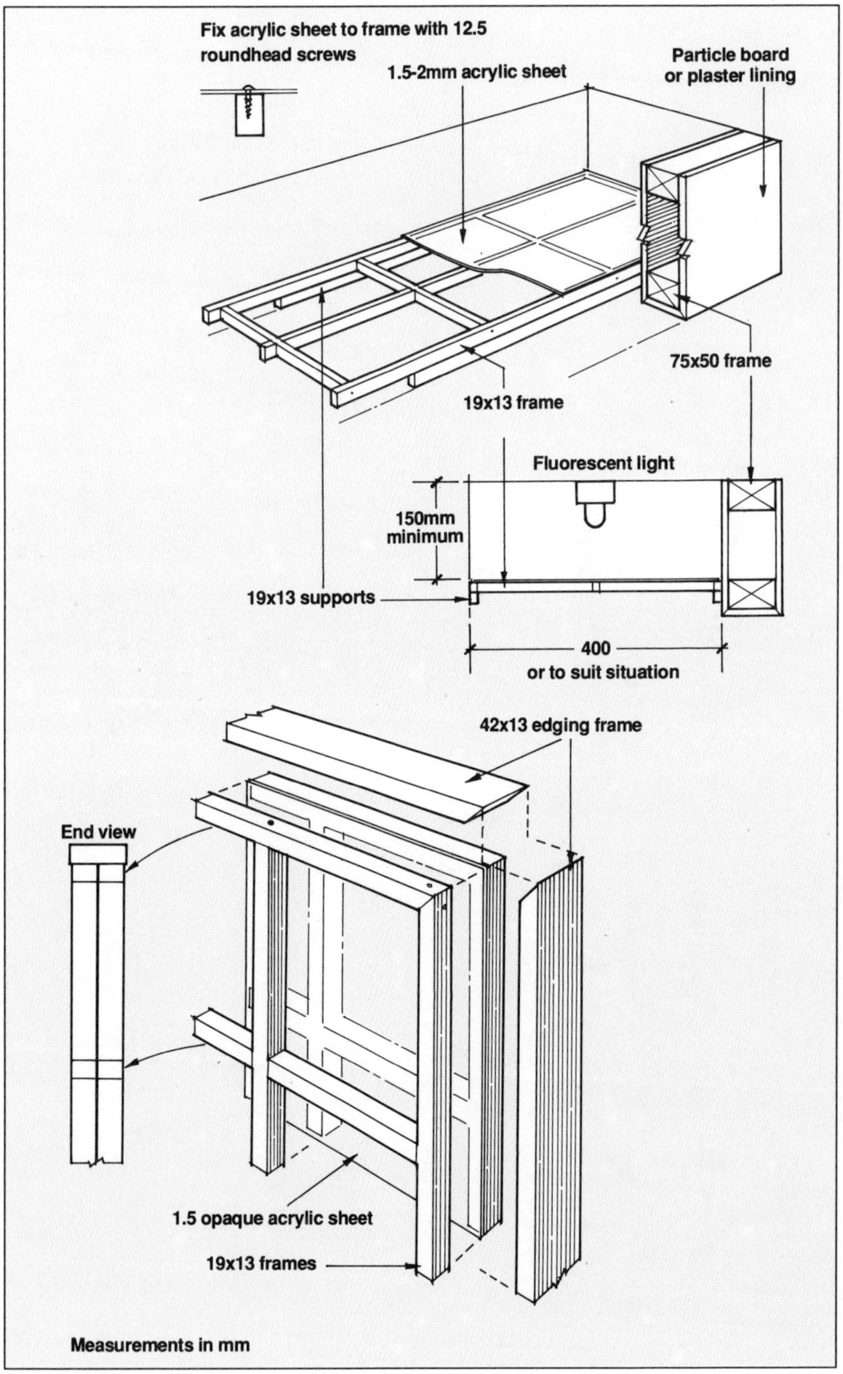

PROCEDURE: SHOJI LIGHTING

This lighting solution is practical, efficient and very striking to look at. Fluorescent tubes are ugly and give out a bright light that's inappropriate in some rooms. Here, their glare is softened and their overall appearance dramatised by the use of a false ceiling constructed of Perspex and supported by an eggcrate-style timber frame.

The diagram shows the basic construction. You will need to build a false beam across the room. This can be done by using conventional wall framing (two plates and jack studs at 600 mm centres) which is fixed to the ceiling joists or battens. If the span is bigger than 1800 mm, the bottom plate should be turned on edge and a batten nailed on one side to make it equal in width to the top plate. This false beam is then covered with gypsum plaster. The edges are reinforced with metal angles and the joints cemented in several increasingly wide layers, each one being feathered off to nothing.

Once the beam is finished, nail a batten of 19 x 13 mm (finished size) around the perimeter of the room, making sure it is at least 150 mm below the ceiling line. This allows the ceiling to be removed when tubes have to be replaced. Have an electrician install banks of fluorescents if conventional lighting has been used.

Make up the ceiling frame, again using 19 x 13 mm dressed battens which are glued and nailed together. It should have 2 mm clearance all round. The sides are full-length and the cross members are nailed into them. The centre divisions are supported by these cross members.

Once the glue is dry, ensure that the frame fits. Sand and finish it with varnish or paint. Black gives a par-

ticularly striking result. When the paint is dry, fix the 1.5 to 2 mm thick Perspex to the top of the frame with 12 mm roundhead screws. Make sure you drill adequate clearance holes in the Perspex so that it doesn't crack. Lay the frame in position, stand back and be knocked out by the great effect – and the many compliments that you'll receive.

This style of lighting has more applications than simply the ceiling one shown above. You could build two identical timber frames and sandwich the Perspex between them. Used vertically, this would make an interesting room divider.

CHAPTER 4

SECURITY AND PRIVACY

Modern society has many advantages, but, as with everything, there is a downside. Security, safety and privacy are matters of concern to us all, particularly in tough economic times. Where once we could be casual in our use of lock and key, most of us now consider it essential that our homes be locked securely – not only to protect our belongings when we're absent, but to protect ourselves and our families when in residence.

Security hints

1. Illuminating the grounds of your property helps deter burglars (50 per cent of robberies take place after dark). As well as manually operated lights there are lighting systems which switch themselves on when a trespasser approaches – very off-putting to a potential intruder.
2. Don't leave ladders lying about to provide easy access to unlocked high windows and the roof; an enterprising burglar will think nothing of lifting a few tiles and breaking in. Unfortunately, in 30 per cent of robberies, the intruders gain entry through windows or doors that have been left unlocked.
3. Don't create handy shrub or tree-clad nooks around windows and doors. You're playing into the hands of the burglars if you provide them with places where they can conceal themselves. Make sure anyone who comes to your home can be seen from the road and/or the house, if at all possible.
4. High fences and lock-up security gates at entry points and in side passages make it very difficult for the television-carrying burglar.
5. Unlocked garages and sheds provide a would-be intruder with a wonderful array of housebreaking tools. Lock up your outbuildings.
6. A dog of the right breed and with the right training can be a great deterrent – but it must not be a nuisance or a danger to the innocent. Nor should it attack a burglar too enthusiastically; the way the law stands, the intruder could end up suing you!
7. Don't put addresses on key rings. If you lose them or give them to people in service and parking stations, you run an obvious risk from an opportunist.
8. If you go away, cancel papers and arrange for trusted neighbours to collect your mail and occasionally check the property. Give the impres-

sion that you are still in residence; have someone mow your lawn, use time switches to activate the lights and radios at various times, leave some curtains open. Turn the telephone down, and tell as few people as possible that you are going to be away.
9. Make a list of your valuables complete with make, model and serial numbers. Engrave your licence number on them, where appropriate. Secure expensive jewellery or anything that is of great sentimental value to you or your family in bank safe-deposit boxes or in a properly installed home safe.
10. If you're in a high-risk area, install an alarm system.

OPERATING A HAND DRILL

A hand drill is easy to operate and is ideal for the beginner. To drill a hole that is about the same size as your screw, you need some twist drills. Insert one in the neck of the hand drill and tighten the chuck (diagram 1) while holding the turning handle until the twist drill is firmly held.

To make a hole, first study a screw carefully. It has three distinct parts: the head, the shank and the thread. To ensure proper fastening, drill one hole to suit the shank size and one to suit the average diameter of the metal core around which the thread turns. Choose a twist drill the same size as the shank diameter. Hold it against the shank and check it is equal or fractionally larger (diagram 2). Insert it into your hand drill as explained.

Practise on a spare piece of timber; you must master getting the drill to enter the wood without moving off the marked spot. Also, you must learn to drill no deeper than the length of the shank. The screw will not hold if you do. Keep pulling the drill out as a check, or mark the depth required on the twist drill with masking tape. You must change the twist drill to suit the diameter of the thread core to complete the hole (diagram 3).

Diagram 1

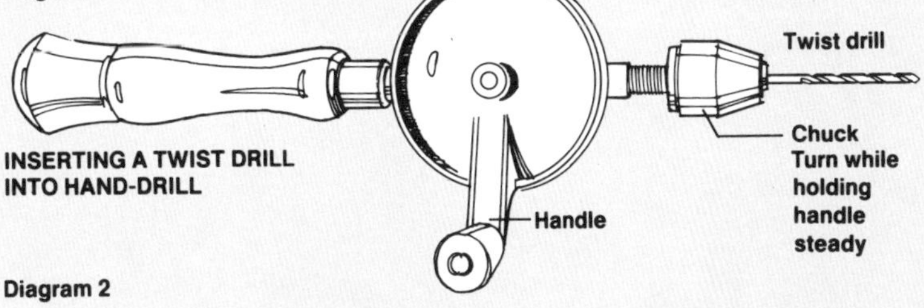

INSERTING A TWIST DRILL INTO HAND-DRILL

Diagram 2

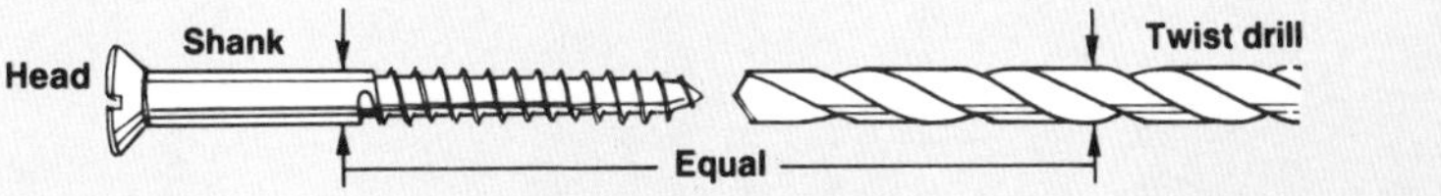

MATCHING THE TWIST DRILL WITH THE SCREW SHANK

Diagram 3

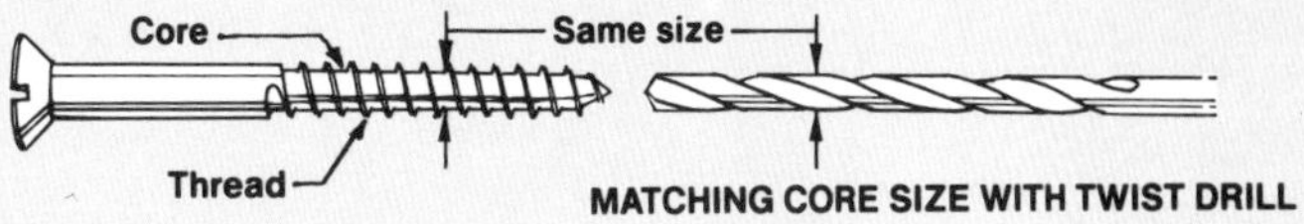

MATCHING CORE SIZE WITH TWIST DRILL

INSTALLING A DEADLOCK

A cylindrical deadlock on all your external doors (or a cylindrical lock set on a home office or bedroom door) gives a sense of security that more than compensates for the effort and cost involved in its installation. You will need to bore two holes and do a little chiselling to install a lock of this kind. Mortice locks, on the other hand, need many more holes bored.

A deadlock ensures that, even if an intruder gains access via a window, he or she can't open the door. A deadlock has no handle and can only be opened with a key (inside and out) and the idea of having to haul your heavy valuables through a window may well see the would-be burglar on his way. Keyed locks on the windows are worth considering.

MATERIALS

A good quality lock; putty; touch-up paint or varnish. Study the installation instructions for your lock.

TOOLS

A brace and bits to suit the lock; you'll need an expansion bit to cut the big hole (alternatively, use an electric drill and buy a 'hole saw and speed bit' set – one made specifically for fitting cylindrical locks); tape and pencil; 10 mm and 20 mm sharp chisels; hammer; nail punch; a fixed or ratchet screwdriver to suit the screws supplied.

PROCEDURE

1 If the door is framed or solid-core, you can install the lock at any height on the opening edge. If the door is hollow-core, you must put the deadlock within 100 mm or so of the other lock to make sure you are fixing it into the lock block. Tap door with a hammer wrapped in a tea-towel to find where the block ends; listen for the hollow sound.

2 Use template provided to mark the hole positions on the edge and both faces of the door (see a).

3 Use your brace or electric drill to bore the two holes (the big one first) to the correct diameter (see b). For a mortice lock, bore a series of holes and clean out all the waste with a chisel. When boring the hole in the door face, it's best to come in half way from both faces to avoid the wood splintering.

4 Slide the lock into the edge of the door and then mark around

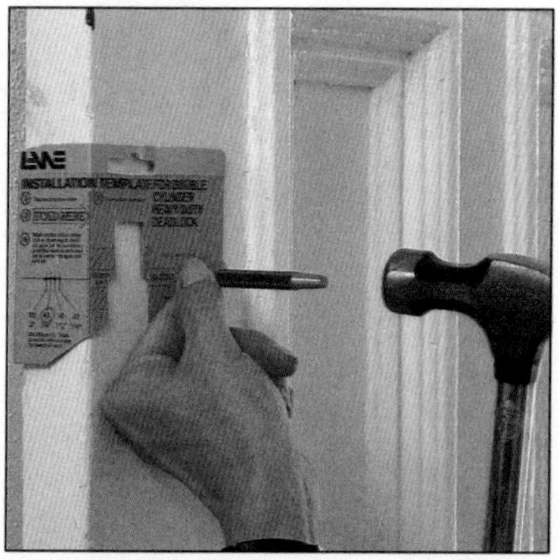

a. *Mark hole positions with template.*

b. *Drill holes in door face and edge.*

c. *Mark latchplate; chisel out for it.*

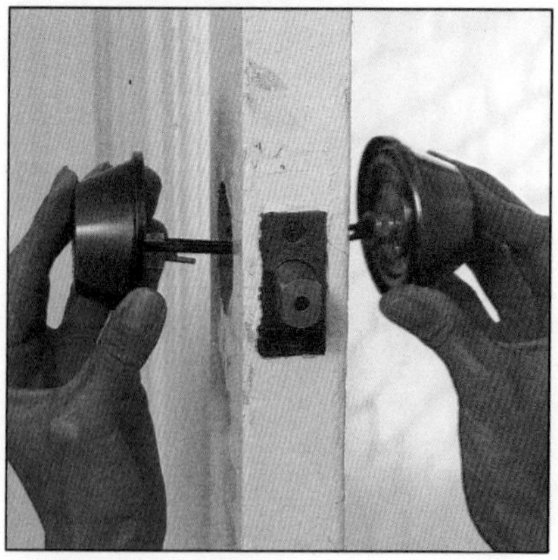

d. *Read instructions; fit cylinder*

e. *Mark door jamb for striker plate.*

f. *With sharp chisel, fit striker plate.*

the face plate with a sharp pencil.

5 Using a sharp chisel and a hammer, carefully check out a recess into which the face plate can fit, making sure you don't go any deeper than the thickness of the face plate itself (see c). Slide the lock in and adjust the check out until the face plate fits flush with the edge of the door. If you've gone too deep, you must cut some pieces of cardboard to pack it out.

6 Use the nail punch and hammer to make a space for the screws of the face plate to be inserted. Screw the lock in place. Put on the key cylinder (or handles for a lock set) carefully following the instructions provided (see d).

7 Open the lock slightly and mark the jamb (the frame into which the door fits) at the point where the dead-bolt or latch strikes it (see e). Measure the distance between the back of the door and the front of the dead-bolt and, marking from the rebate, draw a line to represent this position. Place the striker plate over these marks and, with a sharp pencil, mark around the striker plate. When the striker plate is sunk in, the dead-bolt should go in the hole provided when the door is closed.

8 Check out for the striker plate, place it in position, then make sure the dead-bolt lines up with the hole (see f). Mark around the dead-bolt, remove the striker plate and chop out the hole to a depth that will allow the dead-bolt or latch to be fully extended.

9 Screw in the striker plate. Fill any irregularities or chips with putty; touch-up the finish.

Note: It is important to keep the deadlock key hidden, but it must be in a readily accessible place. Make sure that all your family members know where to find it in a hurry. In case of an emergency, such as a fire, it is vital that everyone is able to get out of the house quickly.

SAFETY CHAIN

A safety chain on a timber front or back door allows you to open the door marginally to see who's calling, but won't afford an opening sufficient for anyone to enter. It also doubles the security of a lock and makes you feel a great deal more comfortable about being home alone.

MATERIALS AND TOOLS

A hefty safety chain, preferably one made from stainless steel – the screws supplied with it must be stout and at least 38 mm long (50 mm is better); hand drill (an electric drill can also be used); a set of suitable drills; screwdriver to suit the screws; pencil and rule.

a. *Position safety chain close to lock on hollow core door (so that you'll have something solid to screw to) and mark screw holes. With solid timber doors, the height is up to you. The fitting with the chain goes on the jamb side (the frame the door hangs in).*

b. *Pre-drill one screw hole to suit the shank size (see diagram previous page) and one to suit the average diameter of the core around which thread turns. Drill no deeper than shank length. Now use twist drill to drill rest of hole slightly longer than the length of the screw.*

c. *Select a screwdriver that fits the head of the screw. It should be slightly narrower than the head diameter and fit tightly across the width. Excess movement could cause the screwdriver to turn out of the screw head and damage the slot.*

d. *Sink in all the screws until they are tight. Slip on the chain. The chain should be long enough to reach between the two fittings, allowing the door to open a few centimetres so that you can see who is there without allowing them to enter.*

DOOR BELL

Most of the many types of bell on the market can be installed in a couple of hours. Try to avoid the ones which play a symphony; their charm wears thin rapidly. Units that have adjustable volume are handy if you are often in the garden.

Buy a bell that comprises a bell unit, push-button assembly and batteries. (Keep a supply of batteries on hand.) If wire is supplied, check that it is long enough to reach from the front door to where you want the bell installed. You can run the wire on top of the skirting; at its base; tucked down behind the carpet; under the floor. Bring the wire up to the bell unit alongside a convenient architrave. Don't install a bell close to sources of heat or steam.

TOOLS

Fasteners for the fine wires; hammer; electric drill and drill set; tape and pencil; pliers; screwdrivers.

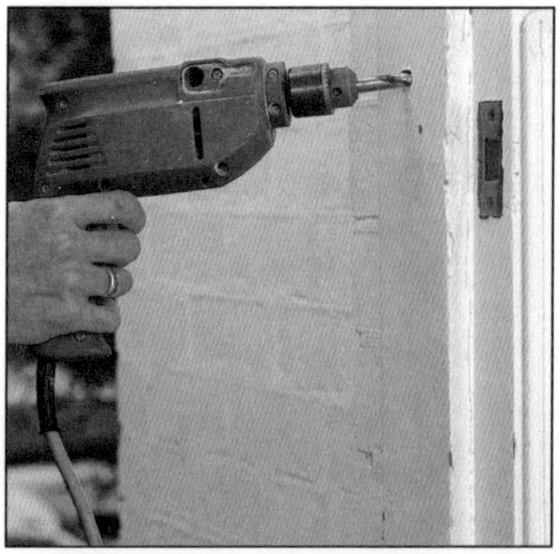

***a.** Mark position of push-button; drill 10 mm holes through the jamb in two directions so that wiring can reach the inside in an unobtrusive place.*

***b.** Thread the wiring through the holes. A bent piece of wire with a loop in one end may have to be used because the hole is two-directional.*

***c.** Bare the two strands of wire and wrap them clockwise around each terminal of the button assembly. Tighten screws well to ensure good contact.*

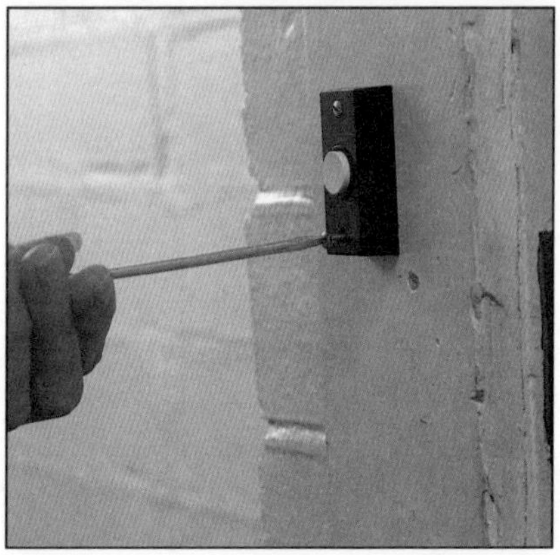

***d.** Screw the button to the jamb with the screws provided. Use putty to fill the hole on the inside, then run the cable down the jamb to the floor.*

***e.** Using the small wire clips spaced at about 150 mm centres, run the wire along towards the bell location on top of skirting as shown. Alternatively, you can tuck it down along the edge of the carpet if you prefer.*

***f.** Mark the fixing holes for bell unit on the wall and drill to suit your fastenings – a stud or spring toggles. Poke the wire through the unit and screw bell to the wall With masonry walls, drill a hole, plug it, then fasten.*

***g.** Bare the two strands of wire as before and fix the ends to the terminals, following the wiring diagram supplied. Then install the batteries and put on the front cover. The bell should now be in working order.*

WINDOW LOCKS

a. *Carefully read the instructions supplied with your chosen lock. Place the fitting in its recommended position and accurately mark around the screw holes with a sharp pencil or, alternatively, use a punch.*

b. *Using the correct-sized drills, pre-drill the holes, first for the screws and then for the locking bar. Drive the nail 3-4 mm into the centre of each screw position before drilling; this will help keep drill holes in the correct place.*

c. *Screw the fittings on with the 'one way' screws and test. Continue until all the windows are lockable*
Note: *Drill hole for locking bar with drill of a largeish diameter which will be easier to turn with an electric drill.*

The extensive use of glass in our homes makes it relatively easy for burglars to smash or cut their way in. However, you can make it difficult for them to remove your belongings if you install deadbolts on external doors and keyed locks on all the windows. Unless the burglars can locate the keys, they can't open anything and are forced to clamber out through a window edged with broken glass.

Putting locks on timber windows is relatively easy; it may even reduce your insurance premiums and, better still, may considerably reduce the likelihood of burglary.

Purchase a system with a single master key. Keep the key in a secure, secret spot. Locks featuring one-way screws are the easiest to install; a one-way screw can be screwed in but can't be screwed out.

Establish what type of timber window you have. A timber window consists of a number of sashes (the frames that hold the glass) which are fixed by a variety of fittings to an outside frame. These sashes will be either horizontally or vertically sliding; casement (opening outward from the side): awning (opening outward at the bottom); or hopper (opening outward at the top).

Make sure the type and number of locks you select will suit your windows. If you're unsure, ask at your hardware store.

TOOLS

A hand drill (or electric drill); a set of drills that suit the fittings; screwdriver; measuring tape; hammer; a 50 mm nail (or fine nail punch); a pencil.

PEEP-HOLE

Before purchasing a peep-hole from your local hardware store, check for clarity and the range of visibility it allows. Where you position it must be determined by the height of those most likely to use it. Keep in mind that people who knock on the door may stand in a certain place because of a flyscreen or other object, so position the peep-hole opposite this point.

The device consists of two parts which screw into each other; all that is required is that a hole of a suitable diameter be drilled through the door. When drilling a ply-faced door, make sure you come in from both sides. Should you come in from one side only there is a chance that the ply could break out on the opposite side. Once drilling is complete, screw the peep-hole in place.

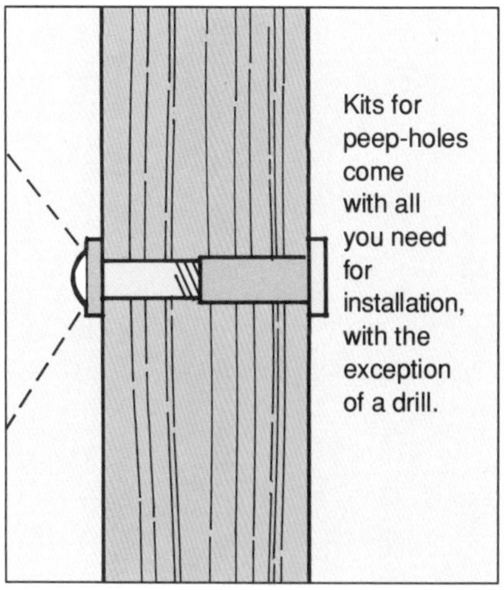

Kits for peep-holes come with all you need for installation, with the exception of a drill.

HANGING A DOOR

There are times when even the most gregarious among us cries out for privacy. Create a quiet retreat just by adding a door and lock to what was once a walk-through space.

To establish the size of the door, measure in between the jamb rebates for the width, and from the floor to the door head for the height. Check in a few places to make sure the frame members are parallel.

Your supplier will determine the exact size door you require but keep in mind the finished door must have 2-3 mm clearance on either side and the top to prevent it sticking. It needs 5-15 mm clearance at the bottom so that the door will clear the floor covering. Even if you don't intend putting carpet down for some time, allow for it; it's a nuisance cutting a door down at a later stage. Getting it off its hinges causes damage to the paintwork.

MATERIALS AND TOOLS

Hammer; sharp chisel; marking gauge (optional); screwdriver; smoother plane; hand drill and drills; tape and pencil; a hand or circular saw (if the door has to be cut down); brass or steel hinges and screws to match existing doors. For convenience, buy loose pin hinges in preference to fixed. If you want the door to open against the wall, buy broad butt hinges.

PROCEDURE

1 If the door is oversize, lay it on a table or set of stools and mark the amount that has to come off. With a solid-core door you can remove the surplus from any point you like. With a framed door, you must take half the required amount off each of the stiles (the vertical members). To achieve the height you need, cut waste off the bottom rail.

A hollow-core door with its flimsy frame (as thin as 25 mm) must be reduced evenly all around. You can't remove more than 3-5 mm or there will be no frame left. Make sure you keep the lock stile (clearly marked) to the lock side; if not, you'll have nothing to which to fix the handle.

If the amount to come off is small, planing is the best method. For amounts over 6 mm, use a saw. If the door is ply-faced, you can saw 'with the grain' with impunity. If sawing 'across the grain', as would happen if reducing the door's height, cut the door with a trimming knife on the underside before sawing to stop the grain tearing. Cut 1 mm away from your line so you can plane the edge smooth without making the door undersize.

2 Once the door is approximately to size, fit one edge. Push this edge against the jamb and scribe it with a sharp pencil. When planing, slightly undercut the edge so that it won't bind when the door closes. Push the door into the corner of a room so it will be held securely while you are planing it.

3 Once one edge is fitted perfectly, make a small block that is equal to double the required clearance. With the door hard against one side, scribe the other side (see photo b). Plane to your line, again slightly undercutting the edge.

4 Fit the top against the door head. Mark and plane the bottom. When the margins are correct, put a small chamfer (a 45° bevel) on all sharp edges.

PUTTING ON THE HINGES

1 Block the door in position with the correct clearance at the top and hard against the hinge stile of the jamb (you will find that two chisels are handy for this task).

a. *If the amount of waste to be removed is small, push the door into a corner. Then, propping the door up on an old phone book, use a sharp plane to bring it to size.*

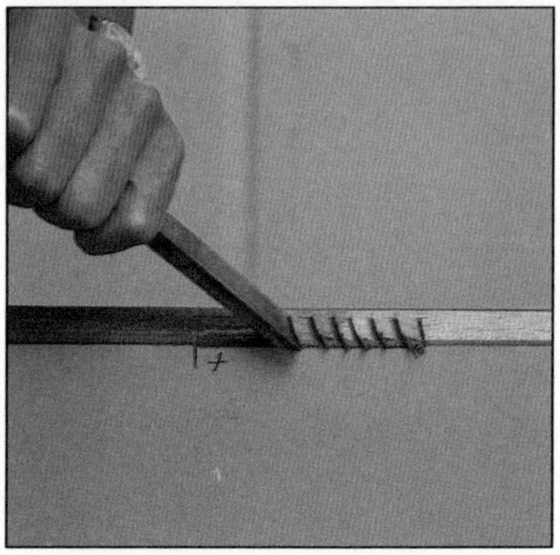

e. *To loosen as much of the waste as possible, hold your chisel, bevel down (as shown), and then tap the handle with a hammer. It will peel off the waste in little sections.*

2 Check the other doors in your home to see where the hinges are placed. Measure these distances and draw a small, level line across the jamb and door (photo c). Put crosses where the hinges are to go.

3 Again put the door in a corner and, opening the hinge up, lay it against the mark and trace out the length of the leaf. Mark how far the hinges should go in from the door face (photo d) – check this distance on one of the other doors. Mark this width with your gauge, it will give you a shoulder against which to chisel.

b. *Once the edge is fitted, use your scribe block to mark the clearance on the other side. Because the block follows the exact line of the jamb, the clearance will be perfect.*

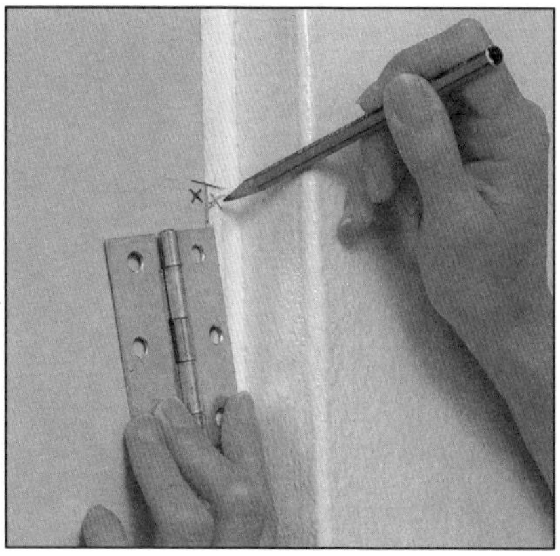

c. *By using crosses where the hinge is to go you will ensure that you don't cut out one leaf of the hinge on one side of the line and the opposite leaf on the other.*

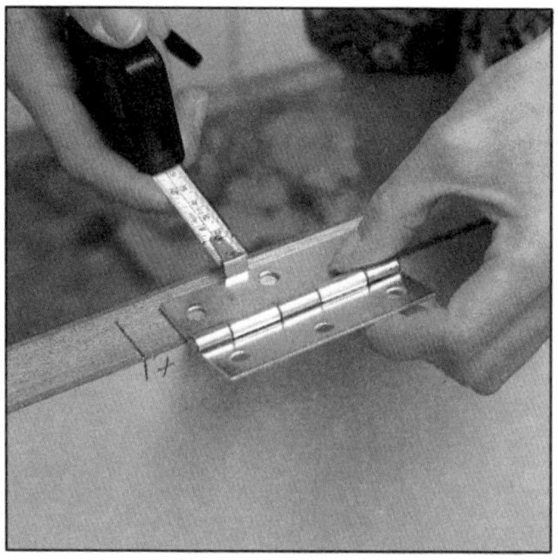

d. *Establishing the hinge position on the edge of the door can be done by measurement (as shown) or by turning the hinge over and using the knuckle as a guide.*

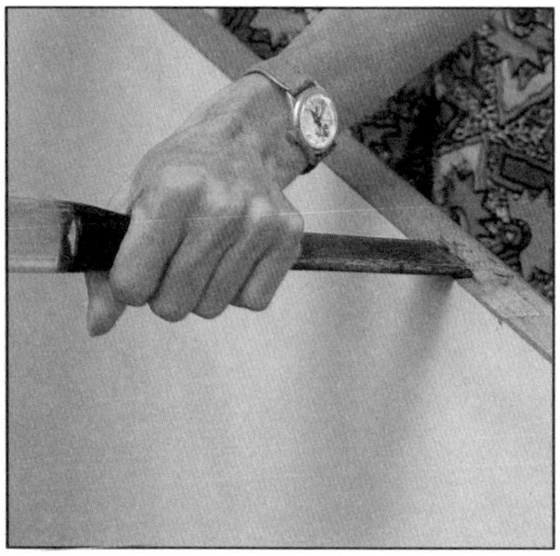

f. *When chiselling in from the face of the door, take great care that you don't hit the chisel too hard; you might break off the solid timber on the far edge of the recess.*

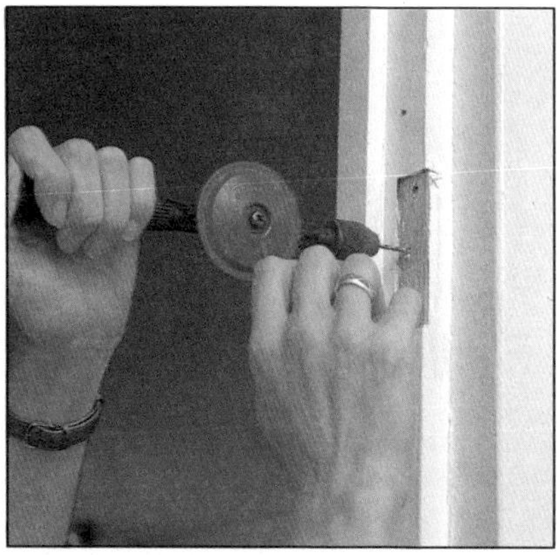

g. *Once you have marked and chiselled out the recess for the hinge leaves on the jamb, mark the screw holes and pre-drill the holes so that driving them is easy.*

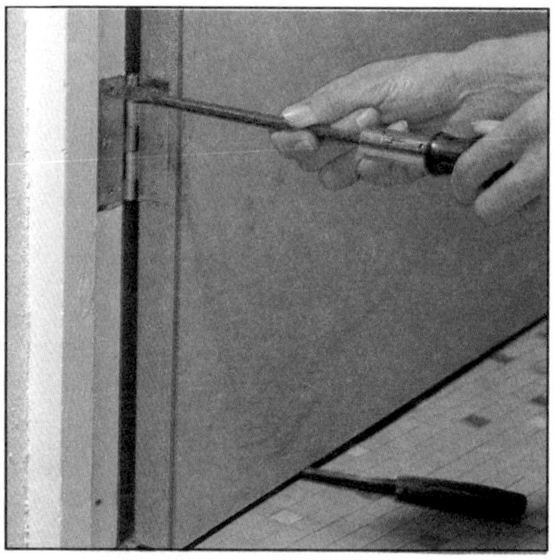

h. *This is the moment of truth. Screw the door to the jamb using one screw only in each hinge and test to see if the door fits. If you've followed the instructions carefully, it will.*

4 Mark the depth the hinge must be set in. Normally, this will be equal to the thickness of the hinge leaf. To check, close the hinge and measure the gap between the leaves near the pin. If your required clearance is greater, don't set the hinges in as deeply. If your desired clearance is less, make the hinge recesses slightly deeper.

5 Carefully chop out the hinge recesses with your hammer and chisel (see photos e and f) watching the lines and making sure you don't chisel 'with the grain' (otherwise you could accidentally split the door).

6 Mark out the hinge positions on the jamb. Everything is done the same way, with the exception of the hinge width position.

To mark this, measure the distance between the back of your door and the hinge. Add 1.5 mm to this measurement and mark it from the shoulder of the jamb rebate to the edge of the hinge recess.

This will push the door away from the rebate 1.5 mm, giving clearance that will prevent the door becoming hinge-bound (and difficult to close in the process) in the rebate. Gauge this line.

7 Chop out the hinge recesses on the jamb. Mark the screw holes and pre-drill (see photo g). Screw the hinges to the door and, using your chisel to get it to the correct height, screw them to the jamb. If you have followed the instructions carefully the door should now swing neatly in the opening. If the clearance margins are uneven, you can either unscrew the door and take a little more out of the recess in the jamb or cut a little piece of cardboard and pack behind the hinges.

Sand off all the pencil marks and apply your chosen finish.

PRIVACY SET

Installing this privacy set to a door involves very little effort in relation to the security it offers. It requires little more than boring a couple of holes and doing a spot of chiselling. An important feature is its safety device whereby the lock can be released fromthe outside should a small child inadvertently lock itself in.

MATERIALS

A good quality lock; putty; touch-up paint or varnish to finish.

TOOLS

Brace and softwood bit to suit the lock (an electric drill and speed drill will also work); measuring tape and pencil; a sharp 10 mm and 20 mm chisel; hammer; hacksaw; nail punch; screwdriver (either fixed or ratchet) to suit the screws supplied.

PROCEDURE

1 Read the installation instructions for the lock several times. Planning and understanding what you have to do is the secret to any successful project. For hollow-core doors, the lock will have to be located somewhere in the lock block. Tap the door with a hammer wrapped in a tea-towel to determine where the block ends: you'll hear a hollow sound.

2 Once the height is decided, mark the hole positions on the edge and both faces of the door, using the cardboard template (if there happens to be one).

3 Put the bit in the chuck of the brace (or a speed drill in the electric drill) and first bore the hole in the face of the door (see photo b). You may have to clear the hole periodically should the bit become choked with waste. Bore in from one side until the feed screw on the bit just emerges on the other side. Complete the hole from that side to avoid splintering. Do the edge.

4 Now slide the tubular lock into the edge of the door and then mark around the face plate with a sharp pencil.

5 Use a sharp chisel and a hammer to carefully check out a

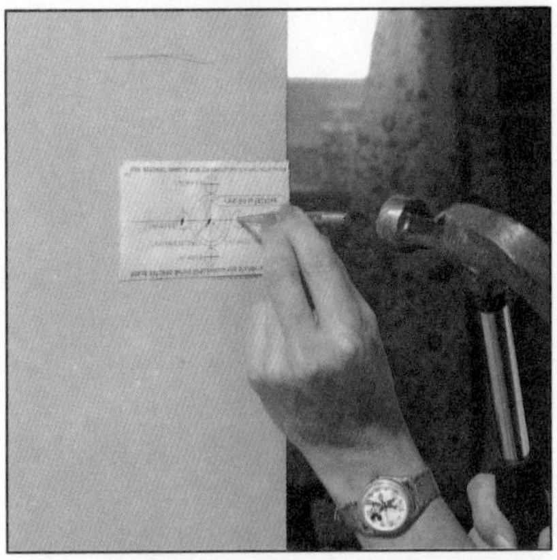

a. *Using a cardboard template, mark hole positions with a hammer and punch.*

b. *With a brace and bit, or speed borer and electric drill, drill holes.*

c. *Mark the latchplate position and chisel out recess; screw into place.*

d. *Fix handle to one side of door and check that it turns; fit other handle.*

e. *When screwing striker plate to jamb, ensure screwdriver doesn't slip.*

f. *If you have been careful and followed instructions, the door will close.*

recess into which the face plate will fit. Slide the lock in and adjust the check out until the face plate fits flush with the edge of the door (see photo c). If it's too deep, cut a piece of cardboard to pack it out.

6 Use the nail punch and hammer to make a space for the face-plate screws to be inserted. Screw the lock in place, put on the handles (see photo d). You may have to shorten the handle bar with your hacksaw.

7 Mark where the latch strikes the jamb. Measure the distance between the back of the door and the front of the latch and, marking from the rebate, draw a vertical line to represent this position. Place the striker plate over these marks and, with a sharp pencil, mark around the outside of the striker plate.

8 Check out for the striker plate, place it in position, and make sure the latch lines up with the hole. Mark around the latch hole, remove the striker plate and chop out the hole so that you allow the latch to fully extend.

9 Screw in the striker plate (see photo e) and test that the release device works. Fill irregularities with putty; now touch up the finish.

PRACTICAL POINTER

When selecting a privacy set, keep the following in mind:

☐ You only get what you pay for. You'll find that a cheap lock will often break down.

☐ Smooth, round handles are a problem if you have wet hands. In a kitchen or bathroom, it might be better to avoid them.

☐ Brass handles look great when new but, as a rule, quickly tarnish. As most are only brass plated they can't be polished repeatedly so their good looks are, unfortunately, only temporary.

A touch of oil or some graphite from a lead pencil will keep locks functioning smoothly.

BIFOLD DOORS

Bifold doors are magic in small homes and units for concealing those not-so-attractive workplaces such as laundries, home offices and sinks. A metal track is installed along the head of the opening you wish to close off. Smaller than conventional-width doors – louvred, flush, or framed and panelled – are suspended from this track and, like a piano accordion, they open out or fold up. But, unlike a conventional door, they only take up half the room. You can cover openings from 915 mm to 2400 mm using doors 19 x 35 mm thick.

The bottom pivot off which the door turns has to be positioned exactly under the top corner of the supporting door to ensure a smooth folding action. Also, if you hinge the doors by fastening the hinges to the edge of the door rather than by recessing them, you will have the necessary clearance to guarantee easy opening.

A bifold kit usually includes the track, top brackets, bottom pivots, hinges and all the fastenings. The instructions enclosed must be read before beginning the project.

Four 650 mm wide louvred doors are used to divide a small laundry area from a main room.

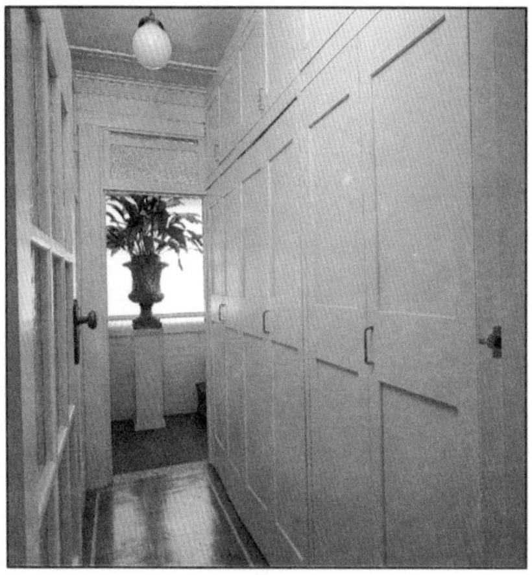

These floor-to-ceiling panelled doors close to leave the hallway unobstructed when its not being used as a dressing room.

These bifolds across the sink match the others which conceal the clothes storage area.

How bifolds work; the inside story. The two outer edges of the hinged pair slide together along the track.

COUNTRY-STYLE DOORS

Modern internal doors, in the main, tend to be plain. You might want to rebel against this trend but find that the cost of framed and panelled doors is exorbitant. Or, you may have an odd-sized opening that doesn't accommodate the standard door sizes (widths 720, 760, 820 and 870 mm and height 2040 mm). If so, why not build your own framed and braced door that has definite character? Look carefully at the style of your house and make sure the design is in keeping with it.

MATERIALS

Two lengths of 90 x 19 mm timber (cedar, Tasmanian oak, oregon, for example) the length of the door make up the vertical frame members (stiles). Two lengths of the same size make up the middle and the top horizontals (rails). The bottom one is 180 x 19 mm, twice as wide as the middle and top ones.

Two more lengths 90 x 19 mm create the braces. Note that the braces are almost parallel and run upwards from the hinged side to stop the door from dropping. The framing lengths will have to be made to suit your particular door size.

The lining boards will typically be 2100 mm in length. The number required will depend on how much each board covers. Allow for removing the tongue and the groove from the two outside boards, or the edges will look unsightly.

TOOLS

Panel saw; electric saw; hammer and punch; electric drill and drills; sash cramps; tape and pencil; square; plane; sandpaper and cork.

PROCEDURE

1 Cut the stiles and rails to length. Erect a work bench out of stools and planks; lay the stiles and rails in place on it (see photo a). Fit the joints with a sharp plane set fine.

2 Glue the joints with a high-strength glue such as epoxy. (It is clear, so you can stain the door if you wish.) Use the cramps to hold it

***a.** A building square is essential for checking right angles.*

***b.** Sash cramps are ideal for a frame of any type; adjust them to any width.*

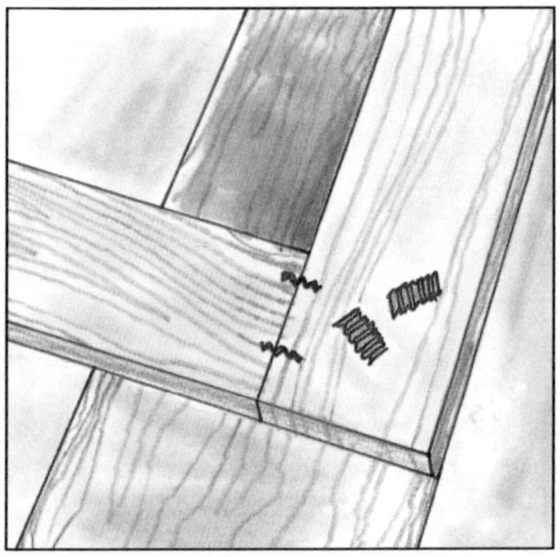

***c.** Reinforce the joints with wriggle nails, two at each corner.*

***e.** Spread more glue; lay the rest of the boards in place for cramping.*

***f.** Use a sash cramp to squeeze the boards together prior to fastening.*

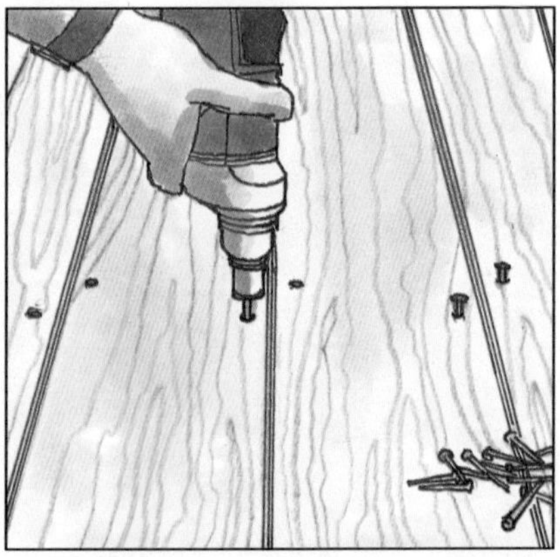

***g.** An electric drill makes the pre-drilling for the screw holes easy.*

Depending on the look you like, hang door with braces hidden or exposed.

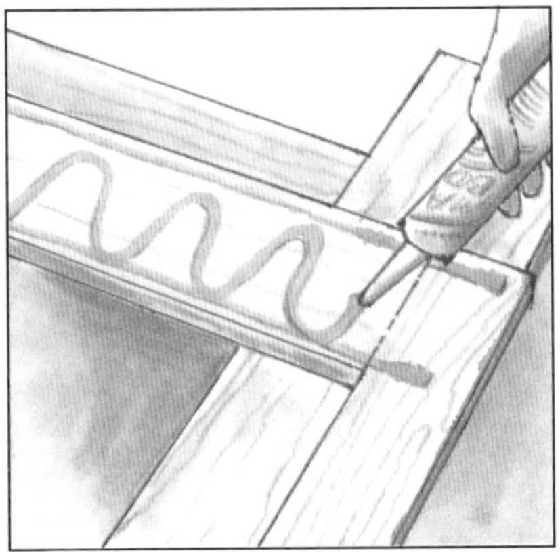

***d.** Once outside boards are to size, glue and fix one of them to one side.*

***h.** Use your square to establish the correct angle for the ends of braces.*

together (photo b). Check for square by measuring that the diagonals are the same. A piece of clear plastic wrap placed under each joint will prevent frame and planks becoming glued together. Place two wriggle nails in each joint to add strength; nail them in from the back of the frame so they won't be visible.

3 Lay the boards on the frame; lightly cramp them. Mark and rip the two outside boards to width making sure they're the same size. Spread glue on the back of the frame (photo d), position the boards (photo f), cramp and fasten them.

You have a choice of fasteners: screws or jolt-head nails, two to each joint where each board touches a rail or stile. Pre-drilling is necessary for screws. In either case, draw a line across the centre of the rails so that fastenings end up in a straight line.

4 Once the glue has dried, turn the door over and fit the braces (see photo g). Line up the centre of each brace with the corner. Glue the braces in position, turn door over, fasten the boards to them, again using two fasteners to each joint.

5 Once dried, clean off excess glue, sand carefully and hang the door.

INSTALLING FRENCH DOORS

Do you wish sometimes that you were able to create the illusion of bringing the outdoors indoors? If you were to break through an external wall and put in a pair of French doors, the effect would be just that. If there's a patio or deck outside, so much the better. The before and after photographs (right) show what can be achieved. If there is an existing window in the desired location, then the job is even easier that you might think.

Check with your local council to see if you need plans and approvals. This is, after all, a structural alteration. However, the council inspector may feel these are not warranted for such a minor job, particularly if a window already exists, which means that the wall, ceiling and roof above are, in fact, properly supported.

Before (above) and after (right). Hard to believe that French doors can make such a difference to a room.

ESTABLISHING THE HEIGHT

Check that the height from the floor to the top of the window will accommodate standard doors. You need 10 mm clearance at the bottom for vinyl or cork and 20 mm for carpet. Allow for the thickness of the jamb rebate at the top plus a 10 mm clearance to make sure that there's no weight on the jamb which might cause it to deflect. If the height is insufficient, you may have to have the French doors made especially for you. If it's too high, you can always fill in the gap.

Note: If the door has no roofed area outside it, as shown in our example, you will need to construct a sill across the bottom of the opening to keep the elements at bay.

ESTABLISHING THE WIDTH

The opening width, if wider than the twin doors, is not so important as you can always put in a few extra studs. But, if it is too narrow, the doors will have to be made to suit. Allow for the two jamb rebates plus 10 mm clearance on both sides. Lay out the height and width of the opening full-size on a piece of timber 100 x 50 mm. Draw in the members and measure the sizes. That done, you can obtain a price from a joinery shop. Keep the piece of timber to help you to get the framing the correct size.

Note: If you intend making your opening wider than a window, or to increase the height of the opening, you must seek the advice or assistance of a qualified builder in case you bring the roof and ceiling down around your ears.

PLANNING FOR THE JOB

How quickly you set about this task depends on whether there is a roof outside and how long you can leave a large opening exposed. Obviously, from the weather and security point of view, the quicker the job is done the better.

MATERIALS

Doors, jambs, extra framing (if required), hinges, 75 mm nails and so forth should be on site before the job begins. If a delay threatens and you're keen to get started, a couple of sheets of corrugated iron or fibrous cement will serve as a temporary cover to the opening.

TOOLS
Pinch bar; hammer; tape and pencil; circular saw; panel saw; chisel; spirit level; screwdrivers; electric drill and drill set; spanner or socket set; hacksaw; plus door hanging tools (see index for Hanging a Door project).

PROCEDURE
The steps will probably have to be modified to suit your situation. In the example here, the window and wall were able to be removed and a new wall constructed without affecting the lightweight roofing.

1 Wait for a forecast of a spell of dry and non-windy weather. Remove the cladding (outside wall covering) and lining (inside wall covering) respectively from below the window (in our case above, as well). If it's lined with asbestos cement, be particularly careful and wear a particle mask and gloves. Bury the asbestos cement or dispose of it in an approved area.

2 Remove the jack studs from beneath the rough sill (the horizontal framing member under the window sill) leaving only the centre one (see b).

3 After removing the window moulds on both the inside and the outside of the window with a hacksaw blade, cut through the fastenings between the window stiles and the studs (photo c). The window should then be easy to remove with the help of a friend.

4 In our example the framing was demolished completely and an entire new frame constructed to suit the doors that had been purchased from a secondhand store (photo d). In other circumstances, new framing may need to be added to only one or both sides of the openings. If you're adding framing, fix it with coach screws (photo e). Use the layout batten to help you get the correct size.

5 In the case of new framing, fix it in position and cut out the bottom plate (photo f). Where there is an old bottom wall plate, cut it out and fill the gap in the flooring with timber of a similar thickness. If it's an external wall and there's no roof, allow for a sill. If you're using a sill, the jambs must be built into it much like a window.

Make sure you prime the ends of the stiles thoroughly or they could rot. There has to be flashing underneath the sill which must be turned up the inside of the sill and on both ends to form a waterproof tray.

6 Once the wall frame is finished, the door jamb can be made. Use your batten or, better still, stand the two doors together and mark the overall width. Mark this width in the rebate, then come outside it the thickness of the jamb (minus the rebate) on both ends. This gives you the back of the jamb stiles. Cut the head to this length and then cut and chisel out the rebate for the head (photo g). Nail the frame together using 60 mm nails; three are needed in each joint.

7 Stand the door frame in the opening, and make sure the head is level. Cut a little off one of the jamb stiles, if necessary. Pack and nail one side at the top (photo h) and bottom until it is plumb both ways. Using a straight-edge to make sure it's straight, pack and nail the

a. The pinch bar shown hanging on window is useful when demolishing.

b. For safety's sake wear gloves long clothing and boots when demolishing.

c. Hacksawing like this requires patience or the blade will bend.

e. If you use coach screws, a socket spanner is handy for driving them.

f. Cut out the excess floor plate with a handsaw and remove.

g. A sharp chisel is essential for making a neat housing in the head.

rest of it at 450 mm centres. Once one stile is correct, you can repeat for the other making sure it is parallel with the first.

8 Once the jamb is solid, hang the doors and put on the locks (see index for earlier project on attaching locks). If the door are exposed, prime them well and paint with two or three coats of a good quality, water-based, exterior paint.

> **PRACTICAL POINTER**
>
> French doors look attractive but securing them satisfactorily can be a problem. Installing heavily made barrel bolts top and bottom plus a quality rebate lock will give good protection. Keyed window locks are another possibility for making your home more secure.

d. If you've prefabricated the frame, this is how you stand it in position.

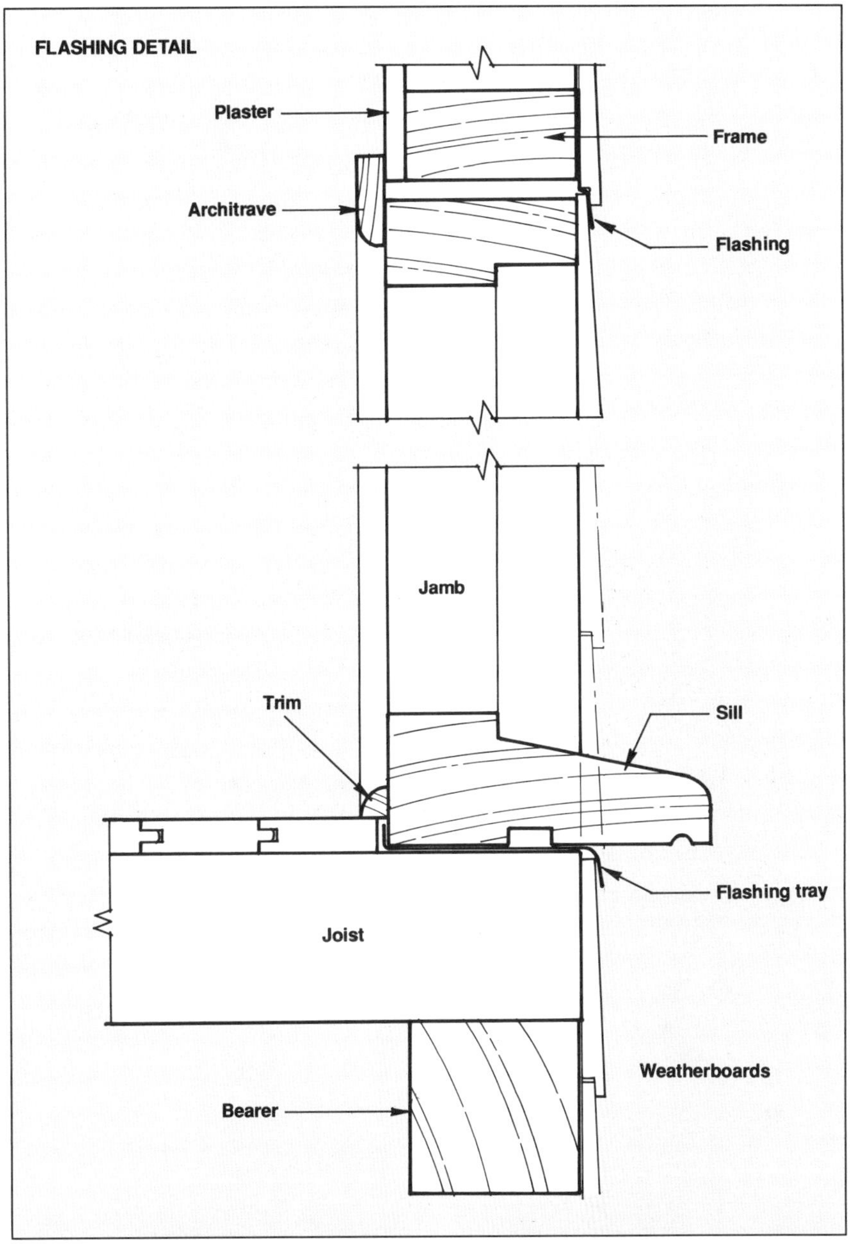

h. When fixing, be careful you don't miss the nail and damage the timber.

i. A mallet is the best tool with which to strike a chisel.

j. When drilling, make sure you keep your hair and clothing clear.

PARTITIONS AND SCREENS

Homes that are short on space (doesn't that apply to just about all of them?) are sometimes difficult to live in. Different activities demand different living areas and the company and the solitude seekers need to be accommodated so that they can live alongside one another with as little friction as possible.

There are various ways in which limited space can be apportioned. Furniture such as a lounge, dresser or screen can be used effectively to divide up the given space. Another solution is to construct a partition.

A partition is defined as an interior wall or barrier that creates an enclosure. The six photographs here show how effective such a simple structure can be. The construction procedure given can be adapted to suit your requirements. Change the size and lining (plasterboard, ply, shingles, for example) and the effect that you create will be entirely different. As a general rule, it's best to choose those materials which match the existing linings.

MATERIALS
Sufficient 75 x 50 mm sawn oregon or radiata pine to make three studs, two plates and two noggings (see photo d). Lining in this instance is of tongue and grooved lining boards. The number will depend on the effective width of each board (the amount it actually covers). Your timber yard should be able to work out the quantities. You'll also need an extra piece to nail on the end of the frame, plus quad or scotia to finish against the floor and ceiling. (If there is skirting and cornice, ideally, you should use the same material so that the partition appears to be an integral part of the room.)

TOOLS
Circular saw; hammer; nail punch; spirit level; tape and pencil; panel saw; combination square; plane; sandpaper and cork block.

PROCEDURE

1 Mark your top and bottom plates (horizontal members) to length and cut them (see photos a and b). Tack them into position by nailing to the floor and the ceiling joists. If there is no ceiling joist, you may have to get up into the ceiling and cut in a couple of trimmers between the existing joists. Measure the lengths of the studs (vertical members) and cut them.

2 You now have two choices: you can nail the studs in situ or knock the whole wall together on some stools (as shown) and erect it when it's complete. It's six of one and half a dozen of the other. The

There are many applications for partitions and screens. They can be used to create intimate corners that are compact and self contained. Or, employ them as a means of breaking up areas while still allowing visual contact with the rest of the house.

Before screening was installed, the refrigerator and kitchen intruded upon the dining area. After screening (see opposite), the two areas are subtly distinct without any harsh breaking up of the area.

noggings should be cut in tight but not so that they bow the outside stud. Notice how they are offset so they can be easily nailed.

3 The frame must be plumb (photo e) and square to the wall. (Use the 3:4:5 rule which states that if you measure along the two arms of a right-angled triangle three units and four respectively, if the angle is a true right angle, the line joining the two measurements should measure five units.) When it is, nail off the plates. The studs which touch the wall should be able to be fixed top and bottom into the wall plates and, in the centre, to the nearest nogging in the main wall. If the walls are masonry, use Loxins or similar. Watch out for wiring and plumbing.

4 Begin to fix the lining; match the main wall joint lines, if any (see g). Tack the capping piece in place first, so that you can fit each board to it. This will ensure you have a neat joint. Use a straight-edge and pencil to give you a straight line of nails. Once the lining is complete, fix off the capping piece and punch all the nails.

5 The quads or scotias (see h) come next; use mitres on the ends. Fill all the nail holes with a suitable coloured filler and finish with a paint or varnish that matches that already in use.

a. *Using a square for marking out will ensure that the members fit neatly. Cut on the waste side of the line.*

b. *A better way to use the circular saw is to clamp timber to the stool and hold the saw with both hands.*

c. *When nailing, if you butt the members against a solid wall, the frame won't bounce around.*

d. *The noggings (in the centre of the partition), help to stiffen up the wall and provide extra fixing.*

e. *To check your level is accurate, plumb the stud; turn the level around. It should give the same reading.*

f. Coach bolts and Loxins are best driven using a socket spanner with a ratchet drive. It makes for quick work.

g. Accurate cutting is essential if the job is to look professional. Use a sharp plane to ease discrepancies.

h. When nailing scotia, don't try to drive the nails right in with the hammer. Finish off with nail punch.

Screens

Screens as dividers have been used effectively for centuries. They have been hidden behind, dressed behind, used as a decorative element or for disguising eyesores and deflecting winter draughts – all manner of tasks where non-permanent screening is appropriate. The screens discussed here will provide you with the basics for screen manufacture.

Slatted screen

This snaky little contraption can go anywhere. Timber strips are nailed back-to-back over a canvas sheet. The strips are standard 30 x 9 mm cover battens 1.8 metres in length and spaced 9 mm apart. To make the one shown (1.8 metres long) you need 92 of them.

PROCEDURE

1 Make sure your sheet of canvas (artist's canvas is the best) is exactly square on the starting end. Cut all the battens to length and round their ends carefully. It will pay you to varnish them *before* you fix them to the canvas, or you'll go mad.

2 Work on a large, flat surface to make things easier. Put PVA glue on the back of one batten and staple the canvas to it (see photo a). Put some glue on top of the canvas and fit the opposing batten to the first one using 15 mm panel pins. Using a 9 mm batten as a spacer to make sure that the battens stay parallel with the end, repeat until the screen is finished (see photo b) rolling up the finished area as you go like a blind. Be very careful that there's no excess glue – otherwise, it might get stuck.

3 When the screen is finished, all you need do is unroll it and place it in position.

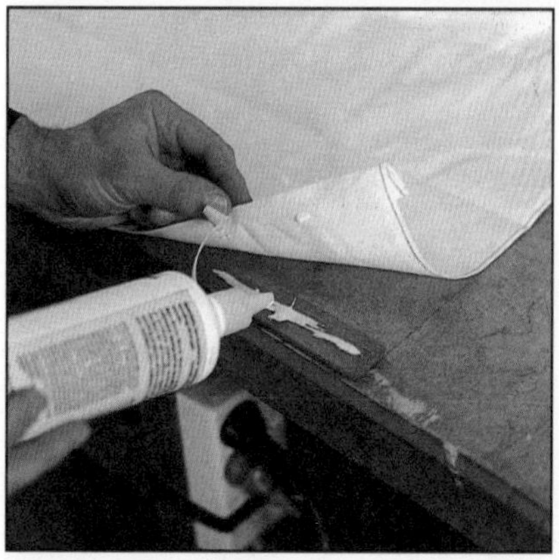

***a.** A glue bottle with a spout will make the spreading easy. Make sure you put the top back on when you have finished so that you prolong the glue's shelf life.*

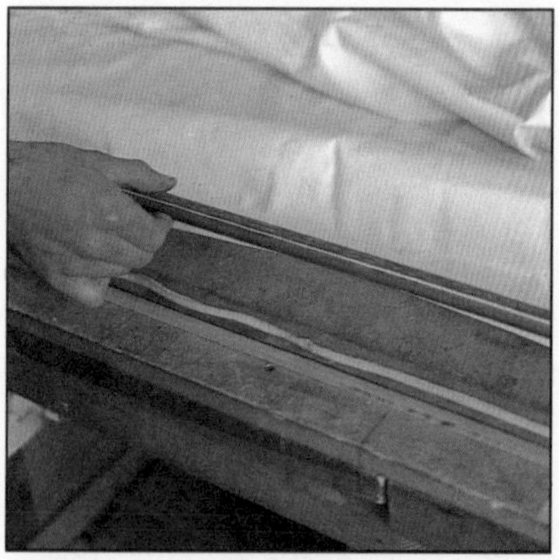

***b.** Note the thinness of the glue bead. It ensures that there is no excess. Work slowly and methodically to guarantee the finished product will be suitably professional.*

Beaded screen

This beautiful screen comprises three stepped panels which are hinged together. The frame joints should be dowelled and glued. The calico fabric is adorned with bows (you could use a different fabric) and the timber is stained brown.

MATERIALS

The three frames are 1800, 1650 and 1500 mm tall and 500 mm wide. They are made from 42 x 19 mm (finished) maple. The fabric dowels (one top, one bottom and one in the middle) are 15 mm in diameter. The

a. *This is a very messy job, one that is best done before the frame is assembled. Use plenty of newspaper to protect the bench.*

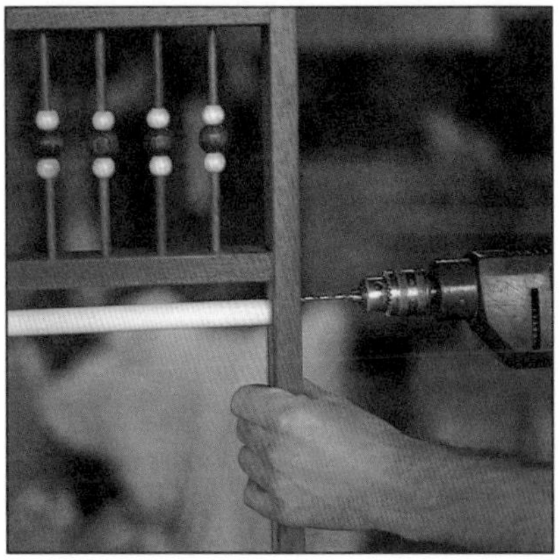

b. *The dowel rods act as braces for the panel frame. They can be screwed at one end as shown. On the other end, screw in from the side.*

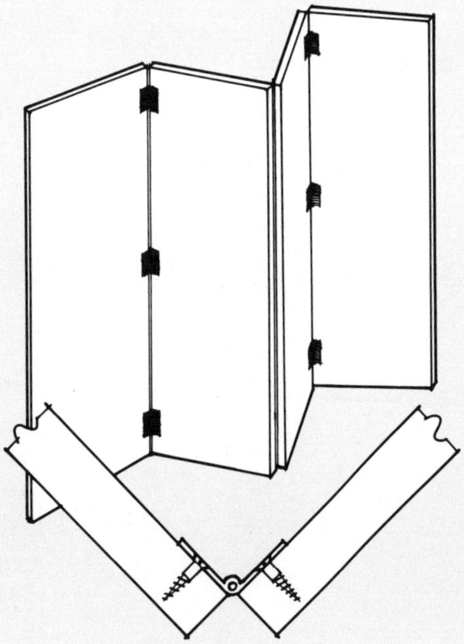

HINGING SOLID PANELS

Ply or particle board panels require piano hinging or 50 mm fixed pin hinges at three points down the panel's length. Fit hinges to the face of the panel if you want one of the screen sides to be hinge free.

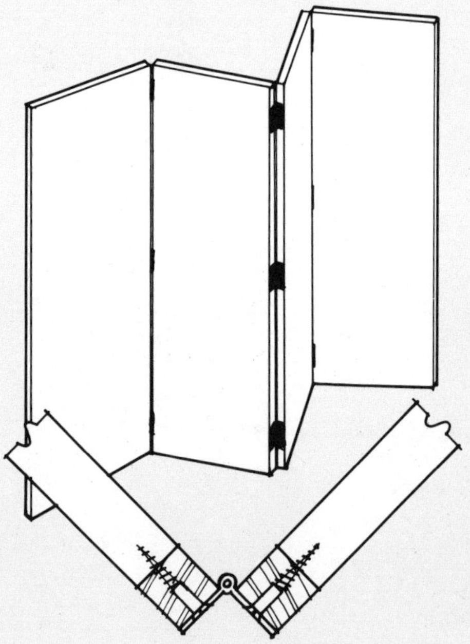

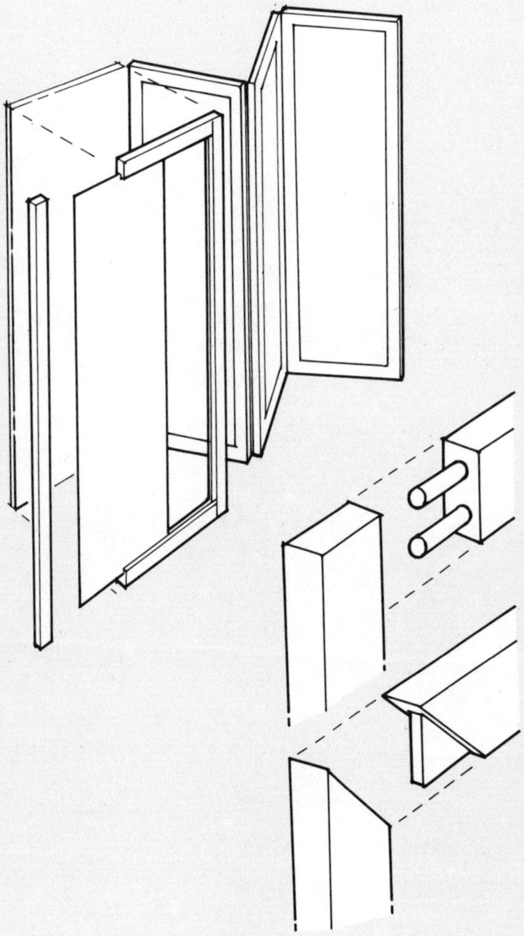

FRAMED PANELS

To make the screens lighter and easier to move around, construct panels on 42 x 19 mm timber frames. The infill panel can be of 3 mm ply or particle board set into routed grooves or of any other sheet fabric you choose. To make solid joints either drill, glue and insert dowel pegs or cut a half-tongued mortise and tenon when sawing a mitred corner. Pin and glue all joints.

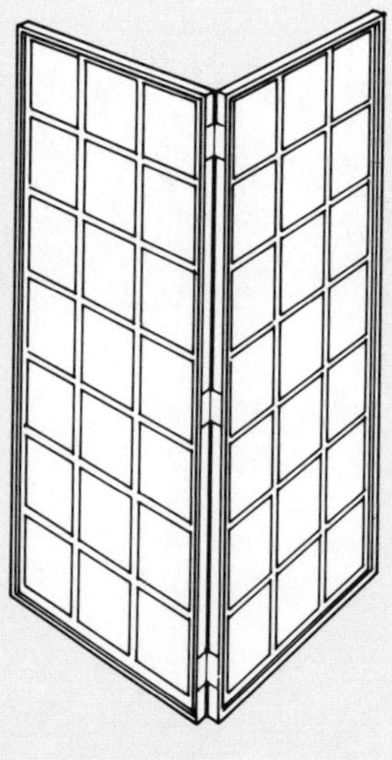

SHOJI SCREENS

The basic frame can be extended to a window treatment – three panels wide instead of two required for a lightbox. Duplicate it for the other side of the screen.

dowels that support the beads (11 to each frame) are 6 mm in diameter and 140 mm long (allowing 5 mm to project into each hole). Two 10 mm brads are needed in each joint. The beads are available from craft shops.

TOOLS

Tape and pencil; electric drill and drills; panel saw; hammer and nails; plane; sandpaper and cork block; screwdriver and glue.

PROCEDURE

1 Cut the six stiles (vertical members) and nine horizontal rails to length; the rails cut in between the stiles. Use a dowelling jig to make the joints; two dowels to a joint, each centred in one of the thirds.

2 Bore the 6 mm holes for the bead dowels in the middle and top rail. Put the rails together when marking the dowels to make sure they are opposite each other. With the 15 mm holes in the stiles for the fabric dowels, set one 10 mm deep in one stile and bore the other one right through (come in halfway from either side) so that each dowel can be easily removed. A piece of tape wrapped around the drill will set the respective depths.

3 After cutting the bead dowels to length, thread the beads onto them and glue the beads into position. (If you have decided to stain the screen, do it before assembly.) Put a drop of glue into each hole in the middle rail and push the bead dowels into them. Repeat for top rail.

4 Once the beaded panels are finished, assemble the frame, remembering to include the 15 mm dowels, but only glue the centre one. Use a liberal amount of glue in each joint. Cramping the frame together while drying will give tight joints; if you don't have cramps, nailing will have to do. Measure the diagonals to make sure each panel is square.

5 Once the frames are secure, hinge them together. Apply your chosen finish. Fitting the calico fabric is easy. Pin the strips in position, folding each end tightly over the top and bottom dowel and pinning in place. Allow enough material to gather one and a half times. Slide out the unfixed dowels and machine the pockets. Refix the calico and screw in the dowels (this allows for easy removal so that the material can be washed). The bows can be made from any cream material and sewn on.

Find the right spot for your handsome screen and prepare to take orders; you might find you have a started a lucrative cottage industry.

Solid panel screens

A variation on the beaded screen uses solid panels. The screens shown here are made from ply or edged particle board hinged together. The hinges can be placed on the edge or on the face of the panels.

Any number of panels could be linked in this way. Another variation could use louvred doors (see photo), while a framed and panelled screen is yet another option (see photo).

The joints for the 42 x 19 mm framing can be butted and dowelled. Or they could be mitred with a half-tongued mortice as shown. The panels can be of three ply or 6 mm particle board which sits in a groove in the frame.

MAIN SW.
STOVE
LIGHT & POWER
HOT WATER
KILOWATT HOURS
84785
WATTHOUR METER TYPE B.A.Z.
10-40
902485
240
400
1
2
50
84785
BRITE-HEAT
FUSE WIRE
TURN OFF MAIN SWITCH BEFORE RENEWING FUSE WIRE
USE ONE STRAND
8 Amp. for Lights
20 Amp. A/C. & H.W.S. Fuse

HOME REPAIRS AND MAINTENANCE

CHAPTER 5

MAINTENANCE PROJECTS

If a home is to maintain its value, it requires some maintenance. The imperfections of their homes make most owners mutter things like, 'I wish I were a carpenter,' or 'If only I could change that!' The spiralling cost of building labour has created an economic pressure on people to do it themselves. Not only does that achieve a monetary saving but the psychological benefit from learning new skills is invaluable.

This section sets out to give you a quick reference guide to enable you to do the typical jobs which you could well encounter in any one year. I have specifically written it to cater for Australian conditions and for people with no prior experience in things practical. The book gives you all the information you need to allow you to confidently undertake and successfully complete small jobs.

If something goes wrong, go back a couple of steps and make sure you've done everything correctly. The solution to all practical problems is in a methodical approach.

Refastening Loose Hinges or Catches

You've had it! A catch keeps falling off or a hinge keeps loosening because the screws won't hold. You've tried to re-screw them but, when you're not looking, they fall out again. If the screws were holding correctly, the thread on the screw should have cut into the sides of the pilot hole, thereby locking itself in. However, if the screws become overstressed, perhaps because someone has put leverage on the door or the catch is sticking, the timber around the screw thread gives way and the thread has nothing to hold to. Fixing it is easy. Here's how.

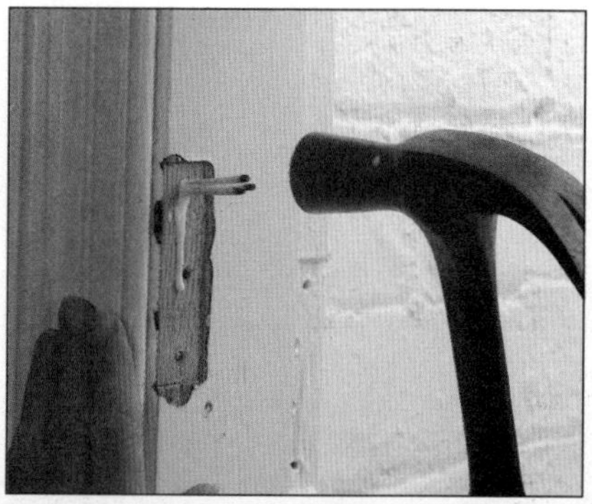

Dip matches in glue and hammer them into the old screw holes.

TOOLS AND MATERIALS

A trimming knife, hammer, nail punch, and a screwdriver will do the trick. You will also need some wooden matches and PVA glue.

PROCEDURE FOR HINGES

1 Open the door until it is at right angles to the frame. Then, using some thin books, scraps of timber, or coasters, pack the bottom of the door off the floor. Now when you take out the offending screws, the door will remain level and in its correct position.

2 With your screwdriver pressed hard into the slot, unscrew the loose screws. If the slots are filled with paint, scratch it out with a nail file or pointed knife. Fold the leaf of the hinge back so you can clearly see the holes.

3 Cut the phosphorus off several matches with a knife. Dispose of it in a safe place because it's poisonous. Depending on the hole size, take two or three matches and dip them in the glue, making sure it covers a distance equal to the length of the screws.

4 Hammer the matches tightly into the screw holes. Let them dry (say two hours).

5 With your chisel or a knife, cut the matches off until they're flush with the surface.

6 Using your nail punch and hammer, make pilot holes for the screws in the centre of the plugged holes (otherwise the hinge won't go back in the same place). Drive the punch in at least half the length of the screw.

7 Carefully rescrew the hinge back into position, making sure you tighten the screws fully. If you can get the slots all pointing in a vertical direction, then it will look very tradesperson-like.

8 Take out the packing and close the door. While you're at it, check the clearance margins around the door. If they're uneven you can make them right by either taking a little more out of the hinge recess with a sharp chisel or by packing behind the hinge with a strip of cardboard.

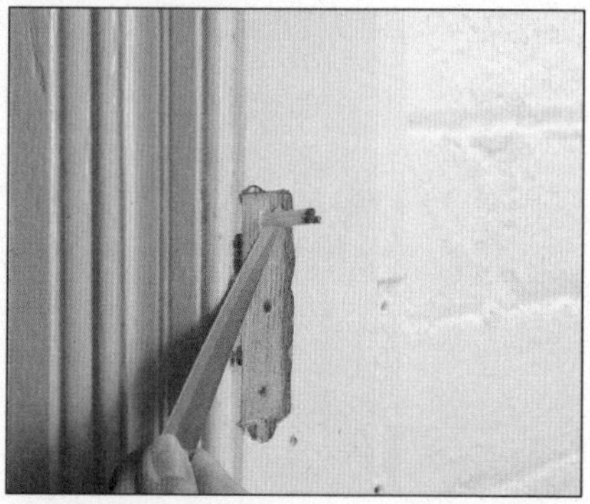

Cut the matches off to make them flush with the surface.

PROCEDURE FOR CATCHES

1 Remove the catch and fill the oversized holes as above. Make the pilot holes.

2 Check another catch to see how it goes on. Put the catch in position and start to turn the screws clockwise. Make sure that you select a screwdriver that fits the screw head properly. If the screws keep falling over, tap them in a little way with your hammer and then screw them in the rest of the way.

Use a nail punch to make pilot holes for the screws.

3 Close the door slowly and check the catch position. The holes in the catch are often elongated to allow for adjustment. Loosen the screws if necessary, move the catch backwards or forwards until the door fits correctly, then re-tighten the screws.

Congratulations. You did it! When the children, spouse or special friend comes home don't gloat. Perhaps another catch or hinge is plotting an escape.

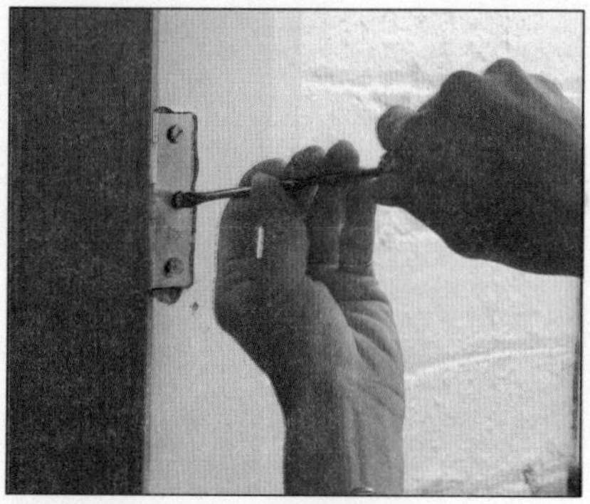

Rescrew the hinge into position, tightening the screws fully.

Replacing a Fuse Wire

There's nothing worse than being home alone at night and suddenly the lights go out. Or the television goes off in the middle of a movie.

Assuming there isn't a blackout, it could just mean a *replaceable* fuse has gone. This fuse is a thin piece of wire which is designed to melt in the event of an electricity overload caused by a faulty appliance or poor wiring. This melting breaks the power circuit. If the fuse weren't there you'd probably have a fire.

Fixing a fuse is easy providing you prepare for it *before* it happens.

The Meter Box

The first thing to do is to find the meter box. For a house it is usually a steel box with a door located on an outside wall. In the case of units, it will usually be in a special meter room along with everyone else's. In all situations it must be accessible to the meter readers.

Once you find it, open the door and prop it up. Typically you will see various dials and a series of white porcelain fuse-holders which are labelled lights, power points, stove, etc. You will also find a main switch which turns off the power supply to the house and perhaps a separate switch for the hot water.

Turn off the main switch and gently pull out one of the fuse-holders. You will see a thin piece of wire stretched between its two ends. If a fuse has blown this piece of wire will be melted; if it's faulty, it will be broken. The wire is fixed at both ends by screws. Just undo the screws, pull the old wire out and replace it with the new. BUT YOU MUST REPLACE IT WITH THE SAME GAUGE WIRE!

If you use a thinner wire it will burn through too easily and if you use too thick a wire it won't burn through when it should, hence potentially setting the electrical wiring in your home on fire. Often the correct gauge (thickness) required is stamped onto the fuse holder.

Make sure you put each fuse holder back in the right place because different circuits require different gauges. Generally, lighting needs 8 amp wire and power needs 15 amp wire. A 3.6 kilowatt hot water system needs 15 amp, while a 4.8 kilowatt hot water system needs 20 amp. Electric stoves require either 20 or 30 amp wire. Check with your supply authority for requirements.

Now you know how it works, put the fuse back, switch on the main switch, and close the meter box.

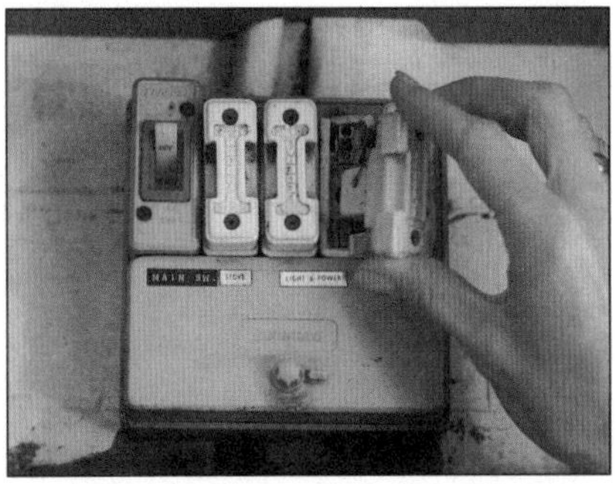

Pull out the fuseholders one at a time to locate the broken wire.

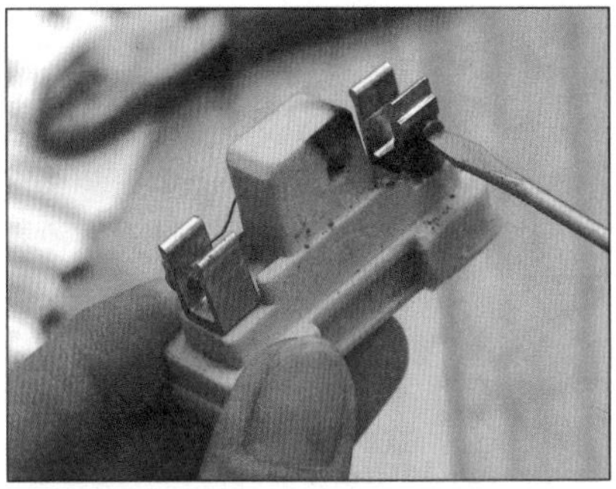

Undo the screws and remove the pieces of wire.

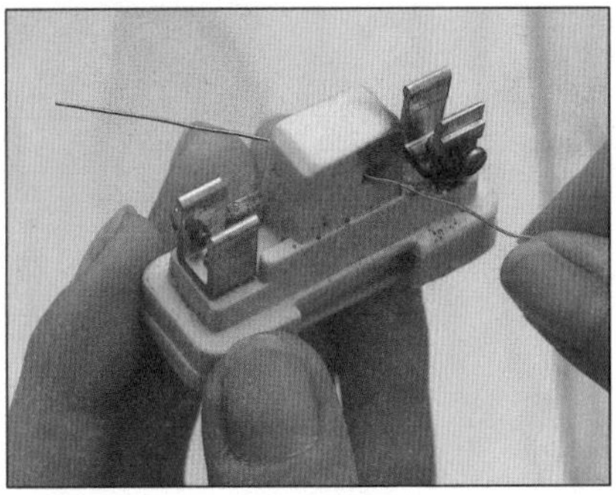

Replace the fuse using wire of the same gauge.

Wrap the ends of the wire clockwise round the retaining screws.

TOOLS AND MATERIALS

Buy a selection of different gauge fuse wires, a torch, and a small screwdriver. Keep them in a place that can be found in the dark.

PROCEDURE

1 First, look outside to see if there is a general blackout. If it's daylight, check other appliances or ring a neighbour.

2 If only your house is affected, collect your fuse kit and make your way to the meter box.

3 Switch off the main switch. This is very important.

4 Check the porcelain fuse-holders one at a time. Replace each fuse until you locate the one with the molten or broken wire.

5 Undo the screws, remove the pieces, and replace the fuse using wire of a similar gauge. Wrap the ends of the wire in a clockwise direction around the retaining screws.

6 Tighten the screws and cut off any loose ends of wire. Replace the fuse-holder and switch on the main power.

7 If the lights or power fuses blow again try to establish the cause of the overload. If an appliance appears to be faulty, disconnect it. If you have a number of double adaptors banked up, remove them. Then do the fuse again.

If it still blows, call an electrician or your electricity supply authority. The latter may be willing to come and investigate.

Fixing Squeaky Stairs and Floors

Squeaking stairs or floorboards can create unnecessary discords in your life. They are fairly easily fixed. Let's go!

Squeaky Stairs

This is usually caused by movement taking place between where the riser joins the treads either at the top or bottom. Diagram 1 shows the usual places. Position yourself behind the stairs and get someone to walk on them until you locate where the problem is. Mark the spot with a pencil.

To solve the problem you can use either nails or glue. If you decide on nailing and the squeak is coming from the top of the riser, drive in 50 mm nails 150 mm apart through the top of the tread and into the riser and punch the heads below the surface. If the squeak is coming from the bottom of the riser, from under the stairs, nail through the bottom of the riser into the back of the tread.

As an alternative to nailing, squeeze some wood glue into the joints and allow to set for twenty-four hours before walking on the stairs. If you really want to be sure, glue *and* nail the offending joints.

Squeaky Floorboards

This is usually caused by movement between the boards and is most often due to shrinkage. First, try sprinkling some talcum powder into the offending joint. If this doesn't work, to permanently stop the movement locate the general area and, if there is room, get under the house and have someone tread about until you spot the squeaky joint.

If it's occurring *over a joist* then measure its position and direction by measuring off the foundation walls or count how many boards it is away from the wall plate. Carefully mark its position from above, then renail and punch the nails down. (See Diagram 2.) If there is carpet you can nail straight through the carpet provided you can accurately locate the position (but don't forget to punch the nails down).

In either case, turn the nails over and flatten the points BEFORE you drive them in — taking the point off the nail minimises the wedging effect and helps to stop the boards splitting.

If the squeak is coming from an area of flooring *between the joists,* screw in some 18 mm screws from underneath the floor. Space them every 100 mm or so along the offending join. Be careful not to sink the screws in too far or they'll project beyond the top of the boards. If you're unlucky, the noise may be coming from several places so be sure you cover them all.

If the squeaks are coming from an upstairs room and you can't get to the joints from underneath because of a ceiling, then lift the carpet where the squeak is and either renail the joints or screw down between them from the top. As an alternative, squeeze some wood glue into the joints between the boards and allow to dry. Then refix the carpet making sure you stretch it tightly. (If you have squeaks in particle board floors the same general principles apply.)

Now turn on the stereo and listen to your favourite records or plan to come home late. The only squeaks will be from mice!

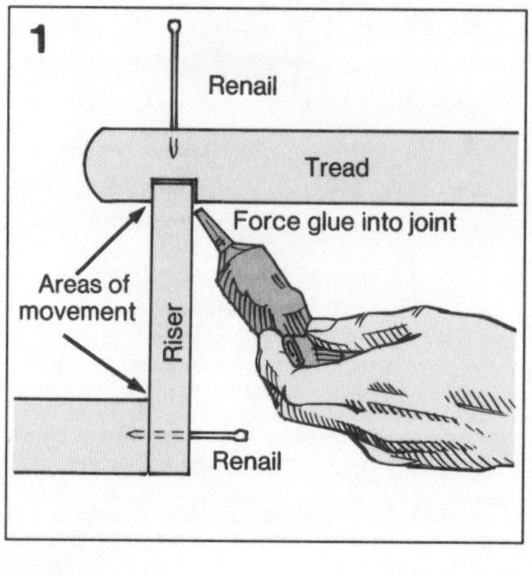

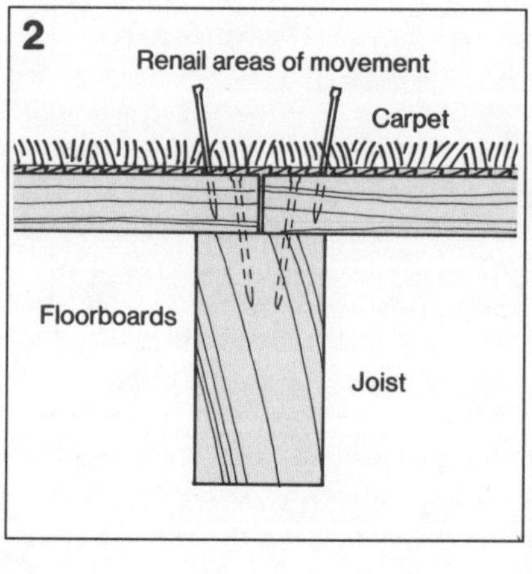

Rectifying Sticking Doors

Sticking doors can be annoying. The sticking sometimes occurs because the screws, being too small or put in incorrectly, become overstressed and partly pull out of the timber. It can also be caused by a build-up of paint narrowing the necessary gap between the door and the frame (the jamb). Another possibility is that moisture is getting into the door and making it swell.

The solutions to all three problems are easy.

Loose Screws

To establish if this is the problem open the door 100 mm and, using your arms, pull and push it towards the hinges. If there is movement then the screws are loose in either the door or the jamb. A telltale sign is cracked paint around the hinge.

To fix loose screws see Refastening Loose Hinges (page 84).

A Swelling Door

Keep an eye on whether the door sticks in humid weather or when the room is subjected to a lot of steam. If so, this means that moisture is getting into the timber through the joints or unpainted surfaces and causing it to swell. Not only does this cause sticking but long term it can lead to rotting. It may also cause the door to come apart because the glue gives way.

With sandpaper wrapped round a block, sand the offending area.

Wait for an extended period of dry weather or until you return from a holiday. If the door is no longer sticking, take it off and paint any areas that are bare or cracked. Pay careful attention to the top and bottom of the door and any joints that show hairline cracks. By sealing the door fully you stop any moisture entering the timber, which should end the problem forever.

Removing Built-up Paint

The solution to this problem depends on the thickness of the build-up and the area of contact between the door and the jamb. If the whole edge of the door is sticking badly you may have to get in a carpenter to plane the door unless you have a plane and know how to use it (see Hand Tools page 276 and later in this topic). For small areas the following procedure is suitable.

TOOLS AND MATERIALS

Screwdriver, cork block, pencil and rule; sandpaper (both rough and fine) and suitable paint.

SANDING PROCEDURE

1 Check where it's sticking. When you are finished there should be an even 2 mm gap to allow for clearance after repainting. Using a pencil, mark how much of the sticking area you need to sand off. Remove the door if it's binding on the hinge side or on the bottom, otherwise sand it in position.

2 Using the rough sandpaper and the block, heavily sand the offending area. Make sure you keep the block flat and slightly angled towards the back of the door (the surface that fits in the rebate). Finish it off with the fine sandpaper. Then use the sandpaper to take the sharp edge off the corners. This is called arrissing and is done to stop splintering and to give the door a neat finish.

3 Screw the door back on (if necessary) and check the gap for evenness and size. Sand further if required, prime and repaint the door.

PLANING PROCEDURE

1 If the whole edge is sticking and you have a plane, mark the 2–3 mm clearance, take the door out of the frame (either by taking out all the screws from the jamb or, if the hinge has a loose pin, driving the pin up with a hammer and a 75 mm nail).

2 Next, set the plane iron. This involves firstly using the depth adjustment knob to wind the sharp blade (see page 276 for parts) out say 0.5 to 0.75 mm beyond the sole (bottom) of the plane. Next, hold the plane up towards the light and, using the lateral adjusting lever, make the blade parallel with the sole.

3 Get a friend to hold the door or push it into the corner of a room. If you're planing on the lock side you will have to remove the lock.

When planing, start with the weight on the front of the plane. As you come off the timber, transfer the weight to the back. This will ensure the timber stays straight. If it's too hard to push, wind the blade back in. If lines appear on the timber, the blade is digging in on one side. Check it again for parallel.

If the wood is tearing you may be planing against the grain. Try planing from the opposite direction. If it tears from both directions, it has 'cranky' grain. Plane the way it tears the least.

4 Make sure you slightly undercut the edge towards the back of the door. Arris the corners to get rid of sharp edges. Then screw the door back in the jamb, check the clearance, and repaint all bare surfaces.

Replacing a Tap Washer

Given that up to 50% of an electricity bill may be attributable to water heating, it is important to ensure that your hot water taps don't drip. Did you realise that up to 45 litres of water per day can flow from each dripping tap? That's money down the drain! Another problem with a dripping tap that is left for too long is that the water may badly stain the surface of a basin or bath.

A leaky tap usually occurs because the internal washer that creates a watertight seal is worn out. Each time you turn the tap off, the soft flexible washer, which is made from rubber or a synthetic substitute, presses against the metal washer seat, wearing a tiny part of itself away. Eventually it becomes thin and irregular in shape. This allows water to seep past and creates the annoying drip.

If you don't replace it but continue to screw the tap down tighter and tighter, eventually you will get metal grinding against metal which will force you to call in a plumber to regrind the washer seating. That can be an expensive business!

Before you attempt the job, first check with your local water supply authorities to make sure you can change the washers.

The reason the water supply authorities have such strict rules concerning plumbing and drainage and insist generally that all work is carried out by a licensed plumber is that they don't want the water supply contaminated by faulty work. You could imagine the health risk if some foreign substance or bacteria got into the water pipes or the drainage system was interfered with.

Before beginning the job of replacing a tap washer, turn off the water supply at the mains tap next to the meter.

Lift the hot or cold button and undo the screw underneath.

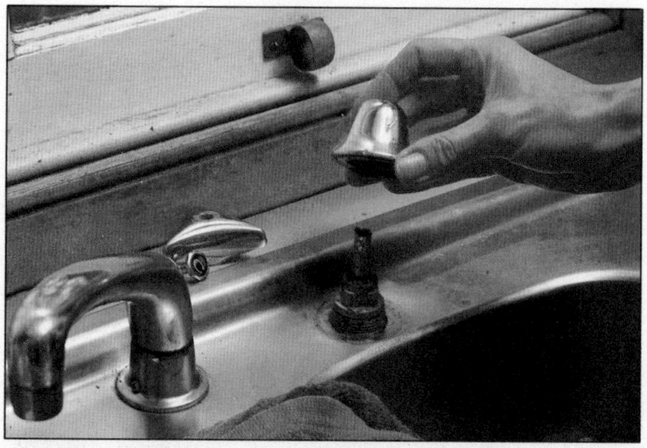

Lift off or unscrew the cover or flange of the tap.

Unscrew the hexagonal collar with an adjustable spanner.

The offending washer is fixed to the jumper by a small nut.

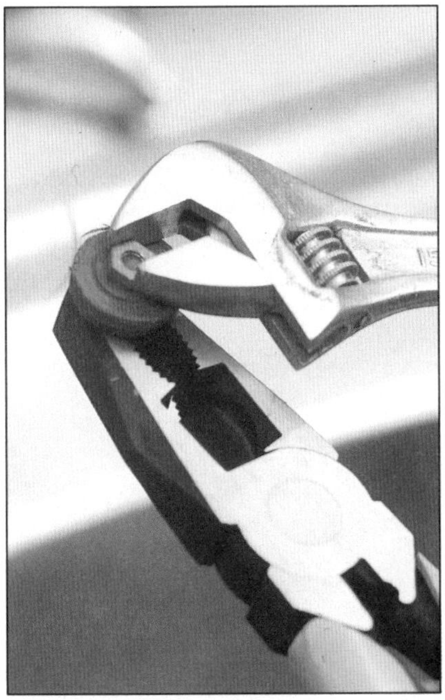

Using pliers to hold the jumper, undo the nut with the spanner.

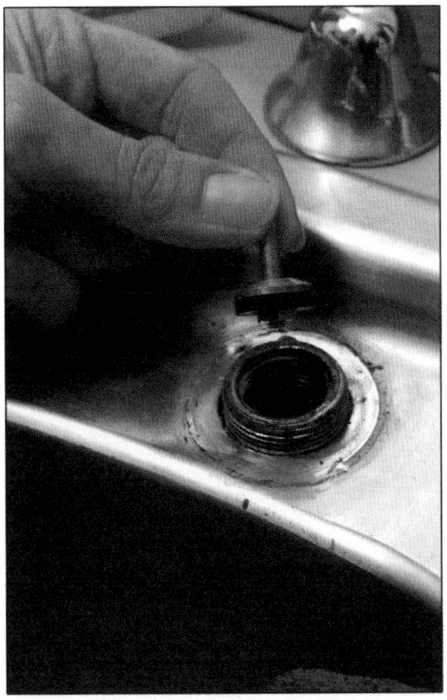

Slip the jumper with the new washer back into position.

To finish the job rescrew the whole assembly back into position.

TOOLS AND MATERIALS

A screwdriver, a large adjustable spanner or wrench, pliers, the correct sized washer (18 mm for most bath and mixer taps and 12 mm for others) and an old towel. You can buy disposable plastic jumpers with washers attached.

PROCEDURE

1 Turn off the water supply to the offending tap. This may be done by:

(a) turning off the main water supply near the meter, or

(b) turning off the supply stop cock (if there is one) beneath the sink or basin, etc.

Note. In the case of a roof-mounted hot water storage system or a hot water system that supplies a tap underneath a house, turn off the supply at the heater (otherwise all the water may run out, which could cause damage to the unit).

2 Turn the tap full on. If you have successfully turned off the supply, the water should quickly stop running. If it doesn't, check the cocks again, remembering you must turn the handle *clockwise*.

3 Put the old towel in the sink. If you drop something it lessens the chance of damage.

4 Remove the tap handle. This is done by undoing the screw at the side or lifting the hot or cold indicator button and undoing the screw underneath. Take the handle off, and then lift off or unscrew the cover or flange. Lay them both on the sink.

5 You will see the mechanism of the tap exposed. Set the adjustable spanner to the size of the large hexagonal-shaped collar and unscrew it in an anticlockwise direction. Remove the assembly.

6 You will find the offending washer (fixed to the jumper by a small nut) either in the bottom of the tap (a pair of tweezers could be handy here) or in the end of the assembly you've just removed.

7 Using the pliers to hold the jumper, undo the nut with the spanner, remove the old washer and, checking it is the same size, put the new one in its place and retighten the nut (but not excessively otherwise you'll distort the washer).

8 Check there are no pieces of the old washer left on the seating, then slip the jumper back into its position and firmly rescrew the whole assembly back into place (making sure the jumper body fits into the hole at the end of the assembly). Also make sure that the tap handle is left in its full-on position.

9 Then put back the cover and the tap handle. Turn the tap off and, with someone watching, slowly turn the supply back on. If it runs, either you've put the assembly back incorrectly or you've used the wrong sized washer. Recheck.

If the drip has stopped, feel proud. You have accomplished something new and perhaps saved yourself excess heating and water bills.

If it still drips there must be damage to the seating and unfortunately you'll have to call in a plumber.

If you are particularly adventurous, you could try reseating the washer yourself, using a reseating tool which can be obtained from hardware stores. If you need a plumber, make sure you get at least four quotes.

Rehanging a Picture

Rehanging a picture (or framed mirror) of any size involves putting up fastenings that must be fixed so securely that they will never pull out of the wall (thus damaging your favourite Monet!). When selecting fasteners, keep in mind the weight that has to be supported. It may be better to use two or even three fasteners for a painting that is extra large or has a heavy frame.

Positioning the Picture

This operation is easier with two people. Get someone to hold the painting so you can stand back and position it to its best advantage. Don't hurry! Wear out two or three friends if necessary. When it's just right, lightly mark where the top and both sides of the frame touch the wall with a soft pencil. Then lay the frame down, pull the wire or chain tight (towards the top), and mark where the fastener(s) should go (see photograph). Measuring from your wall markings, accurately transfer these marks.

After positioning, lightly mark where the top and sides of the picture touch the wall.

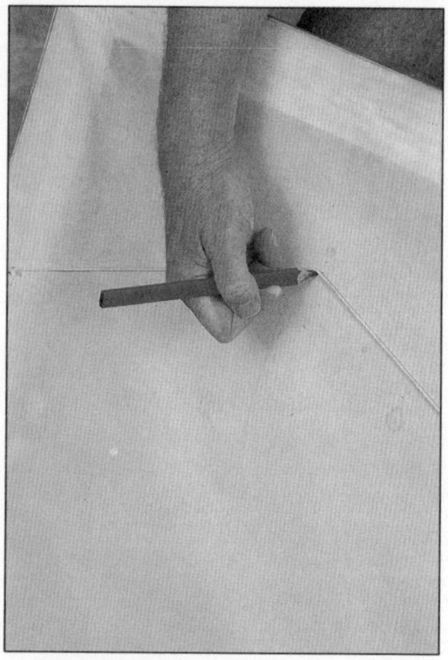

Pull the wire tight and mark where the fastener should go.

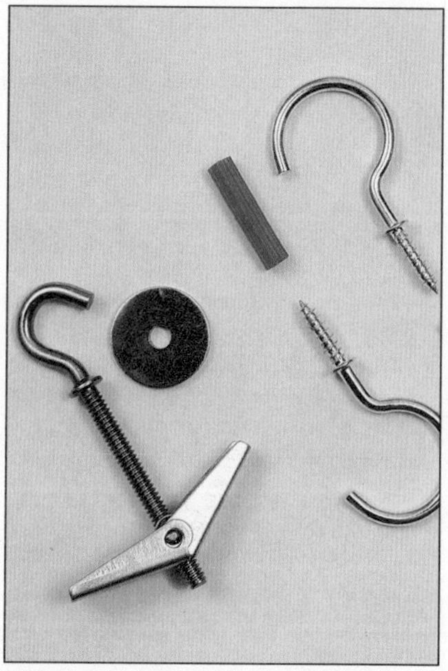

Brass hooks, a wall plug and a hook with a toggle.

TOOLS AND MATERIALS

For masonry walls you will need a 6 mm masonry drill bit plus electric or hand drill, plugs (either plastic or timber), tape and pencil.

For timber frame walls you will need a hammer, tape and pencil, pliers, and a thin nail. If there is no wall framing where the hook is to go, you'll also need an electric or hand drill plus a drill bit to suit the hook / toggle diameter.

A popular fastener is the screw hook or screw eye. Both have a threaded screw section combined with either a hook or an open eye (see page 296). They are made from brass or steel and, if visible, are available in special finishes.

For masonry walls, make sure the thread is at least 15 mm long; where solid fixing is available in timber frame walls, the minimum thread length should be 25 mm (to allow for the 10 mm lining thickness). For hollow walls, a brilliant innovation is a hook which screws into a toggle (see photograph).

PROCEDURE FOR MASONRY WALLS

To provide good fixing you must drill a hole in the masonry and then fill it with a material that the threaded fastener can screw into. Make sure you drill the hole 2 mm deeper than the thread length of the fastener. The hole can then be plugged with a soft timber such as cedar or maple (use a chisel or trimming knife to shape a plug slightly larger than the hole, then hammer it in). Alternatively you can use a plastic plug the same diameter as the drill (see photograph).

Screw the hook or eye into the plug with pliers until the shoulder hits or the thread disappears.

PROCEDURE FOR TIMBER FRAME WALLS

There are two options.

1 If the exact location is not essential, fix into the nearest timber stud. Position the painting as before, then tap along the wall with a hammer in the vicinity of the marks. Where the wall sounds most solid, drive in a thin nail to check if you've located a stud (watch you don't hit any plumbing or electric wiring). Then screw in the fastening. Should two hooks be necessary you'll usually find another stud either 450 mm or 600 mm either side of the first.

2 If positioning is vital and there are no studs, use the hook / toggle. Drill a hole the diameter of the toggle through the wall lining in the exact position, then push the toggle into the hole until the arms open by gravity or spring. As you continue to tighten, the arms will come up against the back of the lining, tightening the hook permanently into the wall (see photograph).

Unfortunately, should you need to remove this hook, the toggle will be lost but, as they only cost a few cents, who cares?

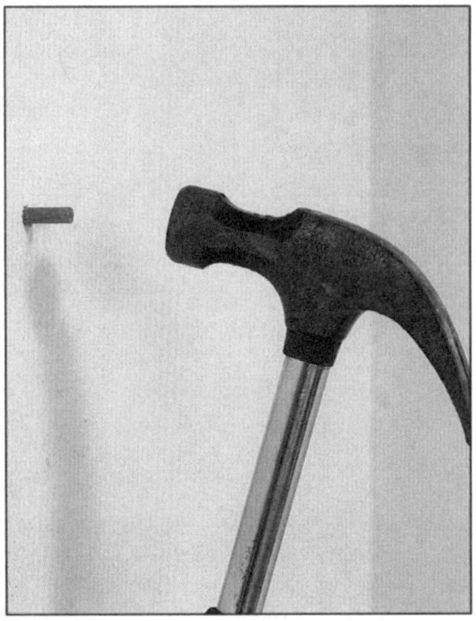

Hammer the plastic plug into the pre-drilled hole.

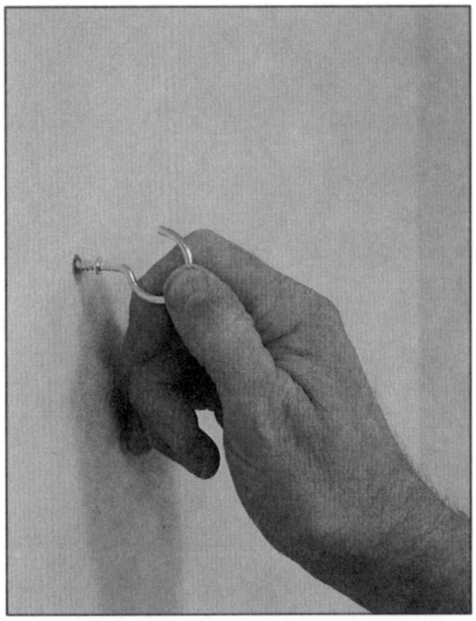

Screw the hook into the plug until the shoulder bites.

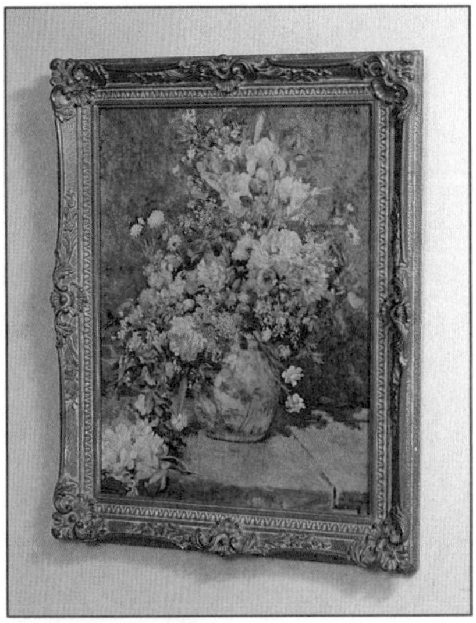

The picture rehung.

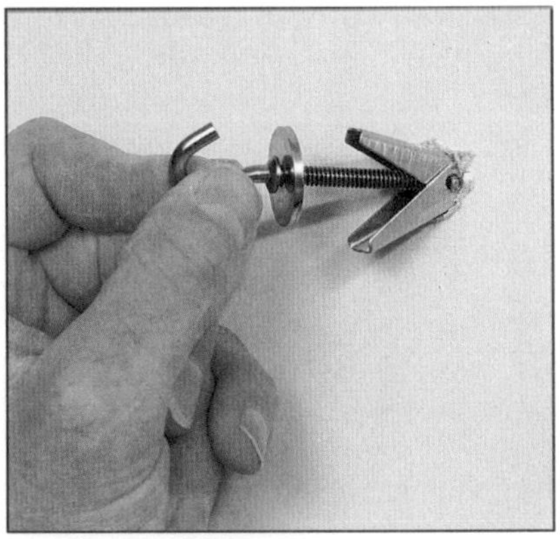

The toggle will fold flat as it goes through the hole.

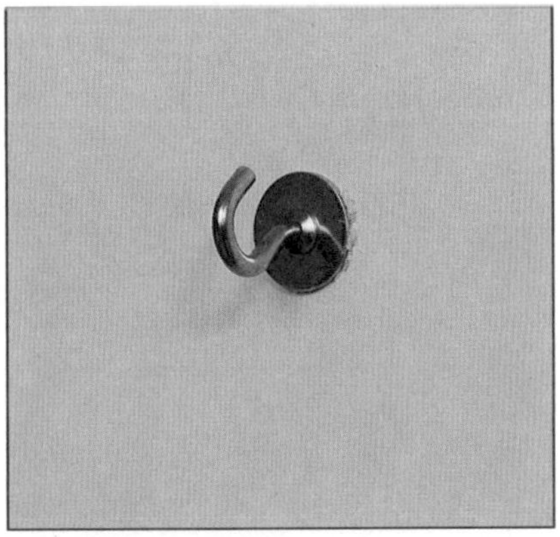

The finished job is very strong.

Rectifying Lifting or Bubbling Laminate

Plastic laminates, properly glued, provide a serviceable and attractive finish for surfaces like kitchen and bathroom bench tops and doors. They excel where there is moisture.

The surface, providing it is not cut or subjected to high temperature, is virtually indestructible. However, because of moisture or faulty manufacture, problems can arise from poor adherence of the material to the backing. The result is that the bench top can bubble or an edge strip can lift. If it's within the warranty period then make some appropriate noises! If not, you will probably be able to fix it quite easily yourself. Here's what to do.

Plastic laminate kitchen benchtops

For a bubble, use a hot iron to warm the whole area.

Laminate Bubbles

Fixing the bubble problem may be easy. The only equipment you will require is an iron or hairdryer plus a hammer and block, assuming that a rubber-based contact glue has been used (see Glues page 298).

FIRST PROCEDURE

1 Using a hairdryer on the highest temperature or an iron set where it's almost too hot to touch (325°F), warm the whole area for at least five minutes. This will soften the glue and make it active again.

2 Using the hammer and block, tap the bubble down. If you are lucky, it will adhere once again and the problem is fixed.

But if it doesn't . . .

The reason could be that a PVC glue (which can't be re-activated) has been applied or there is insufficient contact glue in the offending area. In either case you will have to drill one or two holes in the bubble so you can inject enough contact or PVC glue into the space to cover both surfaces.

TOOLS AND MATERIALS

You will need a hand drill, a 2–3 mm drill bit, a heavy weight, a hammer, smooth block and contact or PVC glue.

SECOND PROCEDURE

1 After drilling the hole or holes (say one every 50 mm of bubble), check which type of glue has been used. You will find that contact glue is a thick yellowy-brown colour whereas the PVC is almost clear. Purchase a small quantity of a similar glue.

2 Pour or rub a liberal quantity of the glue into the holes and press the bubble flat to help spread the glue out.

If using PVC, immediately apply a heavy weight to the spot for at least 12 hours. Watch you don't stick the weight to the bench! Some plastic wrap will ensure this doesn't happen.

If using rubber contact, leave the two surfaces apart for approximately 15 minutes (until touch dry) and then tap the bubble down with your hammer and a smooth block. Apply some weight for a few hours just to make sure.

3 Depending on the colour and pattern of the surface, fill each hole with a spot of epoxy glue and touch it up with matching paint. Alternatively, keep your breadboard or an ornament on top of the holes.

Lifting Laminate

Laminate which peels or lifts off can also be restuck provided you use a glue similar to the original. But remember, to be successful both the underside of the laminate and the backing surface must be completely dry and free from all grease, oil, food matter, etc.

PROCEDURE

1 Wedge the gap open as far as possible (but watch you don't crack the laminate!) with a paddlepop stick, screwdriver or knife. Scrape out all foreign material until surfaces are spotlessly clean (some sandpapering could help), then leave it wedged open for a minimum of 48 hours to help it to dry. If the subsurface is saturated, a hairdryer set on high and blown into the area will hasten the drying.

2 Apply the correct glue and fix following the procedure above.

If you strike any further problems contact your laminate or glue supplier. The manufacturers have printed information on their products which they are only too happy to send to you. They also employ technical people who are eagerly waiting to answer all your tricky questions. The manufacturers want to see you, the customer, happy with their products.

For lifting laminate, clean out the gap with a screwdriver.

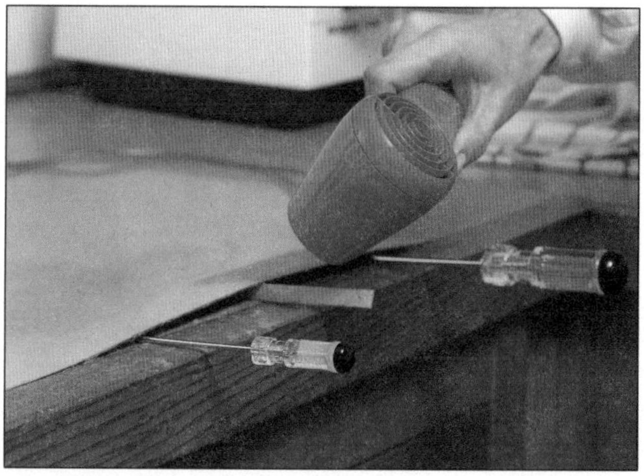

You can use a hairdryer to speed up the drying process.

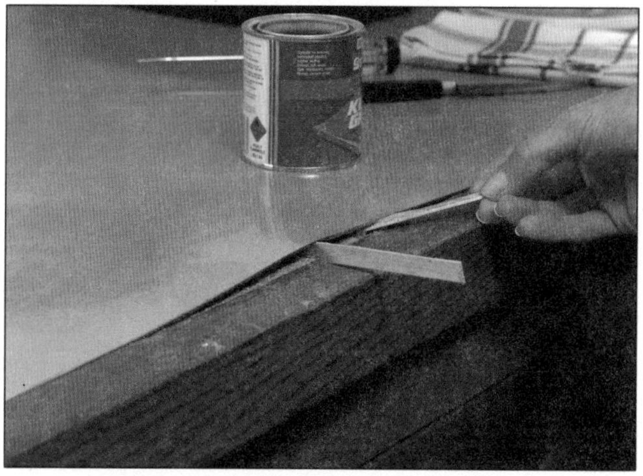

Apply glue with spreader and leave till touch dry.

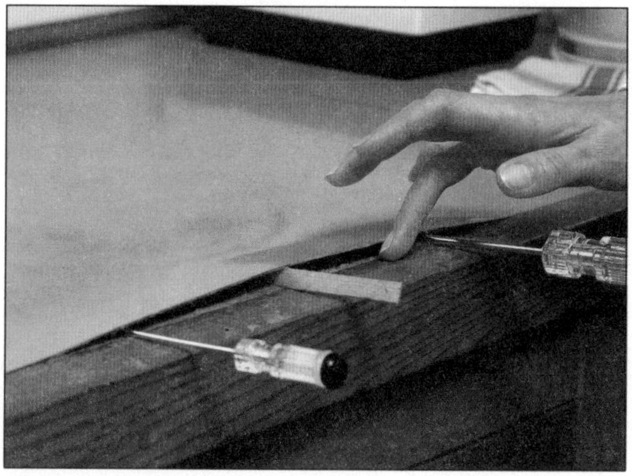

Make sure contact glue is touch dry before joining surfaces.

Tap the laminate down with a hammer and a smooth block.

Fixing a Damp Patch on a Wall

Flaking or peeling paint, crazing or mildewed plaster, or timber decay that begins well above the floor line (assuming it's not caused by rising damp, a broken roof tile, faulty roof flashings or a leaking valley gutter) suggest two things:

- If it's under or adjacent to a window or external door, the window flashings are either not working or are non-existent;
- If it's elsewhere, there may be an obstruction in the wall cavity (if there is one) which is bridging water across from the outside.

Window and Door Flashings

In cavity brick, brick veneer and timber frame construction, all windows and external doors should have head flashings over the top of them. All windows and some doors have sill flashing as well (see Diagram 1). A flashing is a thin, waterproof material such as lead, aluminium or plastic, which is placed in a position vulnerable to weather to stop external water penetration.

Unfortunately, in the hands of poor builders, it is the kind of item that is sometimes forgotten altogether or, all too often, installed incorrectly.

If there are no flashings, other than trying to waterproof the exterior wall by using a waterproofing paint or clear silicone sealer, and using silicone caulking to try to seal off any gaps, the only proper way to fix the problem is to get a builder to take off the internal frame trims, cut the fixings with a hacksaw, completely remove the frame, and then reflash the opening properly.

If the flashings are in place but damaged, taking off the internal trims and using liberal amounts of silicone in the suspect places may effect a cure. If it doesn't, taking the frame out is the most foolproof solution, but well beyond the capability of the average do-it-yourselfer.

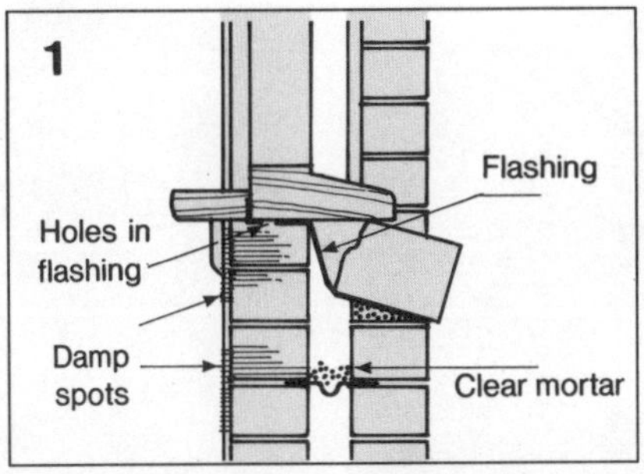

Section showing flashing under sill

Clearing Cavity Bridges

Bridges across cavities in double brick or brick veneer construction are caused either by:

- a brickbat that is jammed in the cavity and left there by a careless builder or bricklayer; or
- mortar droppings that are caught on the wall ties; or
- mortar droppings that are lying on the top of the head flashing.

PROCEDURE

1 To establish the reason, get up on the roof (see Repairing a Leaking Roof page 112) with a torch and lift a few tiles directly over the trouble spot. This should enable you to look down the cavity to see what the problem is.

2 In the case of the last two causes, a long batten poked down the cavity should dislodge the bridge (see Diagram 2). Over a window, watch you don't poke a hole through the flashing itself.

3 A tightly jammed brickbat is a more serious problem. First, try to dislodge it with the batten. If it's stuck, correctly establish where it is (the batten will help), then, with a plugging chisel and lump hammer, from the outside, chop out the brick joints around the brick opposite the obstruction (see Diagram 3). Remove the brick, then the bat, and relay the brick (see Relaying Loose Bricks page 124).

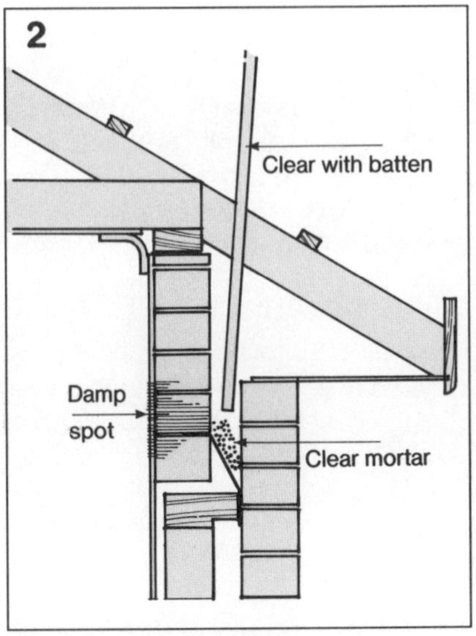

Section showing dampness caused by mortar droppings in a cavity wall

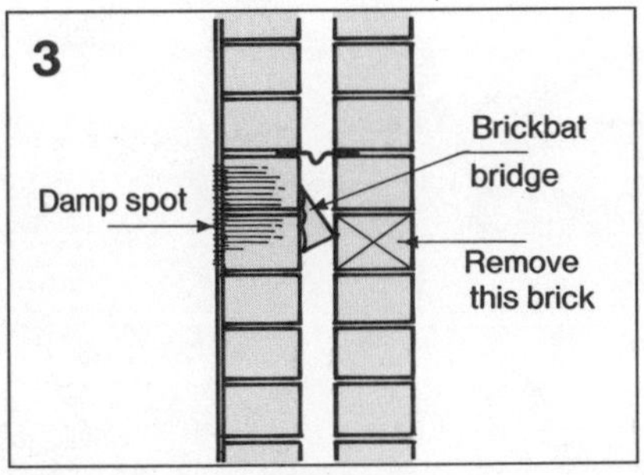

Brickbat jammed in cavity wall

Solid Brick Walls

One solution is to render the outside of the wall to increase its impermeability. This shouldn't be done if the wall has been painted with a sealer because the render may not adhere properly. Although a 1 part of cement to 3 parts of sand mix is strong and fairly waterproof, it is more likely to crack and can in fact lock moisture behind it. This moisture, unable to get away through the outside wall, will (you guessed it!) gravitate inwards.

Use a 1 of cement, 1 of lime, 6 of sand mix and consider using a stucco finish because not only is it less likely to crack, but the surface area is increased, thereby improving evaporation.

If you've tried painting the outside of the porous brick with a sealer or waterproofing paint and you've had no success, then there is another solution. It's called battening out.

What you do is to batten the inside of the wall and apply a separate internal lining. This then creates a cavity which leaves the damp wall to its own devices. The size of the battens and the space between them will depend on the lining you're using. A waterproof barrier should be inserted between each batten and the wall.

The plugs and battens should be of a timber species that won't rot. Western red cedar or a durable hardwood would be suitable. The fastenings should be brass or hotdip galvanised.

Painting the back of the lining sheets with an oil-based paint before fixing will help to seal them off from any dampness. Put a few air vents in the lining to ensure some air circulation behind the lining.

Repainting

Once the problem is solved, the wall should be left until the moisture has dried out. It will require approximately four months for a brick wall to dry out fully but that time can be accelerated by use of artificial heating (hairdryers or radiators). While the wall is drying, the faulty paint should be removed (this will increase the wall's exposure to air and heat). If the paint is oil-based and the rendered area is large it may pay to use a heat gun or blowlamp to thoroughly burn the paint. Then simply scrape it off.

Alternatively, using some rough sandpaper, a cork block and a plentiful supply of elbow grease, sand the patch back to bare plaster.

To lessen the possibility of the patch showing in the finished paintwork, thin the perimeter edges with fine sandpaper on a block so there is no discernible ridge. This is called feathering.

When the patch is fully dry, check that the surface has no whitish deposit on it. If it has, then efflorescence has taken place. This means that soluble salts from within the brick or render have been brought to the surface by the evaporating water. Paint the patch with a 5% solution of muriatic acid and rinse well. Redry the patch before painting.

If using oil-based paint you must apply a suitable sealer, then an undercoat, and finish with one or two layers of a finish coat. With water-based paints (acrylics and plastic) the procedure is greatly simplified. Some can be painted straight on while others only require the first coat to be slightly thinned.

Peeling paint is an indication of dampness in the wall.

Remove the faulty paint with a scraper.

Sand the surface and edges with sandpaper and a cork block.

When the patch is completely dry repaint the wall.

Foundation-based Water Damage

Water is essential for human life. However, if it finds its way into the wrong place in a home it can cause untold damage. A lot of potential water damage in your home can emanate from the ground.

The ground can be likened to a piece of blotting paper. It absorbs moisture in wet conditions and dries out in droughts. Many of the commonly used building materials are porous and also absorb moisture. Therefore, it is essential to stop the moisture movement by providing a barrier.

In brickwork, this barrier is created by building a waterproof membrane such as plastic or aluminium strip into the brick joint during construction. This barrier is called a damp proof course (DPC).

If the DPC is left out or damaged by uncaring or unsupervised bricklayers, water will soak up the wall and, if it is an internal wall, cause the paint to peel off, mildew to flourish, etc.

Unfortunately, the only way to rectify the problem is to replace the barrier. This involves chopping out the joint and inserting an appropriate DPC. It is a time-consuming and heart-breaking job, one that, unless the area is very small, should be done by an expert.

Water Diversion

Another way to lessen potential water damage is to stop it reaching the property. This can be achieved by building retaining walls (which should be designed by an engineer) putting in properly constructed agricultural drains (information on which can be obtained from the CSIRO via their building science notes), sloping the soil or footpaths away from external walls, etc.

Increasing Ventilation

Other common dampness problems, even if the DPC is satisfactory and water is completely diverted, are caused by:

- underground seepage,
- a severe plumbing or drainage leak (which can easily be detected and rectified), or
- insufficient ventilation under a house as a result of having too few vents or because they've been blocked by built-up gardens, paths or even shrubs.

The result of this moisture in the long term is that the under-floor timbers will rot. Short-term indications are cupping of flooring or even swelling that lifts the boards up off the joists.

Periodic six-monthly inspection under a house will ensure that all is well. If rotting (which is caused by fungi that feed on the timber) is discovered, then clearing or dramatically increasing the number of vents will help. For indivertible seepage, laying a cover of plastic membrane over the complete area (making sure you tape the joints) will seal much of the moisture off.

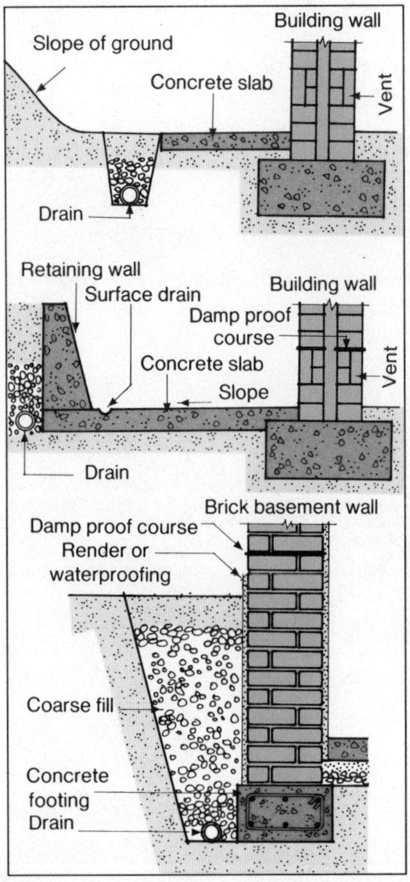

Waterproofing an Existing Wall

Waterproofing can be achieved by painting a wall with a waterproof paint or, if earth fill is pressing against it, by completely removing the fill and following one of the procedures below.

PROCEDURE

1 Waterproofers Made from bitumen, latex rubber, water-based epoxies and silicones, these products are painted onto the wall to provide an impermeable barrier to water. Thus a back-filled internal wall can be painted on the inside or an exposed external wall can be sealed on the outside (the latter being the more effective). The efficacy of the product will depend amongst other things on the severity and pressure of the water penetration; how dirty, wet, mouldy, flaking, crumbly or efflorescent the wall is; and whether the wall is exposed to the sun or not.

2 Waterproofing retaining walls Walls become retaining walls when buildings are excavated into the ground or where land is terraced. They must be properly designed and built to avoid overturning and leaking. If an existing wall is leaking and diversion of the water is impossible then the best solution is firstly to dig out the old fill. Cut it clear of the bottom of the wall by 600 mm and slope it back at an angle of approximately 45°. Apply a waterproofer or, if the flow is considerable, you can stick bitumen-impregnated felt to the wall with bitumen paint.

Then lay a large seepage drain along the wall. Make sure the bottom of the pipe is level with the bottom of the footing. Run it away from the house to a suitable pit or to the street. Then fill the space with a porous backfill such as gravel or crushed stone and cover with a path that slopes *away* from the house.

Replacing a Few Ceramic Tiles

Replacing a few loose tiles is not very difficult. By following the simple step-by-step procedure which follows you can do it yourself and achieve a professional finish as well.

Remember that most tile suppliers love do-it-yourselfers of either sex and will supply you with all materials and lots of free advice. They often hire tools as well.

To the job! Lightly tap the area surrounding the offending tiles and listen to see if the rest of the tiles are sound. If so, breathe a sigh of relief. If they're all drummy (a hollow, echoing noise) call in a tiler. To retile a complete bathroom is too big a job unless you're especially clever and have lots of time.

Next establish the reason for the looseness. It will usually be:

- a water leak in the wall plumbing (you must get a plumber to fix this problem before it causes more damage than just loose tiles);
- the wrong adhesive was used, the adhesive was poorly applied, or the previous surface preparation was faulty.

In some cases it may also be that the grouting (the coloured material in the tile joints) is failing and letting in water. In this situation once you have retiled and grouted the loose area, paint the other joints with a silicone sealer or, if you want a top quality job, rake the joints out and regrout them (see Regrouting a Shower Recess page 110).

Sand off old adhesive from the backs of the tiles.

The completed job with the loose tiles back in place.

Spread the adhesive on the backs of the tiles.

Mix the grout to a paste and rub into the joints.

TOOLS AND MATERIALS

You'll need a putty knife for scraping, a sponge and a notched spreader (which often comes with the adhesive).

Go to the tile shop, describe the situation, and ask for a suitable adhesive, some tile spacers (unless the tiles have spacer lugs on their edges) and a coloured grout to match the existing.

PROCEDURE

For total success, the back of the tiles and the wall must be clean, dry, firm and flat.

1 If a tap is in the way, unscrew it and then remove the loose tiles. Scrape or sand off any lumps of old adhesive and clean each surface with a strong detergent (which must be rinsed off).

2 In the case of new, unpainted gypsum board, it must be sealed by painting the area to be tiled with a multipurpose primer or a polyurethane paint.

If the surface has been painted, scrape off any flaking paint and roughen the old surface with sandpaper. Never use paint stripper, because it leaves a chemical residue which could weaken the adhesive. In all cases, if the surface is uneven, plaster it smooth with a compatible filler.

3 Spread the adhesive evenly over the area to be tiled (2–3 mm thick). In hard-to-reach areas apply a double thickness to the back of each tile.

4 Press the tiles into position working from the bottom up. Push the spacers into place as you go to maintain an even joint. For large areas periodically check that the new tiles line up with the existing ones by using a straight piece of timber or a level. Wipe off any excess adhesive with a sponge and allow the tiles to dry.

5 Mix the grout to a paste and rub into the joints, making sure you clean off the excess *before* it dries. After it sets, polish the tiles with a dry cloth.

Loose Jambs in Brickwork

Fixing a wobbly jamb in an external or internal brick wall looks a daunting task. Loose jambs in a timber frame wall can simply be renailed, but how do you fix into bricks?

The answer is simple: use masonry bolts. You just bore a hole through the jamb and into the brickwork with a masonry drill, insert the masonry bolt, then tighten the nut. The bolt locks itself into the brick by expanding the plastic or metal sleeve that is part of it. Once tightened, the bolt provides secure anchorage and stabilises the jamb.

Secure the jamb in place with a temporary block.

Bore a hole in the jamb with a speed drill.

TOOLS AND MATERIALS

Electric drill, masonry drill bit to suit the diameter and length of the masonry bolt, spanner, tape and pencil, a speed drill bit 10 mm larger than the bolt head (but only if you want the head of the bolt sunk below the face of the jamb), and an old sheet to collect the mess will be needed.

You will also need one masonry bolt for each 450 mm of loose jamb. The length of the bolt must be sufficient to go through the thickness of the jamb and project at least 50 mm into the brickwork. The diameter required depends on the length but will typically be 6 mm.

PROCEDURE

1 Place the jamb in its original position. This can be found by looking on the floor at the old paint line. Secure the jamb with some temporary blocks tacked to both floor and jamb. Use fine gauge nails to avoid damage.

2 If you want the bolt head to finish *below* the face of the jamb (it looks better), use your speed drill to bore a hole into the jamb face or rebate 20 mm deep wherever you have decided to place a bolt (the first one should be around 180 mm from the floor). Avoid brick joints.

Remember, if it's an external brick wall, there is usually a cavity between the two layers of brickwork. A brick is 110 mm wide and render is usually 10 mm thick, so you should be able to position the bolt so it's at least 40 mm away from the edge of the brick. For narrow jambs this could mean that you have to put the bolts in the jamb rebate.

3 Next place the masonry bit in the electric drill and bore through the sunk holes until you hit brickwork. Stop and mark the drill with a pencil line and withdraw it. Mark another location 50 mm higher up the drill and wrap masking tape round this mark. Go on drilling until the timber touches the tape. Complete all the holes similarly.

4 Insert the bolts and, with your spanner or pliers, tighten the nut or bolt head.

5 Check that the door closes. If the jamb has gone in too far, take off the architrave, loosen the bolts, lever the jamb back out to its correct position with a chisel, then pack in behind the jamb with bits of ply or fibre cement. Retighten the bolts and replace the architrave.

If you have sunk the bolt heads in, you could fill the large holes with a suitable filler or, better still, glue in a piece of wooden dowel of the same diameter.

If you haven't, cut off the excess thread with a hacksaw, and paint the protruding fastenings the same colour as the jamb.

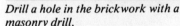

Drill a hole in the brickwork with a masonry drill.

Tighten the nut with pliers until it is firm.

Fill the hole in the jamb with a piece of wooden dowel.

Repairing a Rotting Gate

Gates, because of their exposure to the weather, often rot. This destructive decay of timber is caused by fungi, a minute form of plant life. The spores from rotting wood float through the air and can alight on exposed timber. If the timber is damp the spores germinate and spread, eating the timber away, leaving only a crumbling mass.

The way to avoid rotting is to install a gate made from either a decay resistant timber or a timber that has been treated with a preservative. However, if an existing gate is beginning to decay you must quickly remove the rotting pieces and replace them with a more durable timber.

Of the Australian timbers that have a natural resistance to decay, cypress pine is one of the best. Western red cedar, imported from Canada, though soft, is very resistant to decay and is therefore suitable for exterior use.

An alternative is to use treated radiata pine, which is easily recognised by its greenish tinge. This cheap, fast-growing timber is impregnated with a poisonous chemical that kills fungi and termites, thus preserving the otherwise susceptible wood.

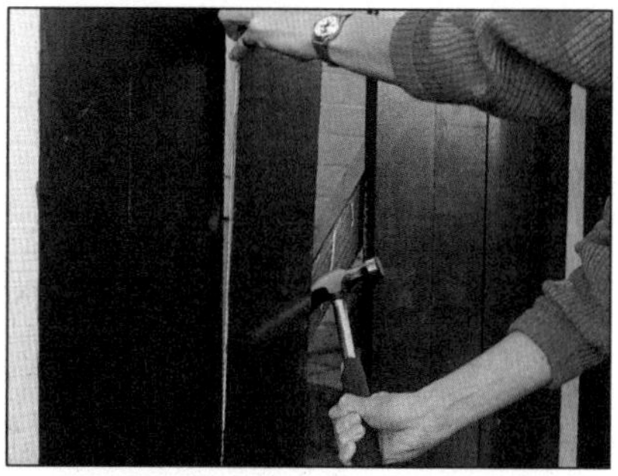

Remove the rotting parts of the gate with a claw hammer.

Carefully mark the new pieces to the correct length.

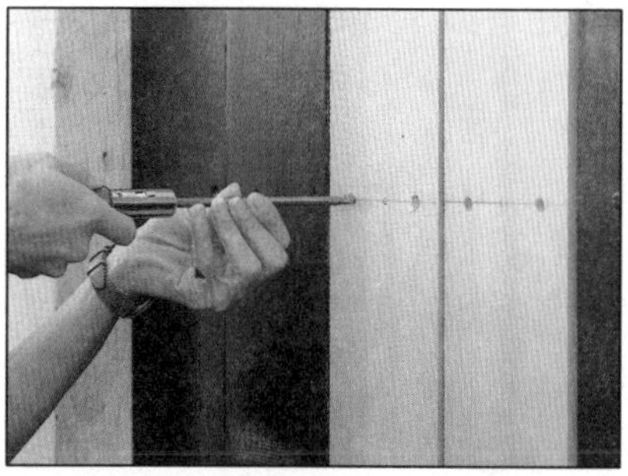

You can fix the new pieces in place using screws.

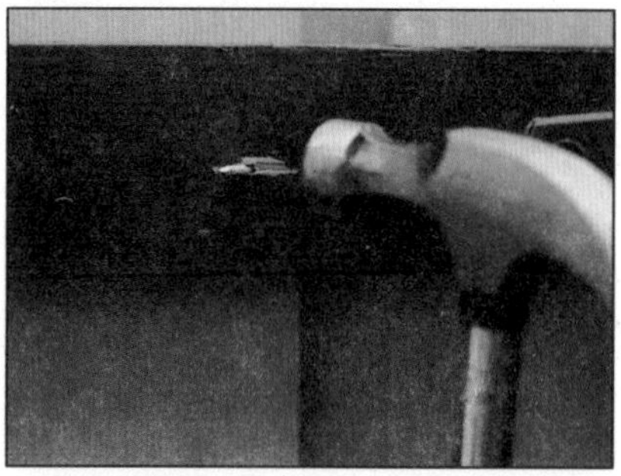

Alternatively use nails and fix the nails by clenching.

TOOLS AND MATERIALS

A screwdriver, hammer and nail punch, a square, a panel or hand saw, tape and pencil and perhaps a hacksaw. You'll need timber of a similar length and section size to the pieces to be replaced. Ideally, fastenings should be brass. Ferrous fastenings must be galvanised.

PROCEDURE

1 Using the screwdriver, take the gate off its hinges. Alternatively the gate can be repaired in position. If the screws have badly rusted you may need to cut them off with a hacksaw. If the hinges are rusty, remove them and either buy new galvanised ones or, if they're in fair condition, wire brush them back to bare metal and paint them with a cold-galvanising paint.

2 A typical gate has its members butted together and is held together with nails, screws or bolts. Assuming it's not a framed gate and has no interlocking joints like the mortice and tenon, it should be possible to remove the pieces that are rotting with the claw on the hammer or by undoing the bolts or screws. Make sure you remove every rotting piece, otherwise the rot could flare up again.

3 Carefully mark the new pieces to the correct length and shape and, laying them on a low wall or bench, cut them to size with your hand or panel saw. Use a coping saw and fine rasp to cut and finish curved shapes.

When cutting the boards, mark a fine line across the face and down both edges. Place the saw on the *waste* side of the line with the edge of the teeth just touching the line. When you're finished sawing the lines should still be visible.

4 Lay the gate on top of some scrap blocks on a solid surface (such as a concrete slab or deck) and, using nails, screws, etc., fix the pieces in place.

To increase the holding power of nails use ones which have flat heads and are 10 mm longer than the total thickness of the gate. When the pieces are well nailed, turn the gate over and bend the projecting nails over in the direction of the wood grain. This is called clenching. Punch the ends below the surface. This will ensure they never pull out.

5 Prop the gate into position using blocks and then rescrew the hinges into place.

6 If the original gate is unpainted and made with a rot-prone timber, either cover the rest of it with some fungus-inhibiting preservative or paint the whole gate with a water-soluble paint. It could help to clear away some of the shrubbery which may be contributing to the humid environment.

Repainting a Room

Repainting a few rooms can be fun and it lends a fresh, long-lasting lease of life to your home. It's easy providing you follow some simple steps.

Surface Preparation

This is always tedious but it's essential for good results. Remember paint will not adhere properly to a surface that is incorrectly prepared.

New work Metal: remove all rust, dirt and oil.

Wood: sand smooth, cover resinous knots with knotting, and fill all small holes with putty.

Gypsum plaster: make sure it's clean and thoroughly dry. Brush or vacuum the wall to remove all jointing cement dust. Fill holes with cellulose filler.

Bricks, concrete and plaster: leave to dry for 12 weeks if using oil-based paints. If using water-based paint, clean thoroughly.

Old work Strip off flaking, crazing or bubbling paint using a blowtorch or heat gun and scraper, but not on fibrous or gypsum plaster for obvious reasons. Alternatively use a chemical stripper (wear rubber gloves and make sure the room is well ventilated). Small areas can be scraped clean, sanded or wire-brushed. Fill all cracks, dents and chips with a cellulose filler or putty and sand smooth. Remove any mould or efflorescence (a white, salt deposit that leaches out of damp bricks).

Some wallpapers, if sound, may be painted over (but a sealer may be required). Check with the wallpaper supplier or manufacturer if known or try a small area first to see if the colours leach out or the wallpaper glue is affected. If any doubt exists, strip it off with a wallpaper steamer which you can hire. Alternatively, soak it off with warm water.

If paintwork is sound just make sure you clean off any grease spots, stains, etc., with detergent or sugar soap, and rinse clean. Sand lightly to increase adhesion.

With nail pops in gypsum plaster, punch the nails heads further in and fill the hole with cornice cement. Then, when dry, skim over it with a generous layer of jointing cement applied with a broad knife. Sand with fine adhesive paper.

HANDY PAINTING HINTS

- Check that paint is sound by sticking some cellulose tape onto the surface in several places. If paint adheres to it when you pull it off, the surface should be stripped.
- If you're in the middle of painting and lunch intervenes, or you want to stop for a cup of tea, simply wrap the roller or brush in a plastic wrap or a plastic bag to seal it from the air — it will keep it from drying out for an hour or so.
- Rollers should be hung up to dry otherwise you'll get a flat spot in the nap.
- Brushes will also retain their shape better if after you've cleaned them thoroughly (paying particular attention to the area near the handle), you shape the wet bristles to a proper brush shape.

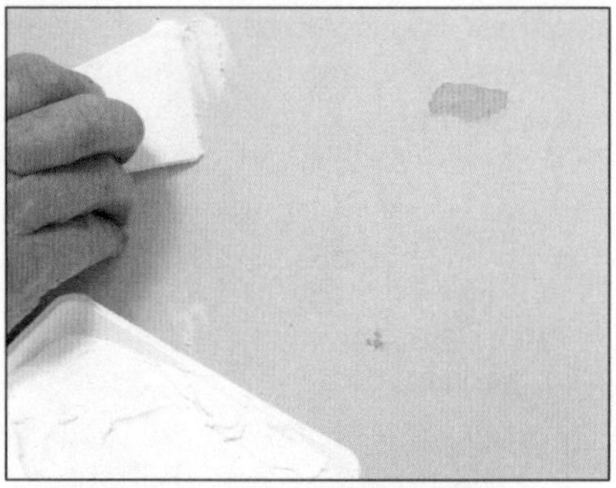

Fill holes in gypsum plaster with cellulose filler.

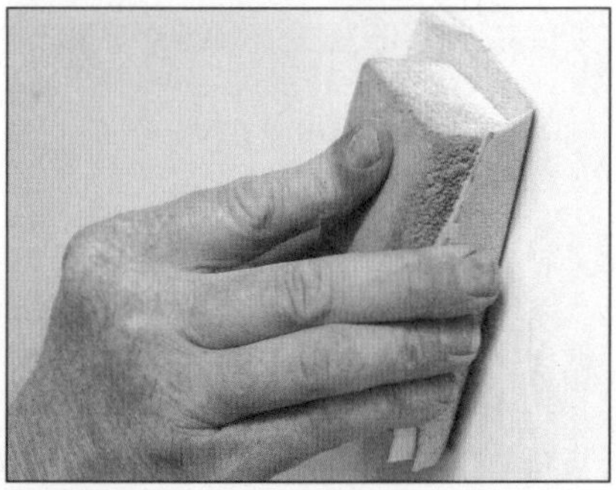

Sand painted wood lightly to increase adhesion.

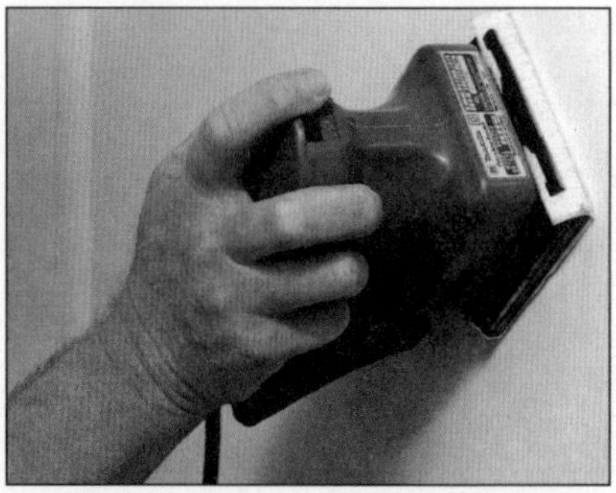

An orbital sander makes the job easier.

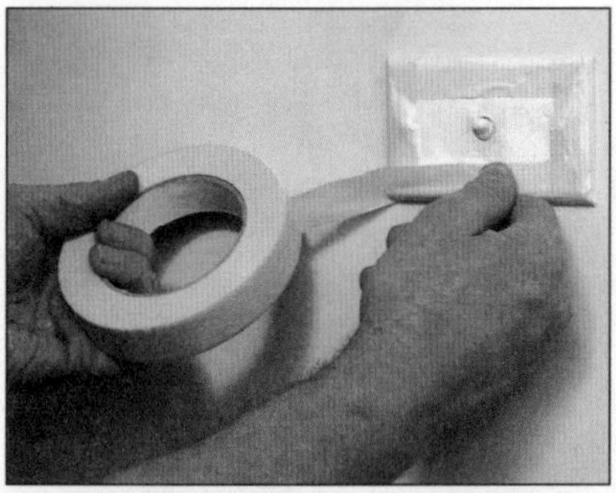

Masking tape round light switches facilitates cutting in.

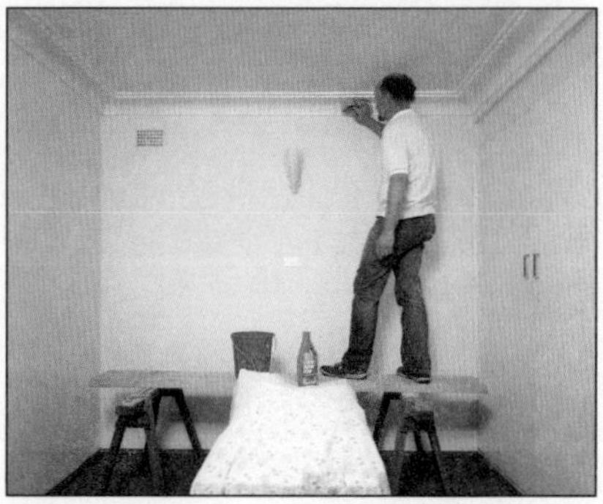

If the old paint is sound, washing may be the only preparation needed.

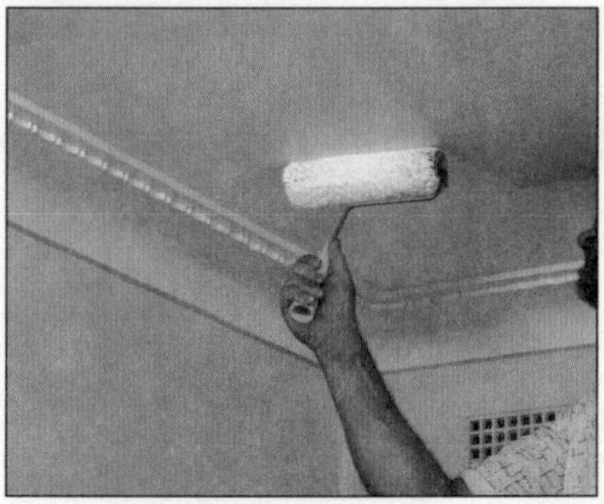

Use a roller to paint the ceiling, working towards the light source.

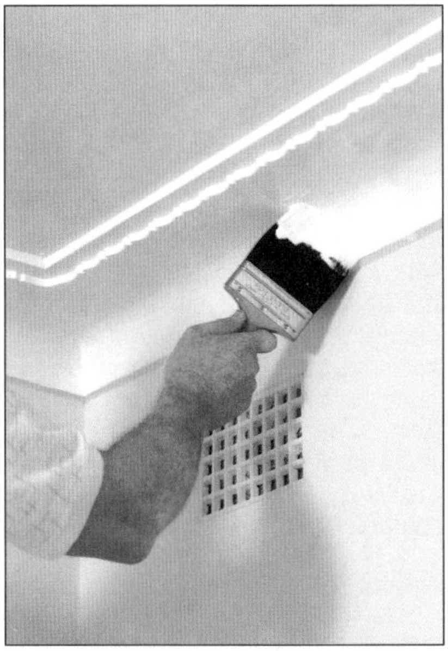

Use a brush for cornices and cutting in.

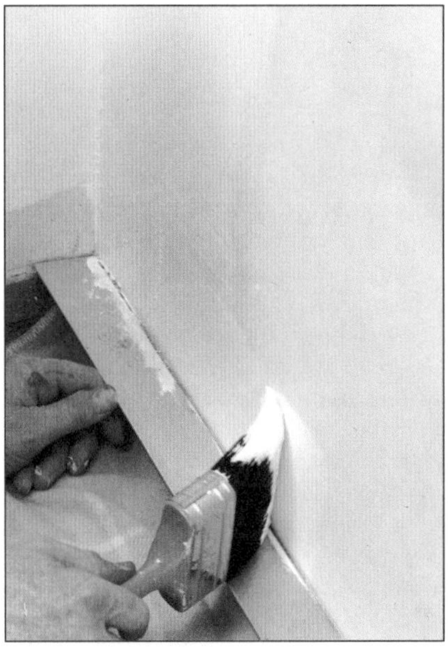

A strip of thin metal is useful when cutting in.

Use the narrow brush for cutting in round windows and architraves.

TOOLS AND MATERIALS

Use a brush for all wood priming and detail work. A good quality 50 mm and a 100 mm cover most jobs.

Rollers with a tray are especially quick for walls, ceilings and flush doors and give a good, slightly textured finish. Rollers (made from foam, lambswool or mohair — different ones suit different paints) and brushes should be well cleaned and dried after each use in the appropriate cleaner to ensure long life.

A plentiful supply of old rags and sponges should be on hand to wipe up spills and drops. A handy item is a 600 × 100 mm strip of thin metal or plastic. This strip can be pressed against skirtings, etc., so that cutting in is easier and faster. Paint quantities are shown in the chart below.

PROCEDURE

1 Begin with the ceilings, then the walls, and finish with the windows, doors and trims. Empty the room as much as possible and cover the remaining furniture (pushed into the centre of the room) and carpets with old sheets, etc. Masking tape around power points and switches facilitates cutting in, but don't leave it for too long in case it sticks permanently! Make sure there is plenty of natural or artificial light to reduce the likelihood of missed or thin spots.

2 Ceilings A plank laid across two stools or strong wooden boxes makes a convenient scaffold. Alternatively use a step ladder. Stir the paint well and fill the tray halfway up the slope. Work the roller into the paint until it's covered and then roll it evenly against the textured tray surface to stop dripping. Apply working from the corners out. Roll out any overlaps. Keep a brush on the tray for painting cornices, getting into corners and finishing against trims. Move towards your light source in 800 mm strips.

3 Walls Follow the same procedure as for ceilings except that you begin in a corner and work from the ceiling down. Paint a thin strip with your brush along the cornice and skirting first and then fill in between with the roller.

4 Doors, windows and skirting Do the trims (architraves) first, then the frames, then the sashes or doors. Flush doors can be done with the roller providing you take off the door handles. Moulded doors, architraves, and window frames and sashes require a brush. Doors should be finished on the edges first, then the faces. Paint around handles first (though it is better to remove them), and then finish the rest.

Again stir the paint well, dip the brush in, remove excess paint by stroking once against the side of the tin, and then, using 300 mm strokes running parallel with the wood grain, apply evenly. Too much paint will cause runs and too little will expose the undercoat, primer or previous finish. Brush out overlaps. When using enamel, finish as you go because it dries quickly, especially on a hot day. Don't attempt to go back over a sticky area!

For cutting in against walls use a thin strip of metal or plastic but watch that you keep wiping the edge clean or the paint will run in underneath.

If you experience any difficulties ring or write to the paint manufacturers. They employ experts who are paid to assist with technical advice or send printed information. But first, read the directions on the tin carefully. It will save you much embarrassment!

Repairing Timber Floors

Before new floor coverings are put down, old coverings have to be removed and the floor carefully prepared. Any marked unevenness will clearly show through linoleum, sheet vinyl or vinyl tiles. Carpet will wear unevenly if the surface is irregular. It is therefore necessary to make the floor smooth and even by filling any holes in the boards, removing nails that stick up plus any bits of the old covering material, and then sanding.

First step is to lift and remove the old covering. A pinch bar is a useful tool for levering up carpet and sheet vinyl, although the claw on a hammer will also do the job. Use the wedge-shaped end to lever it up, and then the curved end for removing the fastenings. If the head of the nail should snap off then simply drive it in level with the floor. If you don't have a pinch bar, a pair of pincers could be used to remove headless nails or staples. For lifting vinyl or cork tiles, a spade is useful.

After the covering has been lifted and removed, examine the exposed flooring carefully. If it is badly split in many places, or the boards have shrunk excessively leaving gaps everywhere, or there are countless holes, it would be better to cover the whole floor with a layer of tempered hardboard or fibrous cement rather than to attempt to fix it (see Laying Cork or Vinyl Tiles page 146).

If it's in fair condition, punch the heads of all protruding flooring nails below the surface of the floor about 2 mm. Use a nail punch that has a tip the same diameter as the nail head. Using a finer one will only damage the tip, while a larger one will make too large a hole. Be careful of your fingers! Make sure the face of the hammer is clean by lightly sanding it. This will prevent it slipping off the punch.

Once all the nails are punched the next step is to fill the holes. Small holes can be filled with a hard-drying, non-shrinking cellulose filler. Your hardware store will advise you which is the best type. Mix carefully and slightly over-fill the hole. Sand off flush when completely dry. If the filling compound keeps dropping right through the hole it may be necessary to get under the floor and nail a scrap piece of fibro or tin over the hole until the filler dries. Watch out for spiders!

Large Holes

Large holes or missing boards may need to be filled with a piece of similar flooring or timber. Cut the offending piece 10 mm clear of the joist at either end with the tip of a tenon saw (alternatively, bore a hole and use a fine keyhole saw) and lever it out. In the case of tongue and groove boards you will also need to use the tenon saw to rip off the tenon.

Nail a scrap piece of hardwood batten on the sides of the joist to give support to the new piece. Make it level with the underneath of the flooring to provide support. Then neatly cut in and fit the new piece, again ripping off the tenon. Nail it in and punch the nails.

A light sanding of the floor with a cork block and garnet paper or, better still, a belt sander, will remove all minor irregularities and any substances which may interfere with the adhesive bond.

The preparation is now complete and should ensure your new carpet or vinyl looks perfect when it's laid.

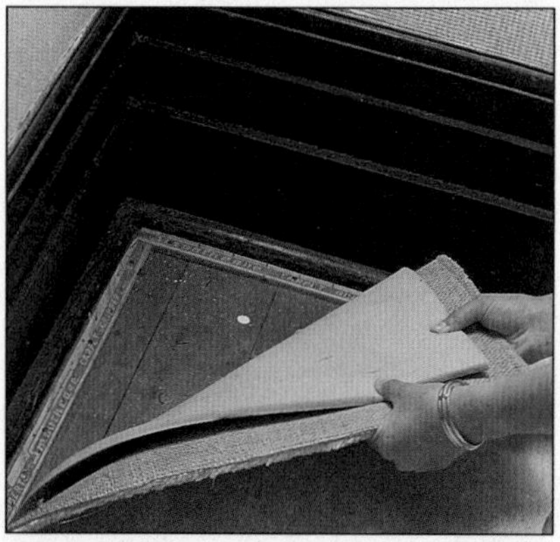

The first stop is to lift and remove the old floor covering.

Lift the smooth edge, if any, with a pinch bar.

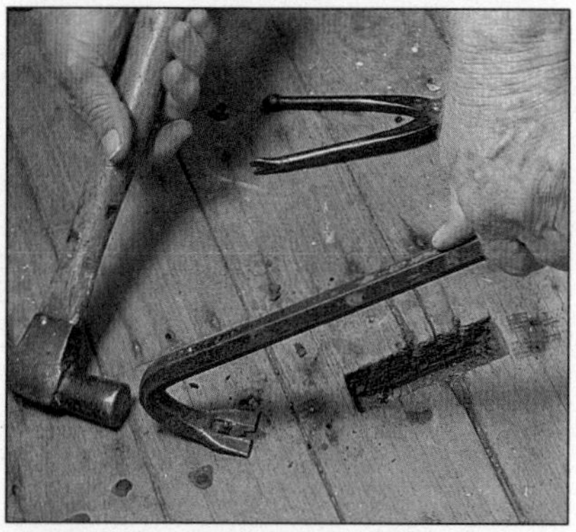

Extract protruding nails with a pinch bar.

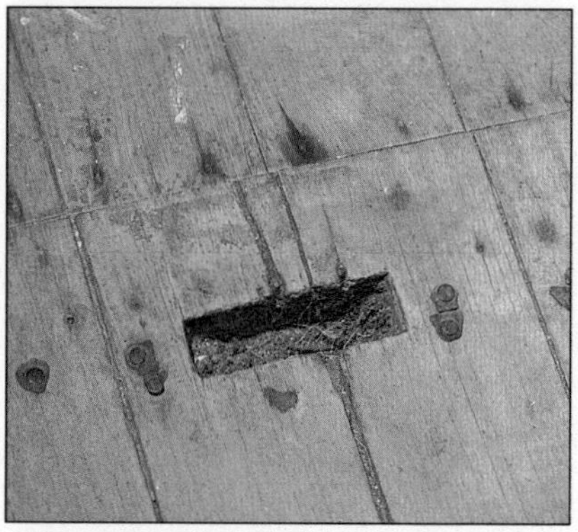

You may find a hole like this in your floor.

Fill the hole with a scrap piece of timber.

Clearing a Blocked Sink

I'll bet you looked disbelievingly at a sink full of lukewarm, greasy water and then you reached for this book muttering, 'Help!' For weeks the sink has taken longer and longer to empty and now, just when visitors are coming, it's finally stopped. Typical, eh?

There are three ways to attack the problem: using chemicals; using a rubber plunger or sink pump; or unscrewing the S-bend under the sink (assuming it doesn't have a cleaning eye).

Chemicals

There are on the market proprietary products designed to be put down the drainage system to eat away some of the things which may be blocking the line. Read the instructions carefully before you use the product. Chemicals are usually dangerous.

Their success varies depending on their quality, the type of chemical used, what is causing the problem, how early you attack it and, most importantly, how long you can afford to wait, assuming the sink is blocked. Often the chemicals must be left overnight.

For a quicker reaction in your sink you may have to buy or borrow a plunger (or a sink pump).

Plunger

The idea of a plunger, which is like a huge suction cup, is to create a pressure which may dislodge the object that is blocking your sink. By placing the plunger over the waste hole and vigorously pumping it up and down you create a force which, if you're lucky and the blockage is minor, may send the tea leaves or food matter on their way. The more efficient and more expensive sink pump gives greater pressure.

If, however, after much effort, the plunger doesn't work, then your last course of action is to disconnect the S-bend under the sink and manually clear the blockage.

The S-bend is a remarkably simple but effective way of sealing off bad odours which might come back up the plumbing pipes.

Removing the S-Bend

TOOLS

You'll need a bucket or basin to catch the sink water. If the large plastic nuts are too tight to move by hand you may also need to borrow a large pair of multigrips or wrench.

PROCEDURE

1 Clear the items from around the under-sink plumbing.

2 Place the bucket or basin in position.

3 Begin to unscrew the nuts on either side of the bend. (If it's an old metal type there may be a small eye on the bottom of the bend which can be unscrewed with a spanner. The blockage can then be cleared with a small piece of wire or a bottle brush).

4 Remove the bend, clean out the blockage, then screw it tightly back in place. Most plastic fittings are self-sealing. Metal sometimes needs to be caulked with Vaseline or thread tape.

5 Run some water and check the joints for leaks while saying a few prayers. If the water flows away quickly you've solved the problem. Clever you!

If it doesn't, then there is obviously a blockage further down the line which could be caused by such ominous things as tree roots, a blocked grease trap, etc. Ring your favourite plumber and leave a 'Help!' message on the answering phone.

Unscrew the nuts on either side of the S-bend under the sink.

Remove the bend.

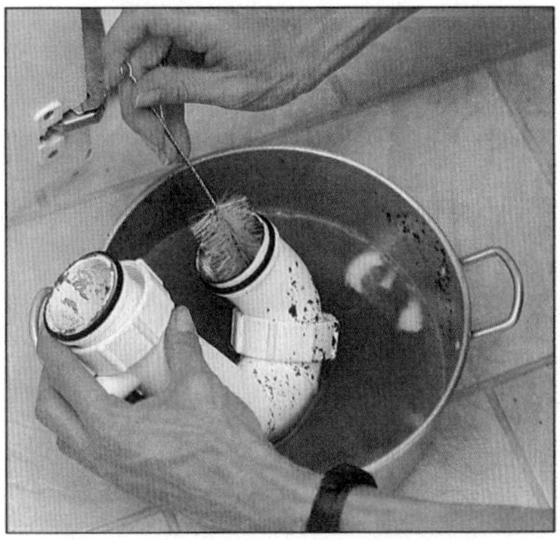

Clean out the bend with a flexible brush.

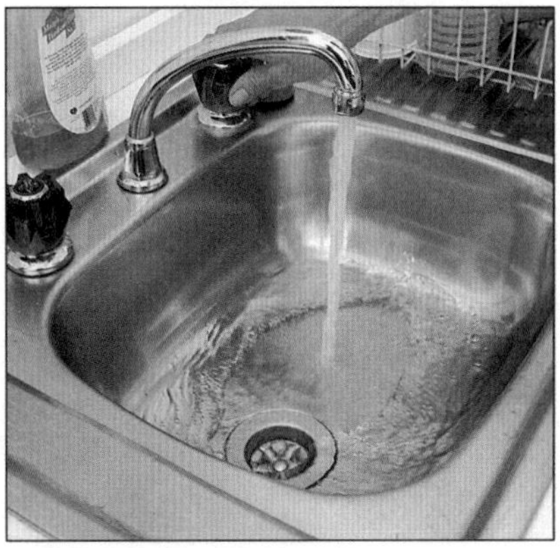

After replacing the bend run some water and check for leaks.

Repairing and Leaf-proofing Gutters

Major problems with gutters, besides rusting, are that the brackets come loose, they hold water, or they leak at the joints.

Leaks

Check all joints in the gutter. For leaking ones, spread the joint, clean the overlapping metal surfaces thoroughly and dry them. Then, using a flexible silicone caulking compound, reseal the joints.

Leaves

Leaves hold moisture, increasing the risk of rusting. They can also eventually block the downpipes, which will cause the gutters to overflow. This could lead to damage to gardens or the risk of dampness in external walls. You can clean them out from a ladder or from the roof surface. Use a putty knife and bucket (the mulch is good for the garden). If there is an excessive number of leaves you would be well advised to purchase an anti-leaf system from your hardware store (see photographs) and install it in accordance with the manufacturer's instructions. These products are specially designed to fit over the top of the gutter to stop any leaves entering it. There are a number of types at varying prices. As with everything, relate the rapidly escalating cost to the often marginal benefit!

Use a flexible silicone caulking compound to seal leaking joints.

Fixing Loose Brackets

Loose brackets usually occur because the nails in the gutter brackets have rusted through or the fascia has rotted or split and the nails have nothing solid to grip into. If the gutter is loose it may no longer fall correctly to the downpipes, meaning water lies in the bottom. This will eventually cause a ferrous metal gutter to rust out. Also if it's loose, it could come adrift in a high wind or heavy rain.

PROCEDURE

1 If the gutter is not too high, borrow or hire a ladder and get up to see what the cause is. Remember that ladders are potentially dangerous if they are not set up properly (see Repairing a Leaking Roof page 112).

2 With a pair of pliers or multigrips, undo the front of the brackets where they clip over the edge of the gutter for the full length of the run. To do this you will have to move the ladder several times unless you have a good head for heights and the roof is not too steep. In that case, wearing sandshoes and walking on the front edges of the tiles, you can walk along the roof and unclip the brackets.

3 With a long piece of timber push the gutter up off the brackets where it's loose and prop it up. Alternatively, lift it out of the brackets while you sit on the roof and lay it on the tiles.

4 Move the loose brackets along a bit and renail them into solid timber with galvanised clouts. Make sure you nail them back at the same height as they were (a level is handy for this). If the fascia is rotten or badly cracked along its length, you will need to call in a carpenter to replace part or all of it and then a plumber to refix the gutter with the correct fall.

5 Replace the gutter and carefully bend each clip back over the nose of the gutter.

With a pair of pliers, undo the front of the brackets.

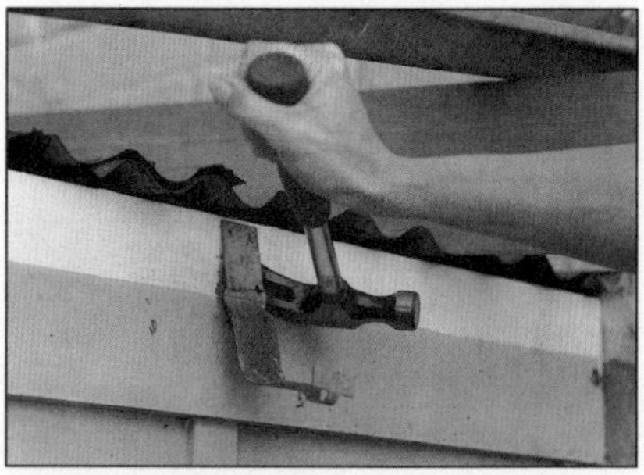

Remove the loose brackets from the fascia board.

Move the loose bracket along and renail it into solid timber.

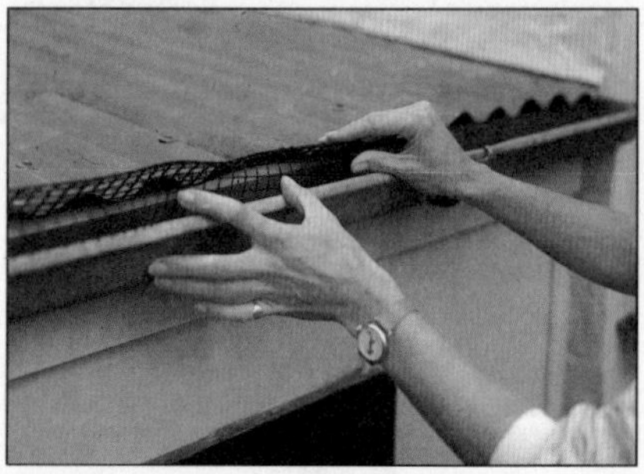

Install a leaf-proofing system to keep leaves out of your gutter.

Fixing Sticking Drawers

Are you having problems with your drawers? Sticking or coming-apart drawers create an unwanted eddy in the flow of household affairs. Fixing them is easy if you have a few minutes to spare.

First you have to identify the problem.

Why Drawers Stick

There are six typical reasons why drawers stick.

1. The drawers may have been accidentally put in the wrong place. If they're the same size, try rearranging the order to see if that helps.
2. Dampness, caused by such things as a plumbing leak, rising damp, or prolonged humidity, may be swelling the timber or particle board members. Check the under-sink plumbing if the drawer is in a kitchen or bathroom and rectify if necessary. For other rooms, move the chest of drawers or dresser out from the wall and feel the wall surface. If it is very damp or mildewed check the under-house drainage. If everything seems to be in order, call in an expert to check the damp proof course.

   To lower the moisture content, put the drawer in a warm, dry place for at least 24 hours.
3. A nail or screw, because of wear, may be protruding into the slide area. Pull the drawer out and inspect the slide assembly, using a torch if necessary. Remove the nail with pliers or pincers or take out the offending screw. If the drawers and runners have been glued, the removal of one fastener should cause no problem. If there is any doubt, put in another one where it will do no harm.
4. Too much friction between the drawer and runner (the member the drawer slides on) can make drawers difficult to operate. Rub on some dry lubricant (candle wax is good).
5. The drawer bottom, through overloading, may be sagging and rubbing on the drawer front beneath it. Depending on the drawer construction, you may be able to take out a few nails, slide the bottom out, and reverse it.

   If the bottom is fully enclosed, simply place a piece of 50 x 18 mm dressed batten across the *inside* of the drawer and nail or screw the drawer bottom to it.
6. A worn drawer bottom or runner (or both) can cause jamming. If the runner is worn too severely, replace it with a new hardwood runner screwed to the side of the drawer (see Diagram 2). For a badly worn drawer bottom, plane it straight, then stick a thin strip of hardwood (or several strips of plastic laminate) to the bottom edges to build the drawer side up.

Repairing Coming-apart Drawers

The construction of most modern drawers is flimsy to say the least. Gone are the days when they were made with solid timber and the intricate, intriguing, interlocking dovetail joint. If your drawers are falling apart, nowadays the only solution is to reglue them.

PROCEDURE

1 Knock them apart using a hammer and a scrap block of wood. Or you can use a nail punch to remove the nails.

2 Clean off all the old glue and then, using some old newspaper to protect your working surface, liberally coat all joint surfaces with PVA glue (or use epoxy glue if you want super strength).

3 Reassemble the drawer and cramp it. Check the corners are at right angles by using a large set square (or simply make the diagonals equal). This is essential otherwise the drawer won't fit.

If you don't have a cramp, either nail the glued joints together with some 38 mm nails or stand the drawer on its end and lay some heavy books on the front. Wipe off the excess glue, allow to dry and then put the drawer back, sanding or planing it to fit as necessary.

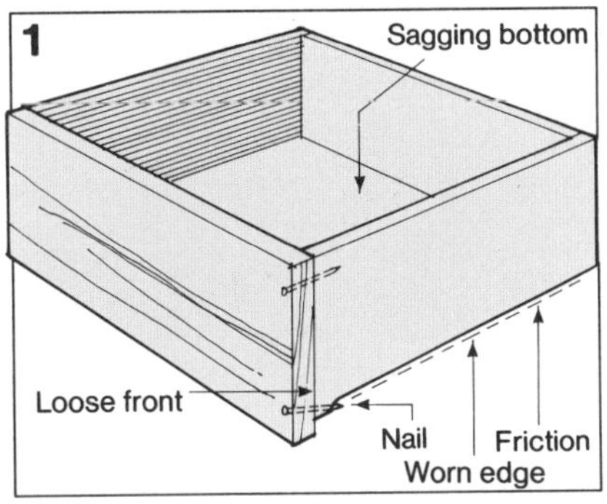

Diagram 1: a faulty drawer.

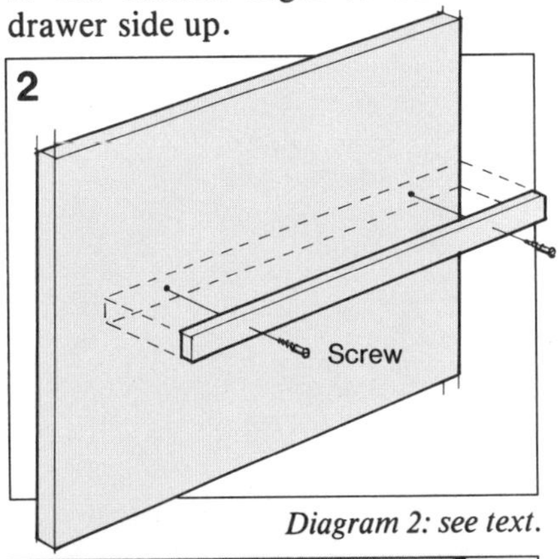

Diagram 2: see text.

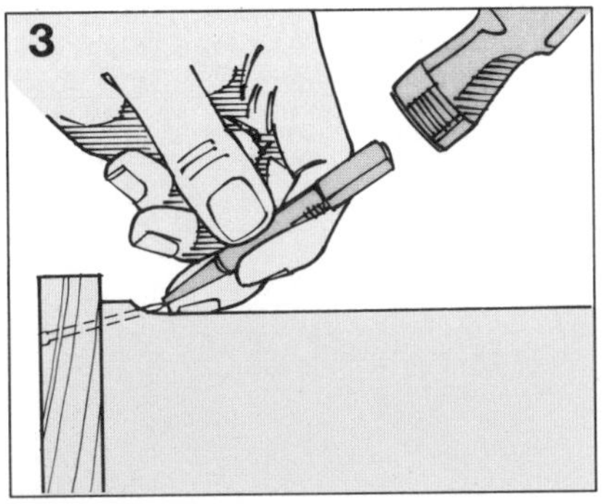

Diagram 3: removing a nail using a nail punch.

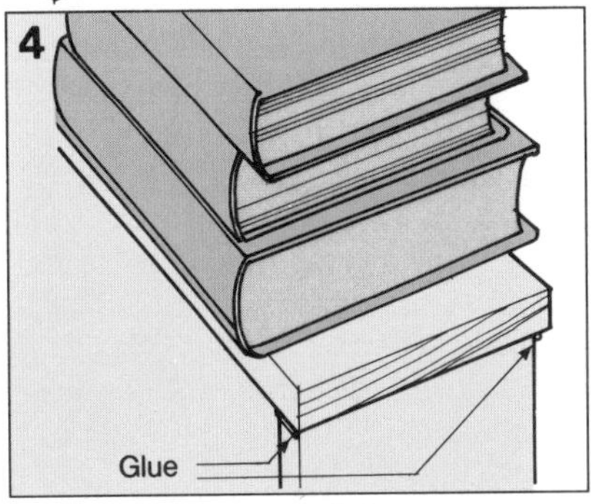

Diagram 4: if you don't have a cramp, lay some heavy books on the front.

Repairing Rotting Handrails or Door Frames

One of the enemies of timber is rot (see Repairing a Rotting Gate page 99). In windows, door frames, handrails and posts, rotting is principally caused because the end grain of the timber has not been glued with a waterproof glue or properly primed with an oil-soluble primer. This oversight allows moisture to soak up the end grain of the timber and before you know it, the rotten little fungi begin their destructive cycle.

The sight of peeling or cracking paint around joint lines or near the bottoms of stiles or the tops of posts should alert you. Maple or oregon are susceptible but western red cedar is not. Push a penknife or skewer into the timber around the joint or end. If it's still solid, heave a sigh of relief, strip the paint off, then reprime, undercoat, and apply several finishing coats as quickly as possible so that further moisture can't get in.

If the knife blade sinks into the timber as it would a sponge cake, you've got real problems!

Depending on the extent of the rotting and the member it is affecting, you may be able to cut away the rotting section and glue a new piece in. Of course, if it's in more than one place, it would be better to replace the whole member.

Note that the joints used in window and door frames are usually housed, whereas handrail joints are either butted or mitred. The procedure for fixing them all is basically the same.

Door Stiles (or Handrail Posts)

The procedure for mending vertical members like door stiles or handrail posts is similar to Handrails. Pay special attention to the priming of the bottom of a jamb. Give it three coats of primer to make sure the problem doesn't recur. Then prime the rest of the new timber (plus any bare patches), undercoat, and apply two coats of water-soluble exterior grade paint.

If the jamb is loose, renail it into the timber framing.

Repairing Handrails

The rotting here is most likely to be found in the top of the posts or where the rails are joined.

PROCEDURE

1 Using a penknife or steel skewer, probe along the handrail until you locate solid timber. Then go another 300 mm and, using a square and sharp pencil, mark across the section.

2 To make a scarf joint, measure back 150 mm and mark again as in step 1. Then set up your gauge or combination square to half the thickness and mark both edges.

3 Make a series of saw cuts down to the gauge line. Ensure the two at either end are square both ways. Carefully following your lines will ensure this. Next chisel out the waste coming in from both sides. Don't take too much off at one go. When the waste is removed, check that the surface is level, using a square or the edge of your chisel.

4 Then cut the piece through and remove the rotten segment. Then simply repeat the scarfing process on the replacement piece leaving the other end long. When the scarf fits, cut the other end and fit it with your plane.

5 Glue or double prime the joint and fix together with galvanised nails or screws. A cramp will help to make it tight.

Push a steel skewer into the wood to test for rot.

Ants and fungi which have made a meal of this handrail are exposed.

Probe along the handrail until you locate solid timber.

Using a square and a sharp pencil, mark across the section.

Then go another 300 mm and mark again.

Set up your combination square to half the thickness and mark both edges.

Make a series of saw cuts down to the gauge line.

Chisel out the waste, coming in from both sides.

Check that the surface is level, using a square or the edge of your chisel.

Cut the piece through and remove the rotten segment.

Repeat the measuring and cutting on the replacement piece.

Try the new piece for size before gluing and nailing.

Spread glue on the joint.

Fix the joint with galvanised nails. A cramp will make it tight.

After the glue has dried, plane the edges of the rail smooth.

Finish by painting thoroughly to exclude damp.

Repairing Gypsum and Fibrous Plaster

Over-exuberance by children, or even over-indulgence by adults, could result in a gaping hole suddenly appearing in your gypsum plaster wall or ceiling (assuming, that is, there isn't the odd one already). Instead of hiding it with a pot plant, why don't you fix it? It's very simple to do — here's how.

Note: if your linings are fibrous plaster, the procedure for fixing a hole is somewhat similar — merely adjust the materials and jointing cements.

TOOLS AND MATERIALS

Some 120 grit sandpaper, saw, trimming knife, pencil and straight edge, a cork block, brushes or rollers and enough paint to do the patch or, better still, the wall, are needed.

Next obtain a straight-sided rectangular piece of gypsum plaster that is slightly larger than the hole. However, don't buy a full sheet! You may be able to get a small piece off a building site or an offcut from a firm that installs gypsum plaster. Make sure the piece is the same thickness as the existing wall lining.

You will also need some cornice cement, plus jointing cement, self-sticking jointing tape, broadknives (some suppliers sell a cheap package which includes one plastic 100 mm, one 150 mm and one 200 mm).

PROCEDURE

You will see that the piece of gypsum plaster has a white core (of calcined gypsum) with a paper linerboard on both sides. It is important you don't damage or scuff this paper lining by oversanding it otherwise your paint finish will be second-rate. Cutting the gypsum plaster can be done either by deeply scoring it with a trimming knife and then snapping the piece away from the cut, or by using a fine handsaw.

1 Lay the piece over the hole (making sure it's reasonably level) and mark around the perimeter. Using a straight edge, draw lines to represent the diagonals, as shown in the picture.

2 With a fine handsaw, cut from the hole along the diagonals into each corner.

3 Then, using your trimming knife and a small straight edge (steel is best), cut deeply around the edges of the rectangle. Keep outside the lines by about 2 mm to make sure that the patch will fit. Snap the pieces out by bending them *away* from the cut face.

4 From the offcuts, make four small blocks (two for smaller holes) approximately 100 × 100 mm. Stick them in position with the cornice cement and allow an hour or so for them to dry completely.

5 Next, push the replacement piece, face out, into place, making sure you put a liberal amount of cornice cement on the blocks. Allow to dry.

6 Sand the painted wall around the patch for a distance equal to at least 300 mm. This will allow the jointing cement to key.

7 Next, stick on the tape and cover with a thin layer of jointing cement 100 mm wide (the tape works in the joint like reinforcing steel in concrete). Allow to dry for 24 hours. Sand off any irregularities, then follow up with a thin layer of cement about 300 mm wide, then, after another 24 hours, one 600 mm wide. Feather the edges off to nothing on the painted section each time. If possible, cover the whole area of the patch with jointing cement.

8 When dry, sand thoroughly, brush all the dust off the surface (otherwise the paint might lift), paint the area with an approved sealer, and finish the wall with a matching paint.

If you've followed the steps carefully and neatly, no one, including you, will ever believe there was a hole there.

The problem: a gaping hole in a gypsum plaster wall.

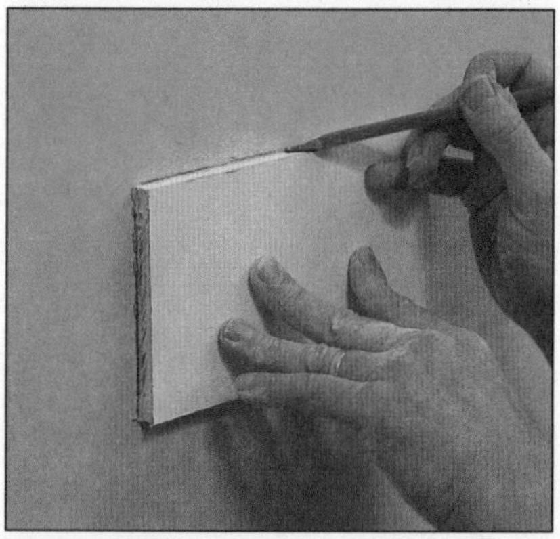

Lay a piece of plaster over the hole and mark round it.

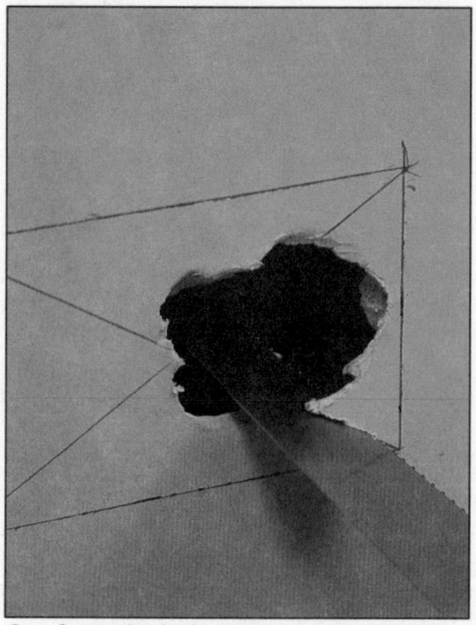

Cut from the hole along the diagonals you have drawn.

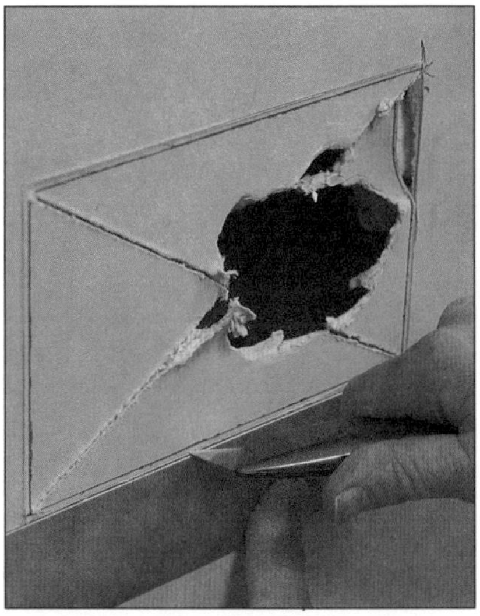

Cut round the edges of the rectangle with a trimming knife.

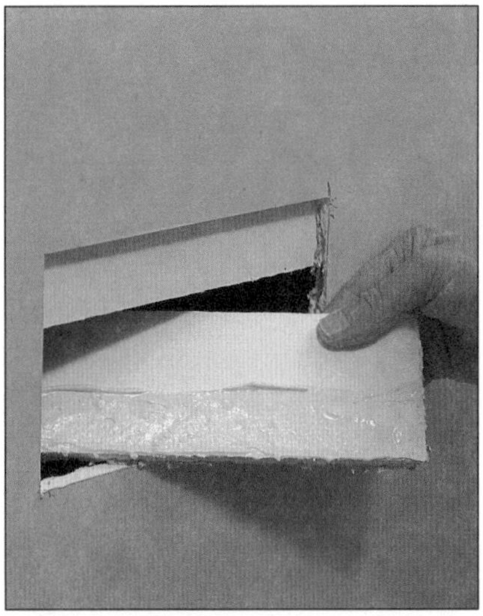

Make two small blocks from the offcuts and stick them in place.

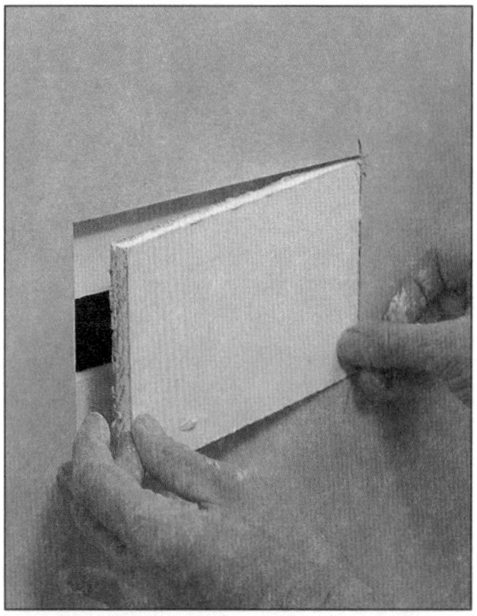

Push the replacement piece, face out, into position.

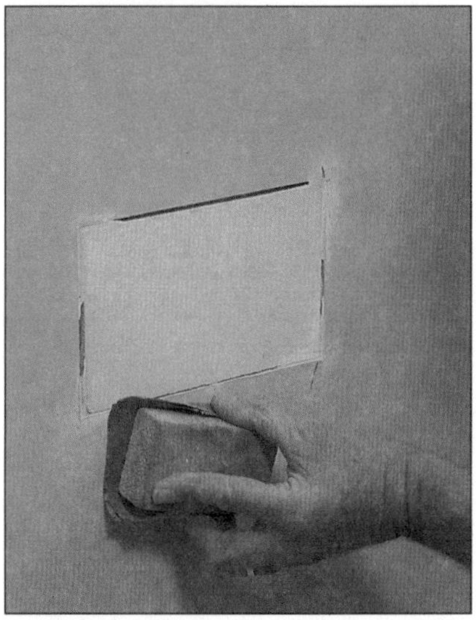

Sand the painted wall around the patch for at least 300 mm.

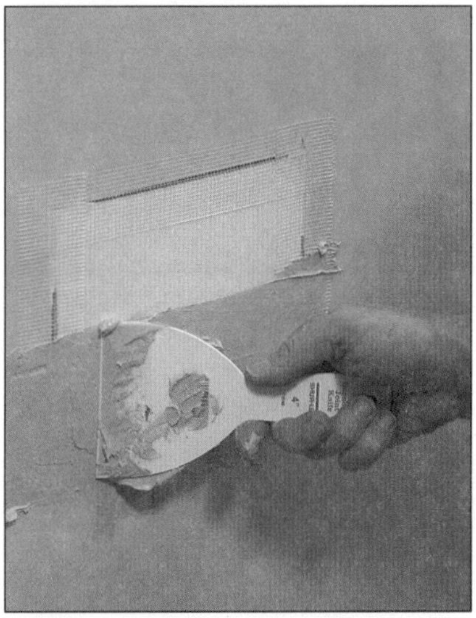

Stick on the jointing tape and cover with a layer of cement.

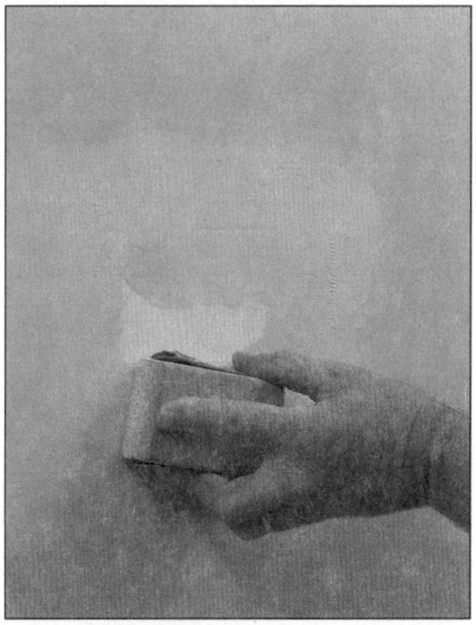

Allow to dry for 24 hours and sand off any irregularities.

Apply a thin layer of cement about 300 mm wide.

Sand the area again and feather the edges off to nothing.

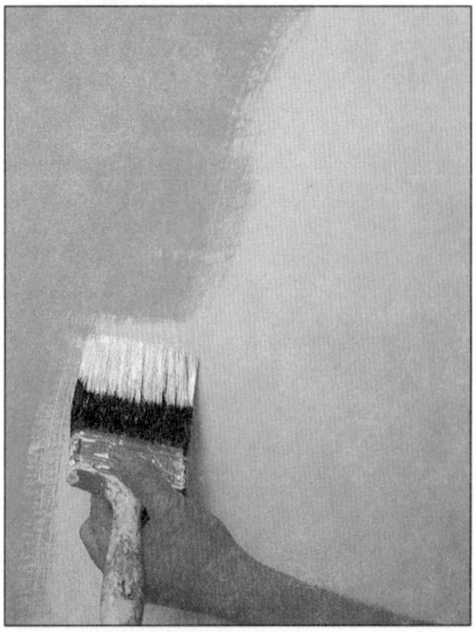

Paint the area with an approved sealer before painting the wall.

Regrouting a Leaking Shower Recess

A leak in a shower recess may be caused by nothing more than the grout having deteriorated. Grout (the material which fills the joints between the tiles) can dry out and crack. Continual exposure to water may also leach out the grout's waterproofing qualities. The result, especially where the walls are brick, can be dampness leading to a breakdown in the paint on the other side of the wall, which often shows up as a peeling or powdering patch in an adjoining room.

The best solution to the problem is to regrout the tile joints to stop the seepage, assuming the problem is not caused by a leak in the plumbing or a breakdown in the flashing between the shower recess floor and walls. Both of these problems require professional attention.

A shower recess showing grouting which has deteriorated.

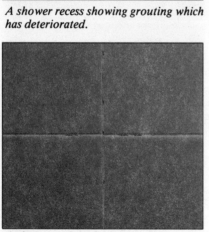

A close-up of the faulty grouting.

Rake out the joints with a tungsten-tipped grout raker.

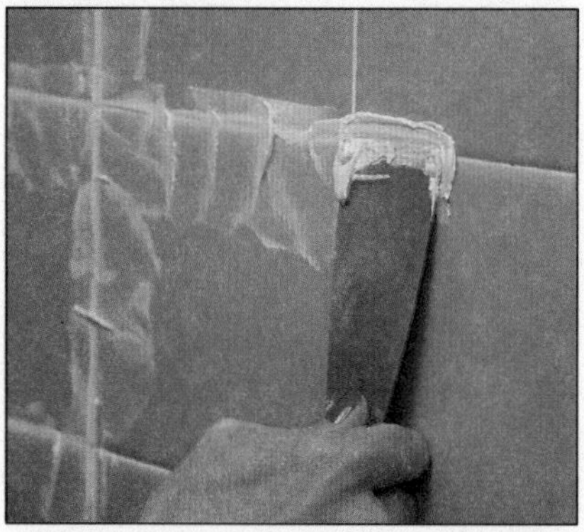

Force the new grout into the joints with a broad knife.

Wipe off the excess grout with a dampened sponge.

TOOLS AND MATERIALS

You'll require sufficient grout to cover the area of tiles (choose a colour to blend or contrast with the tiles and remember white is the most difficult to keep clean). Make sure you tell your supplier what size the tiles are — smaller tiles have more joints.

While you're at the hardware store, buy a tungsten-tipped grout raker. It makes short work of raking out the joints (it's claimed to take around three hours to do a twelve square metre area) and is far safer to use than a screwdriver which will damage or chip the edges of the tiles.

Besides the raker, you'll need some old sheets or blankets to cover the bath and basin, a putty or broad knife, a sponge, an old ceramic dish to mix the grout in, a rainy day and a good sporting event or orchestral concert to listen to.

PROCEDURE

1 Lay the padding over the important items. Either have bare feet or wear soft-soled shoes. Angle the rake into a joint, and, making sure you follow the line of the joint, begin to remove the old grout. Ideally, you must create a cavity at least 1.5 mm in depth by the full width of the joint. Work from the top down and towards the light so that no joints are missed. Be especially careful to create a joint where the tiles join the bath or vanity top and at the bottom of the shower recess. These are two notorious spots for leakages.

2 Clean up the old grout that you've raked out. Then simply mix up the new grout and force it into the joints with the putty or broad knife. Use the slightly dampened sponge to smooth it off and remove the excess. When it's dry, polish the tiles. The bad patch of paint in the next room should be rectified when the wall is thoroughly dry.

Replacing a Flush Cone

Does a mysterious pool of water appear behind the toilet every time you flush the cistern? Don't blame your kids! It could be that the flush cone, the rubber seal that fits over the back of most pans, has perished and is leaking.

One thing is certain — the problem will get worse and worse. Why not replace the seal? It's not a difficult or dirty job (the water is clean) and you'll save money and a lot of inconvenience.

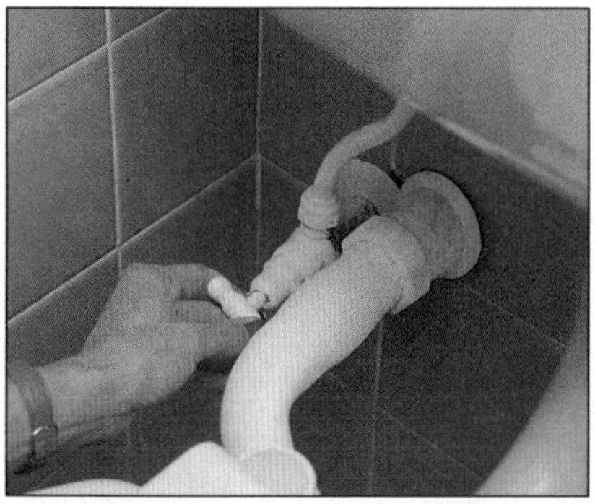

Turn off the stop tap to prevent the cistern filling.

TOOLS AND MATERIALS

Before you begin, check the diameter of the flush pipe, the L-shaped pipe that fits between the cistern and the pan. Then toddle off to your friendly hardware store and get a new flush cone.

You may only need a wrench to loosen the nut that secures the flush pipe to the cistern. If the flush pipe is metal you should also get some thread tape to reseal the joint.

PROCEDURE

1 Turn off the stop tap (the tap that regulates the water supply to the cistern), then flush the toilet. This is in case the flush button is accidentally pushed during the operation and your bathroom floor suffers a flood.

2 Unscrew the nut at the top of the flush pipe.

3 Locate where the rubber seal fits over the horn at the back of the pan then, using your fingers, roll the edge of the rubber back (it's like rolling down a pair of socks or stockings) until the flush pipe comes free.

4 Remove the old flush cone and clean the pipe.

5 Slip the new flush cone over the end of the pipe (wetting the pipe with detergent will help), and then roll the rubber back over itself, inverting it.

6 Push the end of the flush pipe firmly into the opening in the pan, then loosely tighten the top nut.

7 Roll the seal over the outside of the pan horn, then tighten the nut, resealing it if it's metal.

8 Turn on the stop tap, let the cistern fill up with water and then push the button.

If things pan out for you, you will be flushed with success. If the water persists, call a plumber!

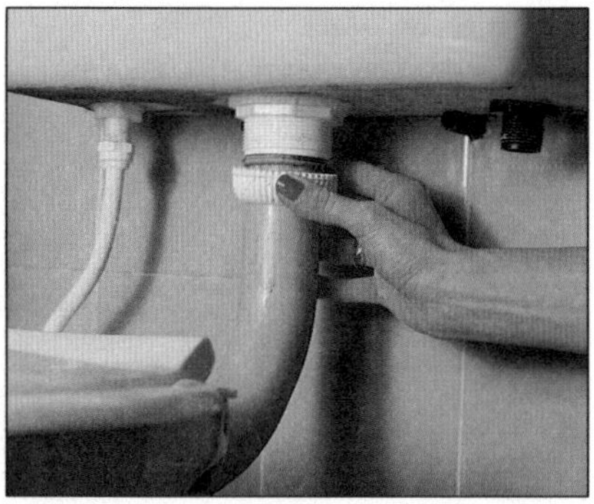

Unscrew the nut at the top of the flush pipe.

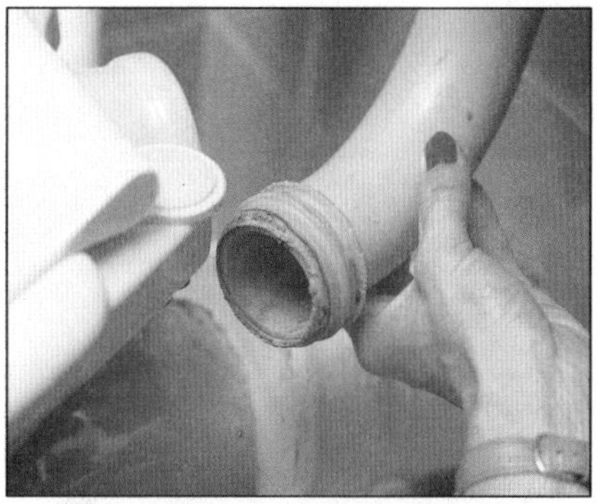

Roll back the rubber seal until the flush pipe comes free.

After cleaning the pipe, slip the new flush cone over the end.

Roll the rubber back over itself, inverting it.

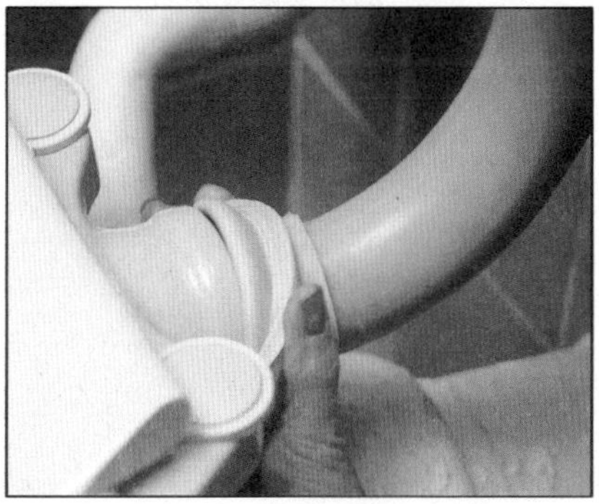

Roll the seal over the outside of the horn at the back of the pan.

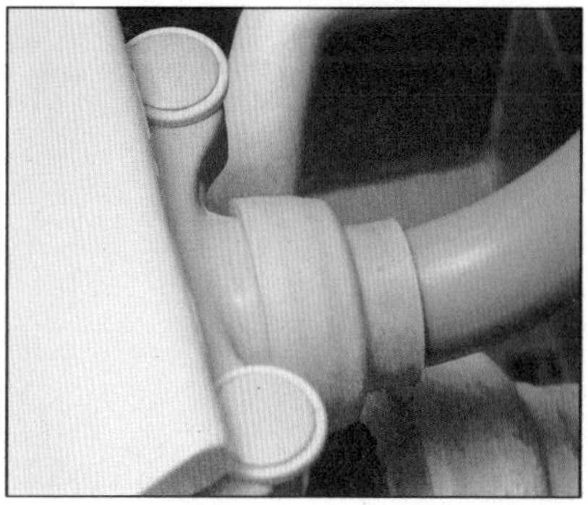

The new flush cone in place — no more leaks!

Repairing a Leaking Roof

A leaking roof, which is evidenced by damp ceilings or water runs down a wall, may be caused by cracked tiles, leaking flashings, rusted valley gutters, or capillary action between the overlapping joints in corrugated iron.

Repairing Flashing

Where various projections such as chimneys or vents poke through your roof, a flashing is used. This is often lead because lead is heavy and its softness enables it to be worked so it fits the shape of the tiles, corrugated iron or the roundness of the vent. However, because of electrolysis, sometimes other materials are used.

Over time and with continual thermal contraction and expansion, the joint between the flashing and the roof surface or vent sometimes leaks. You notice it when drops of water run down the pipe inside your house or when the paint peels off near a chimney.

Get up on the roof and check the flashings are still fitting tightly against both the roof surface and the projection. If the flashing has lifted in a wind or there is evidence of water getting in underneath it, buy some roof caulking compound from your hardware store and, with a putty knife, spread some over the joint. Then press the flashing back down, tapping it lightly into shape with a wooden block. If the flashing has cracked with age it's best to get in a tradesperson to replace it.

If the flashing collar around a vent is leaking, apply a liberal amount of caulking around the top joint. If that doesn't work, call in a plumber.

Making Corrugated Iron Waterproof

Water can get up between tightly fitting sheets of corrugated iron by either capillary action or through the driving force of the wind. If there is evidence of water leaking from around the over-lapping joints in the sheets you may have to undo the screws and, using a suitable caulking compound or silicone sealer, fill the joint, then screw the sheets back down. While you're at it, check that the water isn't coming in through the screw holes. If it is, replace the washers.

When walking on corrugated iron, make sure you put your feet on the area adjacent to the screw holes. This is where the supporting battens are. If you walk in between the battens, you run the risk that you'll permanently distort the sheeting. Should the iron be a bit rusty, you could also go through it.

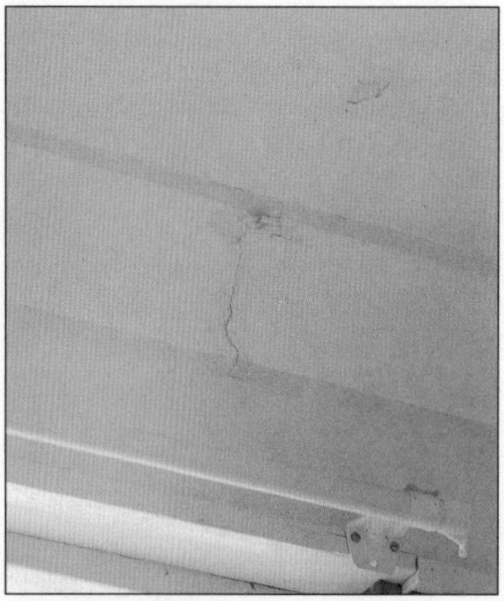

Evidence of a leaking roof: a damp patch on a ceiling.

Flashing round a projection in a roof may lift in the wind.

Spread some roof caulking compound over the joint.

Press the flashing back down, tapping it with a wooden block.

If the flashing collar round a vent is leaking, apply caulking.

The cracked tile which is causing the leak will be fairly obvious.

Lift the front of the row above it and hold in place with blocks.

Slip in the replacement tile, using a twisting motion.

Make sure the new tile fits neatly and lower the higher row.

Replacing a Cracked Tile

You'll often discover the existence of a cracked roof tile when you see a damp spot on your ceiling or the paint starts peeling off in just one place. Hopefully the builders have left some spare tiles under your house for this emergency. If they haven't, and the house is fairly new, you should be able to get some the same from the manufacturer. If it's a discontinued style or the house is old you may have to search secondhand building supply yards.

PROCEDURE

With a replacement tile and a couple of offcuts of 50 x 25 mm batten, carefully proceed to the approximate position of the leak, making sure you walk on the noses of the tiles (their front edge). The cracked tile should be fairly obvious unless it's a hairline crack.

Lift the front of the row above it and hold in place with the blocks. Remove the pieces of tile. If the tile is nailed to the fixing batten, simply lever the piece upwards. The top piece has a lip which must be lifted over the batten to allow removal. If it is wired or the nail won't budge, smash the tile and remove the fastening with a pair of pliers.

Proceed to slip in the replacement using a twisting motion. Make sure it fits neatly, then lower the higher row. This will lock it in place and if all goes well end the problem forever.

LADDER SAFETY

Getting up on the roof to fix the problem involves using a ladder. They are potentially dangerous if not used correctly. When using a step ladder, make sure you stand it on a surface that is level and firm and spread the legs widely.

With an extension ladder, the correct slope should be one in four. This means that the feet of the ladder should be placed outside the gutter line a distance equal to one quarter of the height between the ground and the gutter (see Diagram). Also the top of the ladder should extend at least one metre above the roof line and the top half of the ladder should not be extended more than three-quarters of its length.

Again make sure the extension ladder stands on a firm surface. With both ladders, get someone to hold them while you ascend and descend. Wear shoes with soles that grip (like sandshoes), and wait until the roof is dry before you get up on it.

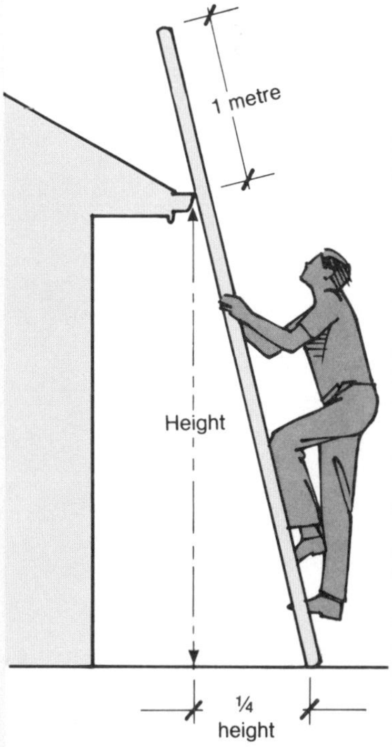

The correct slope for an extension ladder is one in four.

Fixing Wooden Furniture

Over time, excessive wear or poor construction can result in loose-jointed furniture. Other problems that can occur are splits, wobbly legs, rocking tables or chairs, and a breakdown of the finish.

Wobbly Legs

Sometimes legs are affixed to a table or chair simply by brackets or screwed blocks. Look under your table or chair to see if the screws have come loose. First try tightening them up. If they keep turning, then remove them and, buying a slightly larger diameter screw, rescrew them. If the timber is split or the hole too large, then fill the hole with glue and wooden matches. Allow to dry; then rescrew.

Other common joints used in furniture construction are dowelled or mortice and tenon. The best way to fix a loose joint is to knock it apart, clean off the old glue with a file, rasp or sandpaper, then glue (epoxy for clear finishes or PVA for painted) and cramp the article back together again. Make sure it is square and in wind. In wind means the leg or arm, when sighted, lines up with the other ones.

However, before resorting to this drastic step, if the article is painted, first try pouring and rubbing a liquid glue (PVA) into all sides of the offending joint. If all goes well, capillary action will pull enough glue in to hold it. You may also be able to screw a 75 mm metal bracket to the inside of the joint to increase the strength.

If, when you pull the joint apart, you find the dowel or tenon broken, replace it. With dowels simply cut them off flush and then, using a 2 mm drill bit, bore a pilot hole through their centre. Then, using a bit the same size as the dowel, drill out the old dowels, and replace them with new ones.

If the tenon has broken, cut it off flush, rip 50 mm into the member in the same line as the old tenon and chisel out the piece. Then fit and glue a false tenon in position (see diagram). When the glue has dried, fit and reglue the joint.

Rocking Tables or Chairs

Assuming the joints are firm, rocking is caused by legs that have worn unevenly or bowed and are therefore different lengths.

To fix this, select a dead flat surface such as a table (cover it first with newspaper to lessen damage) or a well-laid floor. Pack the two short legs with equal amounts of coins until the table is absolutely steady. Then take a sharp pencil and, laying it hard against the surface, run a line around each leg. With a tenon saw, cut each leg neatly to this line. If there is only a tiny bit to cut off, use coarse sandpaper and a block, or a flat file.

Split Members

A properly glued split should result in the timber being at least as strong as it was before the split, if not stronger. Use epoxy glue for maximum strength. Simply open the split up (or separate the two pieces completely), coat both surfaces with glue, bring them together, and then secure with a cramp until the glue has set. Wipe off the excess glue — otherwise you'll have a long job sanding it back. Be careful not to get the glue on your skin — it's dangerous.

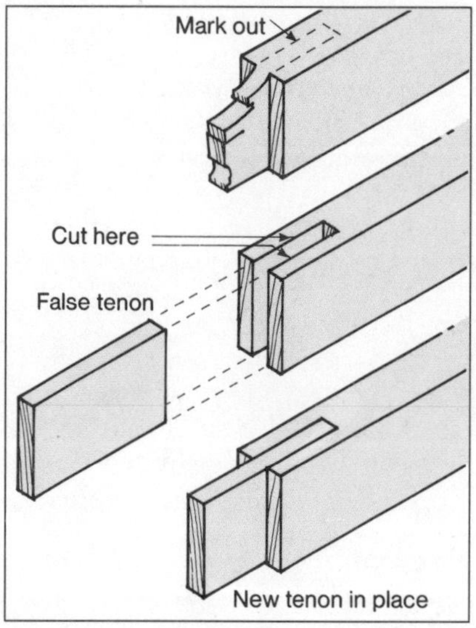

If a tenon has broken you can replace it with a false tenon.

A rickety old table sadly in need of repair.

Open up splits and then coat both surfaces with glue.

Secure joints with a clamp until the glue has dried.

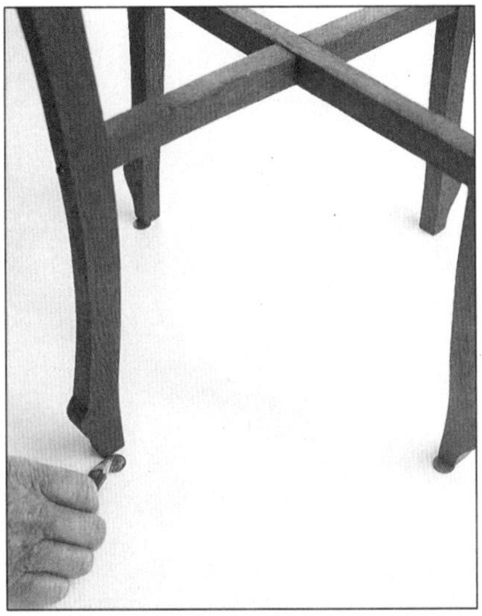

To fix a rocking table pack the two short legs with coins.

Use an old toothbrush to apply stripper on moulded legs.

Fill any gaps with wood putty of an appropriate colour.

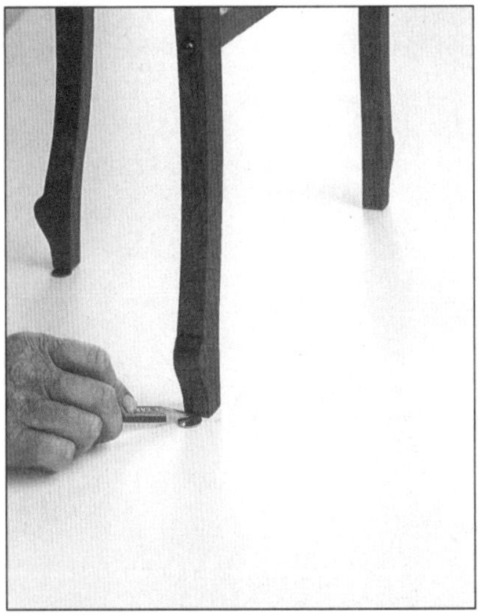

Lay a pencil against the floor and run a line round each leg.

Cut each leg neatly to this line with a tenon saw.

Renewing Poor Finishes

To achieve a good result, the old finish must be removed. This involves stripping. Proper stripping requires infinite patience, especially on turned or moulded members. If the item is a valuable antique, it could pay you to get an expert to do it for you.

To select the right stripper you first have to identify the old finish. Paint and varnish are easy. They can be removed with liquid, paste or water-rinse strippers. Shellac will dissolve if you apply some methylated spirits. Lacquer requires lacquer thinners. A half-shellac, half-lacquer finish requires fifty per cent of each of their solvents.

TOOLS AND MATERIALS

The appropriate stripper plus plenty of newspaper, an old brush, a paint scraper such as a Skarsten, a stainless steel pot scourer, some steel wool, an old toothbrush, gloves and long protective clothing, sandpaper and cork block.

PROCEDURE

1 Select a day when your biorhythm is in an up cycle. If using stripper, take the item out on a verandah or to an open garage. Good ventilation is essential.

2 Read the stripper directions carefully. With all your skin covered, liberally brush on the stripper in 300 mm squares (or 300 mm lengths on legs and rails, etc.), and leave for the required time. On flat surfaces, begin to scrape (or hose) off the wrinkled paint, keeping the tool at a low angle so it doesn't dig in.

3 If using methylated spirits or thinners, keep re-applying it. This gradually melts the old finish. Remove each sticky layer using a plentiful supply of clean rags. On curved or moulded legs, use a scourer, rasp or the toothbrush. (Watch the bristles don't flick the stripper in your eyes.) Finish off with steel wool. A small screwdriver is handy for getting into tight corners. A piece of coarse string or strip of old carpet looped around a curved leg and energetically pulled back and forth will entice the old finish off. When it's finished, it is important to neutralise the stripper otherwise the new finish could peel off. Be especially finicky at this stage and follow the directions carefully. If the old finish is not entirely removed, repeat the operation entirely or just redo the stubborn patches.

4 Then fill any holes and sand the job with coarse and then fine sandpaper (always working with the grain). Dust off, and then carefully apply the new finish in accordance with the manufacturer's directions.

Eliminating Draughts

Eliminating draughts will make your home or unit more comfortable during the cold months of winter. While there are other things you can do such as installing combustion stoves or gas heaters, putting down carpets, covering windows with heavy drapes, installing skylights, insulating your ceiling and trimming trees that block the northerly sun, lessening chilling winter draughts will help. Keep in mind, however, that some fresh air is essential for good health.

Sealing Strips

For starters, you can put stick-on sealing strips around all ill-fitting doors and casement window rebates. These easily installed heat savers are sold by the metre or in rolls, so simply measure the length around each rebate and total them up. You'll need some methylated spirits and a rag to clean the rebates thoroughly, plus a sharp knife.

Open the ill-fitting window or door as wide as possible and clean the rebate thoroughly. Measure and cut each piece to length and *then* pull off the backing and stick it on. There is no need to do the area on the side of the casement stays as, if they have been fitted properly, there is hardly any gap there to allow a draught in.

Caulking Gaps

Finish off your draught proofing by caulking all draught-creating external openings such as those that occur under window sills, around plumbing pipes, etc. For most applications, silicone is ideal although, as with draught excluders, there are other products on the market. Select a caulking compound that is weather-resistant, non-drying, non-shrinking, and adheres to most materials. If you want the caulking to be inconspicuous then choose one in a matching or neutral colour or one that can be painted over. If you have a lot of sealing to do, a caulking gun makes the job much easier.

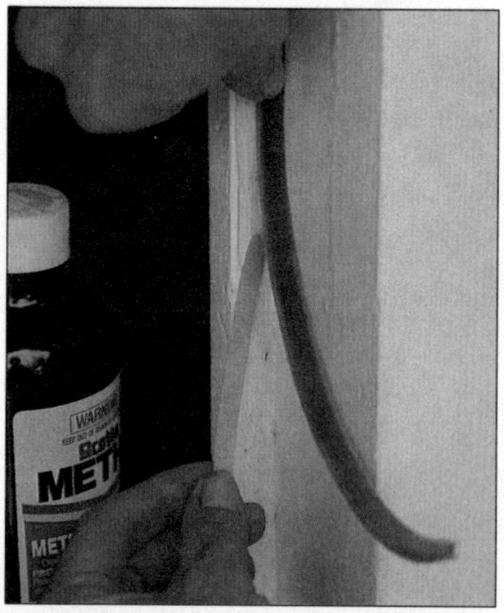

Stick on sealing strips round ill-fitting doors and windows.

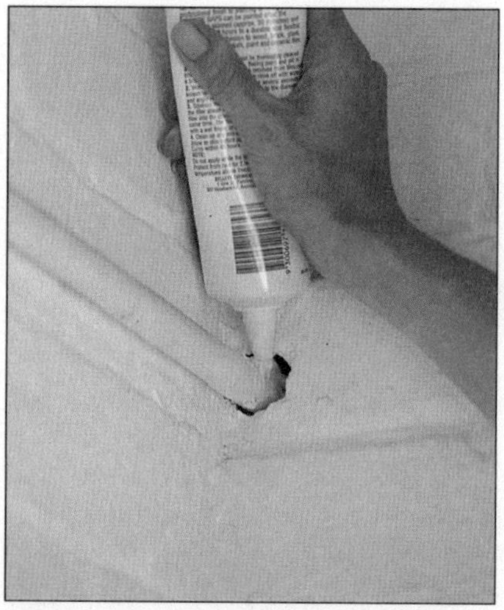
Fill in gaps round pipes with caulking compound.

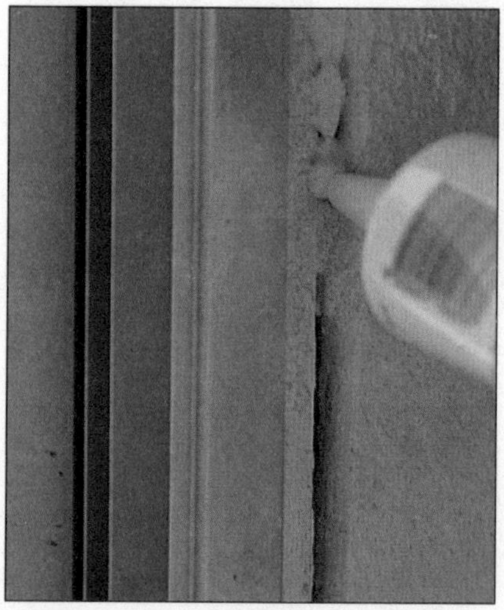
Caulking compound can also be used for gaps beside windows or doors.

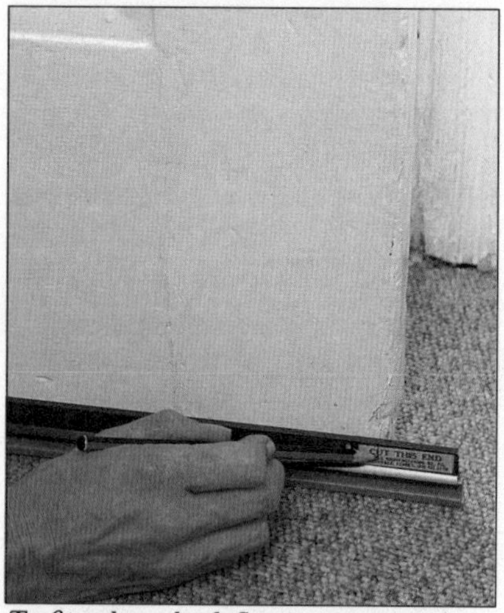

To fit a draught deflector, measure the door width.

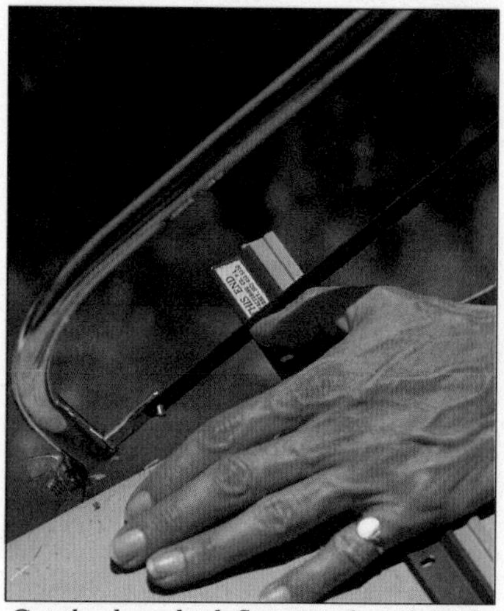
Cut the draught deflector to length with a hacksaw.

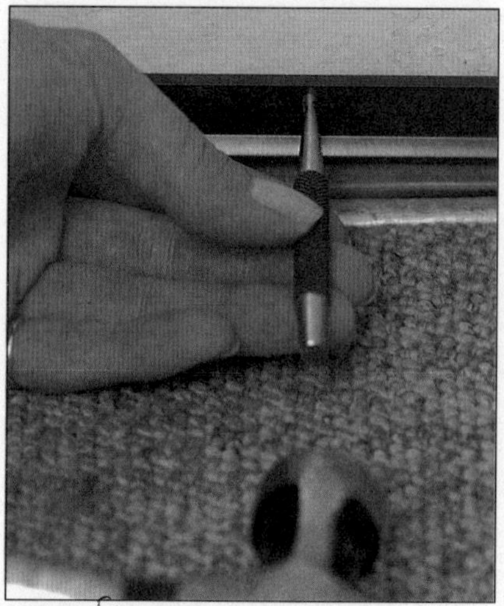
Use a nail punch to mark the screw holes in the door.

First check the outside walls and note all positions where gaps occur (around windows, door frames, water pipes, etc.). Then cut the top off the conical cap and squeeze the compound into position. Smooth off the joint with your thumb. Remove any surplus with a rag dipped in the recommended cleaner. If you are worried about getting a smear of caulking on bricks, etc. put some masking tape around the area, apply the sealer, then simply peel the tape off. If you're painting the caulking, allow the surface to cure a little.

Fitting Draught Deflectors

An effective step in eliminating draughts is to fit draught (which may also be water) deflectors to the bottom of external doors, especially those facing south or west. These come in many types. Discuss your particular location with your hardware storeperson but remember to take along details such as which side the door is hinged (looking from the outside), what type of tread under the door you have, and the door width.

TOOLS

You'll need a hacksaw (to cut the deflector to length), hand drill and drill bits to suit the screws, screwdriver, and a tape and pencil. If you have a terrazzo tread and you purchase a deflector that has a sill, you may need a masonry bit and some plugs to fix the sill in position.

PROCEDURE

1 Measure the door width and cut the strip to length.

2 With the door closed, position the deflector above the tread and mark the screw holes.

3 Drill a hole of a diameter equal to the solid part of the thread or use a nail punch.

4 Screw the fitting on the door with two screws, check for fit, and then complete. The sill, if any, is fitted similarly.

Insulating a Ceiling

Insulating ceilings is like putting a thick blanket over each room. It seals the warmth in and keeps the cold out. It cuts heat loss by 50% while the cost is small. For an average home, $750 should cover it. This is not expensive if you keep in mind that you could well achieve a thirty per cent saving to your winter heating bills. The house will be cooler in summer, too.

If you're handy, agile, sure that the wiring in the roof is safe, and the roof is of high enough pitch, you could insulate the ceilings yourself (and save around $150).

Wearing protective clothing, pack the batts lightly between the joists.

TOOLS AND MATERIALS

Simply calculate the floor area and, getting in through the access hole, measure the average distance between the ceiling joists. Your insulation supplier will calculate the quantity of batts required and the size.

With the batts, a ladder, lead light, a trimming knife (for cutting the batts to size), gloves, a paper particle mask, long-sleeved shirt and long trousers (the insulation can irritate your skin and nasal passages), and two pieces of metre square 18 mm ply or particle board for cutting and kneeling on, you're ready to go. If the roof is a trussed one, use a plank that spans at least four of the chords to spread your weight.

PROCEDURE

1 Choose a cool day (otherwise you'll dehydrate) and begin packing the batts tightly between the joists, making sure you reach right to the external wall plate. Work back toward the access hole. Leave no spaces for maximum effect. Always keep your weight on the joists and not on the ceiling! The short plank or ply square will made the procedure more comfortable.

2 If the pitch is low, a 75 mm slat of wood that just fits between the joists should be fixed to the end of a broom handle. That will provide a useful pushing tool for moving the batts into awkward places.

Be especially careful around any wiring. A stiff cardboard separator should be used to isolate the wire from the insulation material.

Keep the material 100 mm clear of chimneys and flues. Don't forget to cover the access hole but don't block off any ceiling fans, etc.

3 You could, if you have uncarpeted floors, put batts between the floor joists to effect another 10% heating saving.

Let winter come now. Your home is snug! In summer it will be much cooler, too.

Replacing Plastic Laminate

Plastic laminate provides a serviceable and attractive finish for kitchen and vanity bench tops. It excels where moisture is present.

However, over time, the surface may become damaged by normal wear and tear or scratched by the use of over-harsh powder cleaners. Also the pattern and colour may become dated. Why not replace the tops and edging? You can do this by simply gluing new laminate on top of the old.

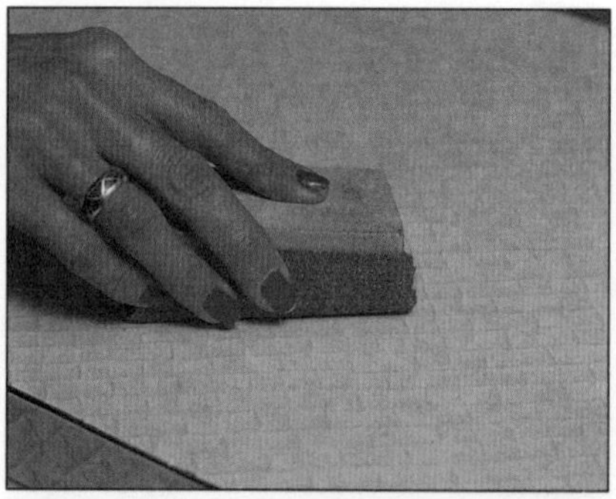

The first step is to sand all surfaces thoroughly.

To cut the edge strips, score heavily with a laminate cutter.

TOOLS AND MATERIALS

You'll need a laminate cutter, a sharp plane, a straight edge, a large flat file (unless you can hire a laminate trimmer), some wooden dowels or slats for separators, tape and pencil, and a square.

Make an accurate plan of the tops and edges so your supplier can help you work out how much laminate and glue you need (keep the figuring so you can cut the sheets correctly). When you make your selection, remember that what looks good in a small sample often looks terrible en masse. Be smart and try to see your choice in someone else's house first.

The adhesive normally used is a rubber-based contact glue (see Glues page 298). For a good job, the existing tops must be solidly bonded and all lifting edges must be reglued (see Rectifying Lifting Laminate page 92).

Heavily sand all surfaces.

PROCEDURE FOR EDGE STRIPPING

1 Carefully (it is easily cracked) lay the sheet, pattern up, on a table and, using a soft pencil, mark out the required width (make it 1.5 mm wider). Make sure you cut the edge strips from the area designated for them.

2 Lay the straight edge along the line and score heavily with the laminate cutter until much of the brown undersurface shows through.

3 Hold the straight edge hard down on top of the laminate directly alongside the cut and, working from one end, carefully lift the edge until the strip cracks off. Repeat until you have all the edge strips.

4 Now cut the strips to length making them 1.5 mm longer than the finished length. Apply contact glue to both surfaces and wait until it's touch dry. Now to the tricky part. It's essential to line them up correctly first time (for long pieces, get a friend to help you). Making it flush with the bottom, push one end into place, then work along to the other end pressing it on as you go. Then go back and tap the strip firmly with a hammer and block. Continue with the other strips and, when finished, leave to dry for an hour or so.

5 Trim the strips flush with the top and on the ends using the flat file, plane, or the electric laminate trimmer (which you should set up and try out on a scrap piece first). When filing, hold the file flat and make sure you file away from the finished surface or you might chip it. The plane is much faster than the file but the laminate eventually takes the edge off it, necessitating more frequent sharpening.

PROCEDURE FOR BENCH TOPS

1 Check whether the benches are square, parallel and at right angles to each other and then mark out and cut the tops, allowing at least 2 mm extra all around. If the bench has a flush or circular sink in it, unscrew the plumbing and the sink clips and lift the sink out rather than try to fit the laminate to it.

Using your plane, fit the top to the bench. Laying the sheet on a table so it projects slightly past it is the best way to plane it.

2 When it fits, apply the glue as before. Then, after it's touch dry, lay the separators on the surface and position the top accurately (see illustration). Slide each separator out (beginning from one end to avoid trapping any air) and when stuck down, tap all over with the block and hammer as before.

3 Trim the excess off with your file or plane (or use a laminate trimmer with a bevelled cutter), making sure you don't damage the edge strips. Incline either tool at 45° to get rid of the sharp edges. Clean off the glue with the correct solvent and give the surface a wipe over.

Looks terrific, doesn't it? If you're feeling especially confident and you want to complete the kitchen transformation, why not do the doors as well?

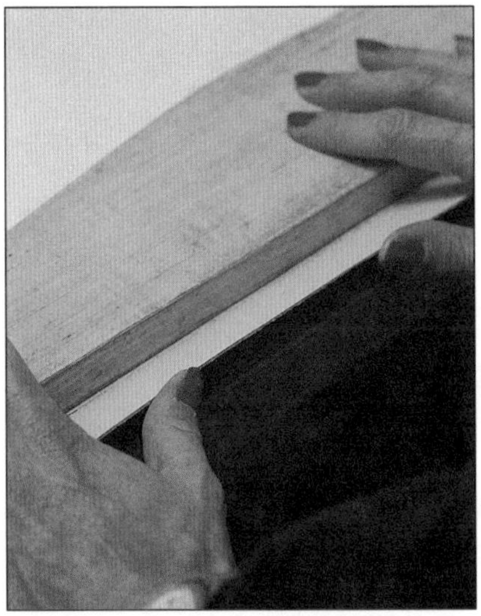

Hold the straight edge down and carefully lift the edge strip.

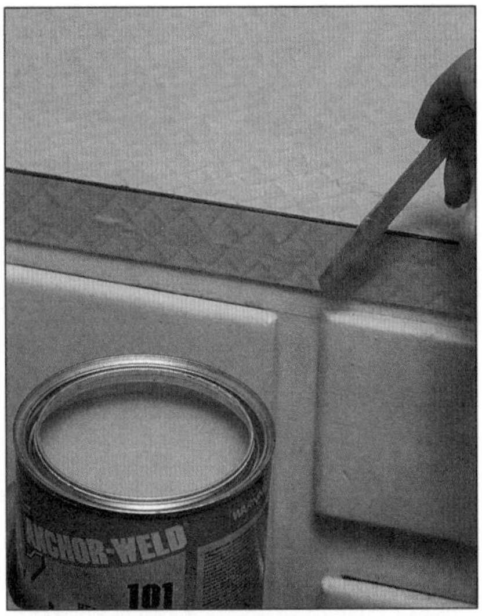

Apply contact glue to both the bench edge and the new strip.

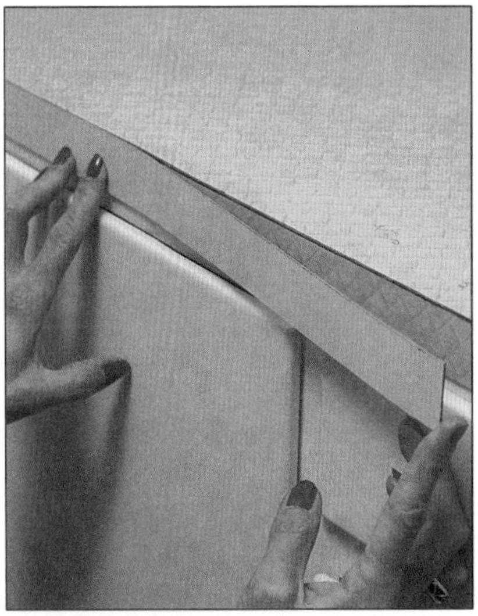

Apply the edge strip making it flush with the bottom.

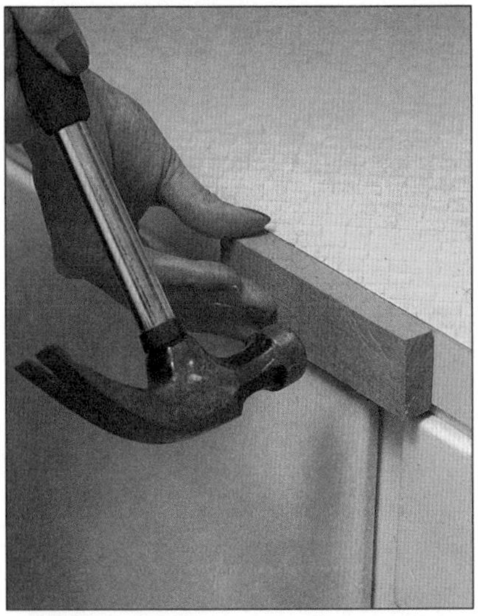

Tap the strip firmly with a hammer and block.

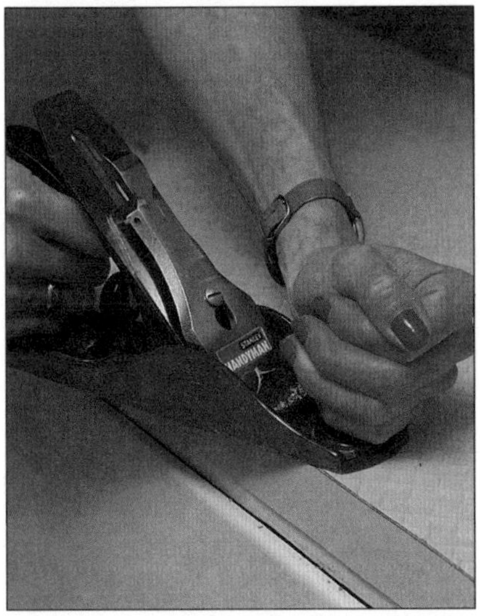

Trim the strip flush with the top using a plane.

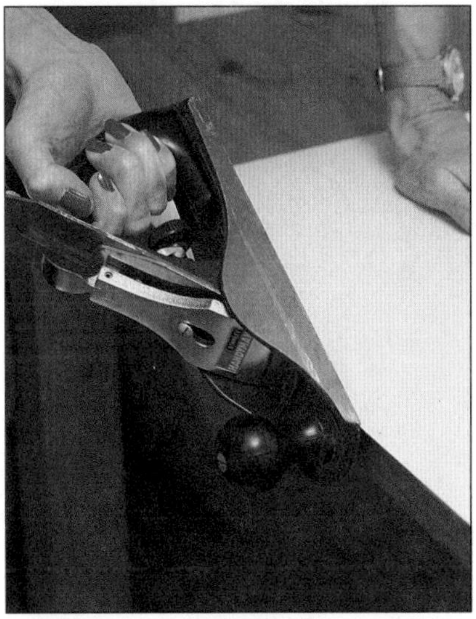

Using a plane, fit the top to the bench.

Apply the contact glue to both surfaces.

Lay the separators on the surface and position the top.

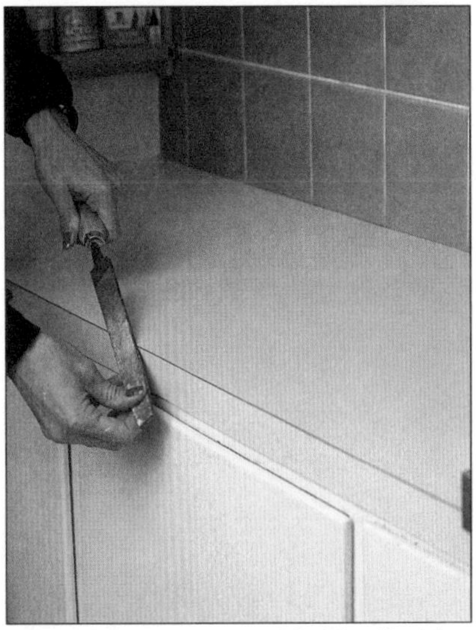

Plane off the excess and finish off with a file. Don't damage the edge strips.

Removing a Cracked Tile

There's nothing more unsightly than a cracked tile in a bathroom floor or on the kitchen wall. It gathers dirt in the crevice, boldly outlining its presence for all your fastidious friends to see. It is also a repository for germs.

Removing it (or a tile that has previously had a fitting screwed to it) is not the impossible task it appears. But whatever you do, *don't* try to lever the offending tile out with a screwdriver or knife. Instead of having to replace one tile you'll end up having to replace a few hundred!

Getting the tile out is easy enough if you follow the steps below. Finding an exact replacement may prove to be more difficult. If the tile you need is out of production and possible replacements are of a slightly different colour, perhaps you could put in a fancy feature tile that has harmonious or contrasting tones. A scout around the tile shops will, I'm sure, result in the discovery of a satisfactory replacement.

There are samples of some of the many tiles available on page 122.

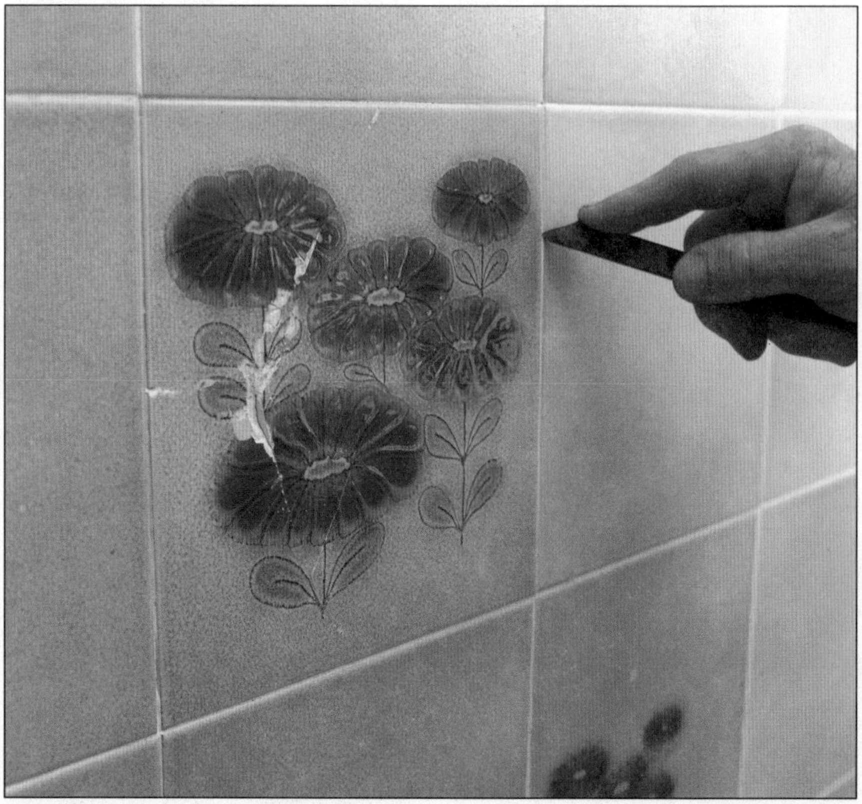

Rake out the grout so that the cracked tile is separated completely from the surrounding tiles.

TOOLS AND MATERIALS

You need a grout rake (which costs only a few dollars), a hammer, fine cold chisel, large screwdriver, putty knife, sponge and polishing rag. If the tile is undamaged except for a hairline crack you'll also need a hand or electric drill (an electric drill is easier) and a small masonry bit.

As for materials, a small amount of tile adhesive (or sand and cement if you're going to lay the tile with mortar), some flexible grout of a matching colour plus a couple of tile spacers should suffice. If the rest of the grouting is hard and cracked, perhaps you should consider raking out all the joints and regrouting the whole area before too much moisture gets behind the tiles and threatens to loosen them. (See Regrouting a Leaking Shower Recess page 110.)

PROCEDURE

1 Cover any bath, basin or vanity top with an old blanket in case you accidentally damage them by dropping one of the tools. Then carefully rake out the grout so that the tile is completely isolated from its companions.

2 Unless the tile already has a hole in it, insert the masonry bit tightly in the drill chuck and drill a hole in the centre of the tile.

3 Working outwards from the centre and taking small bites each time, carefully chip out the tile using the hammer and cold chisel. Make sure you wear safety glasses of some sort to avoid getting razor sharp tile chips in your eyes! Also, when sweeping up the debris, watch that you don't cut your fingers.

4 When the tile is out, carefully clean around the edges and then prepare the undersurface for the new tile. This may involve levelling the surface, sealing porous materials such as gypsum plaster, and making sure that the area is clean, dry and solid (see Replacing a Few Ceramic Tiles page 97).

5 Using a generous amount of tile adhesive, glue the replacement tile back in position. For rendered walls, a 4:1 cement and sand mortar is adequate. Check that the tile is exactly in line with the existing ones and that the joint around it is even. If it goes in too far, pull it out and use more adhesive or mortar.

6 When dry, regrout the joint. Remember to wipe the grout off the tile face *before* it dries. A quick polish with a clean rag will blend the new tile in nicely.

Start from the centre. Bore a hole in the tile if necessary.

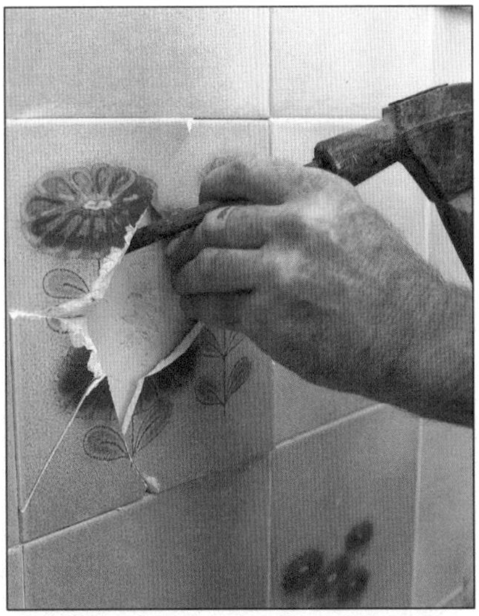

Carefully chip out the tile with hammer and cold chisel.

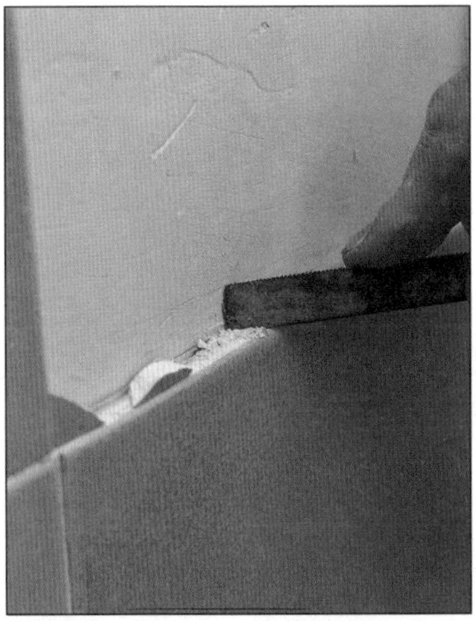

When the tile is out, carefully clean round the edges.

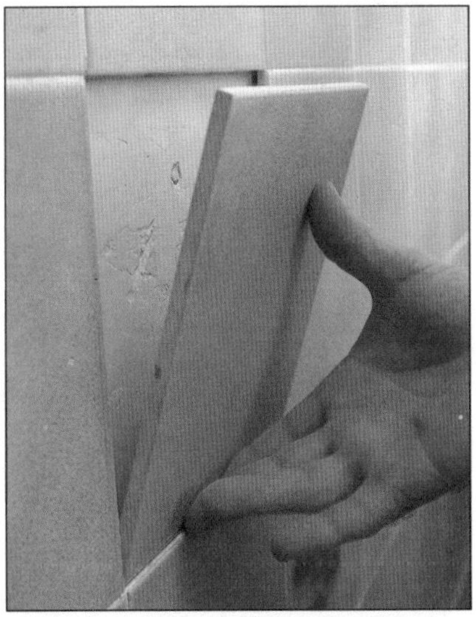

Check that the new tile will fit into the gap.

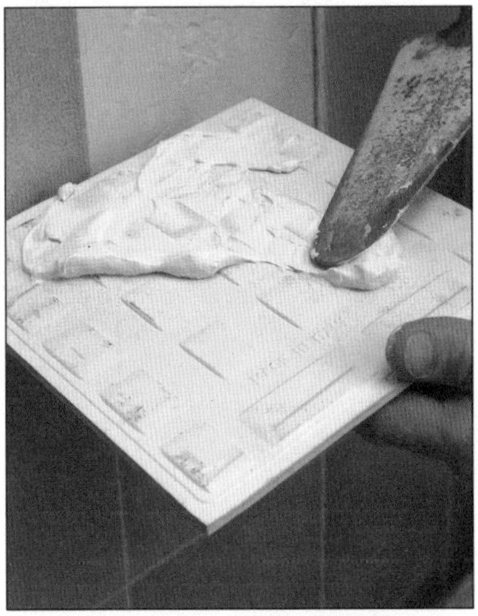

Spread adhesive on the back of the new tile.

Press the new tile firmly into position.

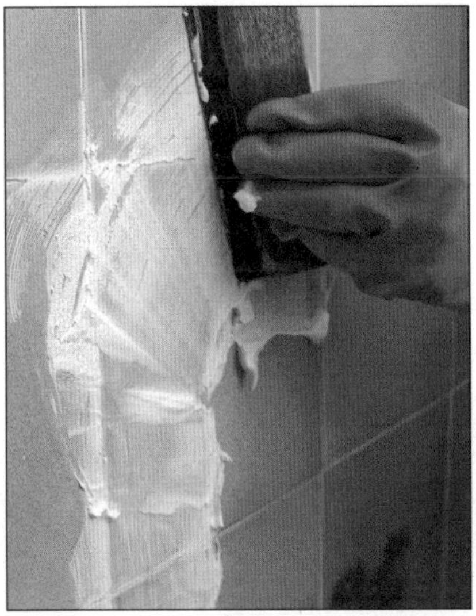

When the adhesive is dry, regrout the joint.

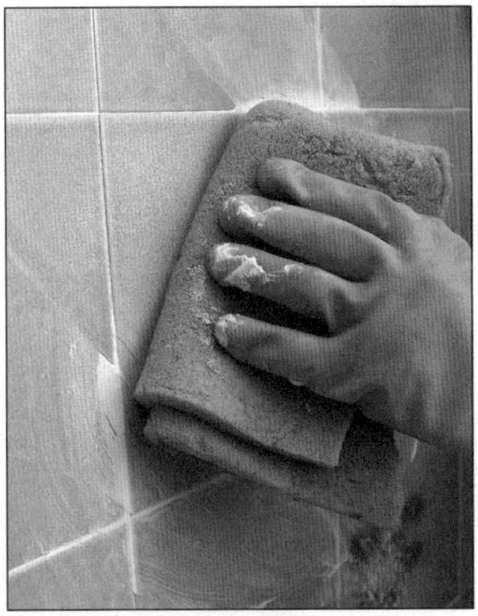

Wipe off excess grout with a damp sponge.

Polish the tile with a clean cloth or rag.

Patching Rendering

Rendered walls or columns give a very serviceable surface. But occasionally, because of dirty or dusty surface, or because of a poorly mixed batch of mortar, or as a result of the wall getting heavily bumped, or the reinforcing steel rusting, the rendering comes off.

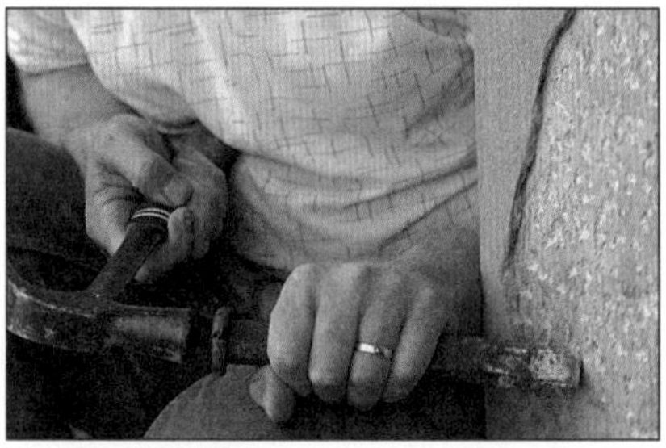

Sparrow pick the concrete where the render is missing.

Wet the patch thoroughly before applying the new render.

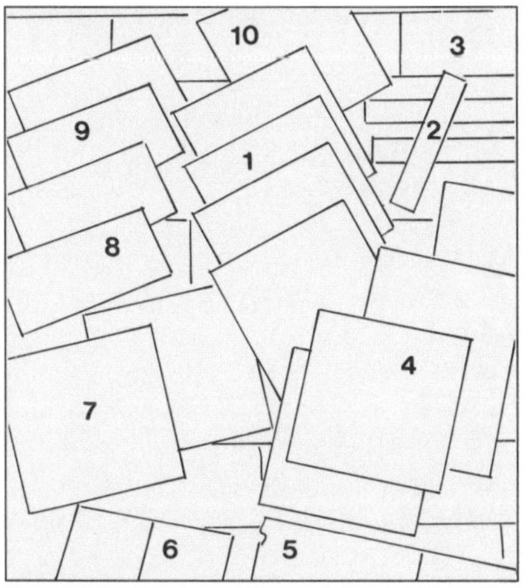

Wall tiles
1. *Plain square tiles*
2. *Narrow edge trims*
3. *Plain white oblong tiles*
4. *Square patterned tiles*
5. *Edge trim tiles*
6. *Plain coloured oblong tiles*
7. *Reproduction old-fashioned feature tiles*
8. *Printed tiles, Art Nouveau designs*
9. *Handpainted tiles* 10. *Feature tile*

Begin to fill the patch working from the bottom up.

Leave it to set a little and then finish off with a float.

TOOLS AND MATERIALS

You'll need sufficient sand and cement for the job using a 3:1 mix. (A mixture of one part of cement, one of lime and eight of sand is better for concrete block walls.) The sand should be suitable for rendering, with little loam in it. Your material supplier should know what is required. As a rough guide, 0.125 m^3 sand and 40 kg cement will make up 4 m^2 of mortar approximately 10 mm thick.

Most rendered walls or columns are finished with a wooden float. This gives a coarse, grainy finish. If they are very smooth, either they have been painted a number of times (possible in older houses) or a steel float has been used.

You'll also need a straight edge which is longer than the widest part of the patch, a hammer and cold chisel (or scutch), a shovel for mixing, a bucket and brush for wetting the wall, and a hawk. This is not a raptorial bird, but a 300 × 300 mm piece of 10 mm ply. In its centre is fixed a wooden handle. You use this hand-held platform for holding the mortar while you scoop some up and press it up the wall with the underside of the float.

PROCEDURE

1 Chop around the edge of the patch with a hammer and cold chisel to make sure there is no more drumminess (loose render) on the wall.

2 Use a scutch or the hammer and cold chisel to sparrow pick the brickwork or concrete where the rendering has come loose to increase adhesion on the subsurface. When you have finished, clean the surface of any oil and make sure it is dust free. If you still have doubts about the surface, use something like Bondcrete in the mix to increase adhesion.

3 Next, lay some old carpet or boards on the floor to catch the mortar droppings. Wet the patch thoroughly before you begin to mix up the ingredients. The mix should be pliable but not sloppy.

4 Transfer some mortar to the hawk with the float. Lay the hawk back towards you, cut away some render with the trowel, and begin to fill the patch working from the bottom up. When it's covered, if the area is large, use the straight edge in a back and forth motion to cut away the excess mortar.

5 Go back over the patch and fill any low spots, then again screed it with the straight edge or float.

6 Leave it to set a little, then go over it with the float (wood or steel) to finish it off.

Before you paint it, allow to dry for at least four weeks (a heater could accelerate the drying), then seal and paint. For best results, do the whole wall or the paint finish could be patchy.

Relaying Loose Bricks

Brickwork relies for its strength on having a good underlying foundation, a properly constructed footing, and a strong mortar bonding the bricks together. However, given that imperfect human beings are involved in all construction work, sometimes a few bricks can come loose. Why not relay them? A few hours' work could return the wall or fence to its original glory (assuming the problem is a minor one). Besides, once you have laid a few bricks and got the knack, you may end up building barbecues, retaining walls . . . who knows where it could end? Look at the Great Wall of China!

HANDY HINT

If you've been a little overzealous with the mortar and managed to spread it over much of the brickwork then it should be cleaned off immediately. Use a wet brush and scrub as much away as you can without wetting the joints (this will wash the cement out).

If when the mortar has dried the stains are still evident, wet the area thoroughly, then clean the bricks with a brush and diluted mixture of hydrochloric acid and water (1 acid : 15 of water is suitable or 1:10 at most). Leave the acid on the bricks for 5 minutes maximum to stop it soaking into the brick and then hose off, using plenty of water. Take care to cover your skin as the acid burns.

TOOLS AND MATERIALS

You'll need sufficient sand (of a type suitable for making mortar), cement, lime (this makes the mortar easier to use) plus perhaps a suitable oxide to colour the mortar to match the existing joints. A good, general purpose mortar mix is 1 part cement: 1 part lime: 6 parts sand measured by volume. For areas below the damp proof course where strength and waterproofness is important, a 1 part cement to 3 parts of sand mix with just a smidgen of lime is ideal. The mortar, when mixed, should have a thick, paste-like consistency.

You'll need a lump hammer (although an ordinary hammer will do), a bolster or comb chisel for cleaning off the old mortar (a cold chisel or old wood chisel might just suffice), a shovel, trowel, level, and perhaps a tool for ironing (making a rounded joint) or raking (making a square joint) to match the shape of the existing brick joints.

PROCEDURE

1 Clean the old mortar off the bricks (both the loose ones and their solidly bonded neighbours) with the hammer and comb chisel. Put the loose bricks on a layer of sand while you're chopping away to lessen the chance of cracking them. Don't damage the DPC (damp proof course, the impervious, continuous layer built into a brick joint to stop moisture from the ground travelling up the wall) should you meet it.

2 When the bricks are clean, wet them either in a bucket of water or by hosing (but don't saturate them). Hose the place where they will be laid as well. This will stop the bricks sucking the moisture out of the mortar too quickly and make it adhere to the bricks better.

3 Measure out the different parts of the ingredients (an ice-cream container will make sure you get the correct volumes of each) and thoroughly mix them with the shovel. Select a waterproof surface to mix on otherwise your cement will soak away.

4 Make a hole in the centre of the mortar (rather like a volcano crater) and begin to add the water. Don't allow it to flood or you'll lose some of the cement and affect the mortar strength. Mix thoroughly.

5 Lay a bed of mortar with the trowel, then, buttering the end of one brick, lay it in the mortar against the existing work. Tap it down with the handle of the trowel and along until it lines up with the existing bricks. The vertical joint should be around 10 mm. Check the brick for level. When it's correct, cut off any excess mortar with the trowel. This excess mortar can be returned to the main lot and reused).

6 Lay another bed and repeat the procedure until all the bricks are laid.

7 While the mortar is still semi-soft, rake or iron the joint. Try to remove any excess mortar from the face of the bricks by scraping and brushing. Don't forget to clean your trowel and shovel thoroughly when you're finished!

8 Leave the new brickwork to cure for a week or more and then, if necessary, remove any stubborn stains by brushing on muriatic acid (a diluted mixture of hydrochloric acid and water). Wear gloves and old, protective clothes. When clean, thoroughly hose the section off.

A gap in a wall where a brick has come loose.

Clean the old mortar off the loose and the bonded bricks.

Replace half bricks with whole bricks wherever possible.

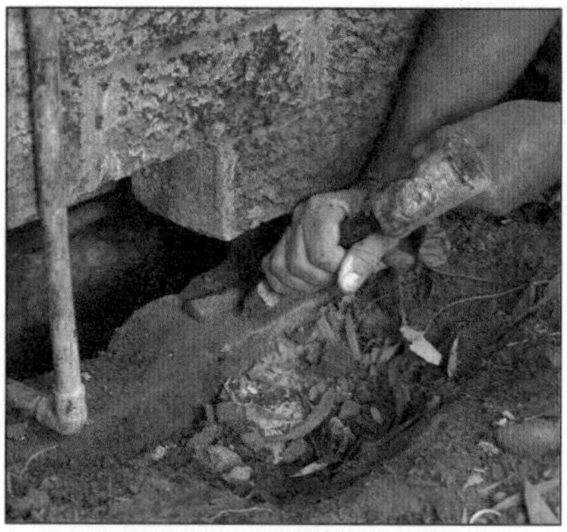

It is important to establish a level bottom line.

Try one of the replacement bricks for size, allowing for mortar.

Apply a generous layer of mortar to the joints and the new brick.

Insert new brick, taking care not to disturb the mortar.

Cut small sections of brick by tapping with the comb chisel or bolster.

Make the top of the split brick level with other bricks; adjust mortar.

The last brick is the hardest — you may need to cut the corners.

Apply final layer of mortar, filling evenly down each side.

While the mortar is semi-soft, iron or rake the joint.

Cutting Down Doors

Often because of poor hanging, swelling in the door, or new carpet, you'll find the door scrubbing the pile off the berber or carving a semi-circular hole in the floorboards. The solution is easy. Shorten the door!

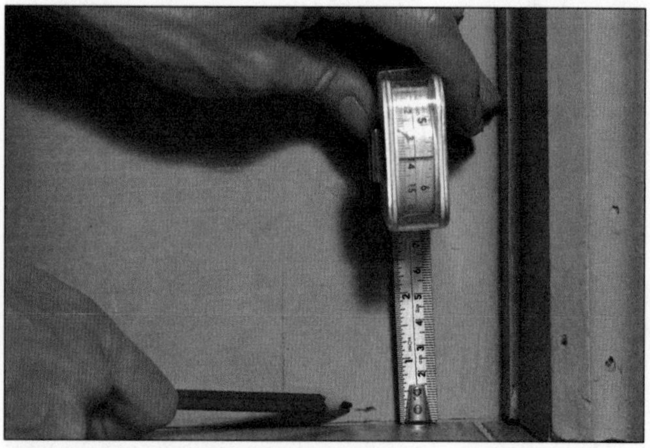

Measure the amount you want to take off the bottom of the door.

Wedge the top of the door and if the amount is small, plane it off.

TOOLS

You'll need: a screwdriver, a plane (for taking off amounts up to 5 mm or for making the bottom of the door smooth), a panel saw (for removing amounts over 5 mm), some glue in case you have to glue the bottom rail back in (only for hollow core doors), a pencil and rule or tape.

PROCEDURE

1 Decide on how much you want to take off the bottom of the door. A clearance of 10 mm above the floor surface is usual but in draughty situations you may want to have less (but don't go below 5 mm). With the door closed, measure the required clearance on both edges of the door and mark clearly.

2 Open the door completely and examine the screws. If the slots are filled with paint, scrape it out with a nail or small screwdriver.

3 Using the correct sized screwdriver (the tip fits neatly in the slot and is the same width as the screw or slightly smaller) undo the screws. Put them in a safe place.

4 Lay the door on a pair of stools or a blanket-covered table and draw a straight line between the two marks. Transfer these marks to the other side of the door.

5 If planing the clearance, wedge the top of the door into the corner of a room to hold it steady (a blanket around it will save any damage) and place two or three thick books under the edge of the door. Then take your sharp plane and begin planing the bottom of the door. Do not plane right through otherwise you may chip the edge of the door. Turn the door over and plane from the other edge, again not running right through. Stop when you reach the line; then, sighting along the bottom to check it is straight, put a small chamfer (bevel) on both edges of the bottom to make a neat finish.

6 Using a block or some thin books, lift the door until the hinges line up with the gains in the jamb, and then replace the screws. Touch up the screw heads with some matching paint.

7 If there is too much to plane off, you will have to rip the waste off with a saw. Using a trimming knife and straight edge, cut through the ply or timber on the back of the door to a depth of at least 1.0 mm. Then when you start to rip the timber will not splinter off on the far side.

8 Lay the door on its back and cut it through keeping just a fraction away from the line. Be careful when you get near the finish that the waste piece does not split off.

9 If the door is a hollow core door and you have had to cut a fair amount off you may find that the whole bottom rail is cut out. In this case, peel the veneer off the offcut with a chisel, plane it smooth (being careful you don't make it smaller) then glue it back in, using plenty of glue. Some heavy objects will substitute for a clamp to ensure a tight joint. Alternatively nail through the face of the door with panel pins, punch, then allow to dry.

10 Set up the door ready for planing, make the bottom smooth, then chamfer the edges, putty the holes and paint all bare surfaces. Painting the bottom is essential because bare timber absorbs moisture from the air. If the rest of the door is sealed and the bottom isn't, you get unequal expansion which can cause buckling, to say nothing of possible delamination. Rehang the door, following the procedure in step 6.

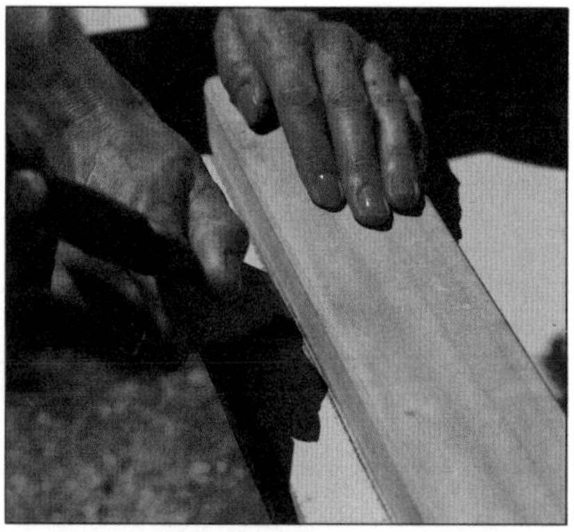

If sawing, mark the line to be cut with a trimming knife to reduce splintering.

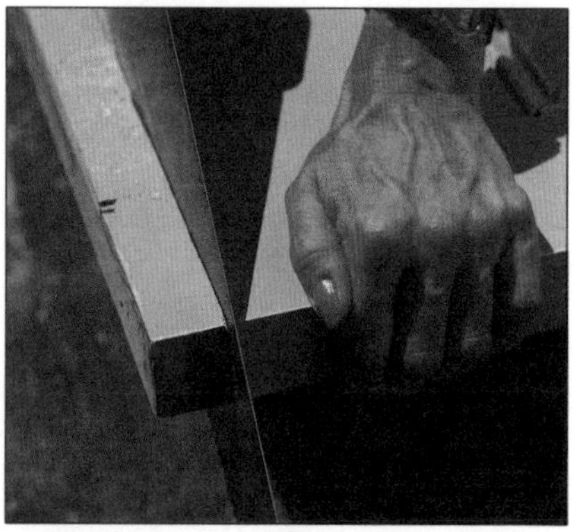

Lay the door on its back and cut it through.

With a hollow core door you may find that the bottom rail is cut out.

Glue the bottom rail back in, using plenty of glue.

Fixing a Springy Floor

The problem of a springy floor can be caused by a bearer twisting or curling off its support. Another reason might be a pier has settled and left the bearer stranded in mid-air. Either way the result is a little like a trampoline — the floor bounces when you walk on it!

To solve the problem get under the house and, with a torch, find what is causing it. To establish whether it is a bowed bearer or sunken pier, simply sight along the bearer. If it looks like the Sydney Harbour Bridge then follow the first procedure.

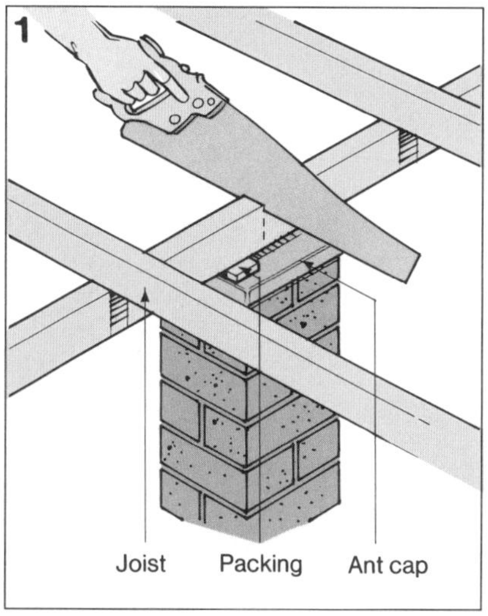

Saw through the bearer until it sits hard down on the pier.

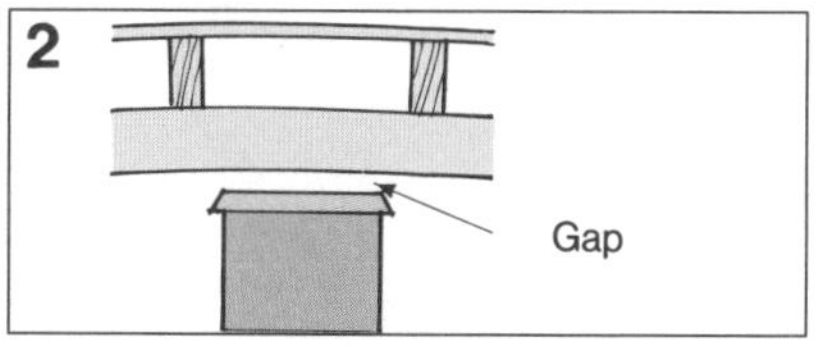

Springy floor resulting from bowed bearer.

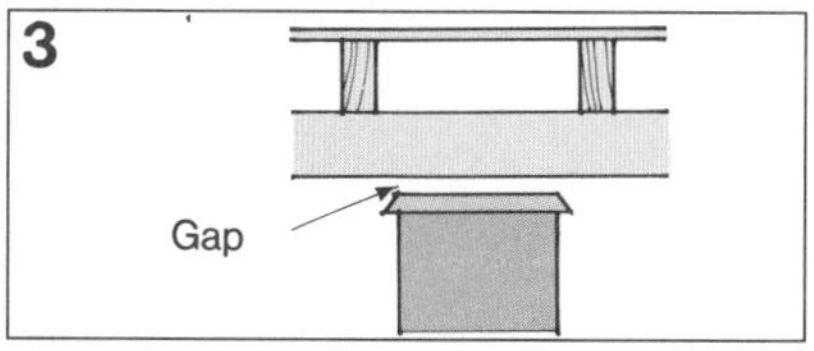

Springy floor resulting from sunken pier.

Underfloor Maintenance

While you're under the house check for white ant trails up the foundation walls. These pesky termites build mud tunnels up the foundations walls and then dine on your timber framing (unless it has been preserved). If you find any evidence, call in a pest exterminator to establish the extent of the damage, if any, and have the ground sprayed with a suitable pesticide.

While you're there, remove any old timber that might be lying around to attract white ants. Also look for damp patches that might be caused by leaking plumbing or surface drainage running under your house. Check for rotting in floor timbers also.

PROCEDURE FOR BOWED BEARER

You'll need a lead light, some packing, and a handsaw. Where the bearer has warped above the pier, temporarily pack it with some fibrous cement offcuts or thin timber shims so it is solid, but remember: you have to get them out again! Then cut the bearer part-way through over the pier with a handsaw. It's an awkward thing to do, but patience will eventually reward you.

Then, using a chisel or pinch bar, lever the bearer up, remove the packing and see if it sits down. If it doesn't, repack it and cut through the bearer even further until it sits hard down on the pier.

If you're not a perfectionist and you don't care if the floor has a camber in it, you could cheat and just pack the bearer tightly!

PROCEDURE FOR SUNKEN PIER

If the pier has sunk down below the bearer, leaving a space, get a piece of fibre cement or other suitable packing material such as metal damp proofing. It must be something that won't rot. Then drive it in tight under the bearer until there is no movement.

Patching Ceramic Floor Tiles

Ever had an annoying spot where you wish the floor tiler had gone a little further? Or moved a door opening and now the tiling doesn't quite go under the door? Putting in a few extra tiles is not difficult.

Fix the screed in position and mark the tiles.

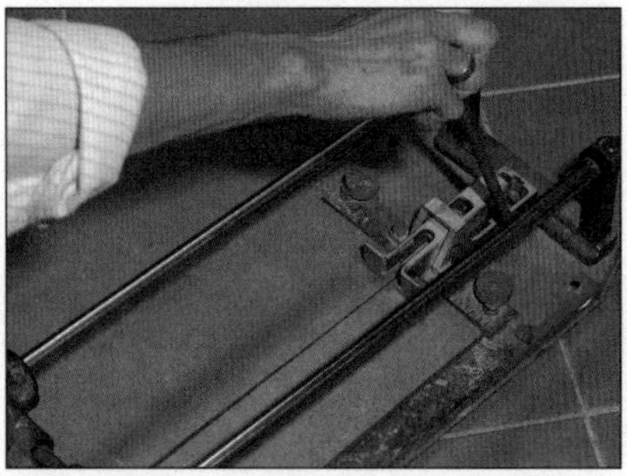

Use a tile cutter to score the surface of the tiles.

Apply the tile bed with a trowel, leaving it slightly full.

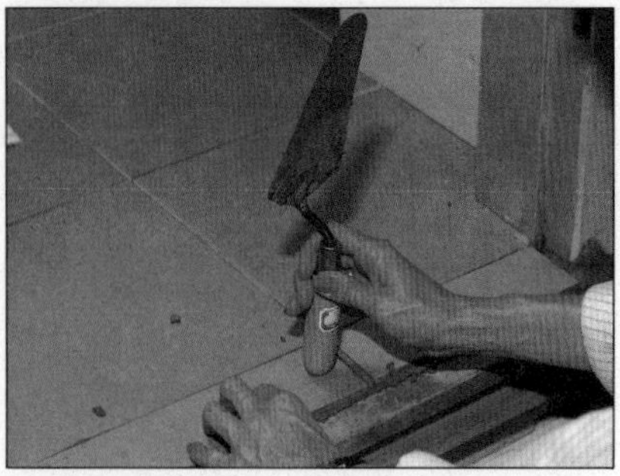

Lay the tiles in place and carefully tap them down.

TOOLS AND MATERIALS

You'll need a tile cutter, small trowel or spreader, a Carborundum stone (for smoothing off the rough edges of cut tiles), a scrap piece of timber (screed) to support the thick bed until it dries (this may have to be temporarily nailed to plugs in the brickwork), a straight edge (to check the new tiling lines up with the old), and a rule and pencil.

You'll also need sufficient tiles to cover the area (allow some extras in case of breakages or problems with cutting). For thin bed joints (up to 3 mm) use an adhesive. For thick bed joints (up to 25 mm) use a cement and sand mix which has some PVA type glue in it (Bondcrete or Semstick, etc.) to increase adhesion.

Because of the number of types and brands of adhesives on the market you would be well advised to consult a few reputable tile suppliers and ask their advice about your particular situation. If using thin bed adhesives, get some grout as well!

PROCEDURE

1 Prepare the subsurface so it is perfectly clean, firm and dry. Roughening it will assist adhesion.

2 Fix the screed (which could be lightly oiled to make sure it doesn't stick to the mortar) in position either by tacking to a timber floor or jamb or, as shown, by drilling the brickwork with a masonry drill and plugging the hole with timber plugs (these plugs can later be drilled out, filled and touched up with paint). If you're butting against a carpet, a brass strip will provide the most attractive finish.

3 Mark the tiles, then, using the tile cutter, score the surface heavily with the cutter. Place a match under the cut and press down. Use the stone to make the edges smooth. A professional tile cutting machine which can be hired makes it easy.

4 Mix up the tile bed to a paste-like consistency and apply, leaving it slightly full.

5 Lay the tiles in place and carefully tap them down with a wooden block or the handle of a hammer until they are level with the existing floor. If there is too much mortar, scrape it out because if you hit the tiles too hard they may crack!

6 Using the straight edge, make sure the tiles line up with the existing floor and adjust as necessary.

7 Wipe off all excess mortar, fill then smooth the joints, and allow to dry fully. Then carefully remove the screed.

Don't walk on the retiled area for at least three days to allow the mortar time to cure.

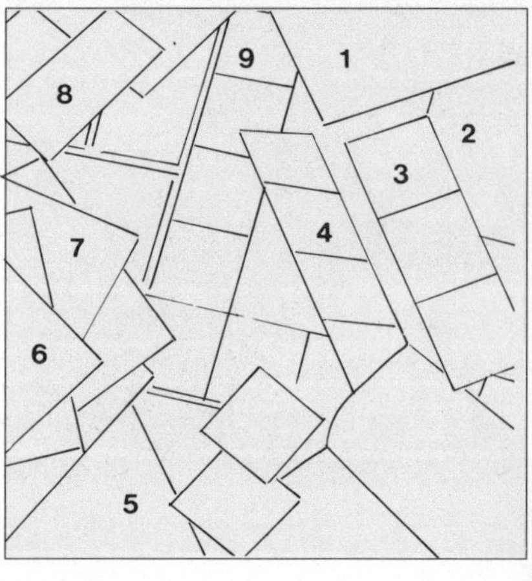

Ceramic floor tiles
1. *Federation-style pattern*
2. *Unglazed terracotta*
3. *Small unglazed terracotta*
4. *Glazed co-ordinates for edging*
5. *Mosaic tiles*
6. *Imitation terracotta*
7. *Selection of printed tiles*
8. *Non-slip stair edge*
9. *Square low-sheen glaze*

GABBIANELLI

Replacing a Rusty Arch Bar

An arch bar, for the uninitiated, is a flat piece of mild steel which bridges across a small window or door opening in a brick wall to support the brickwork above (for larger spans, angle irons are used). Unless the arch bar has been hot-dip galvanised, there is a high chance of rust attacking the metal, especially in coastal areas where there is salt in the air.

Unfortunately, rusting metal expands, creating great pressure. The problem is usually evidenced by a gradually increasing crack in the brick joint on either side of the window opening.

If the opening is small (not more than approximately one metre) and accessible, you could try replacing the bar yourself. Angle irons, because of their size and the amount of brickwork above them, would usually require the services of a licensed builder.

An old steel arch bar which has rusted.

Drill a series of holes in the joint under the top brick.

Use a plugging chisel to loosen the top bricks.

Remove the top brick on either side of the brick reveal.

Thoroughly wet the tops of the reveal and the two bricks.

Tap the new arch bar into position.

Lay a generous bed joint where the reveal bricks will sit.

TOOLS AND MATERIALS

You'll need an electric drill and 6 mm masonry bit (or a plugging chisel), hammer, cold chisel, saw, trowel, shovel, and brick jointing tool.

Order a hot-dip galvanised arch bar the same size as the existing one. Some mortar sand, cement (and oxide if the brick joints are coloured) and a spot of lime will make the mortar to relay the bricks. A piece of scrap timber to temporarily prop up the brickwork in the centre of the opening is a good idea.

PROCEDURE

1 First, carefully examine the bricks over the opening. If they are loose or in a soft lime mortar, it would be better to remove and relay them otherwise they could fall on you. If they are solid and the existing mortar is high in cement (if so, it'll be difficult to scratch out with a nail), they should support themselves during the changeover with the help of the prop.

2 Cut the temporary prop between the floor or sill and the brickwork (not the arch bar) and tap into place in the middle.

3 With the masonry bit (or plugging chisel), drill a series of holes in the brick joint under the top brick on either side of the brick reveal. Then drill out the vertical joint. Carefully remove each brick. Tap the arch bar loose and withdraw.

4 After cleaning any lumps of mortar off the bricks, thoroughly wet the tops of the reveal and the two bricks. Put the new arch bar in position (or wedge it up with another prop). Then mix up the mortar (proportions of 6 of sand and one each of lime and cement are suitable). Lay a generous bed joint where the reveal bricks will sit. Butter some mortar on the ends of the reveal bricks and push them into place (see previous topic). Make sure they are in line with the existing bricks (otherwise the crack won't close up).

5 Fill any holes (but not the cracks) and then use your trowel to cut off the excess mortar. Leave the joint until the mortar is semi-hard, then finish to suit the existing work (ironed, raked, etc.). Clean off any stains and leave the prop for 24 hours, until the mortar has cured sufficiently to take any weight. The cracks should close up when you take the prop out (assuming you haven't left any dags of mortar on top of the bricks). If they don't, mix up some more mortar and fill them.

6 Next paint the arch bar to increase its anti-rust properties. To do this, first wipe it carefully with mineral turpentine, then apply a galvanised iron primer and, when dry, finish off with two coats of suitable exterior grade paint.

Tap the old arch bar loose and take it out.

Finish the semi-dry mortar with an iron or rake.

The new arch bar in place after completing the work.

Hiding Wiring with Timber Conduits

After a house or unit is finished and the occupants move in, it often becomes apparent there are insufficient power points or lights — in fact, one might almost say this is a law of nature!

However, putting in extra outlets sometimes leaves ugly exposed wiring running part-way up walls or across ceilings (either because it's too expensive or difficult to run it down cavities, under floors, or fit it behind architraves). Why not camouflage it?

One way to hide the wiring is to cover it with a small timber section that has a groove in the back for the wiring to fit into. The section may then be painted in with the wall, made into a feature by painting it another colour, or wallpapered over.

If the wiring runs part-way up a wall you should consider running the section the full height of the wall. That looks much better than stopping it half way. If it is a horizontal run, why not make a feature of it and put the wiring at chair rail or picture rail height and run the grooved section right around the room? On ceilings, run it from cornice to cornice.

The groove in the timber can be made two ways:

- by buying a solid section and running a groove in it with a router, or
- by building up the grooved section from three separate pieces.

ROUTER SAFETY HINTS

- Unplug the router while making any adjustments.
- Remember to KEEP BOTH YOUR HANDS ON THE ROUTER.
- Work from left to right (because the bit revolves in a clockwise direction).
- Wear safety glasses to protect your eyes.
- Make sure the cutter and the fence are secure.
- Start the machine with the cutter clear of the timber.

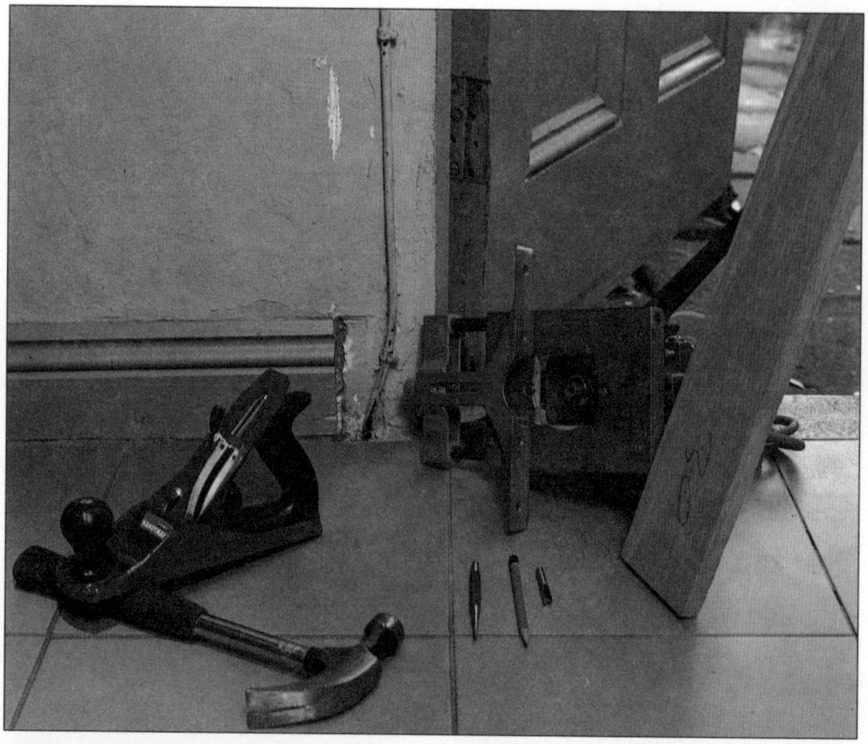

The tools and timber needed for making timber conduits.

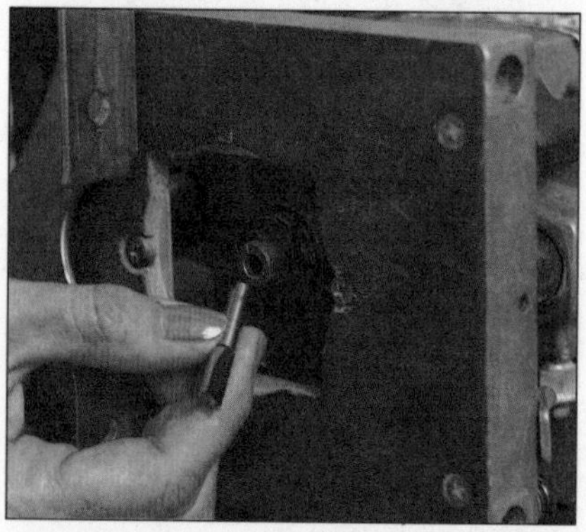

Insert the cutter in the router and adjust to the right depth.

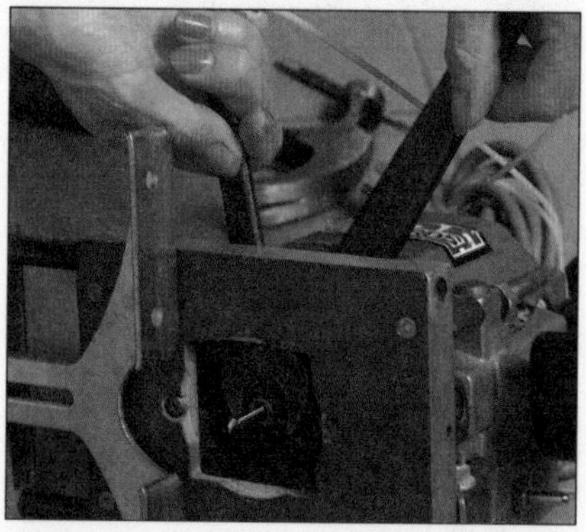

Make sure the cutter and guide are fixed tightly.

Clamp the timber and fix the router in position.

Rout out the groove, holding the router with both hands.

Check the grooved timber for correct fit.

Fix the timber in position and punch nails.

MATERIALS IF YOU ARE ROUTING

You'll require a dressed timber section that is thick enough to be safely grooved to hold the wire (allow for at least 2 mm clearance around the wire) and of sufficient width so that when fixing it, you won't nail through the wiring (but not too wide or it becomes too obvious).

MATERIALS IF YOU ARE BUILDING UP

Buy one length of 50 × 13 mm dressed batten and two lengths of 13 × 13 mm dressed strip. Some wood glue and a few 18 mm brads will make up the section.

TOOLS AND FIXING MATERIALS

For either option, you'll also require 38 mm nails if fixing through gypsum plaster into timber studs, ceiling joists or battens. If there is no timber to fix to, you may have to consider gluing the batten to the wall or ceiling with epoxy glue or contact glue. Hold the batten in place with masking tape until the glue dries. If fastening to masonry walls, you'll need plugs and a masonry drill. Whatever type of wall you have, you will need putty and paint.

If using solid timber, you'll need an electric router with fence and a suitable cutter. This can be hired from most hire outlets but make sure you tell them what size groove you want to cut and get them to show you how to set up the fence and adjust the depth of cut.

A hammer, nail punch, plane, masonry bit and electric drill (for plugs), pencil and rule, and sandpaper will also be required.

PROCEDURE

A. If ROUTING, mark out the desired width of the groove and then set the router up so the cutter extends to the right depth. If it's a deep groove it may be better to take two or three shallow bites at it.

Try the router out on a scrap piece of timber first but make sure the piece is securely held by temporarily nailing it to a bench or stool so it can't move (use a couple of 38 mm nails). If it's correct, remove the scrap piece, temporarily secure the full length timber section in position and run the groove.

B. If MAKING THE BUILT-UP SECTION, lay the two 13 x 13 mm dressed strips side by side, and spread a generous layer of glue on an edge of each one. Using the brads, nail the 50 x 13 mm dressed battens on top of them, keeping them flush with the outside edge. When the glue is dry, lightly sand the section and take off the sharp corners.

FIXING PROCEDURE

1 Cut the grooved batten to length and try it over the wire. Adjust the groove if necessary. You may find it easier to fit if the wire clips are removed. Use tape to hold the wire in place. Check also that the back of the section fits neatly against the wall surface on both sides. Plane it if necessary.

2 Fix the batten in position watching you don't nail through the wire! Punch the nails, fill the holes, then apply a suitable finish. Alternatively, glue it on.

If you still consider the camouflage too obtrusive, hang a large picture on the batten or allow a climbing vine to grow up it!

Glazing

Getting broken glass replaced in timber windows can be a real pain! It's expensive too if your insurance doesn't cover it. Why not do it yourself? Replacing the glass in a small accessible frame can be easy if you follow these steps. Removing a sash from the frame will make the job easier. But remember, glass cuts like a surgical knife, so be careful!

Preparation

The first thing to do is to hack out the old facing putty. Use your second-best chisel and a hammer. Choose a day when your patience is good because, if the window is old, you will probably find that the putty has gone hard and will be stuck like glue to the rebate. Care is required or you'll damage the frame.

Next remove the headless nails (sprigs) with a pair of pliers, and then carefully remove the old back putty, again taking care you don't damage the frame.

Tap out the remaining glass and put it in an old ice-cream container. Don't just put it in a plastic garbage bag — it's dangerous.

Liberally paint the rebate with oil-based primer otherwise the timber will suck the oil out of the putty causing it to crack and fall out. Allow to dry overnight. Some plastic taped over the opening will stop rain and wind if necessary.

Carefully hack out the old facing putty.

Pull out the old sprigs with a pair of pliers.

Use a paint scraper to remove the back putty.

TOOLS AND MATERIALS

With a steel tape or folding rule, measure the exact size of the opening, then go to your hardware store or nearest glass supplier, give them the sizes and tell them where the glass is to be used. They will make the necessary allowances for clearance (2 mm all around) and give you the correct weight (thickness) and type of glass (some situations require safety glass). Buy also some glazing putty, some new sprigs, and a putty knife. It is best to carry the glass on its edge.

PROCEDURE

1 Take a handful of putty and keep squeezing it until it grows soft. Add linseed oil if it's a bit old. Squeeze the dough-like putty around the back of the rebate.

2 Carefully pick up the glass and press it into place (but not in the centre) making sure you maintain an even clearance around the perimeter. Use a couple of matches at the bottom as a spacer. There should be at least a 2 mm thickness of putty at the back.

3 Tap in some sprigs (say every 250 mm) sliding a small hammer or large chisel gently across the face of the glass.

4 Again softening some putty, press it liberally along the front of the rebate using your thumb or putty knife.

5 Using the putty knife, smooth off the facing putty making the bevel approximately the same as on the other windows (that is, in line with the inside of the rebate). Work from the corners into the centre. The bevel gives a neat finish and helps the rain to run off.

6 Using the putty knife, scrape or cut off excess putty from the outside and inside and clean off all marks with a rag dipped in methylated spirits. Leave to cure for a week or so before painting. Make sure you eventually paint it otherwise it will dry out and crack. This could allow water to get into the timber, potentially leading to rotting.

Steel windows can be glazed similarly, providing you cut out any rust and treat the bare metal with metal primer (you'll find clips are used instead of sprigs). However, never use wood putty on metal windows — they need special metal putty.

Aluminium windows, unfortunately, generally require professional attention.

Gently press the new sheet of glass into place.

Press putty liberally into the front of the rebate.

Smooth off the putty with the putty knife.

Repairing Windows

A window generally consists of a fixed frame to which lighter units called sashes are fitted. These sashes hold the glass and move in a variety of directions (sliding, outward opening, etc.). Windows are generally made from timber, aluminium or steel.

The major problems associated with windows are:

- broken glass (see Glazing page 134);
- rotting or rusting of the frame or sash (see Repairing Rotting Door Frames page 106);
- the sashes become difficult or impossible to open. It is this factor that we will look at.

Timber Casement Sashes

These sashes open outwards on hinges (like doors) or by the use of friction stays. If the sashes are difficult to open it will usually be for one of the reasons given below:

Continuous painting has closed the clearance gap. If this has happened, treat the same as for Sticking Doors (page 87).

Water has penetrated into the joints because of cracked glazing putty or peeling paint and the glue has given way allowing the sash to sag. The only effective way to correct this problem is to take the sash out of the frame, tap the joints apart and, after cleaning off the old glue, reglue them with a waterproof glue such as epoxy.

Unfortunately you'll require a sash cramp to pull the joints tight, although you can also do it by nailing a series of blocks to a bench or old table and using wedges. Check that the frame is square by making the diagonals the same.

When dry, carefully repaint the joint and surrounding area with primer, undercoat and finishing coats and reputty where necessary.

The screws may have also pulled loose. The holes should be replugged the same way as for loose catches.

Friction stays that are difficult to operate require lubrication. Clean any grit or dirt out of the fitting with turps, then use Vaseline or one of the dry lubricants obtainable from your petrol station to lessen friction. Some candle wax will do in an emergency.

If rust has damaged the stay it should be replaced. Make sure you get two of a similar size.

Horizontal Sliding Sashes

These may be of timber or metal and run on a metal track using either nylon or roller bearings. If they are sticking, clear away any dirt that has built up in the track, then re-lubricate the bearings with grease or graphite.

If this doesn't work, check whether the top of the window frame is rubbing on the top of the sash. If this is happening then some settlement has taken place (quite normal). With a timber sash, you can remove the beading or trim which holds it in place, then lift the sash out and plane the top of it until it has 2–3 mm clearance.

Alternatively, locate the area of deflection and drive a nail up through the timber lining into the window head to try to pull the top of the window frame upwards.

If neither of these solutions works, call in a builder to help you with the problem.

Vertical Sliding Windows

The two most common ways to make these windows work are spiral balances or weights and cords. In the case of a spiral balance that is weak, undo the bottom clasp and, turn the clasp several times to the left. That should retighten the spring. Screw the clasp back on and see if it works.

If the spring is broken, replace the balance but make sure you get two (if one's gone, it's likely the other one won't be far away). They must be the same size or they may not support the weight of the sash.

Replacing broken or badly rotted cords in wooden box frame windows is a fairly tricky job. Check first in your piggy bank to see if there isn't enough money to pay a carpenter to do it (assuming you can find one who is willing and knows what to do!).

Vertical sash window sometimes become difficult to open.

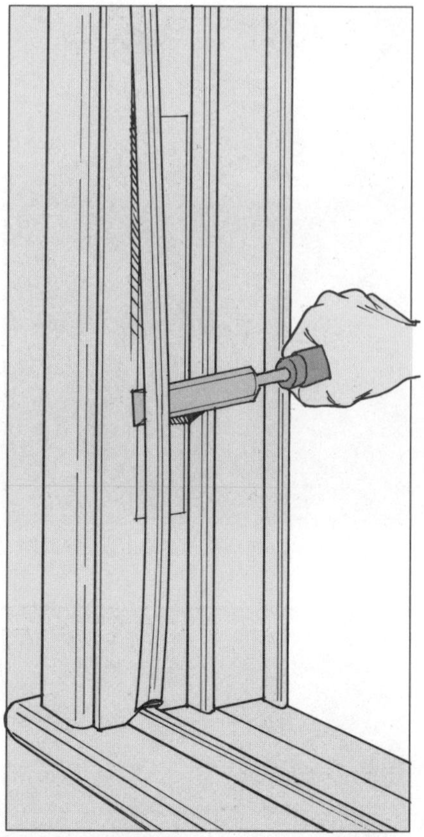

2. Insert a chisel under the middle of the side stop bead.

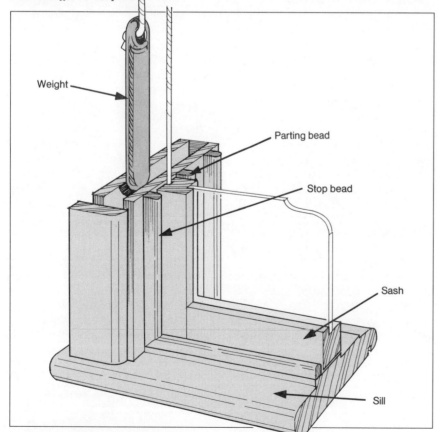

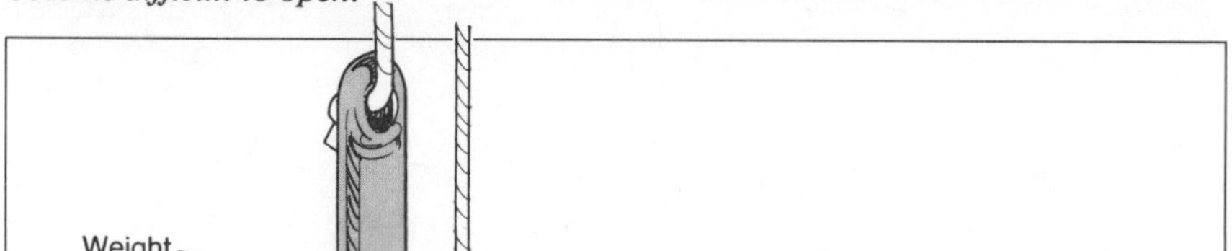

1. Section showing the parts of a double-hung sash window.

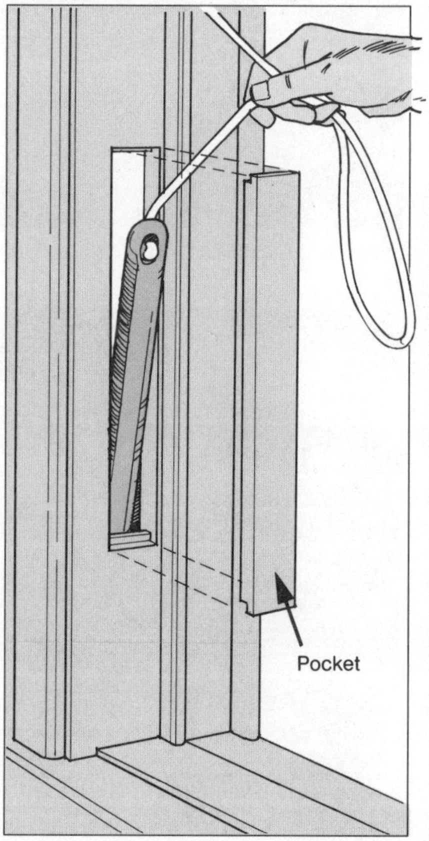

3. Lever out the pocket and retrieve the sash weight.

Replacing Sash Cords

TOOLS AND MATERIALS

You'll need an old chisel, hammer, paint scraper, a few 38 mm nails, a handful of 25 mm galvanised clouts and a roll of sash cord. A roll might seem too much but, if one cord is broken, others will surely follow.

PROCEDURE

1 First study Diagram 1 and identify all the parts on your window. Then carefully insert a chisel under the middle of the side stop bead and, tapping it under with the hammer, begin to lever it off. With a pencil, clearly mark where it goes; then repeat for the other side.

2 Next, cut the bottom sash cords, if any, with a trimming knife and carefully lower the weights down inside the box. Then remove the bottom sash (work the chisel or screwdriver into the joint if it is stuck because of built-up paint).

3 The parting beads, which fit into a groove in the pulley stile, have to come out next. Insert a fine chisel or screwdriver and carefully prise them out (if they or the stop beads break, you may have to make a quick trip to the timber yard to find a replacement — make sure you take a broken piece with you so you can match it). Label them also to make sure they go back in the same place.

4 Lower the top sash, cut the top cords, and remove the top sash. Remove the nails and offcuts of cord from the sash stiles. Scrape or plane away any paint build-up so the sash will slide easily.

5 Next, lever out the pockets with a chisel or screwdriver and retrieve the sash weights. Mark where they belong. If one is bigger than the other, the larger one belongs with the bottom sash (assuming they are both the same glass size) because it has a wider and therefore heavier bottom rail.

6 Make a 'mouse' to help thread the sash cord. This is achieved by attaching a small piece of sheet lead (a thin sinker could also work) to a 1.5 metre length of string. Fix the other end of the string to the end of the new sash cord. Push the mouse through the top pulley hole and allow it to fall to the bottom of the pocket. Retrieve it, then pull the cord through.

7 Fix the top weight to the end of the cord using a figure-of-eight knot, and then push the weight back into the box. Put the top sash in the outside channel and let it rest on the sill. Then pull the cord tight until the weight bumps up against the pulley. Lower it a fraction, then tack a 38 mm nail through the cord 150 mm below the pulley (to hold the weight up).

8 Swivel the sash outwards and nail the cord into the groove in the edge of the sash using the clouts. Four should suffice. Repeat for the other side; then remove the 38 mm nails.

9 Then repeat the procedure for the bottom sash but watch that you lower the cord approximately 100 mm below the pulley before you tack it in place (this stops the weights hitting on the pulley). Then replace the pockets, parting beads and stop beads in that order.

10 Check that the sashes slide before you nail the stop bead off.

If everything works properly, you can have the rest of the day off. We've earned it. If there are other cords to replace, don't leave it too long or you might forget how it's done.

4. Thread the new sash cord with the help of a 'mouse'.

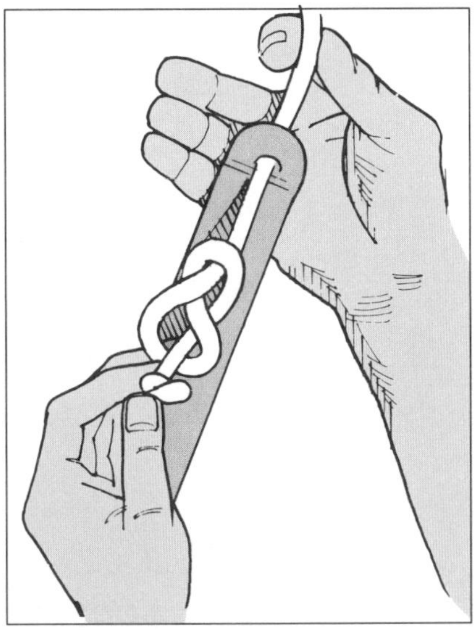

5. Fix the weight to the end of the cord with a figure-of-eight knot.

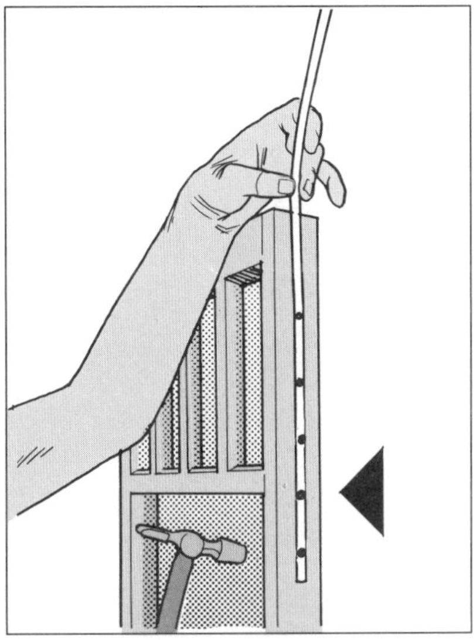

6. Nail the cord into the groove in the edge of the sash.

Removing and Replacing Wallpaper

Wallpapering is a messy job that brings most people unstuck. But it needn't!

Before you begin, remember, what looks attractive in a small piece can look disastrous in large areas. It is helpful if the book you choose the paper from has photographs of rooms as well as small samples of the actual paper.

The type of paper you select (vinyl, textile, etc.) should be governed by the room use. Areas that are to be subjected to water, steam or continual cleaning require a washable surface. Various different types of wallpaper are illustrated on page 140.

If you have never hung wallpaper before, choose a small room to start with. A child's bedroom is ideal for the beginner.

You can hire steaming equipment to remove old paper.

Work down the wall in consecutive strips.

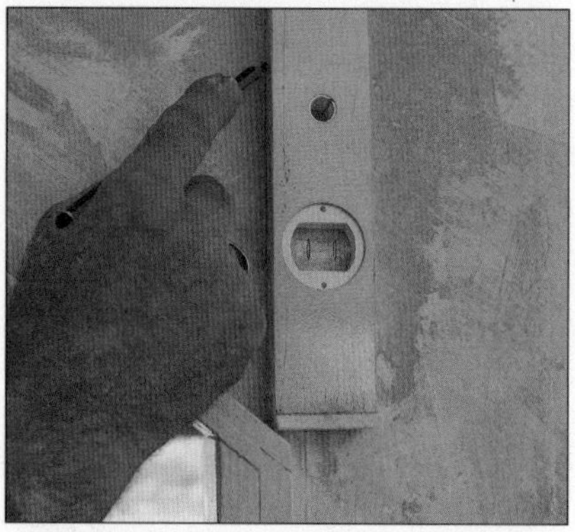

Mark a vertical starting line with a level or plumb line.

Cut measured lengths of paper, always allowing extra.

Pull length of prepasted paper through water trough.

Fold each end to the middle of the drop.

Surface Preparation

It's best to remove all old wallpaper and glue. This can be done by soaking it in hot water that has detergent or stripping solution in it. A better method involves steaming it off (equipment to do this can be hired). Well-bonded, non-vinyl, non-textured paper can be papered over (ask your supplier for advice).

If stripping, score the surface of the previously painted wallpaper with a wire brush or coarse sandpaper to assist water penetration. On plasterboard surfaces make sure you don't overwet the paper or you may lift the lining paper on the plaster. This is not a problem if the plasterboard has been properly painted in the first place.

When the wallpaper is properly dampened, begin to scrape it off with a wide stripping knife, being careful you don't damage the wall surface. When the wallpaper is removed, fill all holes and paint any bare patches with an oil-based sealer.

New plasterboard and cement render must be properly cured before sealing. Previously painted surfaces must be free of flaking paint, totally clean (use sugar soap) and lightly sandpapered. All cracks must be filled and sanded. Any mould must be removed and the wall treated with an anti-mould solution.

Size the walls to slow down the adhesive setting time. This gives you a chance to position the paper properly before it sticks!

Apply the first drop to the wall against the marked line.

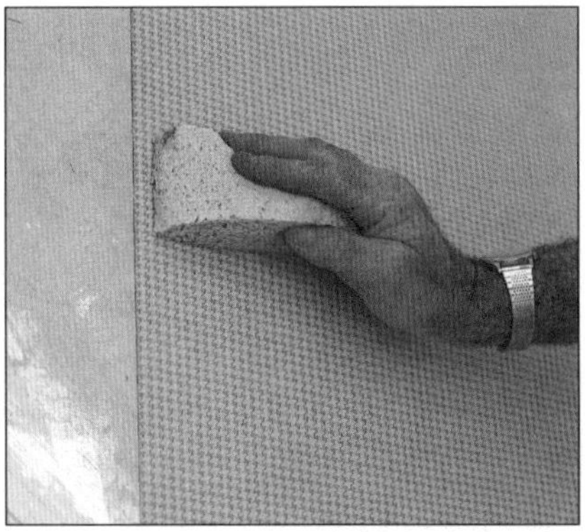

Smooth paper from top to bottom with a damp sponge.

Trim the top edges using a metal edge as a guide.

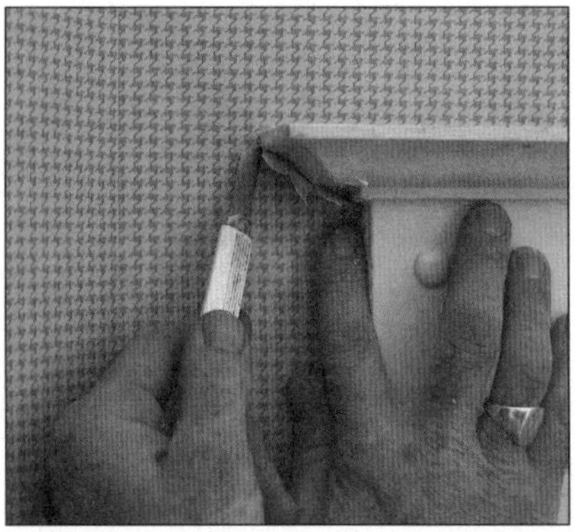

Trim around difficult edges with a knife or scissors.

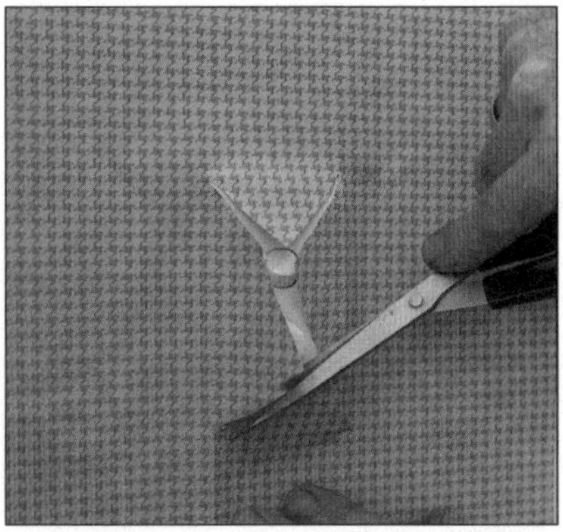

Cut paper diagonally to corners over light switch.

Hanging Wallpaper

TOOLS AND MATERIALS

Carefully measure the width and height of each wall and draw a small sketch of each. Make a note of any large windows, doors, and the type and condition of the wall finish. From your drawings the supplier will calculate the number of rolls you'll need and advise on the surface preparation, the paste required (though most wallpaper is now pre-pasted) and whether you'll need to put up lining paper first (if so, hang it horizontally).

If using a non-pasted paper, a kitchen table or an old door makes a good pasting table while a 100–200 mm paint brush can be used for pasting. A water trough is almost essential for pre-pasted papers. A broad hanging brush or smoother helps to work out any bubbles. Scissors should be as large as possible and a trimming knife is handy for fitting the paper in awkward places.

A sponge, bucket, rule and pencil, spirit level or string with weight attached, drop sheet and stepladder complete the essential equipment.

PROCEDURE

1 Select a day when you're at peace with the world. Cut the paper into full lengths allowing 100–150 mm waste. Match the pattern on each strip as you go and number each one.

2 To ensure the sheets are perfectly vertical, make a plumb line. Use a spirit level or tie a heavy nut or piece of lead to a length of string. Tape it to the ceiling where required, then, when the line is still, mark it in several places with a pencil. Then remove the line and simply join the marks with a straight edge to achieve a perfect starting point.

3 Begin next to a window and continue right around the room. Hanging away from a strong light will help to disguise the joins and avoid glare. If the window is not exactly plumb and straight, trim the first sheet around it until the other edge hangs vertically.

4 If you're pasting, start at one end. Do the middle first, then the edges. Fold the end in towards the centre while you do the other half. Fold similarly, then carry the folded strip to the window and, getting up the ladder, release the top half. Smooth into position with the hanging brush making sure the top overlaps the cornice 40–50 mm. Work from the centre out to avoid trapping air bubbles. Then release the bottom half. Don't overwork thin paper as it may tear.

For pre-pasted paper, place the trough against the wall, roll the paper with the pattern inside, then place in the water. Slowly draw the length past the bar and hang.

5 Next run the back edge of the scissors along the skirting board and ceiling (treat architraves similarly), then peel the paper back far enough to enable you to cut it to length. Clean all excess glue off then brush the paper back into position.

Alternatively, cut it in position using the smoother to steady the paper while cutting with a sharp trimming knife. Check for air bubbles and creases by looking along the sheet towards the light and brush them out.

6 Corners are rarely plumb or straight so cut the last strip so it goes around the corner just 15 mm. Paste into position. Then use the offcut to return along the next wall, overlapping it on top of the 15 mm until the far edge is vertical (but only if the pattern allows it). Paste into position and continue. On all external corners allow 25 mm overlap also. Paper around window reveals first.

7 With light switches and power points, first switch the power off at the meter box. Hang the paper and then, from the centre of the fitting, cut four diagonals to the corners. Trim as for cornices. You've done it! I knew you could.

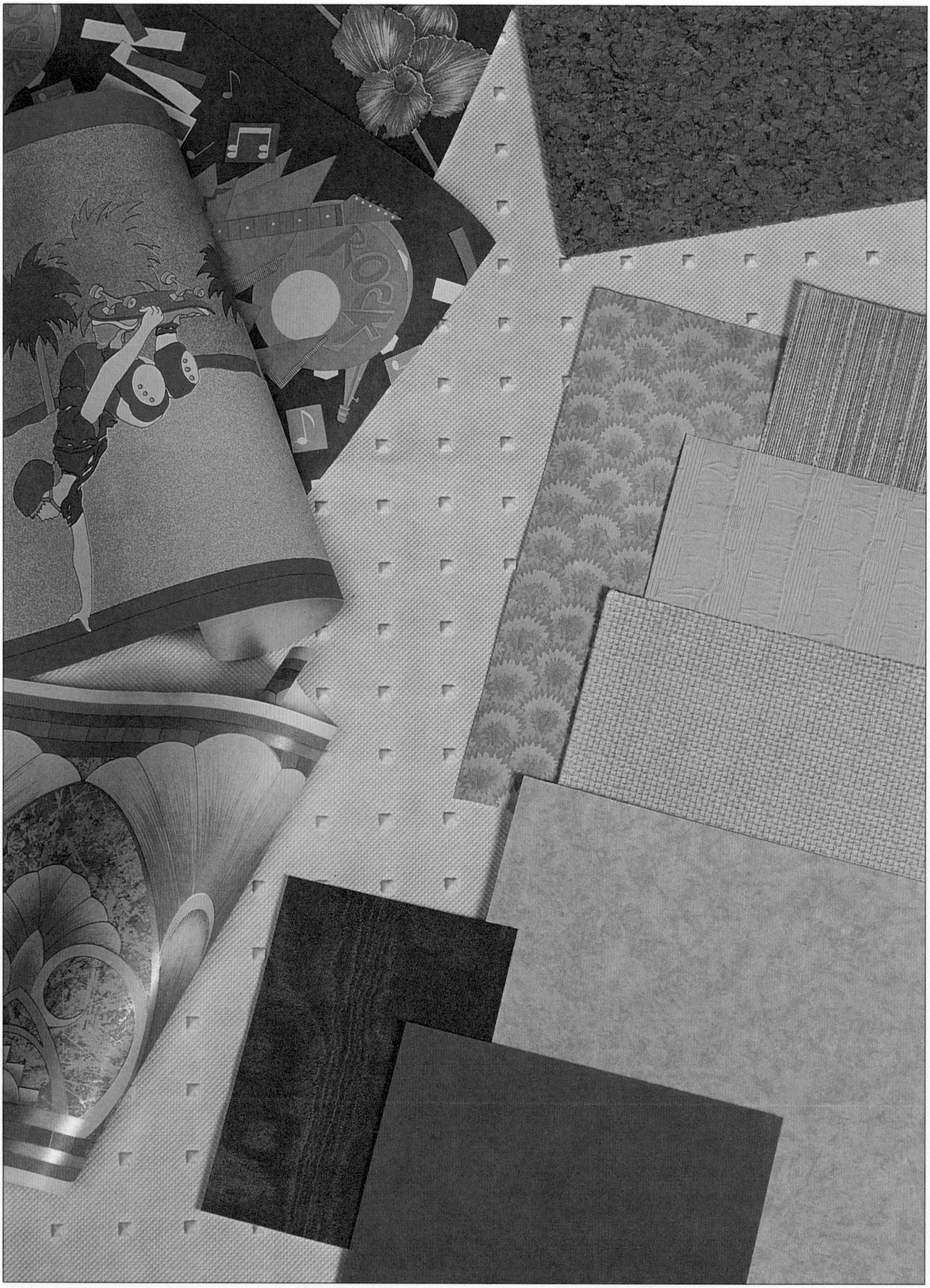
ROCK

Moving a Cupboard

Ever had the feeling that your kitchen's appearance would be greatly improved if the top cupboards were located somewhere else? Why not move them? It's not such a difficult job and the end result could be brilliant, to say nothing of a potential increase in kitchen efficiency.

Cupboards are normally fixed to the wall by screws. In the case of timber frame construction, the screws usually go into studs. With masonry construction the wall is drilled and plugged to provide solid fixing. All that has to be done, therefore, is to undo the screws, remove the cupboard or cupboards, and refix the unit in the more favoured position (but first carefully measure the area to make sure it will fit).

Remember also to check with your local authorities as to how many millimetres you should keep above a stove (and a refrigerator) should they be involved. And above all, when nailing or screwing, watch you don't hit any electrical wiring or plumbing!

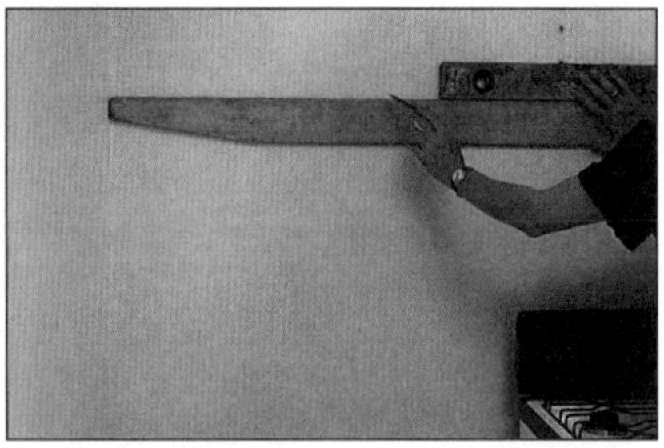

Mark the new position of the cupboard, using a level.

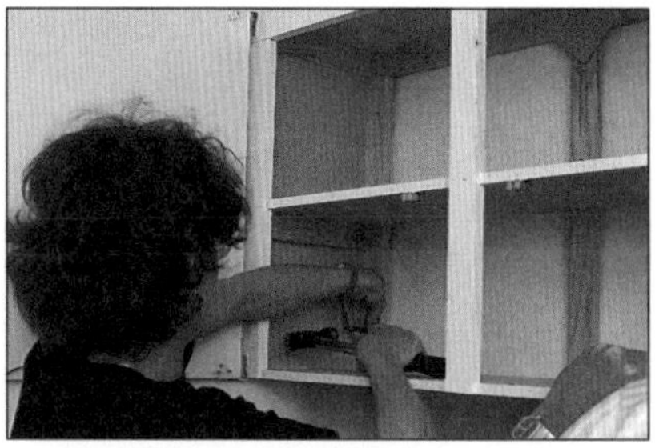

With cupboard held in new position, punch through screw holes.

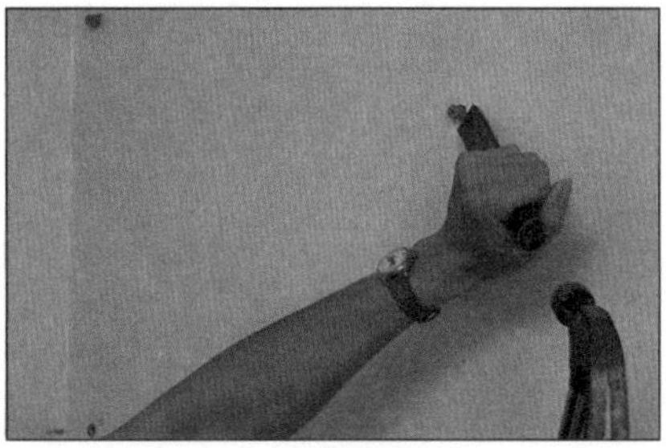

Plug walls and cut off excess plugs with a chisel.

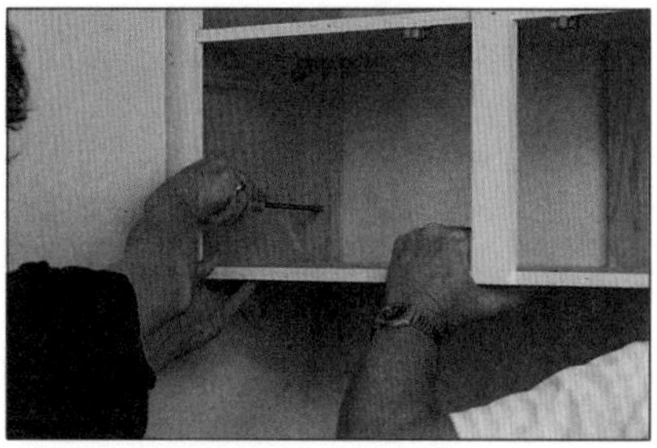

With a friend's help screw the cupboard in the new position.

TOOLS AND MATERIALS

Buy new screws (unless you can get the old ones out without damaging the heads) and plugs if necessary. You'll need a hefty screwdriver (ratchet if possible) that neatly fits the screw heads, a hand or electric drill plus drill bits (include a tungsten-tipped masonry bit if drilling brickwork), a tape and pencil, level, hammer, 50 mm nails, and half a kilogram of fortitude.

PROCEDURE

1 Remove the contents of the cupboard and then clear the screw heads of any paint with, say, a nail file or steel skewer.

2 Look to see whether the top cupboard is a single unit or several units fixed together. If in sections, undo the side fastenings (but check each unit is secured to the wall).

3 To support the cupboard, enlist the aid of a sympathetic and robust friend or build two pillars of support under each end using say books or paint tins. Then undo the screws and remove the cupboard (if you're by yourself and it's too heavy, it may pay to remove the cupboard doors to make the unit lighter).

4 Mark the position where the bottom of the cupboard will go, using the tape. Level this line across the wall (if you haven't got a level, you could measure off the floor cupboards).

5 With the help of a friend place the cupboard in the new location. Use a nail punch or narrow screwdriver to mark the existing screw holes on the wall; then remove the cupboard. Drill and plug the holes (make sure they're at least 3 mm deeper than the amount the driven screw will project past the cupboard), and then fix the cupboard in place.

For timber frame walls you can locate the stud positions by tapping the wall while listening for a solid sound. Drive in a nail to verify solid fixing. Mark these stud positions (usually at 450 or 600 mm centres) *below* the level line, then, with the cupboard in place, drill new screw holes in the back of the cupboard opposite these positions and rescrew the unit to the wall.

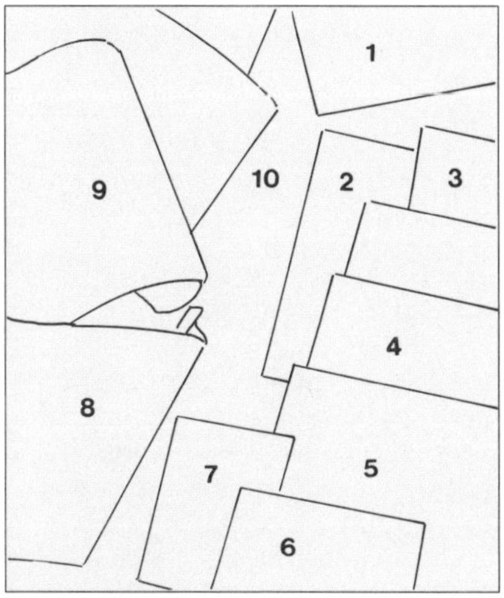

Wallcoverings
1. *Wall cork*
2. *Pastel print paper*
3. *Synthetic grass-like wallcovering*
4. *Pure linen weave, paper backing*
5. *Rag roll print*
6. *Suede-like wall covering*
7. *Moiré textured wall covering*
8. *Art Nouveau border*
9. *Selection of borders*
10. *Heavy textured vinyl*

Relaying a Concrete Path

Concrete paths, because of bad proportioning or mixing, inadequate reinforcing, or incorrect jointing between slabs or poor foundations, can crack. Taking up the old concrete and laying a new path is not very difficult but it is not recommended for anyone with a bad back!

Removing the Old Concrete

First, break up the old concrete. The best hand tool for this is the sledge hammer. If there is a hire outlet nearby, an electric Kanga makes the job easier. Before you begin, check if the path has expansion joints. If it has, these will provide a convenient spot to join the old with the new.

If it hasn't, then you may have to cut through the path at both ends of the cracked section with an electric saw that has an abrasive disc in it, one suitable for cutting concrete (read the section on electric tools). While doing this make sure you wear goggles. Take two or three bites rather than try to cut right through the slab in one go. This will lessen the chance of the blade twisting and shattering.

Begin to break up the slab into pieces that are small enough to carry. When removing the waste, remember to lift with your legs, not your back!

Once the old concrete has been disposed of, remove weeds and fill any low spots with gravel or chips of concrete. A heavy roller, which can be hired, could also help to consolidate the foundation.

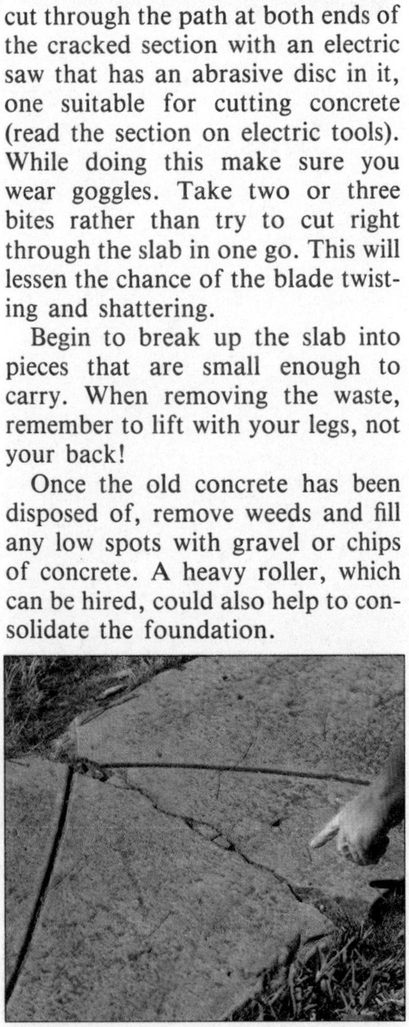

For various reasons, a concrete path can develop cracks.

TOOLS AND MATERIALS

You'll need a lump hammer to drive the pegs, a shovel for mixing and spreading the concrete, hacksaw to cut the mesh, a straight edge for levelling the concrete and a wooden float for finishing.

You'll need sufficient concrete for the job. The volume can be established by multiplying the length in metres by the width in metres by 0.075. This will allow for a path 75 mm thick. If it's a drive, which should be 100 mm thick and well reinforced with steel mesh, multiply by 0.100. Refer to Materials (page 293) for calculating the amount of dry material per cubic metre. Consider using ready-mix if you don't have or can't hire a concrete mixer. Small areas can be done in a wheelbarrow using dry-mix.

You'll also need two screeds 75 x 25 mm long enough to cover the length of the new path plus sufficient hardwood pegs to hold them in place. A handful of 50 mm nails, light reinforcing mesh, and some strips of 75 x 12 mm timber (to make expansion joints) they can be spaced anywhere from one to three metres both for aesthetic reasons and to control shrinkage cracks). Some bitumen impregnated fibre board to fill the joints completes the requirements.

PROCEDURE

1 Compact the underlying soil using a tamper (this can be made out of a 100 x 100 mm post or pole which is used like a battering ram).

2 Lay the screeds in position, making them flush with the top of each end of the existing concrete. Check they're straight both ways. Use a string line to straighten long lengths. When correct, hold in place with well driven pegs spaced so that the screed can't deflect. Cut the pegs off level with the top of the screed. Any timber that is in contact with the concrete could be lightly oiled to lessen the chance of it sticking.

Between the screeds, tack the timber stops where the joints will be made. Make sure they are at right angles to the screed. Next cut the reinforcing mesh in position. A hacksaw will do this (although bolt cutters are faster).

3 Begin to mix the concrete (see Materials page 293 for correct mixing). Pour into position and, using the shovel to help consolidate the concrete and to remove any air bubbles, spread it making sure it is slightly full of the screeds. Lay concrete either side of the stops. Remember to lift the reinforcement.

4 When the concrete is laid, use your straight edge in a sawing action to level the concrete. Fill in all low spots. Leave it until there is no free water on the surface before you attempt to finish it with the wooden float. On cold days this may take an hour or more. Never throw neat cement on the concrete to hasten the drying or the surface will crack later.

5 If the day is hot, once the surface is finished (you may wish to go over it with a sponge to increase the surface roughness and decrease the possibility of slipping), cover it with some old plastic or a tarpaulin to delay drying and potential cracking.

If you don't have a cover, wait for three or four hours, then sprinkle it periodically with a fine spray to slow the drying process.

6 Remove the screeds and stops after 24 hours and fill the gap with the joint material. Continue to wet the concrete for several days. Don't allow foot traffic for at least 36 hours.

Break up the old concrete with a crowbar or sledge hammer.

You may have to cut through the path with an electric saw.

Compact the underlying soil with a wooden tamper.

Lay the screeds in position, using string to make them straight.

To keep the screeds in position, secure them to well driven pegs.

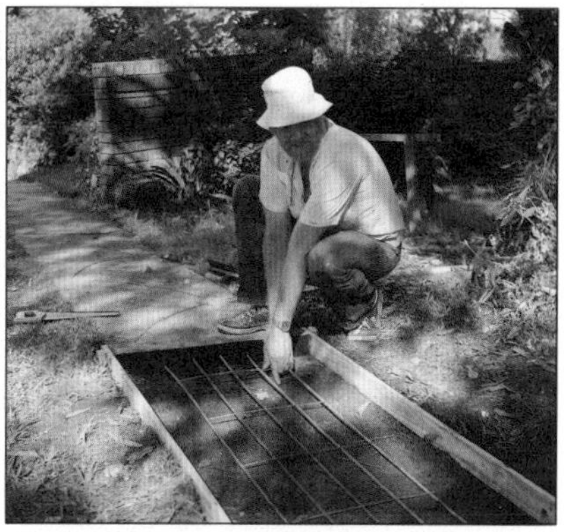

Lay the reinforcing mesh in position.

Mix the concrete (see Materials Section for correct mixing).

Pour the concrete into position and spread it.

Lift the reinforcing mesh after pouring the concrete.

Use your straight edge to level the concrete.

Finish the surface with a wooden float.

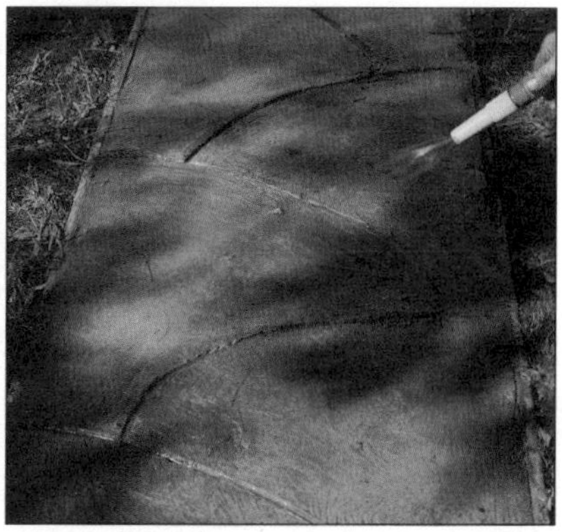

When set, sprinkle with a fine spray to slow the drying process.

Painting Fascias and Eaves

The outside of a house has a hard time because of sun, wind, rain and humidity and temperature extremes. Many materials, such as brick, terracotta, fibre cement and concrete, handle this with ease. Others, like timber and ungalvanised ferrous metal, don't. Certain materials therefore need to be painted periodically otherwise they quickly deteriorate.

Preparation

At the risk of being repetitious, let me make the point that the final success of the job will only be as good as the preparation. Unfortunately, if you're like me, you want to get on the end of a brush or roller and slap the paint on rather than be covered for days in dust, sandpaper grit, rust and sweat.

Proper preparation may be tedious, time-consuming, but it's essential. Unless you are a quick worker, do one side of the house at a time. This is because some primers require undercoating in less than four weeks.

Begin at the highest point (gutter) and move down to the fascia, the eaves, the windows and doors, then any feature boards or cladding. Before you begin, tie back or trim any nuisance tree, take off all flyscreens, house numbers, and cover pavers and paths with plastic sheeting, etc.

Gutters and downpipes Use a wire brush and sandpaper to remove any rust or peeling paint (after you've cleaned out the gutters). (Observe the ladder safety described in Repairing a Leaking Roof page 112.) Treat with rust remover where necessary and then spot prime with an appropriate primer.

Fascias Burn, sand (a sanding disc in an electric drill is handy but wear a particle mask and eye goggles), wire brush or scrape off all peeling or poorly adhering paint. For paint in good condition, use sugar soap or proprietary cleaner to rid the surface of grime, then lightly sand. Spot prime any bare spots, feathering the edges off.

Windows and doors 1. Timber. Treat in the same way as fascias, but pay special attention to joints. That is where rot-inducing moisture can get in. Pay special attention to the sill. If the putty has cracked, replace it (see Glazing page 134).
2. Steel. Use the same treatment as for gutters.
3. Aluminium. Clean with turps and fine wet-and-dry. Apply an aluminium primer.

Cladding 1. Timber. If painted, treat in the same way as fascias but remember to renail any loose boards or sheets. Then punch and fill the holes with putty. If stained, nothing more than recoating should be necessary, providing you remove wasps' nests, cocoons, etc.
2. Fibre or asbestos cement. Scrape off any loose paint and wash thoroughly with sugar soap. Lightly sand and reprime any bare patches. With all of the above don't forget to treat areas of mould or mildew with an anti-mould preparation.

Guttering, fascia and eaves in need of a coat of paint.

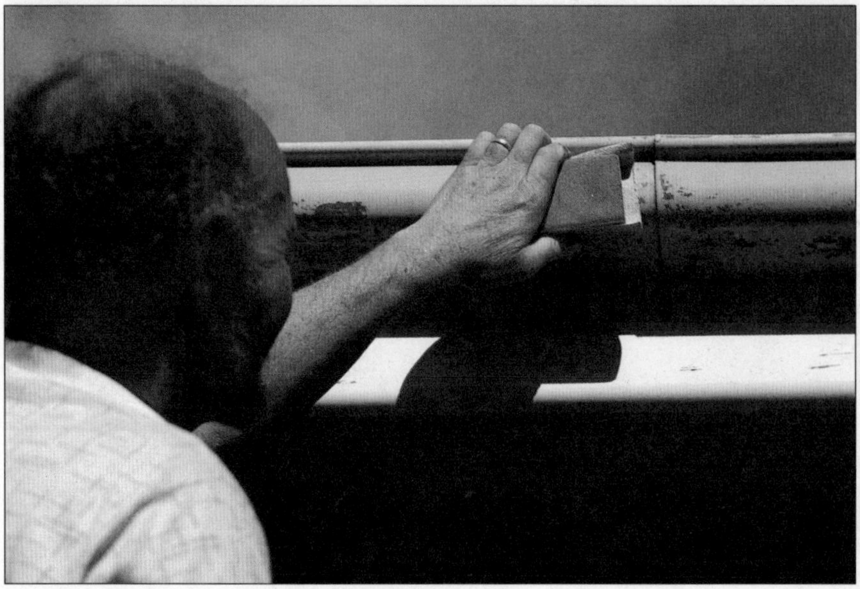

Sand thoroughly to remove peeling paint and rust.

If paint is in good condition it will only need a wash.

Work from the top down. Paint guttering first.

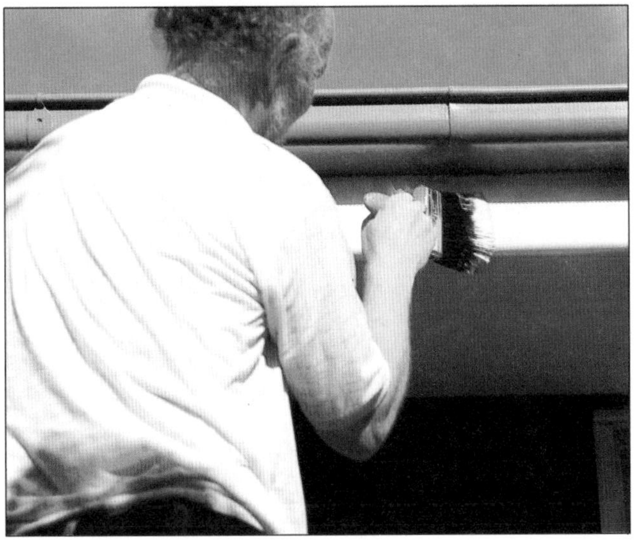

Next paint the fascia and eaves.

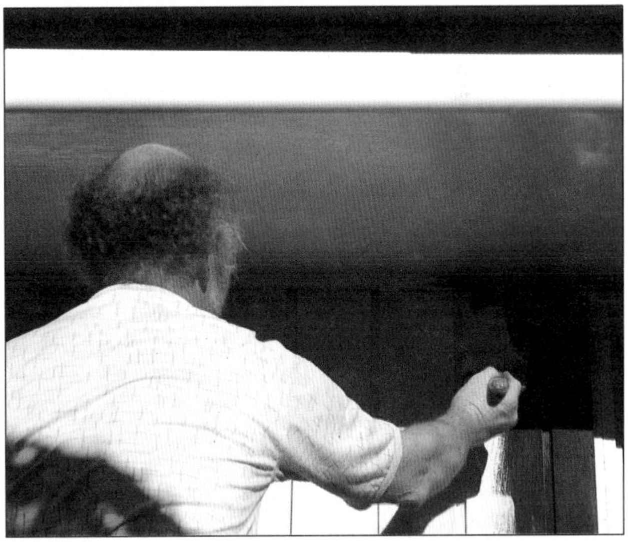

Walls can be painted with a brush or roller.

PROCEDURE

The moment you've impatiently waited for has arrived! Get out the brushes, rollers, rags and tins of beautiful designer colours. Wear some old clothes and a hat.

1 The principle to be applied again is to work from the top down. Do all undercoating if necessary and make sure you use one that suits the finishing paint. Then apply finishing coats to fascias, eaves and porches, gutters, walls, windows and doors, in that order.

Regarding the paint system, can I recommend you use a water-soluble one (for starters you can clean the brushes in water). From my own experience, oil-based paints are a real pain, not only to put on, but because they tend to peel, crack and craze as the oil dries out. A weatherboard house I once owned got painted with acrylic paint once every seven years and the only preparation it required was a wash down with some detergent and a scrubbing brush. The ubiquitous 'man next door', an oil-paint advocate, had to paint his house every two years and spent several days beforehand preparing it.

2 Use paint pots rather than painting direct from the tin. Rollers are obviously far quicker than brushes for large areas and ones with long handles can make an easy job of boxed eaves. Wrap some old cloth around the top of ladders to stop marking or scratching. Brush-paint around the edges of large areas first, and then fill in the centres using the paint roller.

If the walls are too high or the job is too big, get three quotes from members of the Master Painters' Guild and be satisfied attacking something smaller — like the letterbox! If you have any problems or need more information contact the Paint Manufacturers' Association in your state or the technical section of your favourite paint company.

Laying Cork or Vinyl Tiles

Changing the colour, pattern or material used on a kitchen or family room floor can work magic. Two popular finishes are cork and vinyl.

Cork is a warm, softish, honey-coloured material but it can easily be damaged if care is not taken. Vinyl is cold, virtually indestructible and comes in an amazing range of patterns and colours.

Before making your selection of either product, bring home at least a dozen tiles. Lay them together to get some idea of the overall effect.

Tiles are typically 300 mm square and you'll need approximately 12 to the square metre. If you supply an accurate floor plan to your supplier, they will calculate both the tiles and adhesive you require.

Preparation

As with most things, the final success will depend largely on the preparation. Your existing floor will typically be made from polished boards or covered with linoleum, carpet, or vinyl asbestos tiles.

Remove the carpet (or non-glued sheet linoleum) and all staples, tacks, etc.; then check the boards for shrinkage. If the joints are relatively tight, go over the floor with rough sandpaper to clean off any irregularities and to ensure the surface is clean so that the tile glue will achieve a good bond. If there is any dampness, find the reason, correct it, then allow the patch to dry before you apply the new covering. In the case of polished floors, you should sand back to bare timber to ensure good adhesion.

Where the boards have large gaps, knot holes or cracks (or if you have old vinyl or linoleum that is well stuck down), perhaps the easiest way to obtain a good finish is to cover the entire floor with tempered hardboard or fibre cement. This will ensure that you have a smooth, clean, solid surface to stick your tiles to. Use a metal strip at doorways to finish it off neatly. If you're unlucky, you may have to take a few millimetres off the doors to stop them rubbing on the tiles.

Your tile plan will assist the hardware store or timber yard to give you hardboard sheet sizes with minimum waste.

Note. Remember to wet the sheets in accordance with the manufacturer's instructions before use (see Building Boards page 288). Nail it down securely with cadmium-coated nails (or clouts) at, say, 150 mm centres. Make sure you stagger the sheet joints (don't put them opposite each other) otherwise the joint line may show through the tiles.

If you don't lay hardboard, then you have two options. One is to lay the new tiles over the top of the existing vinyl. This involves the difficult job of removing years of accumulated grease and wax, filling large joints, refixing loose tiles, then heavily sanding the entire surface. If the tiles have asbestos in them this could be dangerous!

Remove old floorcovering and scrape off adhesive.

Lay hardboard sheets to create a flat even surface.

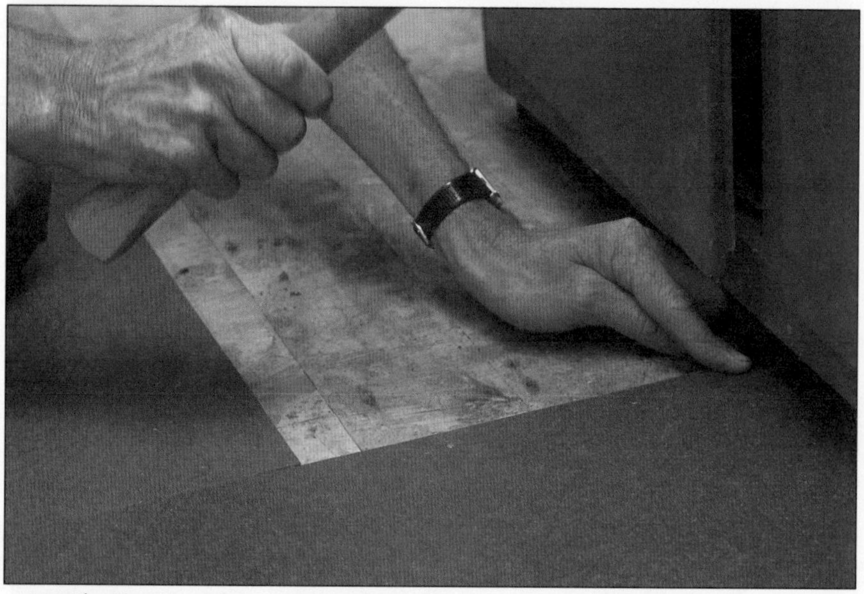

Using hardboard underlay nails, nail sheets to floor.

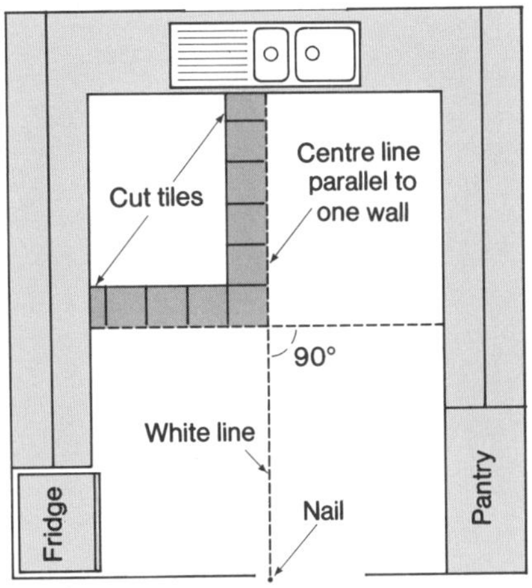

Setting out.

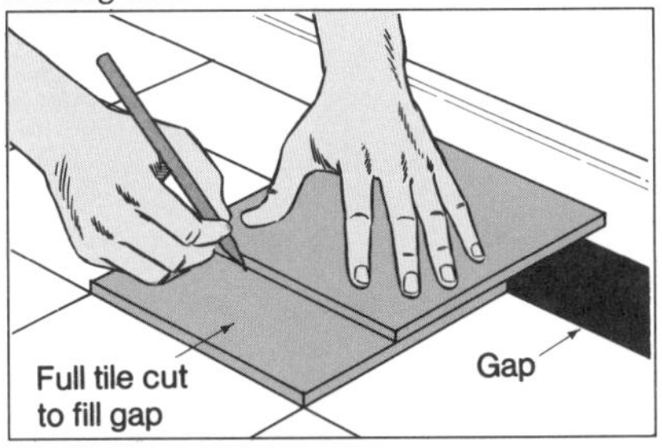

Marking tiles to complete edges.

A laundry floor brilliantly renovated with vinyl tiles.

TOOLS AND MATERIALS

A trimming knife and steel rule for cutting vinyl, panel saw for cutting cork or laying hardboard, string line and chalk, 25 mm nails, hammer, pencil and tape will be needed.

You will also need tiles and a suitable adhesive. If your supplier is doubtful about which glue to use, ring or write to the adhesive manufacturer and seek their technical advice. Sandpaper, plus nails for fixing hardboard if required, completes the requirements.

PROCEDURE

1 Pick a day when you can keep the family out of the kitchen. Look at the room dimensions and establish where the longest run of visible tiles will be. You must create a line which is in the exact centre of this area and one that runs parallel with the longest wall. This will ensure the widths of your cut tiles are roughly even and the cut edges will be against walls.

Once you have accurately established the position, drive in a nail at each end of the room, tightly stretch the chalk-filled line between them, then, pulling the line up, let it go. You should have a clear, white line on the floor.

2 Now carefully measure along this line and accurately mark its middle point. Draw another line at right angles to the white line. Here is the rule to check the lines are at right angles. From the intersection measure 3 units along one line and mark, then 4 units along the other. If the angle is a true right angle, the measurement between the marks should be equal to 5 units. For accuracy use large units. Metres would be ideal if the room is large enough. This will give you the starting position for your first tile. Lay some tiles along the white line and check how big the cut tiles will be against the walls or cupboard. If they're too small (under 50 mm), adjust to make the cut tile at one edge only.

3 Spread the glue evenly over a small area and begin to lay a row of tiles. Watch the edges stay on the white line. Alternatively you could tack down a long straight edge or batten flush with the white line and press the tiles up against this batten, and remove it once you have finished half the room.

Lay row after row of full tiles tightly together, stopping when you come to where the tiles must be cut. Then complete the other half of the room, making sure you clean off excess glue as you go.

4 To get the correct dimensions of a cut tile, lay a dry tile over a stuck one, then, using another tile pressed against wall or cupboard, draw a line. Cut along this line then apply the glue and stick the piece in position. Even intricate shapes can be marked in this way. For difficult shapes you could also make a template out of cardboard. With cork tiles, a coping saw is a useful tool to help you cut around the shape of fancy architraves.

5 Allow to dry overnight, then quickly apply the recommended finish before allowing the troops in to gasp in admiration at your cleverness and the beautiful new room!

42 825
42 854
42 837
42 860
42 847

Plugging a Hole in Timber

Often, when locks are replaced, fittings changed, or a door is removed from a jamb, there are unsightly holes left in the timber. If the hole is small — say 10 mm at its widest point — it can usually be satisfactorily plugged with putty or another appropriate filler. If it's larger than that, it is far better to fill the hole with a small block.

Neatly chisel out the waste, making sure the edges of the hole are square.

Measure, mark and cut a block to fill the hole.

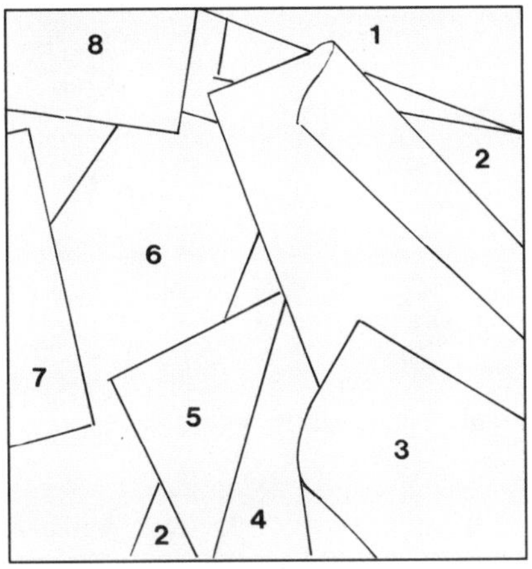

Cork and vinyl flooring
1. Raw cork floor tiles
2. Cork with polyurethane finish
3. Foam-backed vinyl
4. Marble patterned vinyl
5. Subtle Greek Key pattern
6. Inlay detail
7. Colour samples of patterned vinyl
8. Inlaid vinyl floor design

TOOLS AND MATERIALS

A sharp chisel, a plane, rule and pencil, a square, cork block and hammer are all the tools needed.

You'll need a small block of softwood which can be cut and planed to fit the hole without exposing any end grain. Use a similar species to the timber section if the wood has a clear finish. Some sandpaper and glue complete the requisites.

PROCEDURE

1 First sharpen the plane iron and chisel (see Sharpening Planes and Chisels under Hand Tools).

2 The hole must now be carefully marked out with a sharp pencil and square to make it a regular square or rectangle). It must have perfectly straight and parallel sides. Don't make it bigger than necessary!

3 With a chisel (the wider the better) and some light taps of the hammer, carefully cut around the pencil line to a depth of 0.5 mm. Make sure the bevel side of the chisel points towards the centre of the hole. Make sure you stay *inside* the lines. If one side of the hole is close to the edge, tap carefully in case you split the timber.

4 Next chisel the waste out, making sure the edges of the hole are square to the face of the timber. Take your time and don't try to take out too much at one go. Start from one end and make a deep cut. Then lay the chisel over, bevel down, and make a series of cuts working towards the other end. You'll see the timber peeling off in a series of wedges. Make sure you always keep your fingers behind the sharp edge.

Then, using both hands, push the chisel along and clean out the waste. Then, if necessary, make a slightly deeper cut.

5 When the hole is neatly cut out, measure, mark and cut the block to size, making it approximately 2 mm larger than the hole in width, thickness and length. Then plane the sides and ends down until the block fits the hole. Slightly undercut the edges so the block will, with a few taps of the hammer, wedge itself tightly into the hole.

When planing, put the block on a firm, straight surface. If you can't hold the block properly, nail a thin stop to the surface to prevent the block sliding off (see Planing Procedure in Sticking Doors).

When planing the ends, don't plane right across them or you'll split off the far edge. If you come in halfway from both sides there'll be no problems. Another way, if you have a vice, is to put a scrap piece of timber behind the edge of your block and level with it, then plane away to your heart's content.

6 Once the block is fitted, apply a generous layer of glue to the edges and ends of both the block and the hole, then tap the block into place. If it's a little loose, tack it into place with some small brads. Allow a few hours to dry.

7 To finish, plane it almost flush with the surface, then, using a cork block, sandpaper it smooth and flush. The cork block is important because it keeps the sandpaper flat and applies an even pressure which guarantees that the block will be indistinguishable from the rest of the timber section.

8 Fill any gaps with a suitable filler and then apply a finish that matches the original. If you've worked carefully the hole will have disappeared forever and you'll have gained a new and valuable skill that can be applied to recalcitrant knot holes and badly chipped edges.

BACKYARD PROJECTS

CHAPTER 6

PLANNING YOUR BACKYARD

As you sit on the back porch or look out of a rear window and contemplate your existing backyard, you perhaps sigh and wonder what you can possibly make of it all, that dreary piece of land caught between the boundary fences. You ask yourself how you, a mere mortal, can turn it into paradise.

Be assured — you can! If you take it one step at a time, you can achieve a mini-miracle and make a retreat that will succour you, reinvigorate you, cater to your every mood.

The first step in the process is to decide what type of paradise you want to achieve in the end.

In this section, you will find a multitude of practical ideas, hints and step-by-step instructions which are easy to follow and require only average skills. As you learn, you'll acquire more.

Needs and Wants

Paradise, of course, means different things to different people. Your idea will be different from mine. Therefore it is important for you to begin by thinking carefully about your needs. You may be a person who is introverted and private. Such a person probably loves enclosed courtyard areas and screened nooks surrounded by dense foliage.

If you are an extroverted, gregarious person, perhaps a large open area where you and your friends can congregate, have barbecues or play games is your preference. A combination of the two could be ideal if you're like most people, somewhere in between.

Needless to say, unless you live alone, your needs may have to be modified somewhat to allow for the differing ones of your partner or perhaps children. But, unless the yard is very, very small, you can easily create a section that is yours entirely, one where you can totally indulge yourself while the rest of the yard caters for the whims of the rest of the family.

Look carefully at the photographs on adjacent pages. They illustrate what is possible for those who plan — and dare to dream.

What makes a great backyard? All I can do is to help you answer the question for yourself. In the probing that follows, be honest or the result will be disappointing.

What backyards have you liked? Blank off your mind from the shortcomings of your particular catastrophe and think of memorable yards you've been in: those belonging to your friends, neighbours and relatives.

Cast your memory net wider. If you've travelled, you must have special memories of wonderful places you've visited: the grounds of castles and palaces, botanical gardens, other outdoor situations where you suddenly felt comfortable and at peace.

Signs of a well-planned garden: bougainvillea thriving in the sun and impatiens flowering in the shade.

Probably you didn't stop to analyse why you felt so good at the time. If the places are close at hand, it might be a useful exercise to revisit them. Alternatively, drag out those old slides and try to figure out why a particular setting made you feel so good. Identification of the positive elements will help you to plan a backyard to suit your particular needs.

Remember that human beings respond, albeit differently, to certain colours and smells, areas of warmth and coolness, differences in texture, changes in perspective and space, types and volume of noise, the proximity of birds, animals and other humans.

Draw up a list of your likes and dislikes regarding outdoor environments both natural and built. Get your partner to do likewise. With any luck there will be some common ground.

Before we go any further, we now need to look briefly at the items that, combined, make a successful backyard. Keep in mind, however, that a backyard is always more than the sum of its parts.

I have included a full list of items (each of which is detailed more fully in later topics) for your consideration. I'm not suggesting that you try to include them all. You can accept each item, put it on hold, or reject it. This list may help you to identify the things that you liked so much and would like to emulate about some of the memorable places you've visited.

Immediately the list divides itself into two sections: the living environment which covers plants, shrubs and trees, and the inanimate or built environment, consisting of items such as fences, pergolas, decks, paths and garden furniture.

The Living Environment

The living environment is what most creates the feeling of paradise. Sadly we humans, like plants, are mortal. To live in an environment of vigoursly growing plants, shrubs and trees keeps us feeling continually renewed as our gardens go through their own repetitive cycles of life and death.

Plants soften our world, bring naturalness into our often artificial surroundings, harbour hundreds of insects and birds, create oxygen and conjure up a myriad of changing colours that ebb and flow with the seasons.

While the different types of plants, shrubs and trees are more fully covered in a later section, keep in mind the following facts.

- Flowers, whether they are attached to plants, shrubs or trees, bloom at different times. Careful planning can ensure a carousel of colour most of the year.
- Some flowers are annuals, meaning they last only a season and then die. Others are biennials, having a two-year life span. There are also perennials which continue growing and flowering for a number of years.
- Some trees lose their leaves in winter. This can be handy for creating summer shade while allowing the sun through in winter. Others, the evergreen variety, never lose their foliage. Shrubs have similar characteristics.
- Attractive gardens are achieved by careful attention to the arrangement of plant and tree heights, colours and shapes. Think about the places that have impressed you. They certainly weren't achieved by the owner going to the local nursery, buying everything in sight, then planting them indiscriminately. Everything must be carefully placed to achieve balance and harmony.

The variety of plants is infinite. But before you become overawed at the prospects of having to sort through them all, accept that not all of them grow well or even at all in your area. The local nursery will advise on which plants best suit your particular neck of the woods. If you add to this limiting factor your own likes and dislikes, the choices shrink again.

A truly robust garden, albeit a rather grand one.

Styles of Garden

Then there is the important point of creating a gardening theme, one that features certain acceptable combinations of flowers and trees. As you'd probably decorate your house with a theme in mind regarding colour, texture, furniture style, etc., so should you approach the garden. The reason is the same: to avoid a hotchpotch. This thematic concept will again substantially reduce your plant choices.

The topography of your land should be used to best advantage when selecting a garden theme. If the land falls, then terracing can be a feature, along with perhaps a series of cascades or a waterfall. If it's flat, then it would be more practical to opt for a more formal garden with large lawn areas.

Raised and sunken gardens can be used to liven up a site that is level or monotonously undulating. A sunken garden involves creating a separate, lower area much like a minuscule amphitheatre. A raised garden may be an elevated terrace or, on a smaller scale, a raised flower bed surrounded by a brick or timber edging.

Either can be partially paved or covered with lawn and then edged with flowers, rose bushes, etc. For sunken areas, some excavation and steps may be involved but the effect can be entrancing.

To summarise, there is a subtle relationship between trees, shrubs, flowers, groundcover and lawns which either works for psychological harmony or against it. This harmony is achieved by planning. Like a great painting, everything is in a certain place. But of course if you do make a few wrong choices it's easy enough, while things are small, to do a bit of transplanting, trimming or replacing.

Like paintings, gardens come in a variety of styles. As you look at the brief description of the following garden types, you should keep in mind that usually the more formal and structured the garden, the more work. If your backyard is to be a haven of relaxation you may not want to spend one to one and a half days of every weekend maintaining it (unless you find such endeavours relaxing).

Remember that it is not necessary to make the whole garden one type. You can mix several types with success providing you create separate areas with screens.

Bush or Wild Gardens

As the name implies, a wild garden is the opposite of manicured perfection and is characterised by a theme of more or less contrived abandonment, much like a patch of untended bush through which paths meander and wildflowers bloom. It may even look unkempt to many but that belies the careful planning it needs. However, once established, it provides the maximum effect for the least work.

A beautiful formal garden with the beds divided by hedges.

The photographs clearly show there are no neat rows of flowers or lawns like bowling greens. Instead flowers of similar height and vigour burst from random positions. Groundcover is generally used instead of lawn or the grass is allowed to grow long. This, in combination with small perennials or low shrubs, creates areas of openness which contrast with taller shrubs and shady trees. If you're a person who likes an organised underlying structure, this kind of garden will not satisfy you.

Another version of this garden is the cottage garden, based on the gardens which surround English country cottages. This style of garden is characterised by a seemingly random profusion of mixed flowers, herbs and fruit trees and often long meadow grass.

Formal Gardens

Formal gardens are characterised by order and neatness. Lawns are bordered by neat mowing strips, judiciously pruned plants grow in barbered rows, and masses of colour are provided by bedding plants. These are gardens that win prizes and are the result of endless hard work by dedicated owners. This is indeed a garden for those who love order and toil. It brings them pure joy.

Another kind of formality is epitomised in the Japanese garden in which subtle organisation contributes to a feeling of peace and restraint ideal for meditation.

Courtyard Gardens

Used to great effect by the Egyptians, Greeks and Romans, this is the style of garden favoured by inner city dwellers in terrace and town houses. Build a high solid wall around the yard (or a section of it) using something like concrete block or masonry, and then grow medium height shrubs or vines against the wall to soften the hard lines (trees tend to dominate and crowd). A paling fence with or without high lattice and fast-growing vines can create the same enclosed effect at less cost.

The interior area can then be designed to include a pond, fountain, garden beds, a barbecue and seating area with stone or brick paving. With paving, avoid red colours especially if you experience a hot summer climate.

Everything should be kept to a small scale — no giant angophoras here! Judicious use of window-boxes, tubs, planters, lattice-backed shelving, raised garden beds, pergolas and paving combined with suitable and well chosen plant species will create the interest of a much larger garden.

Wild gardens must be carefully planned, but once established can look after themselves.

The easiest garden of all to maintain, a courtyard is the ideal spot for lunch.

The Built Environment

In a successful backyard, the living environment is complemented and enhanced by introducing selected man- or woman-made objects.

There are many possibilities, some large, some small. As you read through the following list, make a tentative decision concerning their degree of importance. Why not make a note of the preferred items as you go?

Consider the following: fences, courtyard walls and gates; ponds, cascades and fountains; decks and pave areas; pergolas, trellises, arches and lattice screens; gazebos and garden shelters; swimming pools and spas; paths and steps, to say nothing of retaining walls, watering systems, rockeries, outdoor lights, barbecues, bridges, play gyms, swings and sand pits, and an area for drying clothes.

Again balance is important. There can be too many things, which clutter the area and spoil its naturalness, while too few make the area less useful and less used.

Planning Basics

Now you have a general idea of the main factors which, correctly chosen, can create a backyard paradise. Selected ones have to be fitted into the available area you have with consideration to:

- the topography of your site (whether it's level, undulating, sloping);
- the aspect of the yard, and whether there is a view;
- the soil quality and type;
- the climate and general situation of your backyard; and
- the style of your house and the overall style of the immediate neighbourhood (these are also important factors that should be considered when deciding which type of backyard will best harmonise with you and your intended lifestyle).

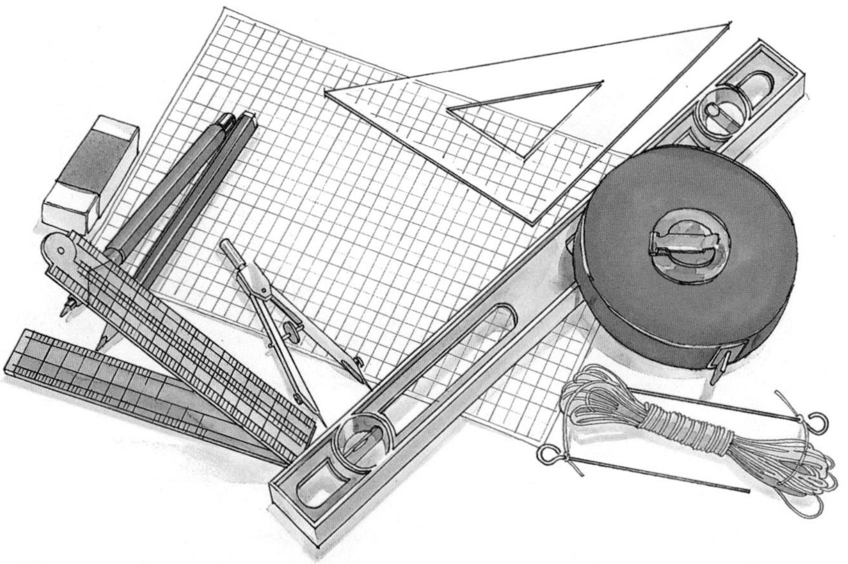

Diagram 1 A few items of inexpensive equipment will help you plan your backyard with a high degree of accuracy.

You could be forgiven for thinking at this point that the whole exercise is too complex, that there are too many things to consider, that you don't have the knowledge and skills to plan it all, let alone do the work.

What follows will help to simplify the whole process by taking you slowly through the vital planning steps, then get you started on the preliminary work. Once you've begun, I'll tempt you to undertake this project, then that. Before you know it, paradise regained!

If it takes two or three years, so what! The main thing is that you have a plan that is worth working towards. When it comes together you'll be glad you undertook it because suddenly you'll have, right outside your back door, an oasis, somewhere safe from the inhospitable desert that life often is.

Earlier I encouraged you to think about your needs and preferences concerning a backyard and jot them down. Now comes the time to translate these vague preferences into something tangible, to match the dream with the reality, so to speak.

Measuring and Drawing the Plan

Before you begin, you must accurately determine how big an area you have to work with. After all, it's not much use planning to include a mini-golf course, a swimming pool and a virtual botanical garden if you only have a pocket handkerchief backyard.

Hopefully you will be able to lay your hands on an up-to-date survey of your property showing the house in relationship to the boundaries (survey plan, see Diagram 2). Reproducing this plan to a larger scale will give you an exact layout of the available area complete with sizes.

If the plans have been misplaced and the block is a rectangular shape, use a 5–10 metre tape to measure the boundaries accurately.

Then, using a rough sketch, locate the house position and size. When measuring, remember that the tape must be held level otherwise your sizes will be inaccurate. Line the tightly stretched tape up with a nearby fascia, ridge or brick fence to ensure reasonable accuracy.

Double check your measurements after you've sketched out the block. Ignore existing items such as hoists, paths, sheds and gates but show exits from the house, windows, and major buildings such as garages and carports. The ability to ignore certain items is important because when you're planning you don't want to be mentally limited by objects that can be easily removed or relocated.

Using a 2B pencil, accurately draw the backyard to scale on as large a piece of paper as you can get. Graph paper is excellent for drawing up regular blocks. Tape it to a plastic-laminated kitchen bench to hold it steady. A scale of 1:50 is adequate. An inexpensive plastic protractor is useful for marking angles.

If the block is irregular, don't try to measure it. Go to your local council and request a copy of the plans or get a new survey done. The chances are that your intended improvements include new fencing and you'll need an up-to-date survey for that anyway.

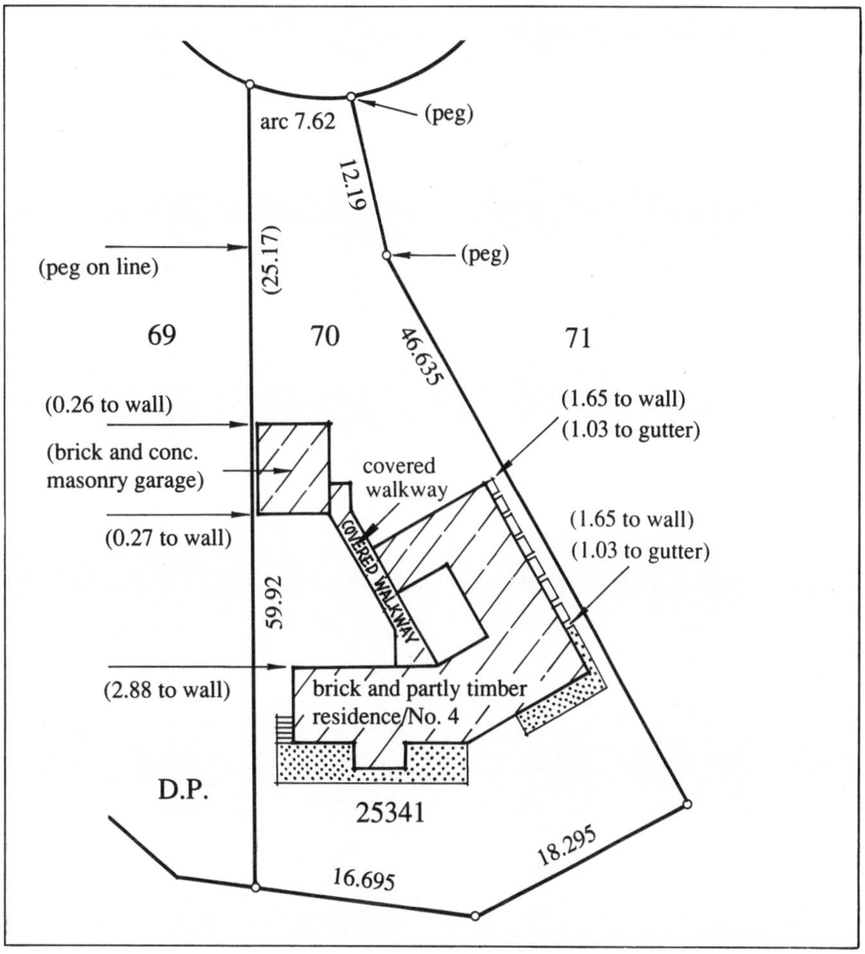

Diagram 2 A typical survey plan

Ranking Needs

Now, begin to relate the available area to your list of needs. Typically, the dog wants a large open area to play on; the children want a pool and some trees to climb or build a tree house in; your partner wants to chat to the neighbours and do a lot of entertaining, and to grow cumquats and roses; whereas you hate gardening and want a secluded low-maintenance backyard, one with high fences, a maze of paths, leafy nooks and ponds. It seems impossible. But is it?

Keep in mind that a yard can be likened to a house. Your house has many different activity areas separated by walls. The person who designed your house hopefully thought carefully about the activities and related them to the available space, space set by the limitations of your or the previous owner's budget. You still chose your house because you felt it best fulfilled your family's needs, given the money you had to spend. Unless you're ultra-rich, some compromises were called for. Why expect different parameters to exist in your backyard?

Cull through your list of needs and preferences (add any extra ones that you may want) concerning the living and inanimate environments and highlight in red the ones that are essential, otherwise divorce or runaway children will result. Highlight in blue the ones that are highly preferred. Use green for the ones that are medium priority. Low priority items should be left untouched. Next go through and numerically rank each colour group in terms of importance beginning at the number one.

If the pool survives this evaluation as red 1 to 3, it must be treated with first priority. This is not only because it will undoubtedly be the most expensive item, it is also the most area-consuming one. The installation of a pool may disturb other features in the yard, too. As well, it usually becomes the focal point of your backyard around which the other factors revolve like moons.

The Preliminary Sketches

Using the same scale as you've used for the enlarged drawing of the backyard, draw the pool (if any) to scale on blue cardboard and, with a trimming knife or scissors, cut it out. Likewise accurately draw and cut out other shapes which represent the plan of vegetable beds, lawns, decks or patios, gazebos, barbecues or ponds — anything in the red and blue zone of your list that takes up space. Use colours that closely approximate the materials you will be using. This will help you to get the big picture of your plan.

Then make up some templates to represent shrubs, planters, pots. If you're unsure of sizes, measure the items. For example, an average shrub will take up a roughly circular shape with a 1–2 metre diameter, a small tree to 3 metres with a larger tree anywhere from 3–10 metres or more.

Draw the circles with compasses or use coins, tops of bottles, etc. Remember that few trees have branches that come right down to the ground. Trees therefore do not occupy ground space beyond the small area taken by the trunk. Don't place trees too close to paths, patios, house footings and drainage pipes unless you particularly like eventual problems, some major. Ask yourself if a tree is needed to bring shade or privacy.

When you draw in a circle to represent a tree, mark on it the maximum height you want it to be. Also mark whether it should be deciduous or evergreen.

The templates, once completed, can be juggled around the plan of the backyard to get the best intermix. Place the items marked in red first, largest to smallest, then blue. If there's a pool, try to put it in a position where it gets maximum sun and least wind (except of course a cooling summer breeze). Keep in mind the design of your house. Protect a view from the windows.

Designate areas of the backyard for different activities. Keep mutually exclusive areas well apart. After all, your bedroom is unlikely to be adjacent to the lounge room so don't put a noisy play area like a pool or open lawn next to a thickly-treed retreat. Create a buffer zone such as a paved barbecue area in between.

Trees

While juggling, keep in mind factors such as maximising the warmth of the winter sun and creating privacy. Use trees, walls and fences to screen out things such as bad winds, ugly buildings and power stanchions. Trees are especially useful for this type of yard enhancement (see Diagram 3) or to frame a view. Keep in mind that trees develop to set heights. Use this fact to create tall borders either side of views creating a tunnelling effect, 3–4 metre high leafy barriers to blot out an eyesore, or 2 metre shrubs or hedges to make nooks and define areas of activity.

With eyesores, if you're uncertain as to what height you need, simply draw to scale a cross section through your yard and the eyesore. Working from your eye level when seated or walking around, draw a line to the top of the eyesore. Then, near the boundary, draw a vertical line to meet the sight line. This approximates to the height you require (see Diagram 4).

Because trees are slow growing, it is also important to use to good effect any trees that are currently growing on your block. Should the converse apply and a tree or group of trees appears to be spoiling your planning, you'd need to inquire at your local council to see what tree preservation laws apply.

Regarding aspect, your house

Diagram 3 A row of trees is an effective way to screen out tall buildings.

plans should have marked on them where north is so you can easily ascertain the compass points and from that mark in the favourable and unfavourable areas of your backyard. You don't want any high trees or walls that will block out the warming winter sun. You may be able to use dense trees on a boundary as a windbreak and create sheltered sunny spots that will not be shaded by the house.

When designing a windbreak, keep in mind that a screen made from a high wall or tall dense trees can in fact create problems. This is because the wind, thwarted by the obstruction, tends to lift over it and swirl turbulently on the other side where you want shelter. In the case of a wall, unless it is especially well constructed, there is also the risk of it blowing over. If room permits, the ideal windbreak is wedge-shaped and slightly open (see Diagram 5). This allows some of the wind to filter through while the wedge shape carries the bulk of the wind gradually upwards, allowing it to pass relatively smoothly over the yard.

If space is limited use a fence like a brushwood fence which allows some wind penetration. If a solid wall is a must, turbulence on the windward side may be lessened by an upward-sloping skillion roof or vine-covered pergola. This not only modifies the effects of the wind but also gives you added privacy that doesn't obscure your neighbour's view or access to the sun.

Small Blocks

You can add depth and width to small blocks by using the optical illusions created by a series of parallel lines. Think of a striped dress or shirt. Vertical stripes tend to narrow the width and extend the length, an important factor if you're more rotund than you'd like to be. By using materials such as paving blocks which have long joint lines, you can create similar visual trickery. Lay the long lines across the land to increase its width. Use long and narrow island garden beds which jut out at random from either of the side boundaries rather than a fringe of bed around the fences to increase the illusion of width. Alternatively use wavy beds which undulate away from the fence then back again (see Diagram 6A). Similarly, trellises or pergolas cutting across the block give the impression of increased width.

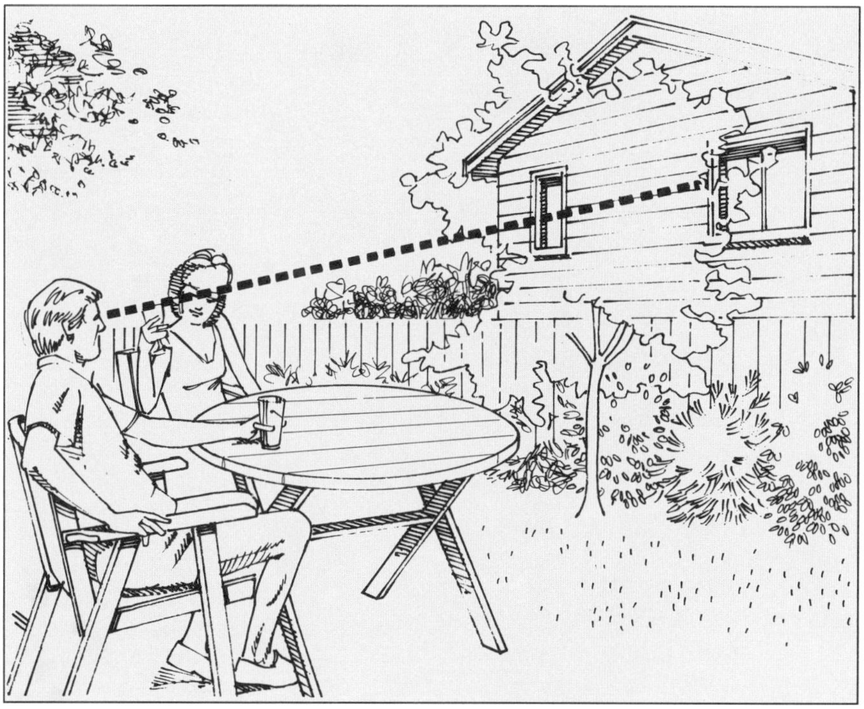

Diagram 4 This proposed tree will hide an unwanted view and provide privacy.

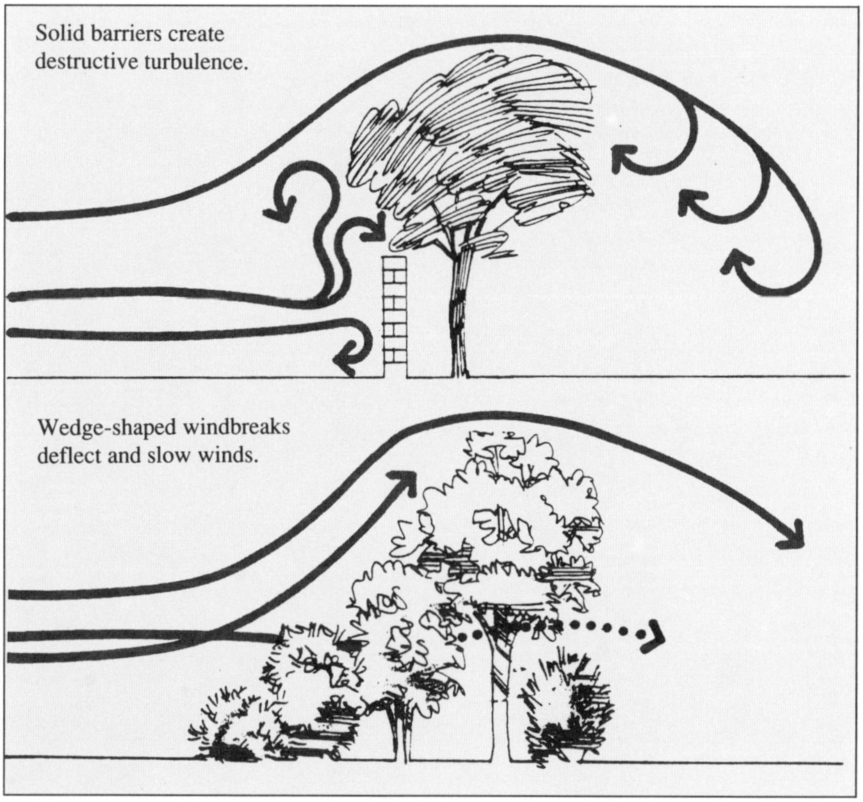

Solid barriers create
destructive turbulence.
Wedge-shaped windbreaks
deflect and slow winds.

Diagram 5

To increase the depth of the yard, run the lines of garden, lawn, edging and paving down the block (but keep in mind that this will shrink the width). By decreasing the height of plants and shrubs as they move down the yard you can also add to the longer yard illusion. This is because the further things are away from your eye, the smaller they get. By artificially creating this effect you trick your own eyes and those of your admiring visitors (see Diagram 6B).

Use the train line effect to advantage (the lines gradually move together in the distance), by making gardens along the fence gradually wider as they progress down the yard and paths progressively narrower. The lengthening effect is further increased. The combination of all these factors could make your tiny yard look like the sixteenth fairway.

Achieving the Final Plan

After a few marathon jigsaw efforts, it may soon become apparent that you are trying to get too much into your backyard. After consultation with the other interested parties, individual items can then be deleted or decreased in size. If you're lucky and there's still plenty of room, make up templates of additional optional items and continue. Don't forget to allow for linking paths.

When planning, also keep in mind the positions of services such as electricity, sewerage lines, etc. Building over services, replacing or relocating them can prove to be very expensive. If you don't have information on the whereabouts of underground lines, seek it out from supply authorities or the council.

A simplified development of a typical plan is shown in Diagram 7.

Some midnight pondering over several glasses of wine may be necessary to select the most suitable plan. Try not to be influenced too directly by the designs that are shown. You and your backyard are unique. The two have to harmonise.

arrange lawns across the block
avoid fence-like garden beds. Have peninsulas jutting out into the centre instead
lay paving units across rather than down the block

Diagram 6A To add width

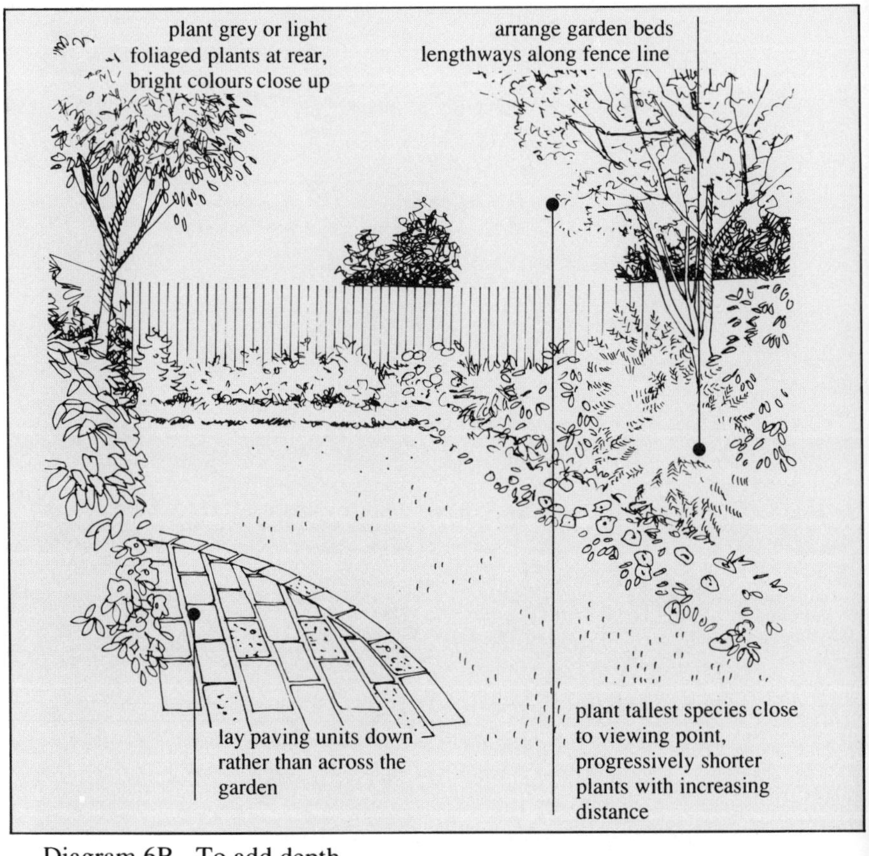
plant grey or light foliaged plants at rear, bright colours close up
arrange garden beds lengthways along fence line
lay paving units down rather than across the garden
plant tallest species close to viewing point, progressively shorter plants with increasing distance

Diagram 6B To add depth

Calling in an Expert

Perhaps at this stage of the planning process, instead of a sense of exultation as you visualise your earthly paradise, you are totally confused. Surrounded by a multitude of dog-eared coloured templates, a score of possible plans complete with a hundred untidy rubbing-outs and several dirty wine glasses, you feel like screaming.

If this is the case, or you simply can't make up your mind, it may be time for you to consult a landscaping expert. There are specialists in landscaping who will undertake to give you some ideas, prepare sketches, draw full working drawings, and even arrange to have the whole job done while you lie in a hammock on the sidelines and give encouragement between sips of your Martini. Like most things, it's all a question of money.

The cost of an expert could range from a few hundred dollars to many thousands but you have to keep in mind the potential value you could add to your home with a professionally planned backyard. Finding the right person is probably the hardest job. As with any work, a recommendation from a friend or relative is a good start. Keep your eyes open when driving around. If you see a spectacular front yard and you're the extroverted type, knock on the front door and ask whether the job was professionally done and, if so, by whom. If the owners did it themselves they'll be highly complimented and there's nothing lost. If all else fails, ring a few landscape designers in your area and have them come over with a folio of their work.

Before you decide on a landscape designer and/or landscaper, make sure you have a contract which stipulates the total price, the maximum time the contract will take (excluding wet weather), the starting date, the progress payments, retention figures and other details.

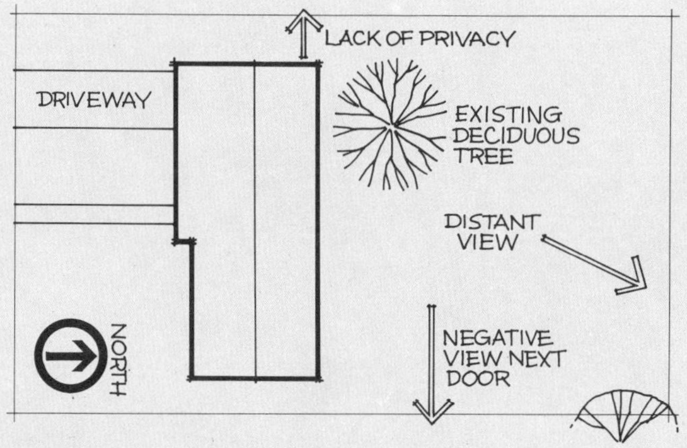

As it is

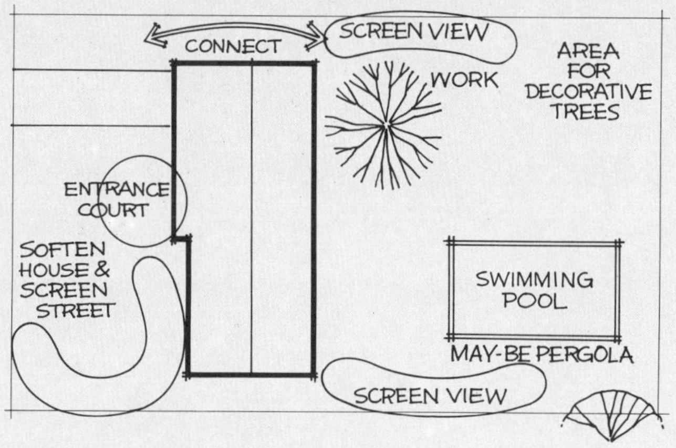

Proposed structural changes

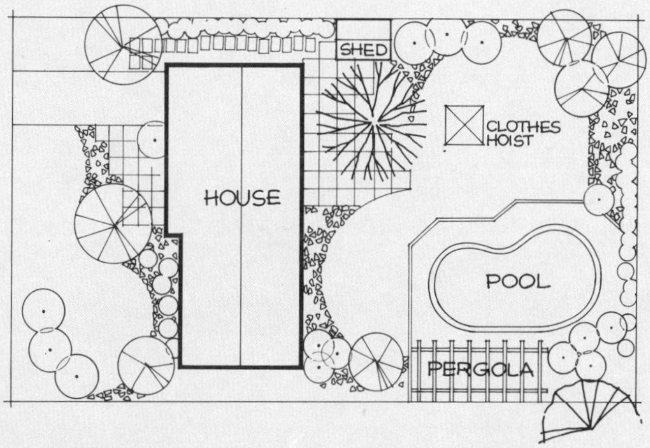

Final plan

Diagram 7

CHAPTER 7

LAYING THE FOUNDATIONS

The next phase in creating your own beautiful backyard involves initiating the actual physical changes. It is probably best to begin by excavating the pool (if any) while simultaneously doing any level changing or levelling off. Build any retaining walls now as well. Then attack the fences, drainage and underground electricity lines (either moving or installing), followed by paved or concrete patios, paths and decks. Once that stage is finished, change direction and start going up by creating trellises and screens, pergolas and gazebos. Then add things like benches and bird baths. The planting of trees, shrubs, flowers and lawns completes the undertaking. Then it's time to sit back and enjoy the paradise you've created.

Identifying Tasks

First you'll need to identify those things which you won't attempt yourself. Projects like high brick and block walls (for such retaining walls, you'll have to get proper engineering design and drawings and you may also need geotechnical reports), elaborate gazebos (unless in kit form), moving sewage lines and building swimming pools are either beyond the capabilities of the average backyarder or require a licence. Crib block retaining walls made from concrete or treated pine can, if you're industrious, be erected but don't forget to get them inspected during construction.

Many structural items require the submission of plans to the local council along with building applications and attendant fees. The plans can be drawn up by a competent draughtsperson fairly cheaply if you know what you want.

It is important to be realistic about what you can achieve by yourself. If you embark on a big job and find you can't finish it you will then have the problem of finding someone who will. A half-finished job is shunned by most tradespeople and builders.

Once you've identified all the jobs in the too-hard basket, consult your yellow pages or local paper and organise to get several quotes. Don't necessarily jump at the lowest quote — it may reflect poor workmanship, faulty materials, etc. Word-of-mouth recommendations regarding tradespeople are the most reliable source of information.

Try to have the work done in a logical sequence where no one undoes the work of another, and where the tradespeople aren't tripping over themselves. While the trade work is progressing, you can get on with other things.

A dark coloured interior gives this pool a moody look.

The plants around the pool have been carefully chosen because they don't drop their leaves.

Pools

If a pool is a possibility, you need to quickly establish four things:

- the approximate pool size you really need (as opposed to what you'd perhaps prefer),
- the pool construction and finish,
- the number of accessories you require such as solar heating, type of filtration, cleaning equipment,
- the approximate price.

An afternoon visit to several pool builders who have demonstration pools will quickly acquaint you with the basics.

Size and Shape

A popular-sized swimming pool is around 9–10 m x 4.5 m. This is long enough to swim in and wide enough for a number of people to enjoy simultaneously. The depth usually ranges from 0.9–1.8 m. Pools of course can be much larger and, more often, much smaller.

Don't be unnecessarily deterred by a smaller pool. Think carefully about what you want the pool for. If you have no ambitions to be a long-distance swimmer or your children are unlikely to be Olympic sprinters then a smaller pool, say 5 x 3.6 m (or even smaller), may prove adequate for the kids as well as for dunking yourself in after floating about in a leisurely way on your air pillow.

Shape is largely a matter of personal choice but typically a rectangular or circular shape would rest well in a formal garden while a kidney or similar free-form curved pool would suit a more casual yard.

Keep in mind the internal finish. A whitish interior will give a blue look that is good for spotting debris and also possibly the occasional funnelweb spider, which can live underwater for several days. A gold or brown interior creates a greenish, creek-type effect which might look better in a bush setting. Try to see your favoured shape and interior colour before signing any contract.

Position

The siting of the pool is important. It should ideally be placed in an area that gets maximum sun all year around, least cold wind, and be well away from leaf-shedding trees. The following photographs show some in-ground pools.

When siting the pool, keep in mind where drainage lines and potential areas of rock are and avoid them. Consider also the effect of noise and splashing on neighbours and the need for privacy.

The topography of your site will probably influence the construction

A pool can be created in any shape to suit your yard.

Bricks make a pleasing pool surround, especially when softened with plants.

technique and materials. If the site is fairly level you have two options: the above-ground pool or the excavated in-ground pool. An above-ground pool has the disadvantage of exposing the sides of the pool although this aesthetic headache can be lessened by surrounding it with a deck.

In-ground pools can be expensive especially if you strike rock. This factor is discussed later. A sloping site allows above-ground construction (which can also be expensive because of the formwork involved) while still creating the in-ground appearance from one side.

Materials

Pools are made from a variety of materials. Concrete is popular although it is very expensive to lay and finish. Fibreglass is another favourite which, like concrete, allows unlimited design but is generally cheaper. The liner will arrive already shaped to your design. An impervious finish added to the fibreglass resists staining and removes the need for tiling or painting. The fibreglass can also be tinted to any colour you choose, although blues, greens and natural rock colours are the most popular.

Fibreglass can also be sprayed onto a concrete shell to give a smooth finish. More typically it is sprayed onto a mould in a factory and then brought pre-formed to your site and lowered by crane into a prepared excavation. This latter method is widely used because of its quickness.

Aluminium or steel sided, above-ground pools with vinyl liners make up a cheaper, third major type. A disadvantage of this construction is that the water depth is restricted to around 1.2 metres.

Price

The eventual price of the pool relates to its size, materials used, the site problems, the method of construction, the equipment required (type and output of filters, number of square metres of solar heating, number and type of lights, etc.). The only way to get some idea of the price is to get a quote. Tell the pool company (select at least three) you want a preliminary estimate.

Keep in mind, however, that the price you get may be understated by many thousands of dollars. Some pool builders come in low to secure the contract then hit you for endless extras. Others may come in high and still hit you for extras. It depends among other things on the integrity of the company, how they cost extras such as rock (costed at nearly $100 per cubic metre), extra cartage to remove spoil over the small allowable limit (in some cases only a laughable 5 kilometres), the possibility of expensive tip fees, any above or below-ground formwork required, piering if the foundation material is uneven, cost of backfilling (unless you do it yourself), pumping out the pool, etc. The list, and the costs should be considered very carefully.

But the costs don't end there! What about landscaping, electrical connections and pool fencing (to say nothing of the cost of repairing all the paths, driveways and lawns that may be damaged but for which many pool builders accept no liability under the 'underfoot' clause).

This pool is bordered by an unusual hedge of ivy.

Landscaping and Fencing

A pool, like a painting, has to be surrounded by something appropriate if it is to look its best. The cost of elaborate landscaping, if you have it done by a subcontractor, could well exceed the pool cost.

This cost can be lessened if you do it yourself. Remember the following: large areas of paving around a pool, unless exceedingly well done, can make it look like a public bath. Regarding plants, don't put prickly ones or those that shed leaves at a great rate anywhere near the pool. Likewise, don't bring the lawn up to the pool because grass clippings will find their way into the water.

Don't forget the mandatory requirement for fencing the pool. The cost of pool fencing is anywhere between $90 and $200 a metre, depending on the materials used. All steel products should be hot-dipped galvanised, especially if the pool is a saltwater one or is anywhere near the coast. Check that your boundary fence meets the requirement if you intend to make it part of the safety fencing. It may have to be changed to comply.

Electrical Requirement

Not only do you need to run electricity to the place where the filters, time switches, etc., are installed but you also have to run the wiring to the pool for the lights. The pool also has to be earthed.

All electrical equipment should be placed in an out-of-the-way position and covered with a suitable box, assuming no alcove or shed exists. Allow $500–600 minimum for this.

Finding a Reliable Builder

Finding a reliable builder is arguably the most difficult part of the pool building process. When selecting quotes, try to get them from members of the relevant swimming pool association in your state. The association offers mediation if disputes arise and can expel members who don't toe the line. The Building Services Corporation or a similar government body gives you a second and more powerful backup.

Lattice can hide a multitude of sensible sins such as fencing.

The greatest recommendation you can get is from a happy client. Ring every friend or relative you have who has a pool and ask a series of searching questions about the construction of their pool.

When the contract is offered, go through it with the salesperson clause by clause. Get the salesperson to give you, in writing, an estimated cost for each variation.

Because rock is such an expensive item, if there is any possibility that it exists, may I suggest you roughly mark out the area where the pool is going, then dig a series of holes at one metre centres with a post hole borer over the whole area of the pool. If rock (under the contract definition) exists, get the salesperson to give a firm price of how much is involved in removing it before you sign the contract (get an independent party to check the figures). Then you know the maximum you're up for.

I'd strongly advise you to employ an engineer to supervise the whole project and to check each variation. His costs are small, the savings high.

Assuming you've bitten the bullet and signed the contract, what follows is typical of pool construction. (I've taken a concrete, in-ground pool as an example.) The pool should be started at the same time as the earthworks. The reason for this is that any fill from the pool may be able to be used elsewhere on the site.

Excavation

Firstly, the supervisor (or contract builder) arrives and roughly sets out the job, putting in a series of steel pegs around which a hose is pulled. Make sure you're happy with the position and shape because once the excavators start, it's a *fait accompli*.

The excavators will begin to dig out the pool, which can be done in a day. Be prepared to have lawns and gardens crushed and paths and driveways broken as large machines move into position. The area will quickly look like a disaster zone.

If the machine strikes rock, which is defined as anything that can't be dug out with the bucket on the machine, the excavators will skim the soil off the area of the pool, then stop. A 'quick' estimate is made of the quantity to be taken out. You may then be forced to sign a variation sheet accepting the quantities they've calculated and agreeing to pay the amount of money involved otherwise the job stops. Sign their form, wait until the excavation is complete, and then call in your engineer to check the quantities.

The excavation then proceeds. Once the pool is excavated, the bottom of the excavation is checked. If it has rock in one area only, you're in trouble. This is because the weight of the pool filled with water will not sit correctly on an uneven footing. A bit of unequal subsidence could crack the pool. Constructing piers that go down to solid rock is the only solution. This could be very, very expensive.

Once the excavation is complete, the steel fixers arrive. They set out for the coping along the top edge of the pool and then begin the formwork, shoring and steel.

Formwork and Shoring

Formwork means the erection of temporary forms to outline the shape of the concrete coping, to fill in any holes or collapses in the earth walls, or to hold any concrete that is above ground.

Shoring occurs where you have non-cohesive soil that could collapse into the excavation. It needs to be shored up until the concrete is poured. Your pool company may again have you sign variation sheets agreeing to pay for so many lineal metres of either or both. Your engineer should check their claims.

Spray-up

Once the steel work is finished and inspected, the concrete spray-up team arrives. An average-sized pool will be completed in less than half a day. The concrete is literally blown onto the walls and because it is both a dryish and a cement-rich mix, it stays there. This operation requires supervision by the pool company.

Finishing Off

Once the shell has cured, the coping will be tiled, the plumbing put in, the lights connected (by your electrician), the filtration and solar system installed (you have to provide power points and time switches), and the backfilling done.

During this finishing off period, you must get your pool fencing done and passed by the council. This is because they won't allow the pool to be filled with water until the fences are approved, and the pool builders won't apply the internal finish unless they can fill the pool with water within a few days, so the pressure is on. To get the fences in place requires you to have the earthworks done, so the finished ground levels can be worked to, so it's a busy time. But with good planning and a level head, it can all be achieved on time.

Steel fixing must be carried out by professionals.

Pool Maintenance

If you've survived the pool building process and the pool has just been filled, you'll no doubt be excited by the crystal clear appearance of the water. Unfortunately, it won't stay that way for very long unless you spend the necessary time maintaining the pool and attending to the water quality.

Of course it's not only the aesthetics of the water that are important. Dirty water can pose a serious health problem. Proper maintenance of a pool requires a two-pronged attack: to remove the solids and to adjust the water chemistry to an optimum level.

Removing Solids

All uncovered pools are subjected to a continual deluge of leaves, dust, insects, hair and, in heavy gales, papers, branches, etc. Obviously most of this debris floats and the skimmer box, which operates when the filter is on, draws the surface water through it and skims off the unwanted items.

Some of the debris, both large and small, may sink before reaching the skimmer box. If it isn't quickly removed, the results will look unsightly, could permanently stain the bottom of the pool, and create conditions favourable to the growth of bacteria and algae.

To get rid of the larger items you can use a hand scoop. This is a time-consuming chore, one hardly compatible with the purpose of the pool. A better way to go is to use a semi-automated, handheld suction cleaning unit or one which works like a robot-controlled vacuum cleaner (both these types operate off the pool pump).

Filters

The filter in your pool is like the petrol filter in your car — if it isn't working properly, the result will be unpleasant. There are three types of filtering systems: sand, diatomaceous earth (DE) and cartridge.

Sand is the most common and relies on forcing the pool water through a bed of sand which traps all but the most minute solids. The sand in time becomes clogged and a gauge on the top of some units shows the amount the water flow is restricted by the clogging. To clean such a unit involves what is called backwashing, that is, forcing water through the sand in a reverse direction and discharging the sediment and dirty water into the sewerage system. This is achieved by a backwash line which is connected to the sewer gully so that the whole procedure can be done by simply turning a valve. The sand doesn't have to be changed for years, making it a very cheap form of filtration.

The DE type uses a series of dacron or polypropylene pads inside a pressurised filter. Crushed DE, a coral-like fossil which has innumerable minute voids, is added to the water. It clings to the pads, forming a 'cake'. The pool water is forced through this cake and minute dirt particles become trapped within the voids. Like the sand filter, the pads are cleaned by backwashing but this involves adding more DE each time to re-form the cake. The pads must be cleaned at least once a year in a light acid solution.

You'll probably need a cartridge type filter if you can't backwash because your area isn't sewered. These filters, which are available as vacuum or pressure types, catch the dirt on the exterior of the cartridge. It can easily be removed for hosing.

Regardless of type, check your filter occasionally and make sure it's clean. In summer, run the filter from eight to twelve hours per day. In winter two to three hours per day will probably suffice.

Chemicals

While the filter and sweeper cleaner remove debris, chemicals are used to remove bacteria and algae. They have a sanitising or sterilising effect. The amount of steriliser required depends on a number of things: where the pool is, the season of the year, the amount of sunlight it is receiving, the rainfall, and the amount of use the pool is getting, so it is a variable factor.

Once the filter and cleaner have done their work, test the pool for alkalinity. This means, in lay terms, checking how much mineral salt there is in the water. An inexpensive test kit obtainable from pool supply shops will check the reading, which should be at least eight to a hundred parts per million. There are more complex electronic monitors which continually test and add what is required. Their price is high but the cost could well prove worth it.

To increase the alkalinity, you add sodium carbonate in accordance with the manufacturer's instruction, then test again. Keep adding until it's right.

Next test the pH factor, which rates the water for acidity and alkalinity. If acidity is zero then alkalinity is 14. If pH measures around 7 then the water is neither too acid or too alkaline. A level of 7½ is preferred, making the water slightly alkaline. If it's higher, then the increased alkalinity decreases the effects of the anti-bacterial agents. If it's too low, the water becomes increasingly acid which leads to stinging eyes, corroded metal fittings, etc. Adding appropriate amounts of acid (a cupful at a time) or sodium bicarbonate controls the pH level.

Chemicals should be mixed in a bucket of water, added to the pool when the filter is going, and checked two hours later when thoroughly mixed.

The final step is to add the sterilisers, which come in granules, tablets and liquids. Chlorine is the most usual one. Two parts per million is usual though more must be added during heavy bathing periods or after storms. If you have a saltwater pool, coarse rock salt is added. In combination with a low voltage current, it forms sodium hypochlorite, an effective sanitiser.

Spas and Tubs

If your finances do not extend to a pool, perhaps a heated spa pool or tub could provide you with a partial substitute. The photographs show just what can be achieved. Spas come in various sizes and can hold up to six or seven adults. The water jets, which work off a pump, can be assisted by a blower. This forces air through the warm water creating a mass of bubbles which play around you, softly massaging and relaxing. The spa pool water requires similar treatment to a pool, that is, filtration and sterilisation. The bigger it is, the more careful you must be.

Tubs, typically made from wood, are similar in construction to a wine barrel. Made from cedar staves held in place by steel bands and stainless steel screws, they provide a totally natural unit that blends in with any backyard landscape.

The timber decking and lattice screen provide intimacy in an outdoor setting.

This spa has the protection of a pergola while still being very much out of doors.

Tools

To do any job properly, you'll require the right tools. Tools for the backyarder can be categorised into three main groups: those for earthworks, building, and gardening.

EARTHWORK TOOLS

Minimum requirements are a mattock, round- and square-mouthed shovel, crowbar, bush saw, a substantial wheelbarrow, axe or hired chainsaw (if the site is heavily overgrown), heavy-duty rake, rock hammer and wedge (if you have to break up a bit of rock) and a water level or spirit level and long straightedge. If the amount of soil to be removed is large, don't be frightened to get a quote for a bobcat. It will achieve in a few hours what will take you weeks. Think of your back! The cost may well be worth it.

BUILDING TOOLS

For starters you'll need a handsaw, combination square, long tape (5 metres minimum) and pencil, jack or smoother plane, hammer, nail punch, 10 mm and 30 mm chisels, various sized screwdrivers (a ratchet one is handy), brace and bits or electric drill and speed borers, adjustable spanner, pliers, cork block and abrasive paper, paintbrushes, trowel, steel or wood float (for finishing concrete), ironing or raking tools (for finishing masonry and stone joints), lump hammer and bolster (for cutting stone and brick).

GARDENING TOOLS

The amateur gardener should gradually acquire: a spade, fork, hedge clippers, hoe, hose with sprinkler and reel, secateurs, clippers, grass rake, handfork, watering can, pump spray, electric or petrol-powered lawnmower and trimmer (whipper-snipper), edger, etc. Some of the tools listed under earthworks and building can also be used for gardening.

Whatever tools you're buying, remember that quality is important. A cheap tool is not cheap if it breaks and you have to buy another. Quality tools, those chosen by professional tradespeople, if used correctly, should last a lifetime. If you divide their price by say thirty years the cost per year will be very small.

Hiring the above tools may be an alternative but, if you're a serious do-it-yourself backyarder, the hire costs will soon exceed the purchase price. This of course doesn't include large items like concrete mixers, electric hammers, chainsaws, etc.

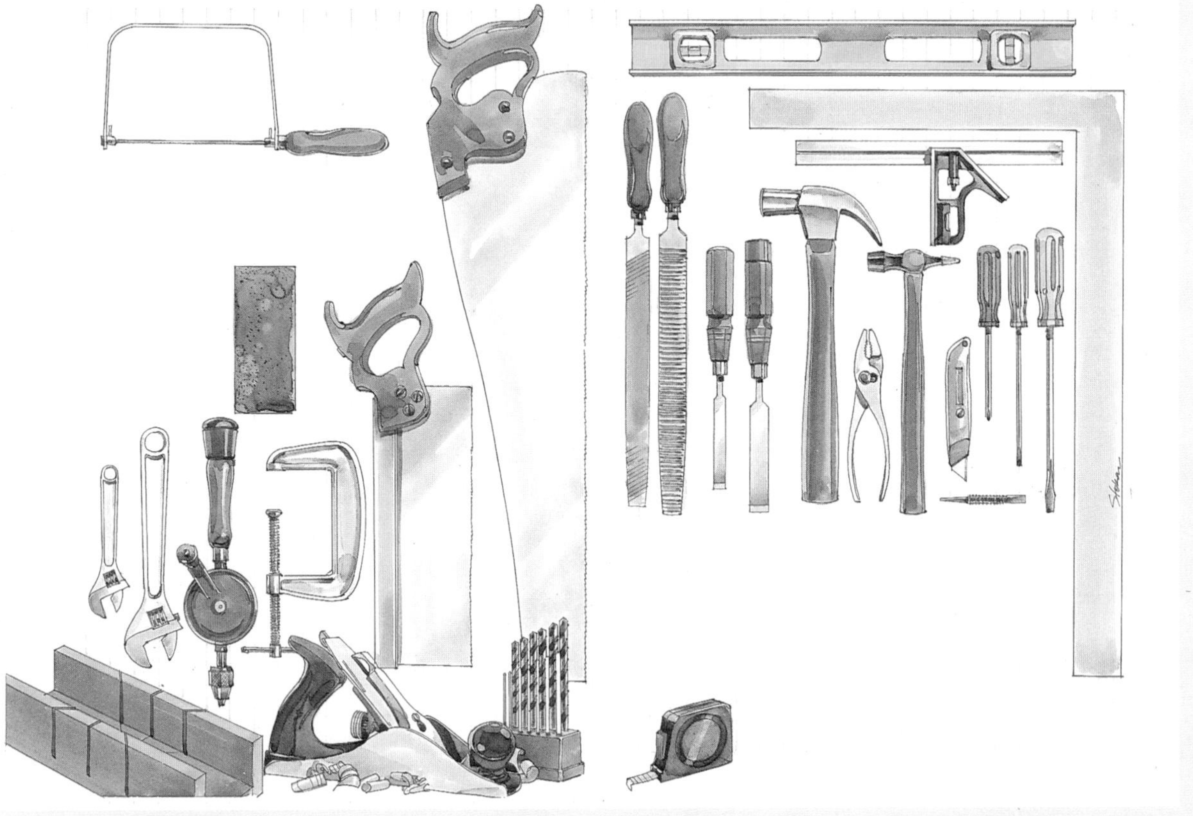

Earthworks

Although this term may sound frightening, it simply means the changing of the levels of your backyard to accommodate plans for level areas, lawns, raised or sunken gardens and so on. Be warned, however — some councils require development applications if the existing topography is to be significantly changed. A phone call to the council will reveal all.

It is important not to be unduly influenced by the existing yard. Unless it is solid rock, often it can easily be changed. On a sloping site, this is done by the cut and fill process (see Diagram 8). You excavate an area out of a slope and throw the fill on the lower side, retaining it with a suitable wall (see page 174). Where you've excavated can be left battered (sloping at 45°) or again retained.

If the site is level and you want to lower an area (watch you don't create a sump which will always be damp or hold water), you have no choice but to excavate and remove the spoil. Raising a garden involves creating a retaining wall (see Terracing page 174), then getting in good quality fill (broken stone or brick and rubble is ideal) and topping it off with good fertile soil.

An important point to remember is that you can't divert surface water onto an adjoining property by changing the natural level of the surface — it's illegal.

This phase, if applicable, is where a cool head is required. You need to look at the amount of physical work involved and relate it to your energy level. Many people, in an attempt to save money, will work for months with a shovel and wheelbarrow and use up all their energy and enthusiasm when the whole job could have perhaps been done in a day with the right equipment.

Earthmoving equipment is admittedly expensive but its quickness offsets that. It ranges in size from the little bobcat, great for situations where access to the backyard is difficult, to large bulldozers. You may have to dismantle a side fence or carport or move some trees to get larger equipment in but it may well be worth it.

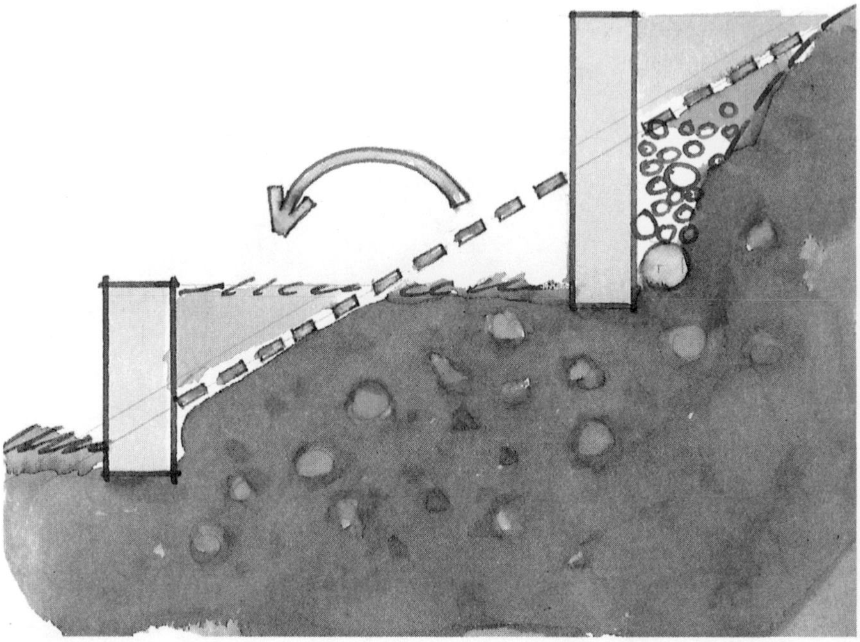

Diagram 8 Sloping sites can be levelled using the cut and fill technique.

Put pegs in to indicate the areas you want filled or excavated and then get at least three prices from local contractors. Make sure they know exactly what you want to achieve and ensure the written quote covers removal of spoil and repairing any damage to kerbs, paths, etc. Keep in mind also that raising the soil level around trees, unless minimal, will kill them. Also remember that fill should be properly retained. Consult with your council regarding current regulations.

In any excavation work, rock is a potential problem. Get a figure from the contractor to include removal of rock, usually quoted at so much a cubic metre. Of course when rock is uncovered you may want to incorporate it into the overall plan (see Rock Gardens on page 176 for suggestions).

Levelling

When setting out for the earthworks (or erecting fences, building pergolas, etc.) you are often confronted with the problem of how to get things level. If they're short, a spirit level can be used. For slightly longer distances, a straightedge and spirit level will suffice. But for long distances such equipment is usually not accurate enough.

One solution is to use a line level. These tiny devices are hung on a taut string line and it is raised or lowered to get it level. The problem with them is that they are not very accurate. A slight knock may throw them out of adjustment. A better solution is to use one of the simplest yet most accurate inventions ever devised: the water level.

The Water Level

The level properties of water have been known about for aeons. Next time you are having a cup of coffee, look at the surface of the liquid. It sits in a level plane with no part higher than the other. Tilt the cup over. No matter how it's tilted the liquid always remains horizontal. It's this principle that was used by the Egyptians for the Pyramids, the Greeks for the Parthenon, and the Romans in their Colosseum. They did it, not using a coffee cup, but by digging trenches around the site and filling them with water. Everything on the building site could then be related to this perfectly level surface.

Of course I'm not suggesting that you build a canal around your property, there's a much easier way. Make a water level which consists of nothing more than some clear plastic tubing, a couple of clothes pegs, and several cupfuls of water.

TOOLS AND MATERIALS

Measure the longest side of the area you need to get level, then get enough 10 mm diameter (or bigger) clear plastic tubing to lay along it plus sufficient extra to allow for a 1.0 to 3.0 m turn-up at each end (this should allow for the fall on most sites). Some garden stakes and a hammer, a tape and pencil, a funnel and some masking tape (should no Person Friday be available) complete the requirements.

PROCEDURE

1 Tape one end of the tubing to the wall, fence or peg that you want to level from. Take the other end to where you want a similar level mark and tape it to the fence or peg, etc.

2 Insert the end of the funnel in the other end of the tube and pour in the water. Fill to within 50 mm of the top with water (you could put dye in the water to make it easier to see).

3 Check along the full length of the tube to make sure there are no air bubbles. These pesky little things, if not eradicated, completely destroy the accuracy of the device. Chase them along the tubing until it is completely filled with liquid.

4 Now take your pencil and mark the height of the water at each end of the tube. These two marks are exactly level. If you measure the same distance above or below these marks, the result will be a perfectly level plane. You can move the tubing to several locations, even around corners and get the same result. You can't do that with a levelling device that relies on a telescope!

When you're finished, simply clamp off each end of the tube with a clothes peg (or cork) and coil up until the next time.

Now fix a level string line between the marks. Measuring down from the string will quickly make any excavation straight. If you want a fall to allow for drainage just make the measurement at one end more than the other and again use the string line to make sure the excavation is absolutely straight.

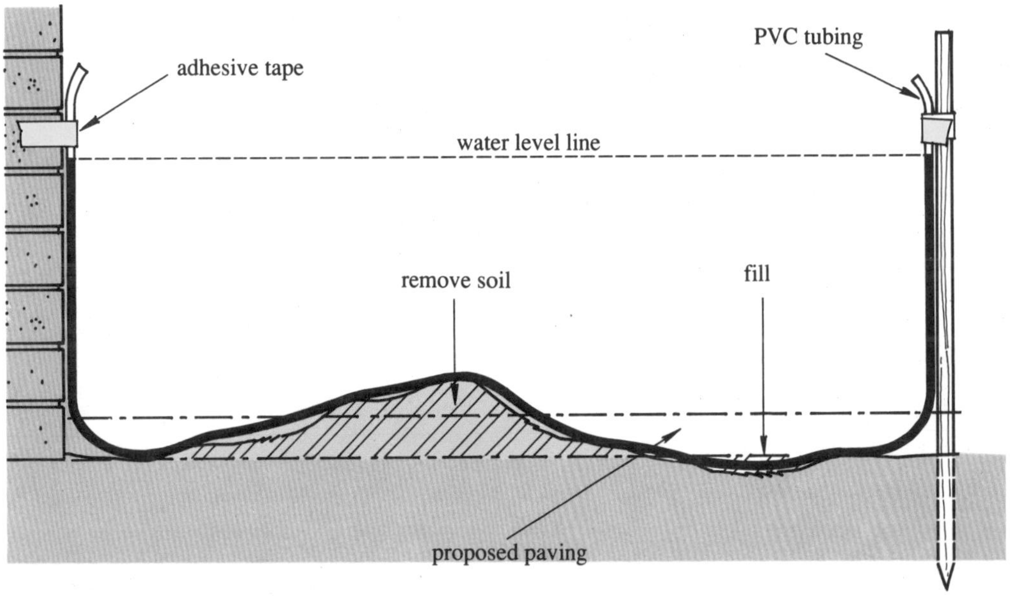

Diagram 9 Using the water level

Terracing and Retaining Walls

If your block is sloping either front to back or side to side, keep in mind that you can quickly create level areas by terracing. That involves the use of retaining walls which, if they're over a metre high, usually require designing by an engineer and approval by your local council.

To establish the potential height, check the slope on your land by using a spirit level and a 3-metre straightedge. Simply lay the end of the straightedge on a representative section of the boundary and level it up. Get someone to measure the distance under the high end. Say it measures 900 mm. This means your block is sloping at 900 mm in every three metres or 300 mm every metre and 100 mm every third of a metre. It is a simple matter then to create a level area that is 3.3 m wide using a metre-high retaining wall which should get you under the council requirement for plans, etc.

Before deciding on the retaining method, think firstly of the aesthetics of your yard. For example, while concrete is a durable, strong product, unless it's painted (which is not always satisfactory if the wall is subject to wetness because lifting paint, salt deposits and mould may result), its grey appearance is more in keeping with roadworks or factories than a backyard paradise.

Stone, brickwork, timber sleepers (laid horizontally or vertically) or treated pine logs create a more natural look.

The theory and design of retaining walls is complex and, if around a metre or more high, become the province of the engineer. But a few elementary principles apply, the knowledge of which will help you to understand what's involved even in making small walls.

Walls are generally either gravity or cantilever. The gravity type (see Diagram 10A) uses more materials and relies on weight to stop overturning. The cantilever type relies more on engineering design to offset the lateral forces. As well as being designed by a professional engineer, a cantilever wall requires extensive formwork for the concrete and is beyond the capabilities of the do-it-yourselfer. Another type of retaining wall is the crib wall, which uses interlocking components.

The type of soil you have will affect the wall design. If soils are cohesive (have a high organic content), there is less force exerted on the wall than if it is non-cohesive (very sandy). Reactive soils such as clay which expand and contract mightily with moisture changes require special treatment.

The success of a retaining wall also depends heavily on the type of backfill behind it and the drainage. A coarse backfill of gravel, crushed brick, sandy soils, graded stone, etc., is necessary to break the enormous natural water pressure which builds up behind the wall. Proper drainage is achieved by introducing a series of weep holes at the base of the wall to allow water to run out and/or the laying of an agricultural pipe behind the wall (see Diagram 10B) which runs to a sump or stormwater line. Your local building inspector should be a great help in advising of local conditions, council regulations regarding materials, height and so on.

A crib wall can provide a perfect bedding for cascading plants.

Railway sleepers or wooden planks can make an effective retaining wall.

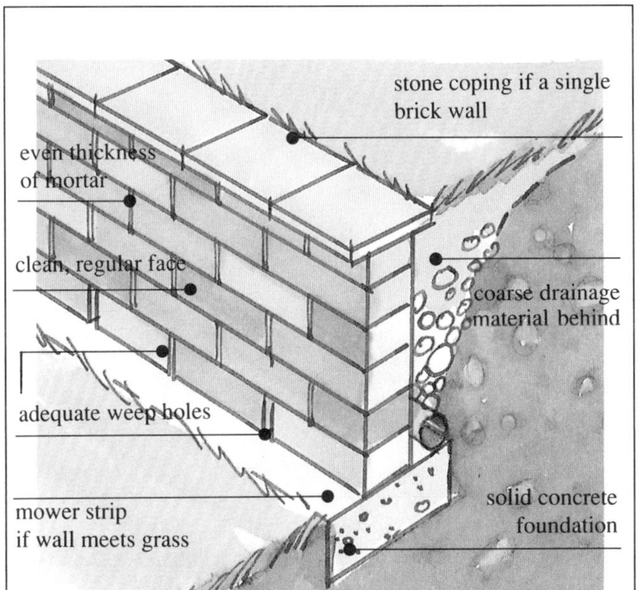

Diagram 10A Gravity retaining wall

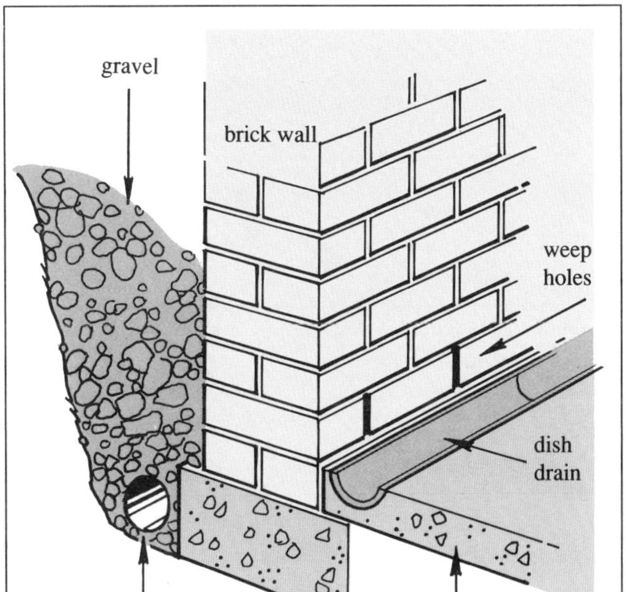

Diagram 10B Retaining wall drainage

Rocks and Boulders

You can add interest to a relatively flat backyard, stabilise an eroding site, or feature changing levels by getting in some huge boulders and arranging them in a collection that looks as if it had been there for millennia. If you already have large boulders on your property, you could consider moving them to a location that will adequately feature them.

Little in life has the permanence of rock. The shape of weathered rock creates a natural sculpture, one that contrasts strongly with the mortal green tissue that, if all goes well, will follow your gardening efforts. Of course, to get rock onto your property involves the use of expensive trucks and, unless they can get to the location, some earth-moving equipment, so don't undertake the project lightly — it won't be cheap. Get a firm price before you begin otherwise the extras may well exceed the cost of the boulders by many times.

If the rock is on your property already and if you are especially innovative, you may be able to move it using large jacks which can be hired. It's amazing how easily it moves once you have cleared its base from the anchoring soil. However this is a slow, difficult process and, if there is a slope involved, you could lose control of your favourite boulder and wipe out several of your neighbours like ninepins!

When creating your rock sculpture keep in mind the following design principles and relate them to your location and personality.

Rock Gardens

Distinct from boulder sculptures is the ubiquitous rock garden. This collection of rocks is designed to become a haunt for plants — trailing perennials, annuals, bulbs, ferns, ground covers and dwarf shrubs. Choose a sunny to dappled shade spot that is out of the reach of strong or cold winds and not too close to trees whose roots could invade the crevices.

The collection of rocks, again some large, some smaller, should not be too high. Big on base and small in height is aesthetically pleasing. Sandstone is a good rock choice because, besides being light, it is porous and holds moisture which helps the plants in dry periods. Arrange the large stones first, burying them between a quarter and a third of their height. A crowbar is handy for levering them into the pre-dug holes.

Try the medium-sized ones in various positions until you have a pleasing result and finish off with the smaller, using their weight or a suitably coloured mortar to lock them into position. Don't make the finishing rocks too small or the rockery will look bitsy.

As you arrange the rocks, allow for various sized depressions and pockets which will entrap soil for the plants to grow in. Unless you live in a near desert environment, allow for the possibility of heavy rain and the eroding effect that can have on new soil. Rockery plants, which come in an amazing range of colours are covered in Chapter 10.

A stunning rock garden overgrown with creepers and perennials.

Fences

While earthworks and large retaining walls are being built, or while you're waiting for any fill to consolidate (an important factor which allows for the inevitable subsidence), fences are the next most convenient project in the building process. They will clearly define the boundaries of your intended endeavours and make planning easier.

A fence is like a frame around a painting — it either complements it, does nothing, or diminishes it. Your local council does not get involved with fences. That is a matter between you and your neighbour. However, the council is interested in the building of small retaining walls on the boundary.

Various types of fences are shown in the accompanying photographs. There is something there to suit every taste but don't be frightened to use more than one material or vary the shape, height, etc. Prices vary according to materials and labour. The cheapest is the humble paling fence. The price then goes up in quantum leaps to cater for elaborate timber, brushwood or metal fences.

Getting agreement on a fence type with neighbours can be difficult although if you offer to pay the majority of the costs, you should have the casting vote. Unresolvable disputes can be taken to the local court for mediation or arbitration, but you should avoid this if at all possible. If the neighbour is difficult or your budget is tight, the existing fence might have to do. Remember

Painted lattice makes a very attractive fence.

that vines such as bougainvillea can quickly cover an eyesore.

Generally, timber fences consist of posts which resist the overturning tendency generated by the wind (and playful children) together with level rails which run between the posts and provide fixing for the palings which can be butted together, lapped over each other, capped on the top, etc. Fixings should be galvanised. The question of which side the palings go on can be resolved by subtle negotiation or heartwrenching compromise.

Natural timber, unless it's expensive cedar or redwood, or the humble hardwood paling, is unfortunately prone to deterioration by the elements, attacks by white ants and borers, etc. The only way to keep it in good condition is to protect it either with a preserving stain or a good exterior paint system. If painting, avoid oil-based products unless you enjoy endless maintenance and frequent repainting.

Other fences are created using steel posts with wire mesh, colourbonded metal panels, brushwood held by wire, etc. The last, though expensive and somewhat drab, is effective in high wind areas.

Erecting a Fence

When putting up a fence remember that the posts should straddle the boundary line. A nylon string line stretched tightly between the survey pegs (or suspended directly above them — use a plumb bob for accuracy) will help you keep the fence straight.

Most fences can be erected fairly easily unless the site is rocky or swampy. Rocky sites mean that the posts can't be dug in deeply with a hired posthole borer — you'll need the aid of a jackhammer. Once they're concreted in, however, the fence will never move.

Swampy sites mean poor soil stability with the chance that the fence could blow over. There is also the increased chance of rotting. Deeply sunk concrete posts in this situation are advisable.

If you're going to significantly change the levels in your backyard near the fences, do this before your fencing work. The reason is obvious. You can't backfill against a timber or metal fence because it may push it over and will certainly lead to rapid rotting or rusting. Lowering the soil level significantly will seriously weaken the holding power of existing posts. In either case, a solid concrete, concrete block, brick or stone retaining wall could be constructed on the boundary and the posts put in as an integral part of it. Alternatively, construct the wall just inside the boundary using a proper footing.

If the fence is an existing one and you're lowering the level by more than 150 mm, then you have no choice but to come in from the boundary at least 600–900 mm depending on the soil type. You can either use a retaining wall or batter (slope) the excavation at 45° to prevent the bank from collapsing.

Once the retaining walls are complete, the next logical step is to do the drainage.

Your fence can be a real feature in your backyard.

Timber fences can be created in a variety of shapes.

A sapling fence makes an attractive background for climbing plants.

Drainage

Poor drainage is something that can affect the success of the overall project. If you happen to have a low-lying block or your backyard is a filled-in watercourse then the result can be a disaster suitable only for swamp-loving plants and mould. This is because most plants require air near the roots. Too much moisture will actually drown them.

Watch for soggy patches that remain long after rain. In heavy rain, watch the surface water. Does it rush across or collect in your backyard? In dry periods, dig a hole and watch to see if it fills with water. In wet periods, fill it with water and see whether it seeps away.

A solution to these problems is possible if the site can be sloped or properly drained. Filling a low area or changing the slope will divert surface water elsewhere (but watch you're not discharging your problems onto someone else).

A network of underground agricultural pipes will effectively collect underground seepage and carry it to the street or to another location. In some extreme situations, there are no real solutions except to plant swamp flora and learn to like it. The other alternative is to move.

Drainage work requires trenches to be dug (as does the installation of garden lights, garden taps, etc.). There is little point in laying paths, paving and lawns if they have to be disturbed later.

Drainage work in this regard does not mean sewage or stormwater (unless your excavations have interfered with them, in which case a plumber should be called). It refers to drainage of the soil where the water table is very high or the soil, through seepage from a higher location, tends to become over moist. In either case the wetness, if atypical, can actually drown the trees because no oxygen can get to the roots. A familiar and dramatic example of this occurs when a

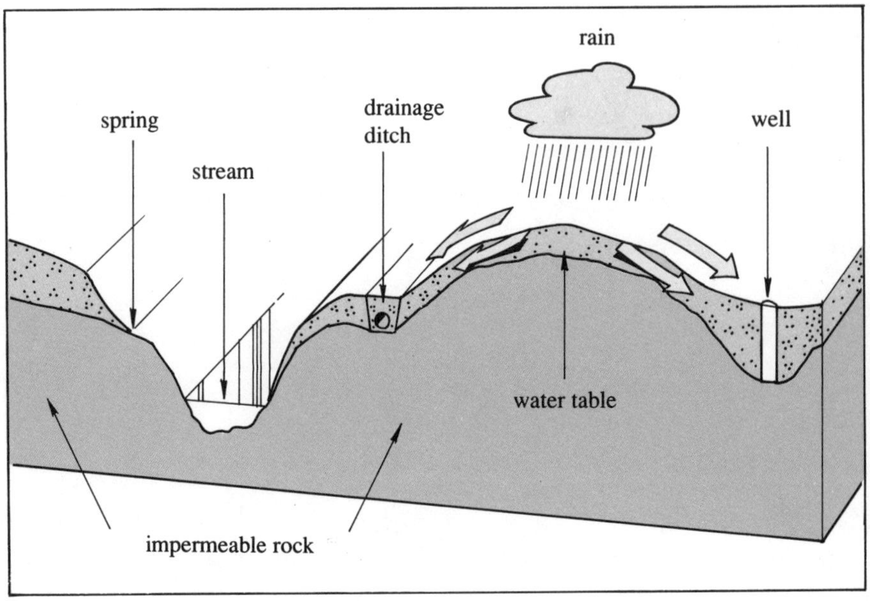

Diagram 11 Groundwater movement

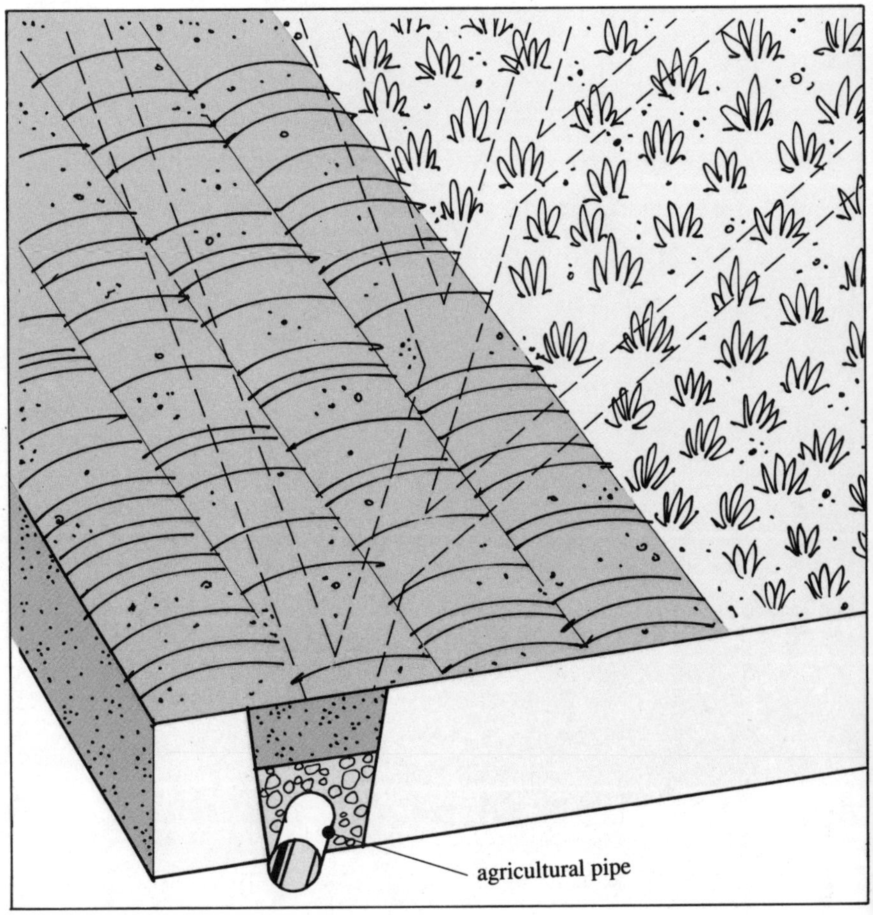

Diagram 12 Laying drainage pipes

wooded area is flooded because of a newly built dam.

The water table, for the uninitiated, is the saturated zone in the subsoil which rises because of soaking rain, subsurface discharge of stormwater pipes and sewers, etc. and falls in time of drought. The water table is not level (like an underground lake) but approximates to the overlying surface and moves similarly to surface water though much more slowly.

Laying Drainage Pipes

The purpose of putting in a drainage system is to collect the underground water and carry it away. This of course means that you have to drain to a spot lower than the bottom of the drainage line. You can't discharge such a line onto someone else's property but must run it to a natural watercourse, stormwater line, or absorption pit.

One drainage pipe widely used is the plastic corrugated type. This is because of its light weight, flexibility and cheapness. The pipe, or network of pipes, is laid with a fall to the disposal area and covered with a coarse fill such as gravel, then a sandy layer, then topsoil. Water then filters through the higher levels, seeps through the gravel into the slots in the pipe walls and runs away leaving the soil with room for air movement. Clay pipes don't have slots but are laid with open joints which collect the water.

Generally speaking, pipes should be laid across steep sites and down fairly flat ones. The spacing and depth depends on the soil type but a rough guide is 0.9–1.2 m deep (spaced 31–38 m apart) for sandy loam and 0.6–0.9 m deep (8–11 m apart) for clay soils. The fall in all cases should be sufficient to generate enough water velocity to stop the pipe silting up (minimum slope 2:100 or 100 mm in every 5 m).

Such lines are of course an open invitation to certain tree roots which will happily block them up. Information on nuisance trees can usually be obtained from the water supply authorities in your state. Specific information on joining and laying plastic and clay piping can be obtained directly from the drainage pipe manufacturers.

A flower display like this depends on excellent drainage.

Tree Lopping and Removal

Existing trees may not suit your plan or lifestyle for a number of reasons. They may be too big for the size of the house or there may be a danger of falling limbs; they may cut out the winter sun or fill the pool with leaves; they may obscure the view or their roots may damage patios and paths. If any of these conditions are occurring or looking as if they may occur soon, then if the council allows it, removal may be the answer. More suitable trees can then be planted. If removal or lopping is permitted, then seriously consider getting in a professional tree removalist. These people, for large amounts of money, will risk life and limb to fell trees in such a way that you, your family and surrounding property (both yours and the neighbours') are not at risk.

The alternative is to get up the tree on a long extension ladder and, wielding a bush saw or chainsaw, gradually whittle it away, working from the top down. Let me tell you, it requires a stout heart, a strong arm and good nerves. Note where the main branches are and try to imagine where they will fall when you cut them and if any damage could occur to buildings, shrubs, electrical wires etc. As you remove each branch, cut underneath it first, then come in from the top. This will ensure a clean cut.

A rope (but not a noose) which secures you to the trunk is a good idea in case a falling branch tries to bat you off the rungs. Make sure the ladder feet are on a solid, non-slippery base and it leans at a 1:4 angle. Don't rest it against a dead, decayed or white-anted limb. And keep all kids clear!

Watering Systems

While the drainage is being done is the time to consider what type of watering system you might want. Watering systems, cleverly planned, can save you hours of mindless hosing, cut down on excess water bills, and ensure the best possible rate of plant growth.

They range from ones that can be run across the surface of the soil or just covered with a thin layer of soil, pine chip or mulch, to ones that need to be put in a trench 150–200 mm deep. It's this latter type that should concern you during this formative stage of your backyard paradise. This assumes, of course, that you have a clear idea of where the plants and trees are going, what type they are, and what watering needs they have. Group together those plants that have similar water requirements.

Watering systems centre on three methods of water distribution: the microspray, the drip, and the pop-up (which requires a trench to be dug). The first two can be left until the garden is fully established.

The microspray. As the name suggests, the water is turned into a fine mist by the spraying heads which are fed by the main line. This lessens water wastage because the volume of water is able to be absorbed by the soil or plant instead of gushing across it to disappear to who knows where.

The drip. This title again accurately describes its function. The water drips from the head at a continuous rate. The heads must therefore be placed close to the plants they are watering. This involves a multiplicity of outlets.

The pop-up. Again a descriptive title. This underground system involves a series of heads which are retracted when not in use but which 'rise to the occasion', so to speak, when the water is turned on and deliver the equivalent of a whole set of sprinklers. Your hardware store carries this equipment and installation directions for each particular brand.

This lush garden has been achieved by deep and regular watering.

There are other pieces of watering equipment you could consider. The three systems can be activated, not by something as unreliable as your hand and memory, but by timers that, motivated by mechanical or electronic brains, take care of the watering automatically. Along with timers, there are moisture meters that stop the system when the moisture content of the soil reaches a predetermined level.

A cautionary word: before you run out and buy thousands of metres of tubing and a miscellany of mysterious fittings, you need to consider your water pressure, which has to be adequate for the system.

Measuring Your Water Pressure

Oviously your watering system has to be fed by the town water and if the pressure is too low all you'll get out of the many heads is a mere dribble. The water pressure is measured by calculating the number of litres per minute coming through a garden tap and relating this volume to the recommendation of the watering system's manufacturer.

To work it out, get a bucket of known capacity, say 10 litres. Turn on the garden tap full pelt (make sure no other taps are on either inside your house or out) and time how long it takes to fill the bucket. Take out your abacus or calculator and divide the bucket size by the number of seconds and multiply the answer by sixty. The answer will give you the flow per minute. For example, say it took 25 seconds.

$$\frac{\text{bucket size}}{\text{seconds}} \times 60$$

$$\frac{10}{25} \times 60 = 24$$

So the flow is 24 litres per minute. Keep in mind that if someone washes their hands or fills a bath, in some areas the pressure will probably drop.

If your water pressure is well under what is required, you will either have to set up a system that works in sections or reduce the number of distribution lines. You could, of course, install a pump.

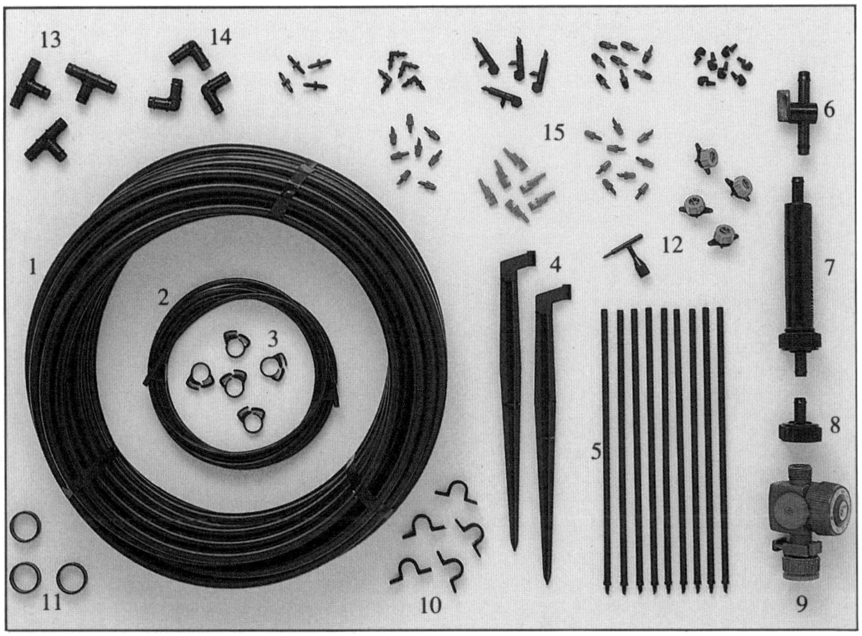

Watering system

1. Hose
2. Thin hose
3. Locking clamps
4. Riser stakes
5. Rigid risers
6. Shut-off valve
7. In-line filter
8. Tube-to-tap connector
9. Timer tap
10. Saddle clamps
11. End stops
12. Punch
13. Tees
14. Elbows
15. An assortment of sprays, jets and drippers

Installing an In-Ground System

Although watering systems vary in specifics, the following general principles apply. First of all plan the position of the pop-up heads. If you work on a 1.8 m watering radius for each head you'll be close. To assist you further, special heads spray in quarter, half and three quarter circles so that you can water exactly where you want (unless it's windy).

Dig the trench and lay the tubing. Mark each head position and then cut a section out of the tube with a sharp trimming knife to take the threaded tee fitting. At the end of the line use a threaded elbow. Push the tubing over the fitting after checking that no soil has entered the line. Putting the tubing in hot water will make it more pliable. Clamp the joints; then screw the spray heads in position. Then simply fill in the trench, making sure the retracted head is flush with the finished ground level. A turn of the tap and *voila*! controlled rain. But beware the drought caused by either no filter or an inadequate one. The fine heads require especially good filtration or they quickly block up.

The procedure for a non-trench system is similar. Simply run the tubing where you want it, seal the end, screw jets or riser tubes into the tubing where required after punching, fit heads then cover the system with mulch or soil. You can branch off the main feeder line wherever necessary using T-joiners.

With either system, make sure it is planned so that it can't be damaged by foot or vehicular traffic. Because it is so inconspicuous, it is easy to walk on. A visitor needing parking could also run over it.

When watering, keep in mind that early morning and late afternoon are the best times, especially in hot weather. The water will not evaporate but will soak deep into the soil where the roots can get at it.

CHAPTER 8

MAJOR FEATURES

The completion of the yard in terms of filling, terracing, drainage and so on frees you to begin the next phase where you rise above the barren ground and, with new interest, make all manner of intriguing and substantial creations to add interest, beauty and comfort to your backyard. The items that follow — projects in timber and other materials — are not presented in any particular order, so attack them as and when you will.

Ponds

Whether your backyard is designed to be a total water garden complete with fountains and cascades or to merely include a simple pond, water — still, running, or spraying — will contribute to a feeling of peace and tranquillity.

Modern pond construction, if moderate in size, no longer involves difficult concrete work similar in principle to a swimming pool. The advent of preformed fibreglass ponds and waterproof liners has made the backyarder's lot much easier.

When designing, keep in mind the following: a pond is a pond, not a swimming pool. Its depth should not exceed 450 mm. Its position should allow for at least five hours of sunshine per day or the water plants will suffer and won't flower. Ponds don't respond well to constant leaf deluges so keep them clear of offending trees. Aim for large ponds with a reasonable water volume if you want to create a proper ecological balance for the fish and plants. Otherwise, because algae love the increased light and warmth of small volumes of water, they will respond by happily making your pocket handkerchief pool murky and stagnant.

Also allow for an overflow from the pond to cater for rain. This can be achieved by fitting a piece of hose under the pond coping and running it away in a shallow trench to a location that is appropriate. While we're on the subject of rain, keep the edge of the pond above ground level to stop surface rainwater filling it with debris.

Moss covered rocks, groundcover and dense planting result in a very natural looking pond.

Fibreglass Ponds

Fibreglass ponds come in many shapes and may be up to 3 metres long. Simplicity of shape has much to commend it though it is purely a personal issue. Some have built-in shelves or pockets at various levels to hold water plants.

To install a fibreglass pond, simply dig a hole to take the unit, set it in flush according to the manufacturer's recommendations and cover the edge with pavers or stones to give it a more natural appearance. If desired, partly elevate the pond out of the ground to give a raised look. The edging which supports it could be of brick or stone.

Making a Liner Type Pond

The principle involved here is to form the pool shape in a level area and lay a waterproof liner over the base. When filled, the water pressure pushes the liner hard against the base, lessening creases and creating an instant pond. The liners are made from materials like polyvinylchloride (PVC), and butyl rubber, the sort of products often used in children's wading pools.

Fish and water plants thrive in this man-made backyard pond.

PROCEDURE

1 Unless you or your partner is a dressmaker and can cut the liner to fit exactly, dig out the shape avoiding sharp corners where excessive bunching of the liner could occur. Make a recess around the perimeter 125 mm deep by 100 mm wide. This will take the brick edging. Put a small slope in the pond bottom to facilitate cleaning.

2 Line the shape and perimeter with 50 mm of coarse sand or fine gravel. This will smooth out any irregularities and cover sharp edges that may penetrate the liner sheeting.

3 Lay the sheeting in the hole, letting it overlap say 900 mm around the edges. Stretch it a little to suit the hole shape but make sure there is no tension otherwise the water pressure combined with aging may tear it. If it has to be joined, use a glue recommended by the sheeting manufacturer. Use bricks or stone to temporarily hold the sheeting in place.

4 After the glue has dried, create underwater terracing or pockets using stone or brick. Lay the material without mortar, watching that there are no sharp edges. Then fill the pockets with rich loamy soil, plant the lilies or other plants and cover with coarse sand or gravel. This will hold the soil in place while the pond is filled and stop the plants floating upwards. An alternative is to put the plants in pots which can be put in place at a later stage.

5 Immediately fill the pond with water or the plants will die, and then leave for 5–7 days to allow for consolidation of the foundation material.

6 To finish the edges, neatly lay bricks on their flat around the recess keeping them 2 mm apart. This allows for brick growth which will be accelerated because of the moisture. Fill in the space at the back with a dryish concrete mix. This will hold the liner in place.

7 Trim the excess liner off flush with the top of the bricks and finish around the edge of the pool with stone, slate or pavers using 4:1 mortar in the joints. Alternatively use bush stones in between which are pockets that hold soil for edging plants. Coloured gravel, sand or river pebbles can be laid in the bottom of the pond to lessen the liner (or fibreglass) impact.

As well as fibreglass or PVC liners, ponds can be created out of all manner of things: old bath tubs, cut-down water or wine barrels, tubs, etc. You're only limited by your imagination.

Once the pond is finished, get advice from nurseries and pet stores on which water plants (see section on water plants) and freshwater fish best suit your particular locality. Some fish varieties you could consider are comets, fantails, shubunkins, lionheads, ranchus and the bugeyed blackamores. With names like that, you'd expect fascinating shapes and colours. You won't be disappointed.

When first introducing fish to your pool, place them, still in their plastic bag, in the pool for at least an hour. This allows the fish to adjust to the change in water temperature slowly, rather than explosing it to a sudden variation which could kill it. Don't overstock the pool. Four fish per square metre of water is ideal. Overfeeding is also detrimental to pond fish.

One problem you can have with fish ponds is that dogs love to disport themselves in water, especially in hot weather. A more serious issue is the possibility of predators. Cats and some species of birds love a tasty goldfish or shubunkin. One way to lessen their interest is to make sure that the pond has a good collection of floating plants under which the fish can hide.

However, if the fish population appears to be quickly decreasing, you have no choice but to cover the pond with galvanised chicken wire or reinforcing mesh. It looks ugly but it foils even the hungriest predator. Alternatively you could try a scarecrow.

To empty the pond for cleaning use a bucket or, if getting a mouthful of pond water doesn't alarm you, use a garden hose to make a siphon. Surface debris can be removed by running a piece of newspaper across the water.

A galvanised iron bathtub pond looks better the older it gets.

Twin ponds with a mini waterfall between.

Cascades and Fountains

The sound of running water is considered by some to be more soothing than the tranquillity of a pond. Why not create your own mountain stream in a corner of the yard? As well as the soothing effect, the mystifying benefits of splashing water create spray which is beneficial to nearby plants, to say nothing of the cooling effect in summer.

If you have a sloping block, cascades are easy to create. Simply form a series of descending shallow pools using stone with coloured joints. A metre drop in height is adequate. Wide and low has a better appearance than high and thin. Zigzag the direction for effect and use a few large rocks rather than many small ones.

Alternatively, the cascade could be created by using a series of small overlapping fibreglass pools suitably edged with rock or large river pebbles. If your block is level, build a sloping mountain of rock joined by suitably coloured mortar that blends in with the stone.

End the cascade with a pond. This holds the submersible pump which uses pressure to move the water up a hose or water piping to the top. The same water is recirculated over and over, an important point in low rainfall areas or during water restrictions.

A sloping block offers its own rewards.

1. Large flat rock as pouring lip
2. Siting pump under last fall prevents unwanted cross-currents
3. Pool liner ends above water level
4. Pipe laid underground from pump directly to top pool
5. Stones
6. Outlet

Diagram 13 Cascade mechanics

The size of the pump you require depends on the volume of water you wish to move, the height it has to be raised, and the distance it has to travel. Some pumps work off a 12 volt transformer — the kit can be bought with full instructions. This allows you to do the full installation. Pumps that require 240 volts must be installed professionally.

While you're at it, why not consider putting in waterproof, coloured lights in various nooks and crannies, again using the 12 volt system. The wiring conduit can be camouflaged with ferns or other plants.

You can quickly enhance the appearance of a pond by putting in a fountain at one end. Fountains can be simple or elaborate. The decision on which way to go depends on the style of the garden and the size of your budget. Decide beforehand on the effect you want to achieve.

An added bonus is the attraction a fountain has for bird life. In the hot weather, birds of all types will be attracted by the spray and will tend to preen and clean themselves in it. If feathered visitors are important to you, make sure you plan on building the fountain and pond in a secluded place, but not one that is heavily enclosed by undergrowth that could hide a cat.

To build a fountain, simply use a submersible pump which discharges into a head attachment (similar to your shower) which gives the type of discharge you want, ranging from a fine spray to a full-throated geyser. The head attachment can simply be propped up on bricks or stones. Special figures such as Grecian maidens, turtles, etc, are sometimes available with a fountain outlet formed inside them. They can add a distinctive touch in the right setting.

Remember that when it is windy the spray will fly about so the fountain should be placed away from main traffic areas.

A classic fountain like this can add a touch of elegance to your backyard.

Decks

There is nothing like a large deck to bridge the gap between the inside of your house and the planned outdoor environment. In fact if the deck is made the same height as the internal floors and there is plenty of floor-to-ceiling glass it can look as if it's an extension of the room, enlarging it dramatically.

As well, a large deck gives you a level area for entertaining or relaxing on, a bonus if the yard is steeply sloping. The photograph shows the effect that a well designed deck can have. It cries out for someone to relax on it.

Of course decks needn't necessarily be attached to a house. They can be erected anywhere to take advantage of a view, a shady tree, a sunny spot, or to create an elevated level area in an out-of-the-way corner of your backyard. Wherever they go, watch they don't interfere with things like drainage lines or gullies, items which may require the attention of your friendly but expensive plumber at some stage.

The principle in deck construction is similar to that of your timber floors. It consists of a system of bearers and joists standing on timber, concrete or brick piers. The framing timbers are usually covered by hardwood decking boards although compressed fibre cement sheeting can be used which can be painted or, preferably, tiled. If the deck is over a certain height (usually 1.2 metres) it will need a 900 mm or so handrail. Check with your council for local requirements.

A deck is a perfect place for entertaining, especially with a view like this.

Designing the Deck

When planning your deck, keep in mind that the aesthetics of the backyard have to balance with the decking size and construction materials. An enormous deck will swallow up a small backyard while a tiny deck will be lost in a big yard. The materials should, as much as possible, blend in with the living environment and be painted with neutral, earthy colours (unless your yard happens to have a Mediterranean or Spanish theme).

Unfortunately, there exists the distinct possibility that even so humble a structure as a deck has to have council approval. The Local Government Act (Ordinance 70) regards anything from a flagpole to a house as a structure and theoretically requires documentation which can range from a simple letter advising a minor change, to the full catastrophe of building applications, plans and specifications. Not only do the council inspectors closely scrutinise the application, but in many localities the surrounding neighbours are given the opportunity to object if aspect of your deck or other structure offends them. Before you complain, look at it from the other point of view. You wouldn't want your neighbours to put up a structure that blocks your view or sunlight, or a deck that overlooks you and destroys your privacy.

Piers and Posts

The supports for the framing system need to be solid and well supported to stop sinking, deflection or lateral instability (these factors are discussed below in more detail). Typical supports are made from concrete, brick, galvanised steel pipe or columns, timber poles and posts.

Sinking. While the weight of the average deck is not excessive, the base of the pier, or support for the post, must be large enough to avoid a punching effect similar to that of the destructive indents of high-heeled shoes on a vinyl floor.

There are three possible ways of achieving this:

- a large footing under a brick pier
- a pedestal footing under a pipe column or 100 x 100 mm timber post or
- the cross-sectional size of the treated posts being large enough to carry the load. This refers to treated poles of 200 mm diameter or more.

In all these situations, the size of the footing or the diameter of the post must relate to the bearing value of the soil on which it's sitting and the weight being supported. If the foundation is hard like shale, then the footing need not be very large, whereas if it is spongy like an organic soil, a larger footing is required to spread the load over a wider area.

Deflection. Put quite simply, the piers mustn't bend, and this is especially applicable when the piers are more than a metre long. The cross-sectional size required is related to the length of the pier, the material it's made from, and the weight it's supporting.

Lateral stability. This refers to the ability of the piers to resist rocking caused by wind, people movement, etc. If the piers are short this is not such a problem but the higher the structure the more exaggerated the rocking effect. Properly designed bracing between the piers will generally offset this movement.

An engineer will happily design a deck system for you taking into account the above factors. Alternatively you can buy a deck in kit form and put in footings as recommended above.

Deck Framing

The dimensions of the bearers and joists depend on the span between the piers and their spacing. A fairly standard convention is 100 x 75 mm hardwood bearers at 1.800 m centres and 10 x 50 mm joists at 450–600 mm centres. Departures from this require engineering design or the use of span tables which can be found in the Building Standards booklet obtainable from some banks.

Connectors

There are a variety of different types which, like any fastenings used externally, should be of galvanised steel.

Connecting timber posts to concrete footings is done by metal shoes. They come in a variety of shapes and generally require bolts to secure the post to the shoe. Two methods of fixing posts are shown in the illustrations on page 202. Avoid any design that fully covers the end of the post or rotting can occur. This is because water becomes trapped and, unless the end of the post is extremely well painted, it soaks up the end grain and rots the timber.

Connecting the joists and bearer is usually done by skew nailing. An alternative is to use triple grips. These handy connectors come in a variety of shapes which allow, among other things, for butt joining.

Preparing to Build

Order all the materials and, upon delivery, carry it to the deck site and stack it in a position that will not interfere with the building. Make sure it is stacked level and straight so that it can't twist or warp. The decking should be stacked with the layers separated by battens to assist in seasoning. This is especially important with hardwood decking.

1 Once the plans are approved, begin to set out the post or pier positions. The easiest way to do this is to make up a level grid using intersecting stringlines and profiles (see Diagram 14). For making them level, a line level can be used. The more accurate water level is even more useful for this task (see page 173).

On the top of the profiles, which should be kept 900 mm away from the actual position of the structure to allow you to dig without disturbing them, you lay out the post positions. Drive in 38 mm nails on the outside marks so you can string lines from them.

Make sure the grid is square by measuring 3 m down one side and 4 m down the other. The diagonal, if there is a true right angle, should measure 5 m. Alternatively, measure the diagonals. Adjust the sides until they're square. Then simply plumb down from the line intersections using a straightedge and spirit level or plumb bob to locate the exact positions for the piers or posts.

2 Next dig the footings out (or holes for the posts or pedestals). If the soil is sandy, you may have to shore up the sides with old corrugated iron, etc. Temporarily brace timber piers or pipe columns so they are vertical.

3 Next pour the footings using a dryish concrete for maximum strength. If there is a large volume it may pay you to get in readymix or hire a concrete mixer. Make sure you place any shoes (to which posts will be attached) in the correct position before the concrete sets. The intersecting string lines will again prove invaluable for this. Leave the concrete for 10 days to ensure

Building a Deck

it cures properly or it might crack when you're fixing the bearers and joists.

4 The rest simply involves constructing or erecting the piers, posts etc. and forming the floor framing (Diagram 15A shows a typical joint between steel column and bearer). Put a waterproof membrane on top of any brick piers followed by an antcap. Clear the area under the deck and fill any depressions that could hold water. Lay black plastic on the ground and/or spray to stop weeds. The black plastic can be covered with gravel to improve its appearance. Skew-nail the timbers with galvanised 75 mm nails or use connectors. The framing timbers could be painted at this stage if you really want to protect them.

5 When laying the decking, which should be no wider than 75 mm or the shrinkage is excessive, stagger the joints and leave a 2–4 mm gap between the boards to allow for shrinkage. When nailing close to the ends, pre-drill the nail holes or flatten the points on the nails to lessen the chance of splitting. Use a good quality paint or stain on the timber to help preserve it.

6 Handrails are necessary to prevent children and tipsy adults from taking an unscheduled dive into the petunias. The handrail should be strong enough to support the leaning weight of your most robust friend.

The posts (suggested minimum 75 x 50 mm) can be fastened to the handrail by bolts, metal brackets etc. (see Diagram 15B). A top rail of 100 x 50 mm and at least one middle rail (say 75 x 38 mm) should be securely fixed to the posts by coachbolts, screws, etc. Pre-drill to avoid the risk of splitting. Put in extra rails or some form of netting if you have small children or they could fall through. Another albeit expensive alternative is to put up acrylic or glass sheeting. This has the advantage of being transparent.

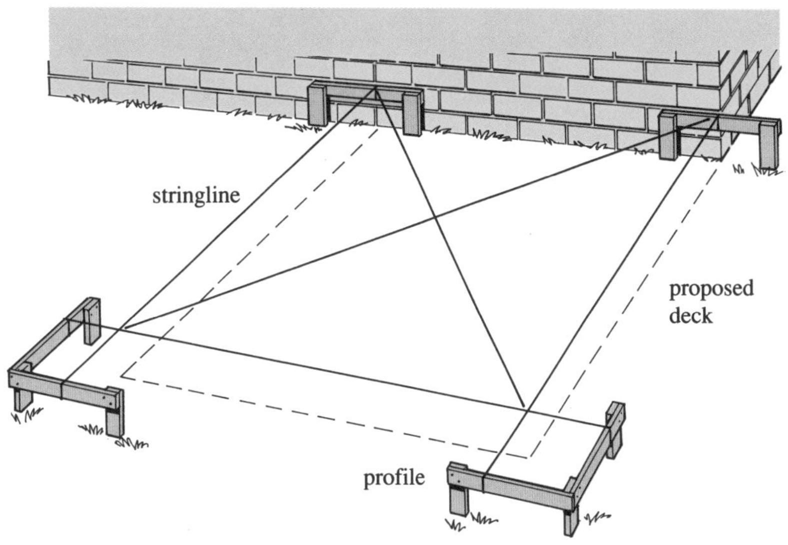

Diagram 14

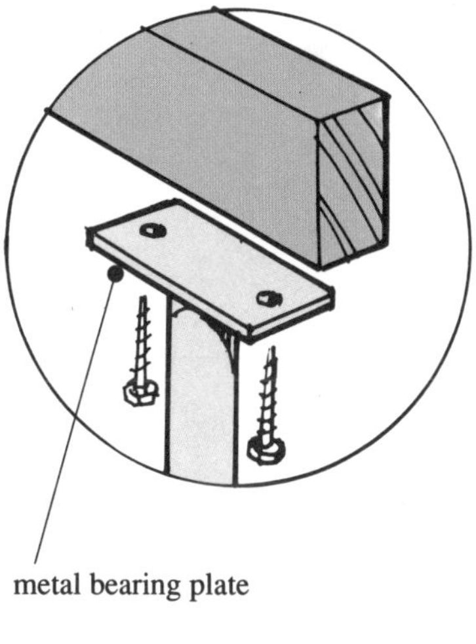

Diagram 15A

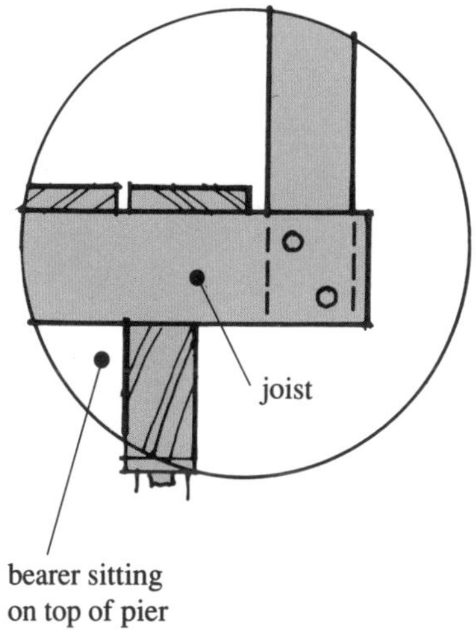

Diagram 15B

Timber Stairs

Having constructed the deck, quite possibly you'll want to get up on it! For a low deck, a few railway sleepers could quickly make some rustic stairs. Alternatively, they can be made from solid brick or precast concrete. If it's a fairly high deck, it could well involve the building of a set of timber stairs.

A quick solution is to contact your local joinery shop or stair manufacturer and have them come out and give a quote to supply a set of hardwood stairs. To get some idea of price over the phone, simply tell them the height the stair has to reach (total rise) and the distance you can project out from the deck (the total run). (See Diagram 16A.)

If you intend building the stairs yourself, before we can proceed any further we have to discuss a few deep and meaningful concepts associated with the mysterious art of stair building. In case you didn't know it, there is a relationship between the height of each step (rise) and the width of the tread (going) which governs whether the steps are easy to ascend and descend or not. Ordinance 70 sets out the following table which shows how, if you increase the height of the riser, you should decrease the width of the tread to compensate.

Looking at the table you can see that the maximum riser height recommended is 190 mm and the minimum is 115 mm. This is because if it were any more than 190 mm it would be an effort for most people to raise their legs high enough to clear the step. The minimum size is there because too small a change in level is not discernible to most people, which greatly increases the possibility of their falling down the steps.

The going or run, which refers to the width of a single tread, is quoted at 395 mm maximum. Any larger would require a person ascending to be a giant or to take two steps on each tread. At 255 mm minimum, the reverse applies. Someone with big feet wouldn't fit because when you descend you don't place your heels hard against the riser so the toe of the shoe would be dangling in space, increasing the risk of overbalancing.

The formula 2R+G is not, as you may have feared, similar in complexity to Einstein's equation for relativity. R is the rise in millimetres and G is the going. The formula states that if you multiply the rise by two and add the going (tread width) to it, the total figure should fall between 585 and 625 mm if the stair is to be safe and easy to use.

For example, if you have decided on a rise of say 150 mm (which is a good height), the ideal tread width should range between 325 mm and 285 mm (2 x 150 (the rise) = 300. 300 from 625 = 325 mm and similarly 300 from 585 = 285 mm). The equation can of course be worked in reverse should you decide on an ideal tread width first.

Although the example may appear difficult, you'll find that once you do it a couple of times, it's easy.

CALCULATING THE SIZE OF STAIRS

Riser Height (R) in mm		Going (G) in mm		Quantity 2R+G (mm)	
Max	Min	Max	Min	Max	Min
190	115	395	250	630	585

If the joinery shop wants a small fortune for making up some stairs and you happen to be a bit short on small fortunes (and assuming that solid bricks steps are not your style), this method of building a basic flight of timber stairs may get you out of trouble.

MATERIALS

You'll need two pieces of 300 x 50 mm hardwood to support the treads. These are known as the stringers. Their length, as you can see from Diagram 16A, is equal to the diagonal which joins the top of the rise to the end of the run. If you measure out the run and then take the tape up to the top of the deck it will give you the theoretical length. Add another 600 mm for good measure.

The hardwood treads can be made out of 300 x 38 mm assuming the stairs are no wider than 900 mm. If they're between 900 and 1200 mm make them 50 mm thick. To work out the number required, divide the total rise (distance between ground level and the top of the deck) in metres by 0.150 (the height of each rise) then take off one because the top tread is in fact the deck.

In the example, the total rise is 1.050 metres which divided by 0.150 = 7. To make the seven steps you'll need six treads (the top one is the actual deck). If the total rise doesn't work out in 150 mm increments it shouldn't be too hard to adjust the ground level by digging a bit out or adding a bit of fill until it works.

PROCEDURE

To mark the checkouts for the treads, make up a ply or hardboard right-angled triangle with sides 150 x 300 mm. Alternatively, if you have one, use a

Building a Simple Flight of Stairs

steel square (see Diagram 16B). Either method can then be used to step off the checkouts. Putting any curve in the stringers up, start from the bottom allowing one rise off the ground as per the diagram.

Note the level cut on the bottom to allow the stringer to sit firmly on a brick or concrete pad which could be bolted to a metal angle (Diagram 16C). Don't let it rest on the soil because rot or white ants will soon make a meal of it! The bottom should also be triple primed with an oil-based primer.

Step off the required amount of treads, then shape the top as shown. Skew nailing, bolting or perhaps a pair of metal anchors will secure the top forever. Cut out the checkouts using a hand or electric saw, then fix the stringers in position, making sure they are parallel and at right angles to the deck. Then prime underneath and nail on the treads with galvanised nails (Diagram 16D). After chamfering all the sharp corners to lessen splintering, coat the whole thing with the same preservative as you used on the deck (but make sure it's not a slippery type, otherwise you may slip on the stairs).

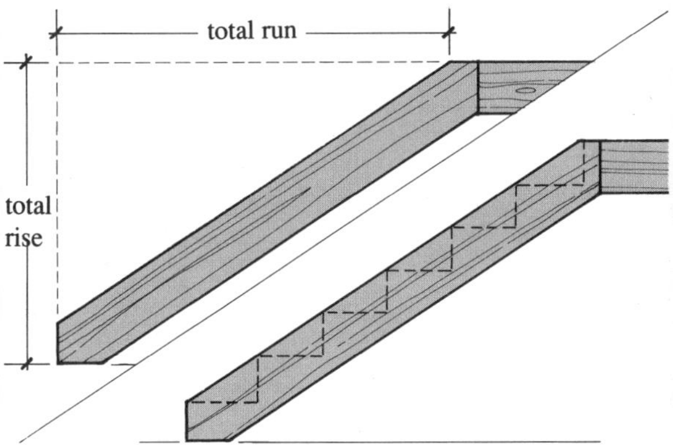

Diagram 16A

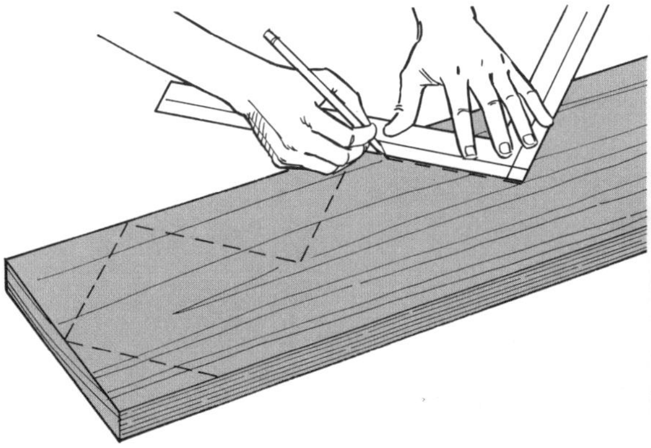

Diagram 16B

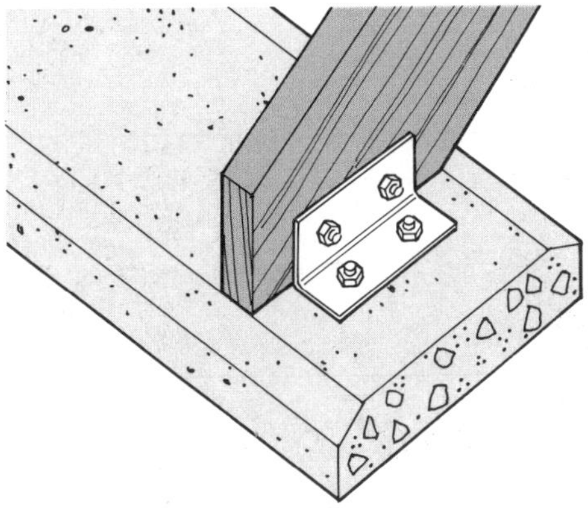

Diagram 16C

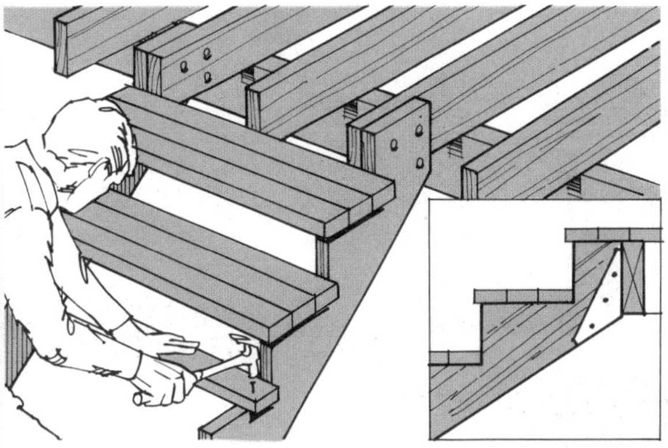

Diagram 16D

Lattice Screening or Fencing

Lattice is an enduring boon to the backyarder. In a matter of a day, you can build an attractive screen. A few days effort gives you a fence that could grace a mansion or an elegant railing to complement your deck. Laid over a pergola, it creates a pattern of symmetrical shadows. Its separated slats give privacy without the heaviness associated with solid stone or masonry walls. It creates shade without the loss of a cooling summer breeze.

The holes, either square or diamond shaped, are created by the spaced slats which allow the wind to pass through it while lessening its force. This makes it ideal for fencing in windy areas because no turbulence is created. It can be bought with the slats spaced closely or well apart. The latter, because less timber is used, is the cheaper. Keep in mind that the diamond shape, because of its lack of horizontal or vertical symmetry, is more visually blocking. If further privacy is required it is an easy matter to grow vines in selected places.

Lattice can be easily shaped. In combination with arched rails, almost any geometrical shape is possible. Add in some turned posts and the effect is elegant. Put a pergola on the top and it'll look a million dollars.

It is generally available in radiata pine, western red cedar and oregon. In treated form, radiata pine lattice begins as light green and, when weathered, ends up as a light grey. Western red cedar, which also goes grey, is vastly superior to pine because it weathers better but it's very expensive. Oregon lattice, of dubious durability, is also available.

Lattice, which can be bought either dressed or sawn, can of course be painted and indeed should be, especially oregon. Its lifespan will be considerably lengthened if it is. Spraying on the paint (in some out-of-the-way place) before the lattice is put in place is the quickest way. People are reputed to have gone mad trying to paint lattice with a paintbrush.

A lattice screen provides privacy without blocking out the light.

A lattice archway can be used to divide sections of the backyard.

Lattice screens can provide shady spots and dappled light in the yard.

Making a Lattice Screen

Basically all you have to do is to form a frame out of solid timber that provides a continuous groove for the lattice to rest in.

This groove can be formed by:

- nailing twin battens around the inside of the framing structure,
- running a groove in the framework with a router, or
- buying a solid timber section of, say, 75 x 50 mm that has a lattice groove already run in it. This latter method is useful if using rounded timber posts.

Curved shapes are more difficult to achieve. They can of course be bought from lattice supply companies along with a range of lattice accessories such as finial posts, knobs (which when fixed to the top of square posts make them look as if they'd been turned) and hardware. However, you can, with a bit of effort, make arches yourself (see Arches and Gateways page 216).

A simple type of screen is shown in the Diagram 17. These screens can be used singly or in multiple configurations. The groove for the lattice in this instance can be formed by routing or, more simply, by nailing two 25 x 25 mm battens to the posts and rails.

Simply fix two durable posts in the ground either by concreting them in or by ramming the earth solidly around them. Then cut and nail the bottom rail in position, making sure it is level and at right angles to the post. Form the groove along the rail and up the two posts, fix the lattice panel in place and then nail on the top rail. If the bottom rail tends to sag because of the span, it may be necessary to provide extra support in the centre. This can be achieved by means of a block of the same material, a brick etc.

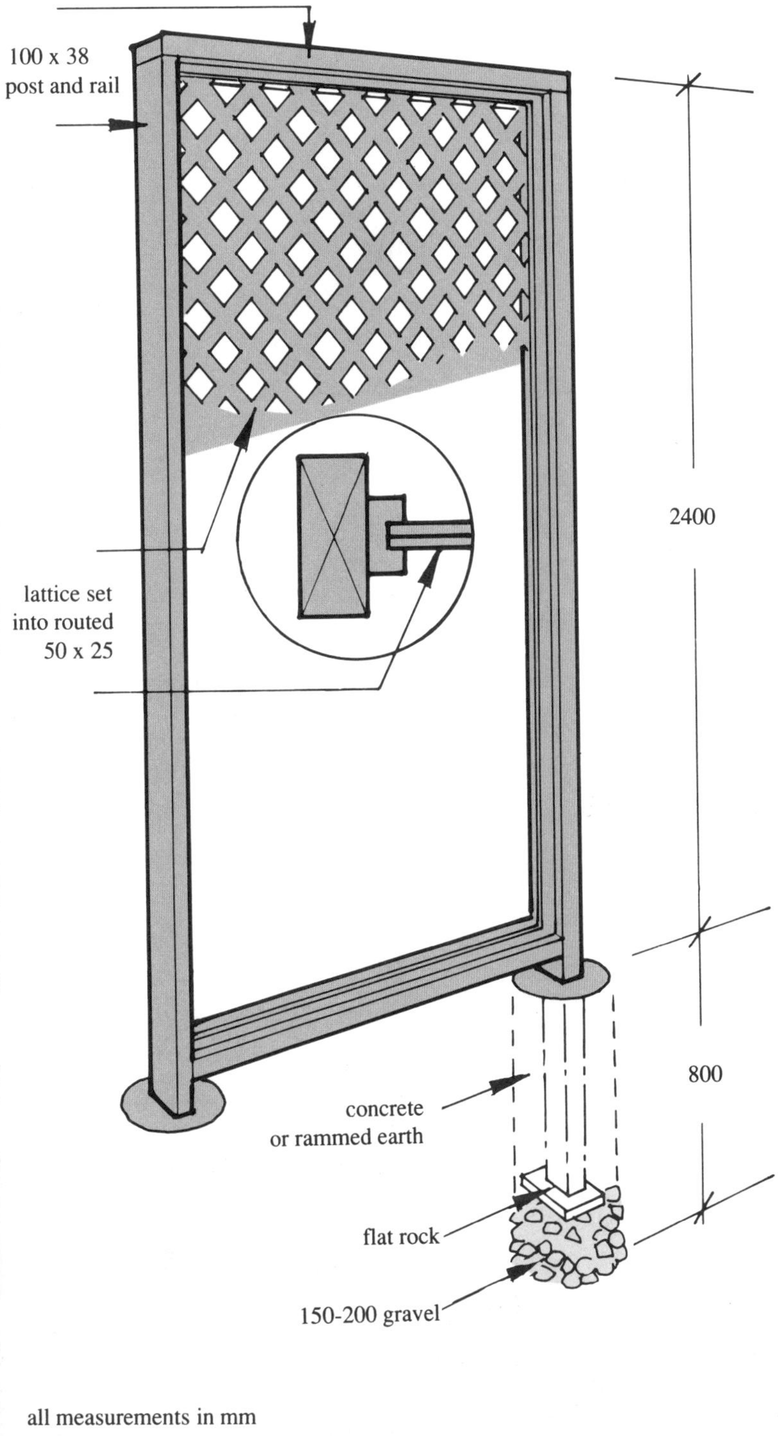

Diagram 17

Though lattice is versatile, virtually anything can be used to screen off an area. The photograph shows how a deck can be shielded from inquisitive neighbours, noise or bad winds. The inclined planks contrast interestingly with the horizontal and vertical lines of the house and deck. The 100 x 50 mm capping gives it a framed appearance as well as protecting the vulnerable end grain from the effects of the destructive summer sun. A few pot plants and a chair and you have a delightful corner in your yard.

Using the same framing principles as used for lattice, any number of different screen finishes can be achieved. Use dowels, steel mesh, battens or colourbond steel (although this would conflict with the natural look). Whatever you choose, think carefully about how it will blend in with the rest of the yard.

An interesting screen created by laying planks at an angle.

A lattice walkway creates charming shadows.

Pergolas

The word pergola comes from the Latin word *pergula*, a vine arbour. That should conjure up in your mind images of drowsy summer afternoons, carafes of chianti, crisp bread, mozzarella cheese, pleasant company reclining lazily on deck chairs or lounges, dreaming of . . .

Seriously, though, 'pergola' in English means a series of columns or posts supporting trelliswork and vines forming an arbour or covered walk. In Australia it often means a plant-covered area suitable for any pleasurable pursuit. It is definitely synonymous with relaxed living and should have a place in your backyard paradise.

The great part about it is that it can be erected quickly. When covered with shade cloth or lattice, you create an instant shady place that would take the average tree years to achieve. If it looks a bit artificial, then a quick-growing vine will colour your sky with all manner of pastel shades. Imagine: the scent of wisteria, lush bunches of grapes, bees buzzing — ah!

Another aspect of the pergola is that it provides geometrical contrast with the softer shape of the plants and trees. As plants in a room bring life to the static geometry of the horizontal and vertical lines of walls, ceilings and furniture, your garden will benefit from the careful introduction of some geometrical structures.

As in all other aspects of your backyard, it's a matter of trying to keep some continuity of theme. If your theme is rustic, don't build a pergola in the style of the Parthenon.

A vine covers this very simple pergola and provides welcome shade in a sunny yard.

Pergolas can be covered with deciduous or evergreen vines depending upon the strength of the winter sun.

The pergola illustrated in Diagram 18 is very basic. The construction principles apply to most pergolas regardless of how elaborate they are. Posts, 100 x 100 mm (dressed or sawn) support a bearer which in turn supports 100 x 38 mm rafters and 50 x 50 mm shade battens (not shown). The bearers are bolted to the posts while the rafters are fixed to the bearer by 75 mm skew nails. The treated poles (or Ironbark and Jarrah posts which should be well soaked in a timber preservative) are set in concrete. This method is self-bracing.

As you've probably noticed, the principle is much the same as the decking construction except that the timbers are lighter and spaced further apart because the weight is less.

If the pergola is free-standing, some method of cross-bracing in the corners should be introduced to stop the whole thing falling over.

Instead of in-ground posts they can rest on galvanised anchors set in concrete (see Diagram 19). Galvanised bolts are used to fix the posts to the anchor.

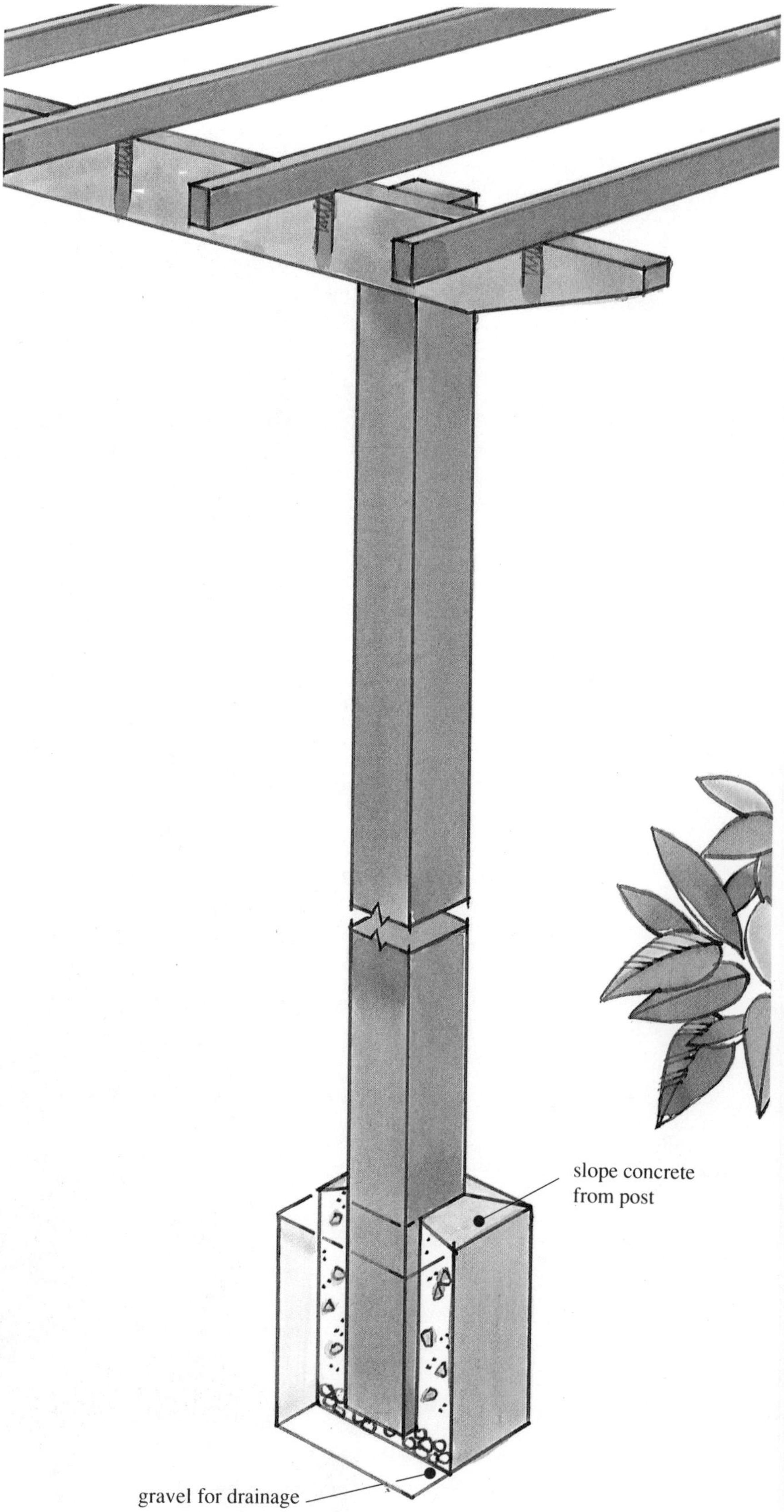

Diagram 18

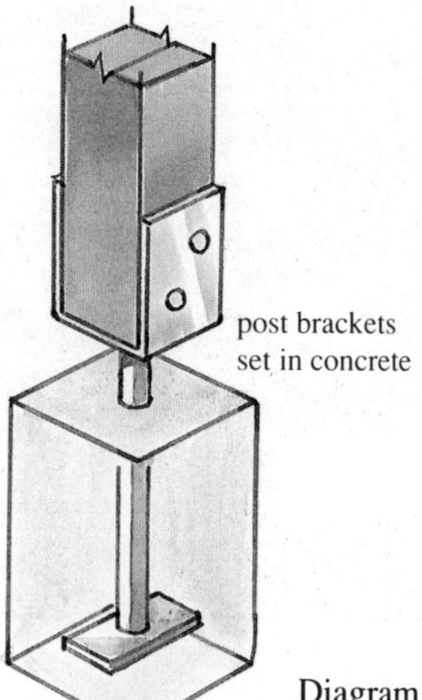

Diagram 19

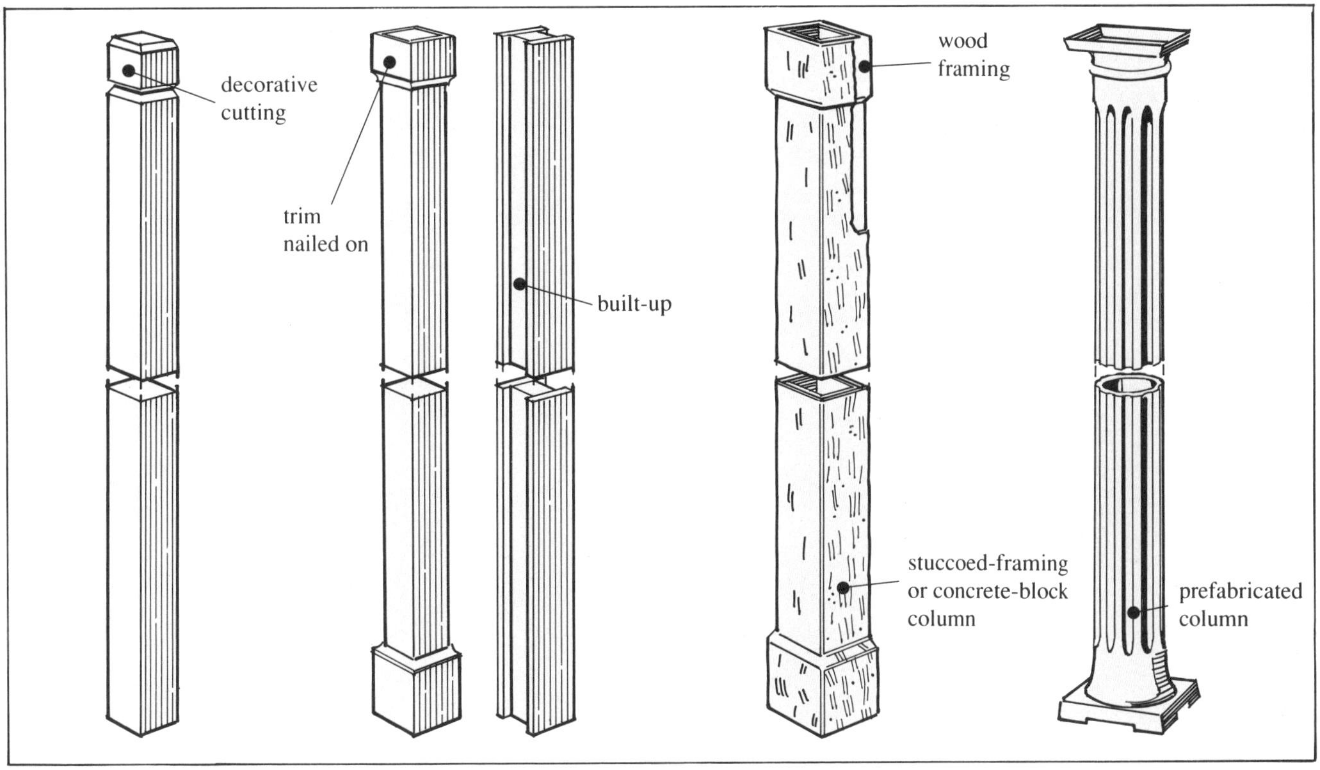

Diagram 20 Types of posts and columns

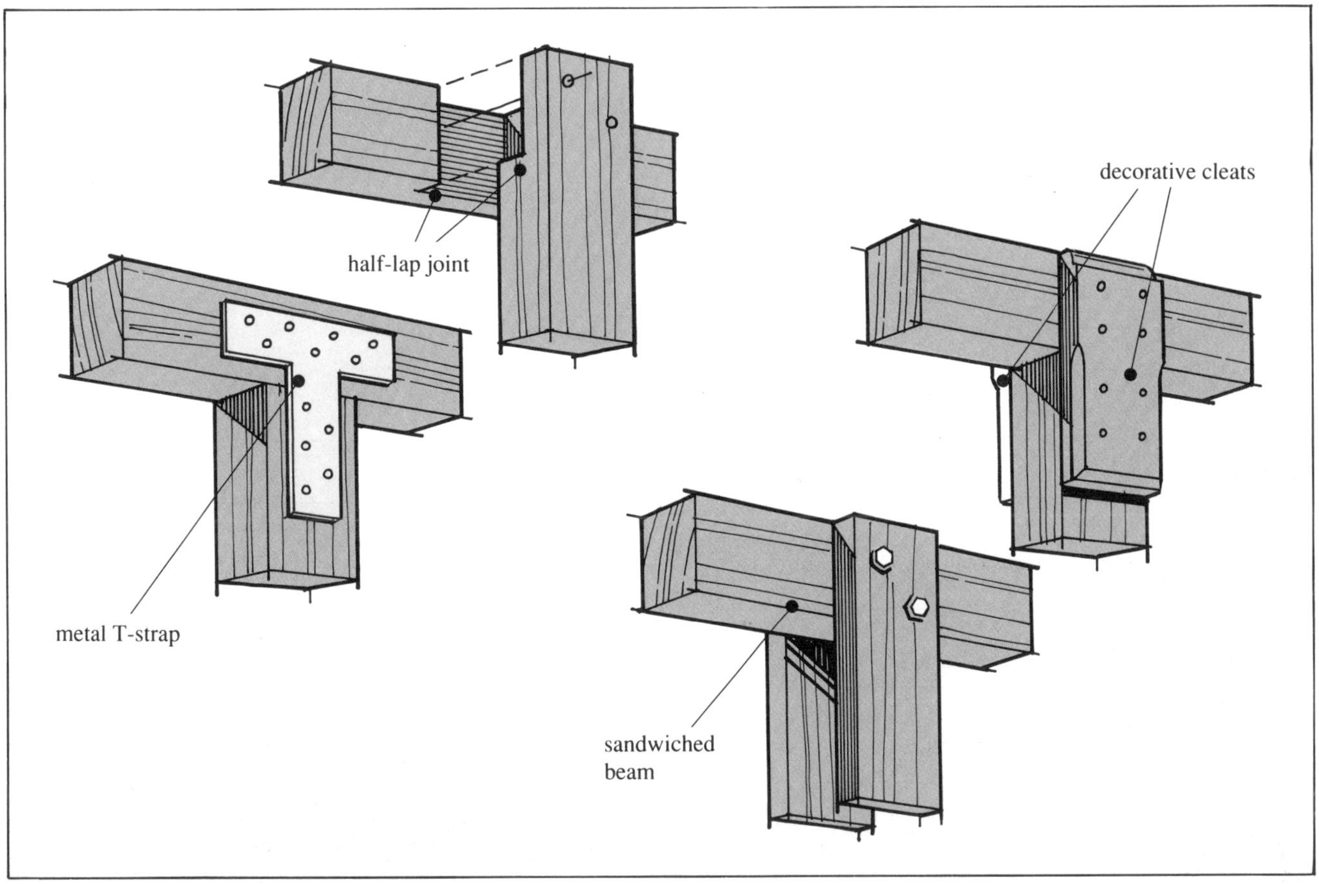

Diagram 21 Post and beam constructions

A slatted roof creates pleasing dappled light under this pergola.

Shade cloths can be used to good effect to cover a pergola.

Building a Pergola

This pergola is simplicity itself to make and can either be freestanding or attached to the house. Concreting the poles into the ground gives the structure a solidity that needs no further bracing and does away with the fiddling usually associated with metal post supports.

MATERIALS

You'll need four 200 mm diameter treated pine poles each a metre longer than the finished height above ground level (allow a minimum clearance of 2.1 m under the beams); two 300 x 75 mm beams, each 4.8 m long; seven 150 x 50 mm joists, 3.6 m long; plus battens to suit the desired roof finish (all roofing timbers to be of durable quality). Some 50 x 25 mm bracing timber, sixteen hardwood pegs, eight 150 mm galvanised coach screws plus a large handful of 75 mm galvanised nails together with sufficient dry-mix concrete for filling in around the poles completes the requirements.

TOOLS

A post-hole borer or crowbar, shovel, electric saw, stout chisel, hammer, tape, pencil, square, adjustable spanner, spirit level and long straightedge.

PROCEDURE

1 Choose a day when you're feeling especially strong. Set out the post positions making sure you check they are square to each other (if they are, the diagonals should be equal).

2 Dig the holes for the poles a metre deep and lay 50 mm of gravel in the bottom to provide drainage. Then stand the poles plumb, and temporarily brace them with timber battens nailed to solidly driven pegs. Next, mark the position of the underside of the beams on each pole, making sure they're level with each other (a line or water level can be used instead of the long straightedge and spirit level). Remove the poles and accurately make the check-outs for the beam.

3 Restand the poles with the check-outs facing outwards. Brace them and then pour the concrete, making sure you tamp it well with a rod to get rid of any air bubbles (a dowel or a 1.8 m length of steel reinforcing is good for this). Leave to cure for at least 10 days before beginning the roof framing.

During this period, cut the beams and rafters to length and shape the ends as shown (or come up with your own design) on both the rafters and beams. The shape shown can be cut either with a circular saw or handsaw. If a circular shape takes your fancy, you'll need to get a jigsaw, one with a blade long enough to cut through the rafter. Make a few patterns out of cardboard before you decide. Then prime the wood (or use a timber preservative).

4 Knock off the bracing, then put the beams in place and bolt them to the poles. Next lay out for the rafter positions (approximately 600 mm centres), lay them in position, and skew-nail them to the beams. Nail on the battens, if any, and then thoroughly and carefully paint the whole structure.

Fix the roofing of your choice or plant grape vines, etc. Then assemble the tables, chairs and guests under your arbour and while away the summer hours with lots of fresh bread, olives, cheese and crisp, chilled wine.

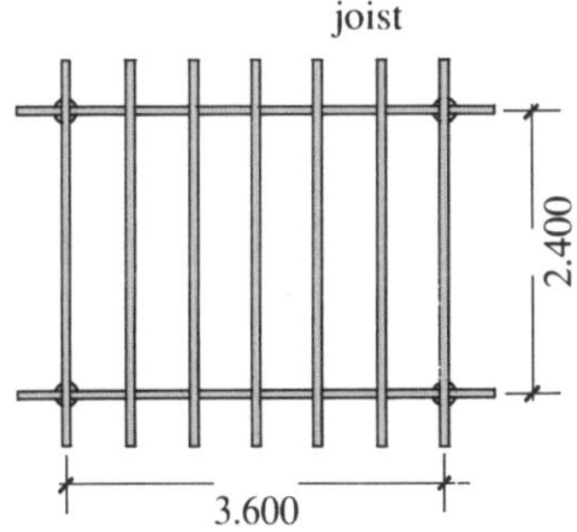

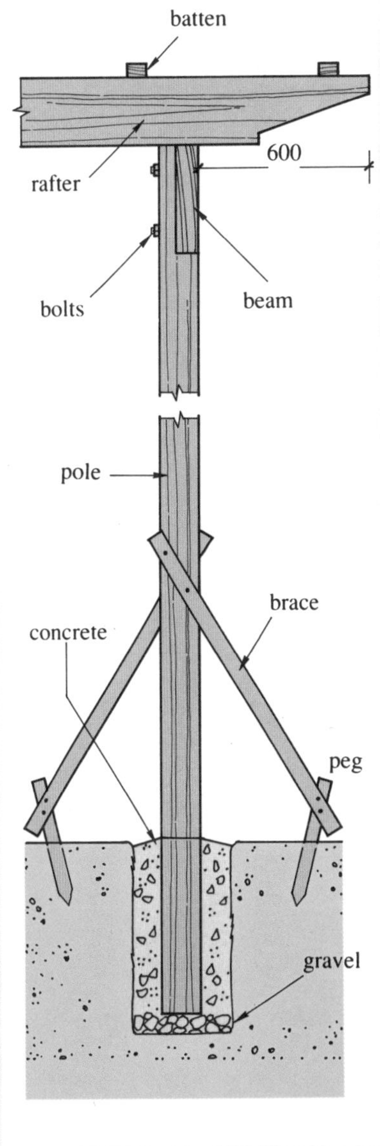

Diagram 22

Paving

Decks create raised level areas that require council approval, are expensive, and need periodic maintenance. Lawns also create level areas but need constant attention in the form of mowing, weed removal, watering and pest eradication. This is where paving comes into its own.

Paving has been used for centuries as an important part of gardens. If laid correctly, it gives a perfectly level area that requires no maintenance other than an occasional sweeping. The range of materials that can be used for paving is large, so any backyard theme can be catered for. You can use bricks or clay pavers for starters. Some of them are interlocking. The range of clay colours and textures is extensive and varied.

Stone flagging such as slate, sandstone, granite, basalt and limestone can also be used. Ceramic or terracotta tiles can be laid on top of existing concrete to give another wide range of colours, textures and designs but check their slipperiness and weathering qualities. Pavers, stone and tiles can, of course, be laid in different patterns. Again the possibilities are endless.

But there are even more possibilities! Concrete slabs can be laid and a colour finish applied. Concrete pavers in squares, circles, hexagons and rectangles are available in either a plain or fine pebble finish. The pebbles can be applied while the concrete is wet (or they can be stuck onto cured concrete).

Timber can also be used. Sleepers made out of tallowwood, redwood or ironbark can be laid in the ground. Alternatively use log discs or treated blocks. With lawn or gravel in between them, the patterned effect is interesting. Then there are cobblestones, river pebbles . . .

Are you exhausted? I sympathise with you. Sometimes having too many choices creates stress.

Bricks make effective pavers and can be laid in patterns of your own design.

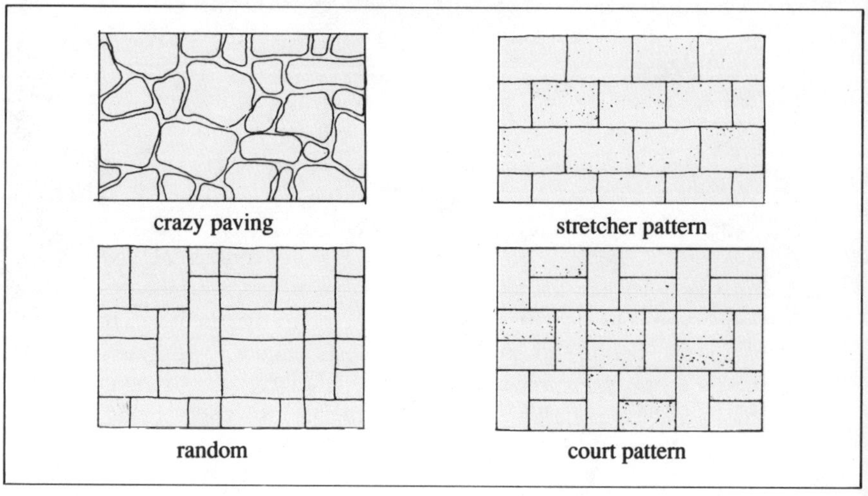

Diagram 23

Materials for Paving

As with plants, trees and shrubs, every material has its advantages and disadvantages that will limit the range somewhat. For example, clay pavers are harder wearing and keep their colour longer than cement ones. Special salt and chemical resistant clay pavers, some with rounded edges, must be used in salty environments. Clay pavers do best in sunny locations, otherwise they soon grow a mantle of moss.

Stone products such as sandstone, limestone and some slates, unless well preserved with sealers, usually weather badly. They either discolour to a bland grey or, in the case of limestone, actually wash away.

Timber products, unless they are of a durable species or have been very well treated, crack and twist if exposed to the sun. They also become grey, which is considered by some to be both natural and attractive. White ants of course love timber and will quickly devour anything that lacks toxicity.

Ceramic tiles are virtually indestructible. Perhaps collectively they have too much of a manufactured appearance to blend in with a natural paradise but that's a matter of judgement. Make sure you get an unglazed type that isn't slippery or a heavily textured glazed type.

While it is not possible to document the laying of every conceivable type of paver in this book, the basic principles involved in laying clay pavers can be broadly applied to some of the other types. In extremely hot areas, a coarse subbase is essential to allow for paving movement. Slate must be laid on a solid concrete base.

The size of pavers varies but common sizes are 230 x 115 mm or 220 x 110 mm. Ordinary house bricks can also be used as pavers. These sizes allow a variety of bond patterns (see Diagram 25). Thicknesses range from 40 mm for paths and patios and 65 mm upwards for driveways. Most bricks can be easily cut with a bolster and lump hammer on a sand bed. Very hard bricks often have to be cut with a diamond saw, which can be rather expensive if there are a lot to do.

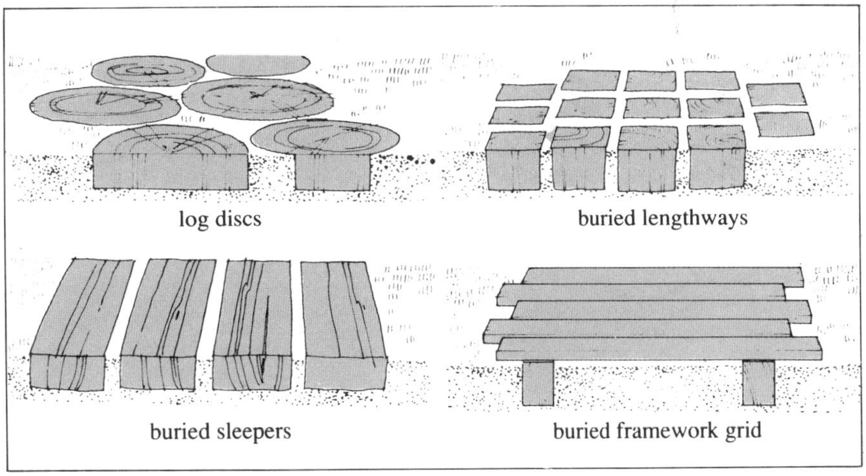

Diagram 24 Timber pavers

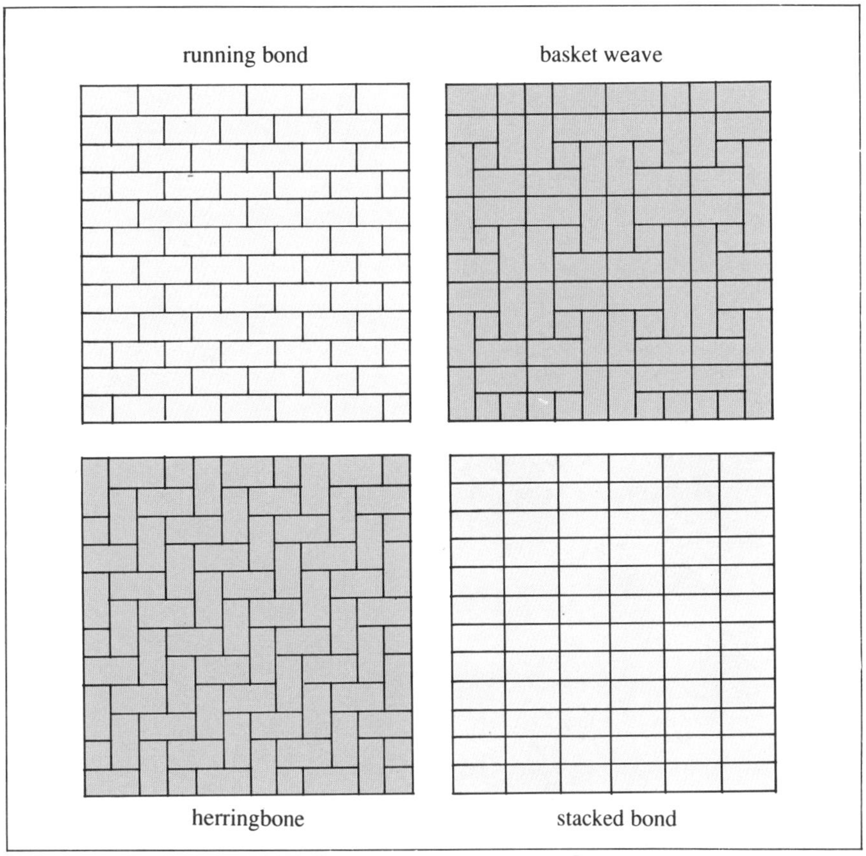

Diagram 25 House bricks

There is a large variety of patterns to choose from. By varying the colour and perhaps introducing curves, the results can be spectacular. With a few sketches and a glass or two of oaky wine, you could come up with your own unique design!

If you want to achieve curved shapes, make the edging out of several layers of tempered hardboard or thin strips of treated timber. When setting timber into the ground use pieces of 150 mm thickness or more for proper stability.

Laying Pavers

MATERIALS

Pavers: measure the length and width in metres. Multiply them together. The answer will be in square metres. There are usually 37 pavers (230 x 115 mm) to the square metre and 42 for the 220 x 110 mm size. Make sure you add between five and ten per cent for waste (this allows for any cutting plus discarding cracked or chipped pavers).

For sand only beds: take the number of square metres of paving and multiply it by the thickness required in metres (remember 50 mm is 0.050 of a metre). Your answer is in cubic metres. For example, 20 square metres of bedding 50 mm thick requires 1 cubic metre of sand.

Calculating cement in mortar mixes: if you want a 10:1 mix then the cement you'll need is approximately equal to one tenth of the volume of sand. One 40 kg bag of cement contains 0.03 of a cubic metre so, for one cubic metre of sand, four bags of cement would be plenty.

TOOLS

Lump hammer, brick bolster (for cutting pavers), string line, tape, straightedge, trowel, shovel, rake, hair broom, softwood block 250 x 100 x 50 mm, timber edging if required and a hose.

PREPARING FOR PAVING

Subsurface: the subsurface must be firm and stable otherwise the pavers will settle unevenly. Remove all topsoil and grass plus any loose fill. Create a fall in the subsurface of between 15 and 20 mm per metre to assist drainage. If the subsurface is soft or unstable, heavily compact it or cover with a 75–100 mm layer of crushed rock. Remember hired rollers that can be filled with water are good compactors.

Concrete makes a good subsurface for pavers. Use a mix of 10 sand to 1 of cement for the mortar. Use a 20–25 mm thick mortar bed.

Drainage: slope the subsurface towards an area where the water will drain away, or discharge into a stormwater line. If this is impossible, use a mortar bed under the pavers because it can't wash out. For badly drained areas you may have to put in a subsurface drainage system or a dish drain.

FORMING EDGES

The paving should be secured around the edges so that any sideways movement is stopped and the bedding can't be eroded. Make the edging work in paving sizes to lessen cutting.

Edges can be restrained by using treated timber boards or hardwood sleepers etc. held in place by hardwood pegs. Make the top of the edging the line for the finished pavers. This enables you to make a screed board for levelling the bedding. Simply nail cleats on both ends of your straightedge (see Diagram 26).

Alternatively, lay the edge pavers in a mortar (8:1 or 10:1 mix by volume). Extend the 50 mm thick mortar 100 mm past the edge pavers and slope at 45° (see Diagram 27). For added strength, use a 1 cement, 1 lime, 6 sand mix of suitable colour between the edge pavers but do it as you go to lessen staining.

Note: With brick houses, the finished height of the pavers should not come any closer than

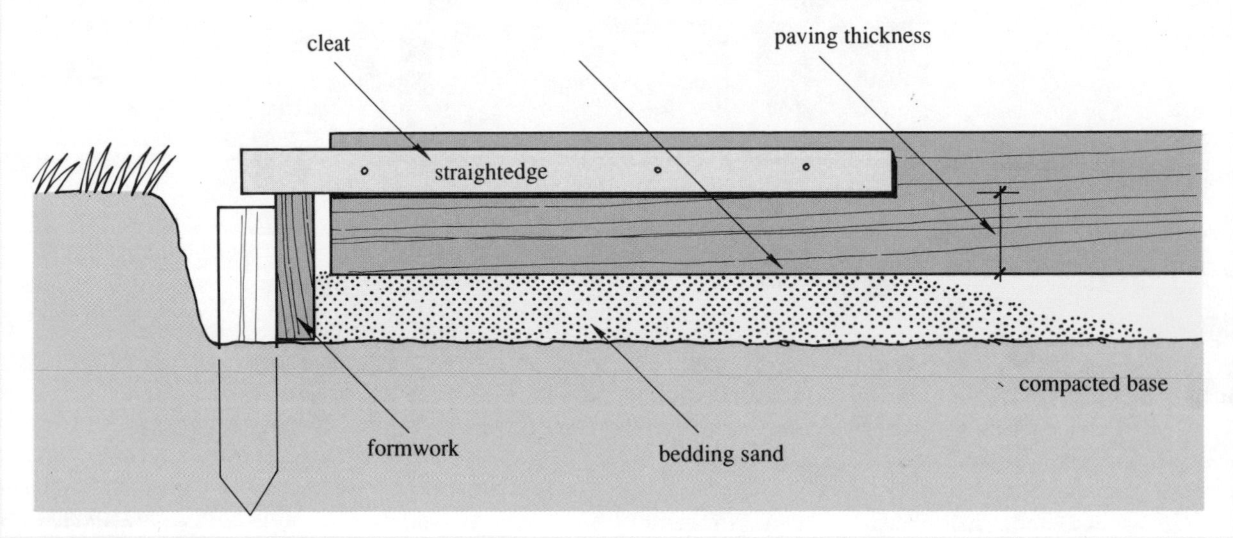

Diagram 26

Laying Pavers

150 mm below the damp proof course. This is because of the danger of moisture entering the wall through splashing or flooding. If this is impossible, make a 200 mm garden bed between the paving and the wall.

LAYING THE PAVERS

1 After the edging is secure, lay the bedding. The bedding provides drainage and a uniform support. Never use beach sand. The salt ruins the pavers. When using coarse concrete sand, spread to 50 mm thickness (minimum 30 mm), screed off and compact. Periodically check the bedding for straightness. Use a straightedge or a string line for this.

If laying a mortar bed, mix up only enough to do a square metre at a time. Don't make the 10:1 mix sloppy — semi-dry is best. Make sure you wet the pavers well before laying. Alternatively the mortar can be dry mixed and evenly spread over the area to be paved. This will provide sufficient moisture to set the mortar underneath.

2 Start laying the pavers. Leave the cuts until last. Work uphill if there is a slope. Tap each one down with a rubber hammer (or lump hammer and a block of soft wood) until firm.

3 Maintain a 2–3 mm joint between the pavers. This allows for the inevitable brick expansion and size discrepancies. For house bricks, use a 10 mm joint. Constantly check the surface with your straightedge and pack up any low ones.

JOINTS

When all the pavers are laid, fill the joints with washed sand by throwing shovelfuls of it across the pavers, and sweeping into the joints with a broom. Then lightly hose. It will take several applications to completely fill the joints. If laying pavers with cement mortar joints, complete as you go, making sure you brush off any excess mortar. Clean off any mortar stains with very diluted hydrochloric acid (1:12). Leave on for a maximum of five minutes, then hose off with copious amounts of water.

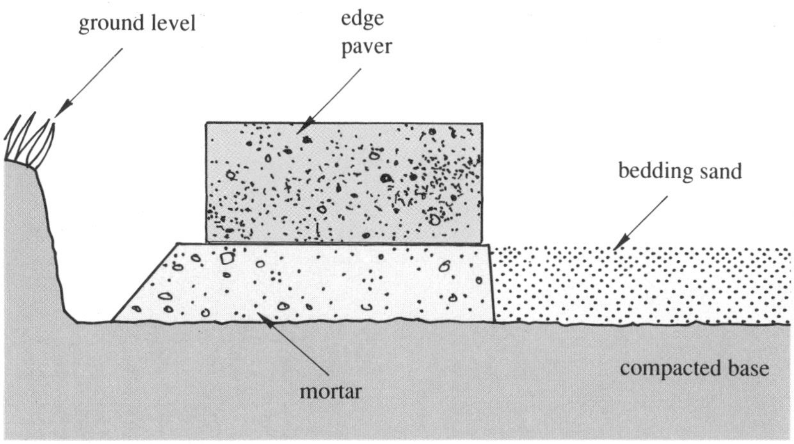

Diagram 27

Stone pavers get better with time and weather.

Paths

Though made from similar materials to paved areas, paths, because of their smaller width and difference in function, need to be planned differently. They are the linking devices that join the various sections of the backyard together. They range from the purely practical path, like the one that joins the clothes hoist to the laundry, to the whimsical, like the one in the adjacent picture.

Paths should tie in with the backyard theme. For example, if you have a geometrical garden, then paths should be regular in shape and have straight edges and regular joints. A wild, casual or bush garden could have paths with gentle curves, random patterned or crazy joints, and have the edges made fuzzy by overgrowing plants and ground cover. Paths shouldn't, of course, be too circuitous, or you simply encourage lawn-scrubbing shortcuts.

Paths are means by which people move through the backyard area and as such they should serve the purposes of the yard.

The materials paths are made from should blend in with existing paved areas and the exterior of the house or a patchwork-quilt effect could result. For example, a house of light yellow brick would hardly be complemented by a path or patio made from dark red pavers.

Unlike large paved patios with their mortar-laid edging, paths can be restrained by using a 75 x 25 mm timber edging that remains in the ground or even by simply digging a shallow trench in the top soil. A sand underlayer should be used.

Concrete Paths

Concrete paths, though plain, are very serviceable. Concrete is one of the oldest building materials, having first been used by the Romans who use crushed shells (lime) as cement and crushed rock as an aggregate.

A path that meanders through dense planting adds mystery to a garden.

Its plainness can be offset by mixing oxide in the concrete itself or, more economically, by adding a coloured topping. Another way to overcome its blandness is to spray the almost set concrete with water to expose the aggregate.

In modern form, concrete consists of three basic components: coarse aggregate (gravel), fine aggregate (sand) and a binding agent (cement). When mixed with water, the binding agent generates a chemical reaction which turns the cement paste into a powerful mineral 'glue' which strongly bonds the aggregates together. Concrete, once it has set, continues to gain in strength throughout its life, though reasonable strength is achieved after 10 days. The main strength of concrete is in compression. Where tension is important, as in paths where shrinkage and uneven settlement is guaranteed, steel mesh reinforcing must be used.

Concrete, if laid and cured properly, is virtually indestructible and usually requires little or no maintenance. Surface cracks can be obscured by forcing a cement/sand paste into the space, which should be cleaned and wet first to assist adhesion. Holes can be similarly filled but if they are more than 50 mm deep, a light aggregate should be used to reduce shrinkage.

Efflorescence stains, which are caused by moisture bringing whitish impurities to the surface of the concrete, can be removed with a mild acid solution (10 parts water to 1 part hydrochloric acid). Make sure you hose the acid off the concrete as soon as it has completed its work. Grease stains are best treated by removing any excess then cleaning the spot with trisodium phosphate or a solvent. Oil stains should be attended to immediately by covering the patch with lime or dry cement. Old stains can be removed with a special scowing solution obtainable from most hardware stores.

Laying a Concrete Path

The secret of achieving a strong concrete path involves three things:

- Having clean, well-shaped, and properly proportioned fine and coarse aggregates.
- Proper measuring and mixing of the dry materials. For small jobs dry, pre-mixed concrete is available. Each bag makes up 0.02 of a cubic metre of wet concrete.
- Clean water. The guiding rule is: if you can't drink it, don't use it!

PROCEDURE

1 Concrete should be laid between timber screeds held securely in place with hardwood pegs. It should be laid on a 25–50 mm bed of sand which in turn rests on a well tamped, even foundation. Expansion joints should be introduced every 5–10 metres to allow the concrete to shrink without cracking.

2 Once the concrete is mixed, transport it to the required location in a bucket or wheelbarrow, taking care not to shake it too much (because the coarse aggregate may sink to the bottom and separate from the fine). Place it in position slowly with a shovel and level off with a straightedge. This will bring air bubbles to the surface and so avoid honeycombing (a series of interconnected voids). As the concrete begins to harden, a wooden float should be used. It yields a gritty surface suitable for paths.

3 When using reinforcing steel, make sure that you maintain 50 mm minimum clearance from the external surface of the concrete to the rods, otherwise the steel may rust and crack the concrete. You can stand the steel on special chairs, or simply pour the concrete and then lift the steel up to the required height. Use your hands or a hook.

4 Don't allow the concrete to dry out too quickly or it may crack. Once the surface has hardened, periodically hose it during daylight hours, especially in hot weather, or cover it with damp cloth, tarpaulins or plastic for several days. If freezing is a possibility, cover the new path with straw, dry earth, etc.

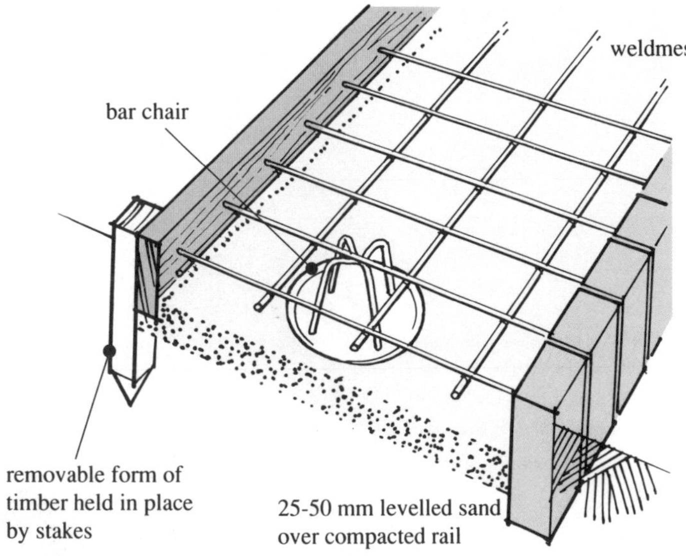

Diagram 28 Concrete path

Timber Paths

Timber for paths should be hardwood. Eucalypts, tallow-wood and turpentine are durable along with suitable pressure-treated pines.

There is a variety of ways to use timber. Consider the use of sleepers or planks laid either transversely or longitudinally. Quite rustic, isn't it? Another great effect is gained by raising the path above ground level. Decking is nailed to joists which can be laid on concrete pads. If the joists are treated, they can be partly sunk into the ground.

Notice the curve which is part of the path in the picture. The planks in this section could be tapered to fit. If so, draw out the corner showing the inside and outside curves on a piece of hardboard or the patio and divide it up into segments to get the right shape.

Another variation on timber is to use wooden rounds or discs which are made by sawing 50–70 mm cross sections off logs. Again set the path up with screeds, lay weed-controlling plastic and then a layer of sand on which the rounds can be bedded. When you're laying them, consider the comfort of the walker and space them relatively close together. Keep them flush with the ground to lessen the chance of tripping. Fill the spaces in between them with gravel, grass or wood chips.

You could, of course, fill the whole space between the screeds with wood chips. It gives a slightly softish, uneven surface that just begs to be walked on. Another thought! Why not consider square 'rounds' without edging.

Other Kinds of Paths

Variations on the log rounds include concrete rounds, flagstones and large river boulders. The last need to be relatively flat on one side and well embedded in the ground so they don't rock. If they're not, make sure your public risk insurance is high and up to date! The gaps between them can be filled

Timber paths look delightfully rustic especially when flanked by creepers.

A simple narrow brick path laid out in a stretcher pattern.

as above or coloured mortar can be used.

Gravel, either blue metal or some of the special reddish coloured ones, can be used effectively for paths. Again it requires edging to stop it spreading all over the garden and plastic to stop the weeds. Poisoning can be used but try to avoid that if possible because of the potential deleterious effect to your health and the environment. Another version of gravel is river pebbles. They give a dried-up riverbed appearance that is great to look at but not to walk on. Perhaps a few rounds could improve things.

Cobblestones, so beloved in squares and lanes in Europe, look good when laid as a path. Use half-bricks on end or virtually any type of stone. Your choice will depend on whether you enjoy symmetrical or random patterns.

Wooden rounds look particularly good when combined with gravel.

Flagstones, placed close together, make an attractive and relatively inexpensive path.

If you're a keen gardener, place stepping stones near the flower beds to protect the lawn.

Stepping stones across a lawn save your shoes in the rain and are less obtrusive than a pathway.

Steps

A path that is the same level along its full length could be fairly accused of being boring. The introduction of steps may well bring problems to the walker, to say nothing of the difficulties of wheeling a barrow, but the visual impact of differing levels even as small as one step high can be dramatic (providing the step is wide enough).

A nicely placed set of steps can draw the eye towards one of your backyard features. The effect is increased if the stairs are wide. Ideally they should be wide enough for two to walk together, say 1.8 metres. Introducing curved steps that follow the natural contours of the land will, like paths, also add interest. However, straight steps are easier to build.

Of course if your block is dead level (a rare occurrence), then putting in steps is a problem. You could get in some fill and slope the land away from the house (but don't come up any higher than the damp proof course otherwise you'll have rising damp problems). This will also assist surface water drainage and give you the fall you need to incorporate some steps. Alternatively you could do a little excavation to get a bit of fall.

When working out how many steps you need and how wide the tread should be, use the same theory and calculations as for timber stairs (see page 194). Single steps which are joined by lengths of paths are exempt from such calculations but the easy going 150 mm riser height should be maintained.

Materials for Steps

As with paths, step materials should be an integral part of the backyard, not a feature. Most of the paving materials mentioned earlier can be used, along with sleepers, timber rounds, etc. The important point is that they shouldn't be slippery.

Bricks make an effective edging to steps.

A decked walkway sets off the steps very well.

Sleepers. A great favourite with landscapers, discarded sleepers are relatively cheap and last almost indefinitely. They can be held in place with 600 x 10 mm diameter steel spikes.

Planks. You could make up a series of small overlapping decks. Simply use some treated joists and nail on 150 x 38 mm planks.

Concrete. Unfortunately a set of concrete stairs is probably beyond the average backyarder. It involves a tricky layout and requires proper formwork and steel reinforcing. The effect is too regular anyway and is reminiscent of fire stairs. However, if you rather like that effect, get in a carpenter to erect the formwork for you and design the reinforcement, then pour the steps, strip off the formwork, and finish them yourself.

Another way to use concrete without the complexity is to lay a series of overlapping paths (at least 150 mm) beginning from the bottom up. All you need for that is a simple riser form around 150 mm wide, held in place with pegs at either end. Screeds can be attached to the ends to form the side thickness which can be as little as 75 mm. A bit of mesh in the bottom, some readymix and a wooden float and you're away. Alternatively use a 100 mm rise and slope the paths upwards 50 mm.

Pavers. These are hard to use for steps because you don't have a restrained edge. You need a firm foundation material cut to suit brick courses. Lay the bricks on a thick mortar bed and tie together with strong mortar (four of sand, one of cement). Begin from the bottom up.

Stone. The procedure differs depending on whether the stone is sawn, in rough pieces or boulders. If in sawn brick-like blocks, lay the same as pavers. Small random pieces can be roughly fitted and laid on a 50 mm mortar bed reinforced with a bit of galvanised chicken wire. Larger pieces of relatively even thickness can be set on a mixture of cement and soil or an ordinary mortar bed. Boulders can be dug into the ground and will look as if they've always been there.

Railway sleepers placed at intervals along a sloping pathway make rustic-looking steps.

These steps leading up to a patio are made from a combination of brick and wood.

Arches and Gateways

If, by using fences, screens or hedges, you've created very separate areas in your backyard, you'll need points of access and egress. You can of course just leave an opening. However, the garden gateway complete with picket gate shown in the photograph shows what can be achieved. Diagram 29 shows how the 150 x 50 mm beams fit over each other and the 100 x 100 mm posts. Note the tapered ends which give the gateway a timeless look. The posts can be spaced at 1.8 to 2 m centres depending on the load the gateway has to carry when the vines grow.

Arches and decorative gateways, though not strictly essential for human activity in your backyard, can add a special touch. Lattice and vines or climbing roses draped over them further add to the charming effect. Making a timber arch is not as hard as it might appear.

This Chinese moongate is an interesting alternative to an arch.

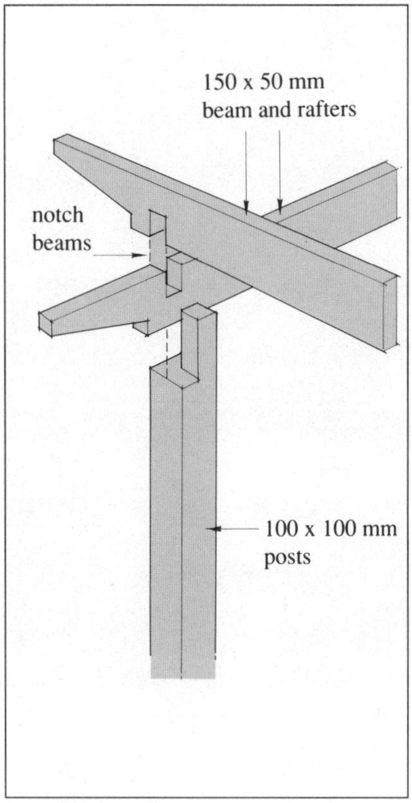

Diagram 29

Climbing roses beautifully frame this simple slatted arch.

Making a Timber Arch

There are many ways to construct arches, some requiring a great deal of skill, to say nothing of equipment like bandsaws, mortising machines, etc. Once the treated or end-preserved posts are installed, the following method can be undertaken by anyone using some simple materials and basic tools.

As Diagrams 30 and 31 show, the arch is built up by laminating a series of thin strips. The glue used to secure them must be a waterproof one such as epoxy.

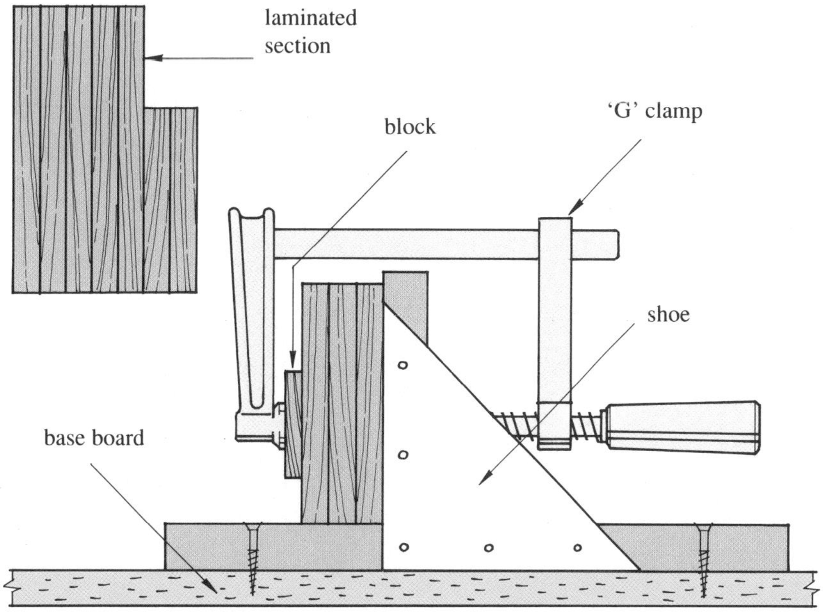

Diagram 30

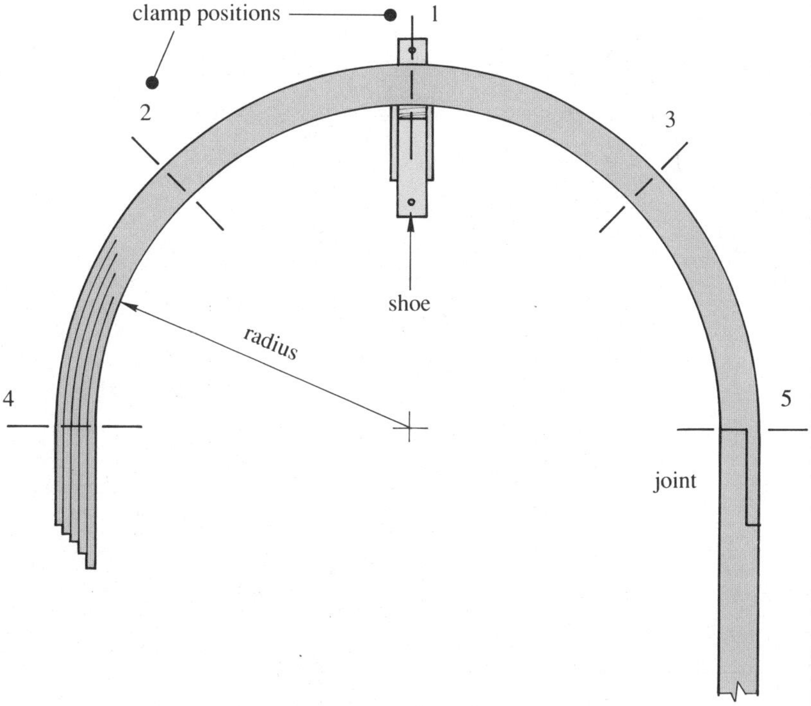

Diagram 31

PROCEDURE

1 On a piece of 20 mm thick particle board or plywood, mark out two parallel lines to represent the distance *between* the posts. Then lay out the required arch shape to fit between them. Use a long strip of timber with a nail driven through one end and a hole in the other end through which a pencil projects to draw the shape of the inside of the curve. Experiment with different radii and centre points until you get the curve you want.

2 Screw the timber shoes (which can be made from 50 by 25 mm batten reinforced with hardboard or three-ply) to the curved shape. Their spacing depends on the sharpness of the curve, the species of timber (clear oregon is excellent for bending) and the width and thickness of the strips (75–1C0 x 5–10 mm is suitable). Bend a piece around the curve to get some idea of how much pressure has to be exerted.

3 Begin to glue the strips together holding them tightly against the shoes with clamps (work your way along from the centre). You might, if the curve is very gradual, be able to glue the whole lot at once. Make sure you remove any excess glue.

4 When the glue is completely dry, remove the curved section, plane the edges smooth and then sandpaper. It is a simple matter to glue a couple of thin strips to the arch to form the lattice groove.

Any number of arches, large or small, can be formed in the way described on page 217. To join them to posts let a couple of the strips project 150 mm at each end and recess out the back of the stiles to take them. If you glue and screw it, it will never move!

As the photograph shows, a combination arched gateway and side screen is an attractive project. Refer to the instructions on page 217 regarding forming the arch which Diagram 32 shows. A quick check of the lattice section (page 196) will also prove beneficial. Note that the lattice is held in a groove formed by nailing (with galvanised nails) twin battens to the uprights and horizontals. Although the uprights can be held by ramming the earth around them, they will be much more solid if you concrete them in.

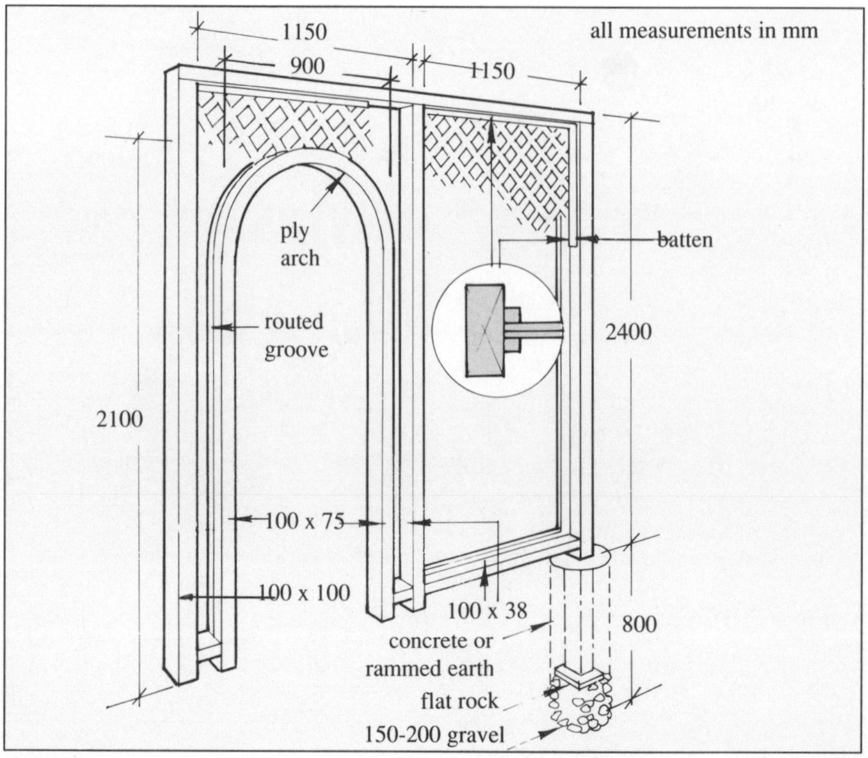

Diagram 32

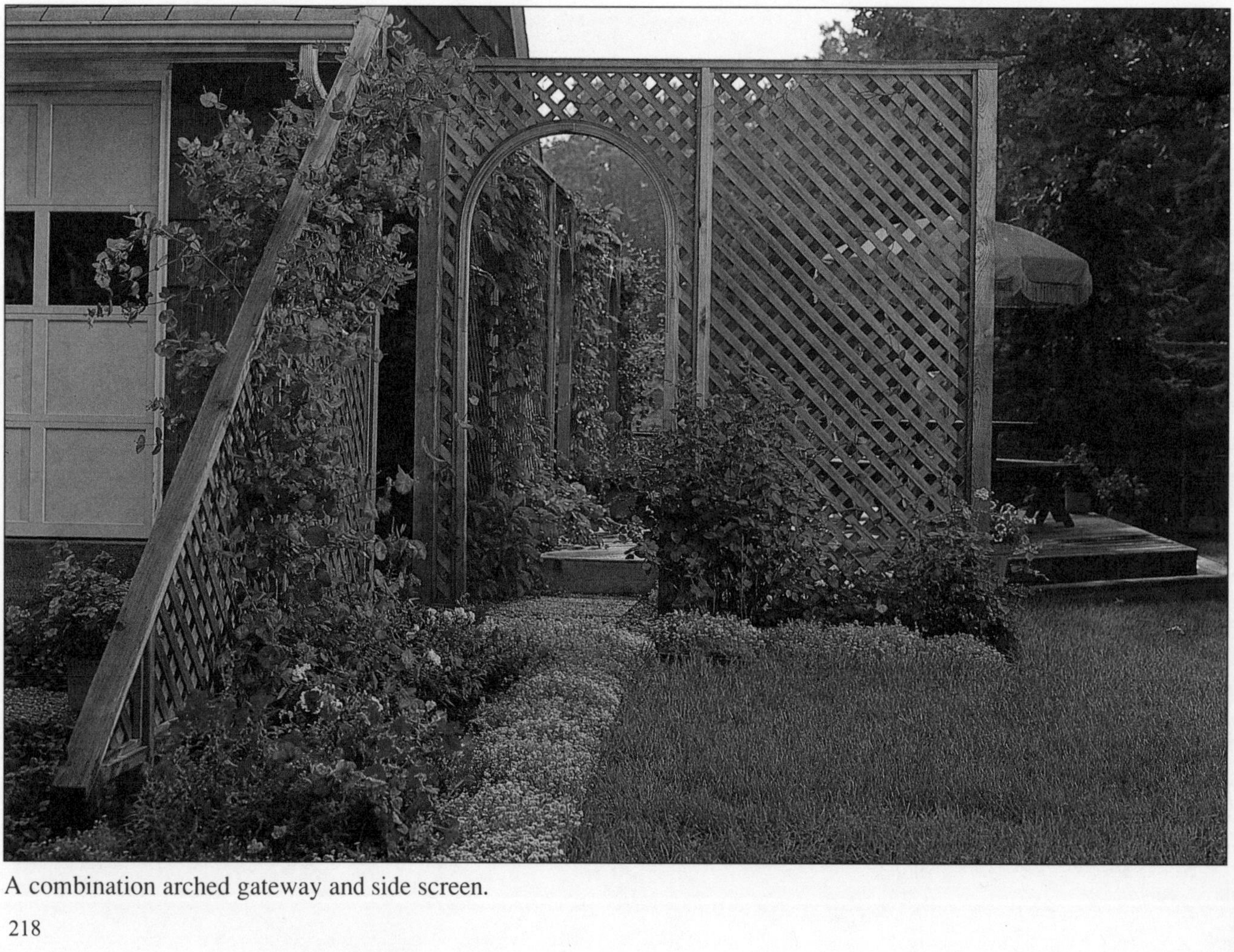

A combination arched gateway and side screen.

Gates

There are a zillion types of gates. In timber, they range from the simple ledged and braced gate up to picket gates. In metal there are any number of different shapes and finishes which can be made to suit any sized opening.

The photograph shows an unusual gate which is made of three layers of western red cedar laminated in a similar fashion to plywood. Diagram 33 shows the alternating layers of shiplap which are glued together with waterproof glue and nailed with galvanised ring nails for better holding power. This form of construction, in combination with the durability of western red cedar, should make the gate last forever. The top of the gate can be cut to a circular shape (or any other shape you prefer) with a jigsaw.

Use large tee-hinges and make sure that the hinging post is strongly embedded. Thickly paint the top of the gate to lessen the chance of cracking.

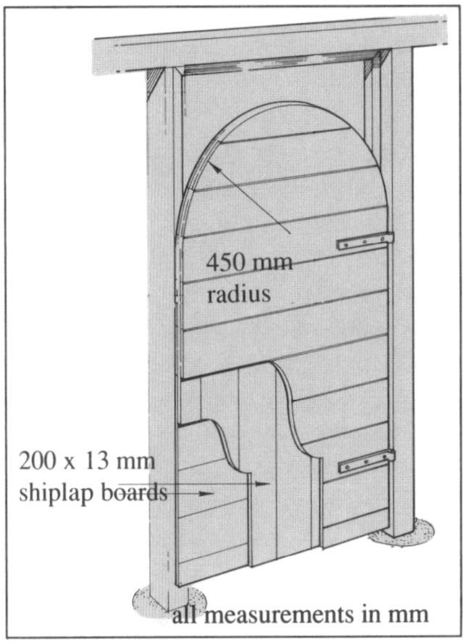

Diagram 33

An unusual but very effective timber garden gate.

Ledged and Braced Gate

As Diagram 34 shows, the gate is made up of tongue-and-groove boards which are fixed to a top and bottom rail by clenched galvanised nails or by screws. The brace, which runs upwards and outwards from the bottom hinges, stops the gate from sagging.

PROCEDURE

1 Cut the boards to length (use western red cedar or cypress pine), then the 150 x 25 mm rails making them 10 mm shorter than the overall width of the door. Chamfer the rails on the exposed edges and ends.

2 Lay the boards on the rails until they overhang equally on both sides, then mark and rip the outside boards so that the tongue and groove are removed.

3 Prime in the grooves, then begin to nail the boards to the rails making sure that the rails are at right angles to the boards and the boards fit tightly. Putting blocks under the rails will enable the nails to project through the other side.

When nailing, put two nails near the centre of each board. If you put the nails close to the outside edges, the timber, as it shrinks, will split. Make sure you punch the nails.

4 When all the boards are nailed on, turn the door over and fit the brace. Notching it into the rails will ensure it never moves. When it fits, nail it into position.

5 For extra strength clench the nails over in the direction of the grain and punch the points below the surface.

6 Fit the door between the posts, screw on galvanised tee-hinges, then affix a suitable latch. Painting the gate will increase its longevity and lessen any chance of it splitting.

Diagram 34

A picket gate can be made on the same construction principles as the ledged and braced gate. Simply substitute shaped pickets for the tongue-and-groove boards. Space them 25–38 mm apart, depending on the width of the pickets.

With the gate in position your yard will acquire new character and convenience.

Shelters and Shade Houses

Your garden is not always a hospitable place. In fact at times tempests come, to say nothing of the heat of summer. A pergola, since it has no roof, is not always adequate, so having some form of protective shelter you can retreat to is a boon. The photographs show what is possible (all subject to council and perhaps neighbours' approval, of course).

A hexagon-shaped rotunda built on treated pine poles is probably one of the easier ones to construct. Of course, if you prefer something simpler, the structure can be made square, still using the same construction principles. A simple layout for a hexagon is shown in Diagram 35. This procedure fixes the position of the posts and also the shape of the hub at the peak of the rafters. Leave the posts long and, when the concrete has cured, mark them for height with the water level and cut them off with a chain or bush saw.

Diagram 36a shows how the beams are fixed to the top of the poles. Framing anchors will secure them against storms. Notice how the hip rafters in Diagram 36b, which

A true summerhouse, complete with shingle roof and weather vane.

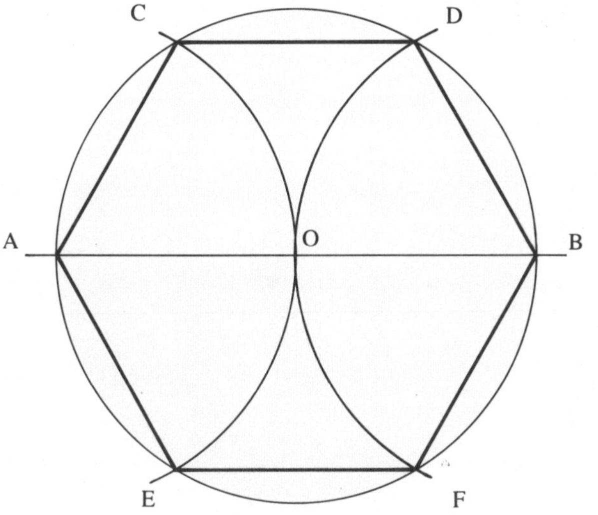

1. Draw a straight line AB, across the given circle to pass through the centre, point O.

2. Using points A and B as centres, scribe an arc to pass through the centre, point O, to meet the circumference at points CE and DF.

3. Draw sides to meet at points obtained on the circumference.

Diagram 35

come in at 60° to the corners, are notched over them to provide a level surface for nailing.

Battens 75 x 38 mm or 100 x 50 mm (depending on the span) will hold shingles, corrugated sheeting, ply, etc.

Diagram 37 shows how the top of the rafters are joined. The hub may project above the rafters or be kept flush with the top of them, depending on the roof covering.

A gazebo or summerhouse placed near a pool, patio or secluded corner is an impressive asset for your backyard. Though similar in basic design to the forementioned structures, it is much more elaborate and a daunting structure to try to build. It is typically a five, six or eight sided structure with a pitched roof and comes either enclosed with glass or flyscreening or at the least with a handrail that is filled in underneath with lattice, laths or boards. The roof can be thatched, shingled, tiled, or covered with copper or galvanised iron.

The structural members can be of new or salvaged timber and there are usually decorative embellishments such as scrolls, arched corners, decorative finials and weather vanes. You could get a price from a builder to construct one. They are also available in kit form from various suppliers. I would recommend you go this route and follow the manufacturer's recommendations regarding a suitable base. The floor finish could be of gravel, slate, pavers, flagstone, wood or wood chips depending on its use and how much money you have to spend.

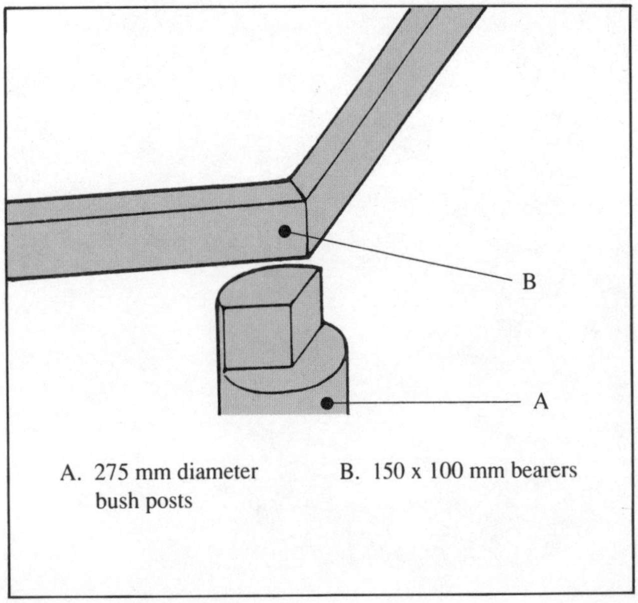

Diagram 36A

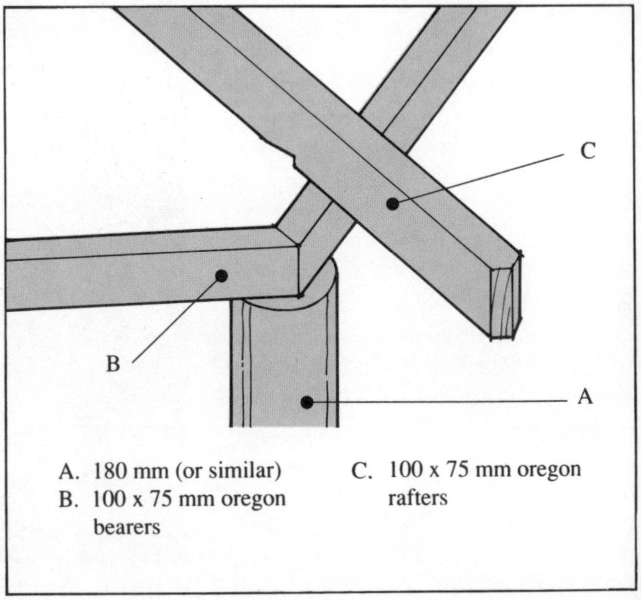

Diagram 36B

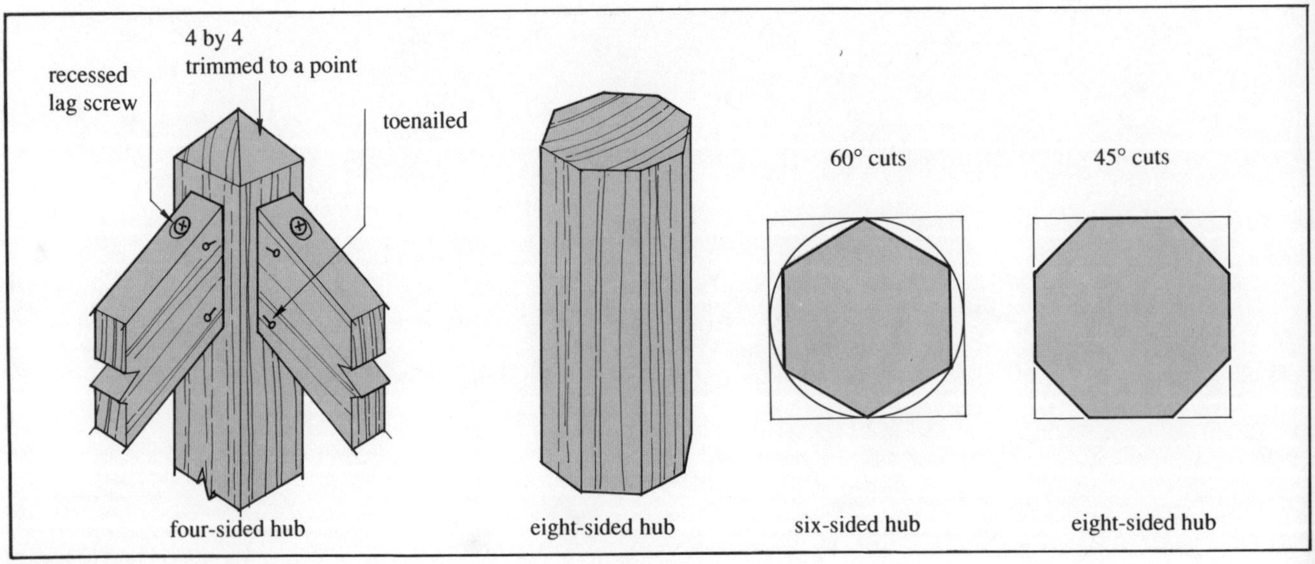

Diagram 37

Brushwood, lattice and thatch give this summerhouse an island feel.

Shade Houses

A shade house is just that: a structure that primarily provides shade, not for humans, but plants. Egocentric and perverse as humans are, they sometimes find pleasure in providing facilities that encourage and pamper other living things.

A shade house can be anything from a lean-to with a slatted roof hanging onto a rickety back fence to a slightly upmarket variety that stands against the house, to an elaborate free-standing structure that has louvred sides and a shadecloth roof.

The trick is to decide what type of plants you want to grow in your shade house. Obviously they are varieties that don't want direct sunlight and perhaps require shielding from cold southerlies or boisterous westerlies. Some require a maximum of rainfall, others very little. Plants, like people, have different needs and preferences.

There are a number of important factors that are common to all shade houses:

- They need strong beams (and thick diameter galvanised steel pipes) to support hanging baskets as well as the shading material.
- They should have a gravel floor with stone flags. This allows good drainage while providing a level, firm surface.
- If using shade cloth, put galvanised chicken wire underneath it to lessen feline indentations. Choose a density of shade cloth which allows in the right amount of light and moisture. Don't make it too dense because most plants need some sunshine.
- A constant air flow must be maintained as well as moisture. For the latter, a misting spray is ideal for some plants, a damp floor with rising humidity for others.
- Slats or shade cloth can be used on one or more of the walls as can adjustable matchstick blinds or lattice to control the elements. Alternatively, put up galvanised steel mesh and use flowering vines to fill in the sides.
- Because of the damp environment, use a durable timber or one that has been treated.

Your shade house, properly constructed, will provide you and your sun-shy plants with a secure retreat, one especially pleasant on a hot day.

This combination shade house and pergola provides protection for your plants and a very pleasant place for you.

Bridges

Where a bridge spans a pond or crosses an imitation dry creek bed, it makes a charming addition to any backyard. The photograph shows what can be achieved with relatively little cost and effort.

The bridge beams are just old railway sleepers. They have been suspended off four posts which are also cut from railway sleepers (or they could be 100 x 100 mm and extend 900 mm above the bridge level and take a 100 x 50 handrail). The posts can be creosoted and driven into the ground as shown, or concreted into position. The fixings used are galvanised coach screws.

The decking could be of 100 x 50 or 38 mm sawn hardwood, depending on how wide you want the bridge to be. A 100 x 50 should easily span 1.00–1.20 metres.

The much softer lines of a curved bridge are not as hard to make as they may look. The technique is the same as described in the section on arches (page 216) and involves laying thin strips of say 75 by 12 mm western red cedar or seasoned hardwood over a curve and gluing them together. You can use the same layout and shoes to make a curved handrail with the same curve as the bridge. Make sure you use waterproof glue and non-corroding fasteners otherwise your bridge will delaminate.

The curved bridge can be fastened at the ends in the same manner as the straight bridge but make sure the posts are well secured so that they resist any tendency for the arch to sag. Paint your bridge with a good wood preservative finish. Paint should not be used unless you sprinkle sand onto the finished coat. If you don't do this you could slip, especially on a curved bridge.

A simple bridge made from railway sleepers.

CHAPTER 9

THE SMALLER TOUCHES

Once the large touches are complete, the next step, if you've still got the energy, is to begin the smaller projects. What better place to begin than that great Australian institution: the barbie. By this I don't mean a blonde American doll but the ceremonial place where, while drinking copious amounts of cold beer and cask wine and simultaneously swiping at flies, bits and pieces of dead animals are grilled to a blackened perfection in a smoky cloud.

Barbecues

Barbecues, like people, can be simple or complicated. A few stones grouped together with a piece of chicken wire over the top will do the job nicely. I've even seen the end of a shovel held over coals used to cook a piece of prime T-bone steak beautifully. The portable barbie made from cast iron or steel is not to be sniffed at either.

At the other end of the scale are barbecues that could almost rival the Taj Mahal. Chimneys that Santa would be proud to descend can arise from the barbecue ashes, so to speak. An old stove can be recycled, antique tiles find a new setting, bricks can be uniform or jut aggressively, steel mesh or grids from stormwater pits can be transformed into super grills — you are only limited by your imagination!

The siting of the barbecue is important. Consider the neighbours from the point of view of smoke and convivial noise. Put it in a sheltered place that gets winter sun. Carefully consider where you'll eat. If you have to make a route march from the barbecue to get there, the food will get cold.

A simple brick barbecue with a built-in wooden bench for preparation.

Fixed Barbecues

Basically, a fixed barbecue consists of a metal plate and/or grill suspended above a hearth which is set in stone or brickwork. Choose the masonry carefully, making sure it blends in with the rest of the materials in your yard. Make sure you get a brick that will stand high temperatures.

The mortar in any barbecue should not be too strong otherwise it will crack under the extreme heat. A 5:1 to 8:1 mix (with a bit of plasticiser in it to make laying easier) is ideal. The mortar should be coloured to suit the bricks. The joints can be flush, raked or ironed. Cut the bricks with either a cold chisel or, better still, a bolster.

A barbecue can be built on a concrete slab or out of solid brickwork reinforced with brick tour. Keep the brick joints to around 10 mm and make sure you accurately level each course with as long a spirit level as you can get. Professional bricklayers build up the corners first, then string a nylon line between them using points or blocks to fill in what they call the 'guts'.

As you lay the bricks, keep checking the structure for plumb (verticalness) or it will resemble the Leaning Tower of Pisa. The most common bond used today is stretcher bond. If you're especially adventurous you could consult a bricklaying manual and try something more exotic but only if you've had previous bricklaying experience.

Tables and Seats

Nothing encourages use of your backyard like tables and chairs. They are synonymous with relaxation, eating and reading. The photographs give you some idea of the effects that can be achieved with both home-made and ready-made garden furniture.

Regarding ready-made furniture, consider it carefully. By this stage of the proceedings your energy and enthusiasm could be waning a little and you might be glad to buy some attractive garden chairs and tables.

If you go this route, keep in mind that in a few months or a year you could well be restored and eager to put some more of yourself into the backyard (besides the sweat). Buy something that has the potential to fit in several locations so that if later on you want to create a unique setting of your own, the temporary setting will adjust well to a new position.

Alternatively, you could create something really temporary. Some railway sleepers laid on top of two stacks of bricks can create a great seat and/or table. An upturned tree log will support the heaviest guest (albeit not too comfortably but, after all, this could result in a slower depletion of your liquor stocks!). A post in the ground with a cask lid on it makes an instant table.

As the photograph shows, split and whole pine logs can be combined to form a seat that would grace any backyard (refer to the play gym later in this section for general comments about using treated pine). The design can be used as is or improvised on. The rougher it looks the better, so you don't have to take as much care with joints and finish as you would with a more formal seat.

For those who want something more permanent the following seats and tables will provide ideas and some construction details.

A home-made but very elegant treated pine garden seat.

A sawn log and two tree forks are used to make this rustic garden seat.

Garden Table and Bench Unit

The trick of balancing a spilling plate in your lap and a can on your kneecap is a bit passé. With this table and seat unit you can sit and eat in comfort. Being portable it can be moved into the shade or under a waterproof shelter or to a position that takes full advantage of the sun or view. Because it is put together with screws it can be dismantled for storage or transport.

MATERIALS

The best timber to use, considering it is for outside use, is treated radiata pine. This has strength as well as durability, especially if given the additional protection of a coat of paint. Western red cedar can also be used but it is much softer and therefore more easily damaged. Considering your comfort and clothes, dressed timber sections are preferable as they are smoother and easier to paint.

The sizes you need to order are shown in the table below. The length of the table or the height of the seat can be varied to suit your individual requirements.

You'll also need galvanised screws for making the frames (36–75 mm roundheads), 20 heavy gauge strong metal brackets (either galvanised steel or brass) and enough 25 mm galvanised screws to screw them on, some 75 mm nails, and 30–50 mm countersunk galvanised screws for the fixing of the slats, etc.

TOOLS

Hammer, tape, pencil, handsaw or circular saw, plane, square, hand drill (or electric drill), suitable drill bits, screwdriver.

PROCEDURE

1 Cut the six legs to the length shown in Diagram 38. The bevel used is 60° and this can best be marked by using a large 60° set square. Make sure the ends are parallel and square to the face.

With a sharp plane set fairly fine (if you haven't one, use rough abrasive paper and a cork block), make a neat chamfer (45° bevel on the edges) around the four ends. The chamfer (say 2 mm across) gets rid of sharp edges which may splinter; it also provides an attractive finish.

2 Cut the top rails to length, nip off the bottom corner (you could make it round if you like), and again chamfer the ends and the two bottom edges.

3 Repeat for the seat rails making sure you keep the rounds down.

4 On a flat surface (a concrete slab is ideal) lay the legs in position and, using the 75 mm nails, tack the top rail and cross rail on top of the legs using the measurements shown. Check the legs are at 60° to the rails.

Then drill and screw three 75 mm screws into each joint in the positions shown in Diagram 38 (use a drill the same size as the screw shank in the rail, and one equal to the thread core in the leg). When complete, remove the nails, and repeat for the other two frames, using the first frame as a template to check the others are the same (if they're a bit out at least they'll all be the same).

5 Fix the metal brackets to the outside of the end frames and either side of the middle one, positioning them in the centre of the tops and seat. Make sure you keep the top of the bracket flush with the top of the rail.

6 Then cut the seats and table tops to length, again chamfering the ends and all edges.

7 Mark the rail positions on the underneath of the seats and tops and square the lines across.

8 Lay the top boards upside down on the slab with their ends flush and, with a friend, stand the two end frames in the positions you've marked, and screw the brackets firmly to the top (see Diagram 39).

9 Repeat for the centre frame. Check that it lines up with the other two.

10 Carefully roll the table over the right way up, then fix the seats in position, again using the brackets in the positions shown.

11 Leave the assembly for a few weeks to allow for shrinkage, then fix the top and seat down more securely with the 25 mm countersunk galvanised screws (put them midway between the brackets and the edges). If you put them in before

NO.	ITEM	LENGTH	WIDTH	THICKNESS
6	Legs	1000	100	38
3	Top Rails	900	100	50
3	Seat Rails	1800	100	50
3	Tops	2400	300	38
2	Seats	2400	300	38

All measurements are in millimetres.

Garden Table and Bench Unit

the shrinkage takes place you'll find the timber will split.

12 Then apply a suitable finish. You can of course paint the seats and top a different colour from the frames for variation but this will involve more cutting in.

If there is an end-to-end wobble in the table (because the brackets are not stiff enough), fix a 100 x 25 mm stiffener in the position shown (hard against the top rail).

You may find, as the timber in the table shrinks, that you have to retighten the screws to make sure the table stays rigid. It is also important to set the table on a level surface otherewise it could develop a permanent twist. A small paved area is the ideal base, one that stays relatively dry, even in the wettest weather.

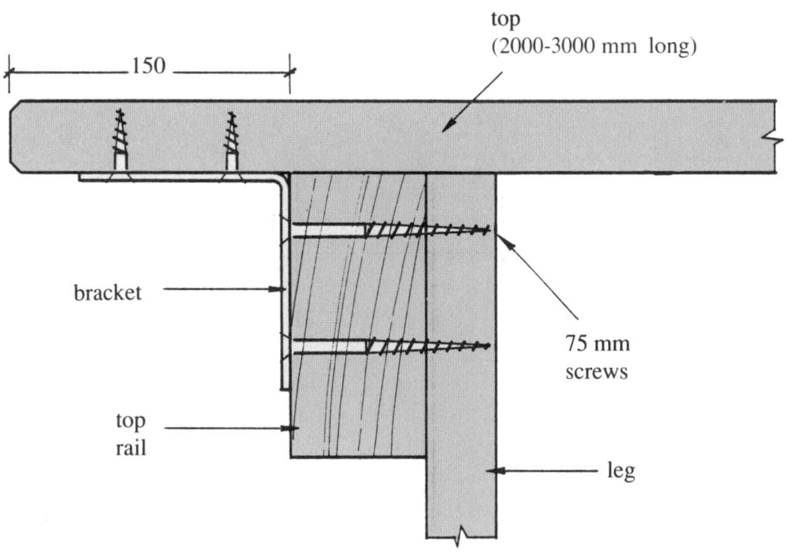

Diagram 39 End detail

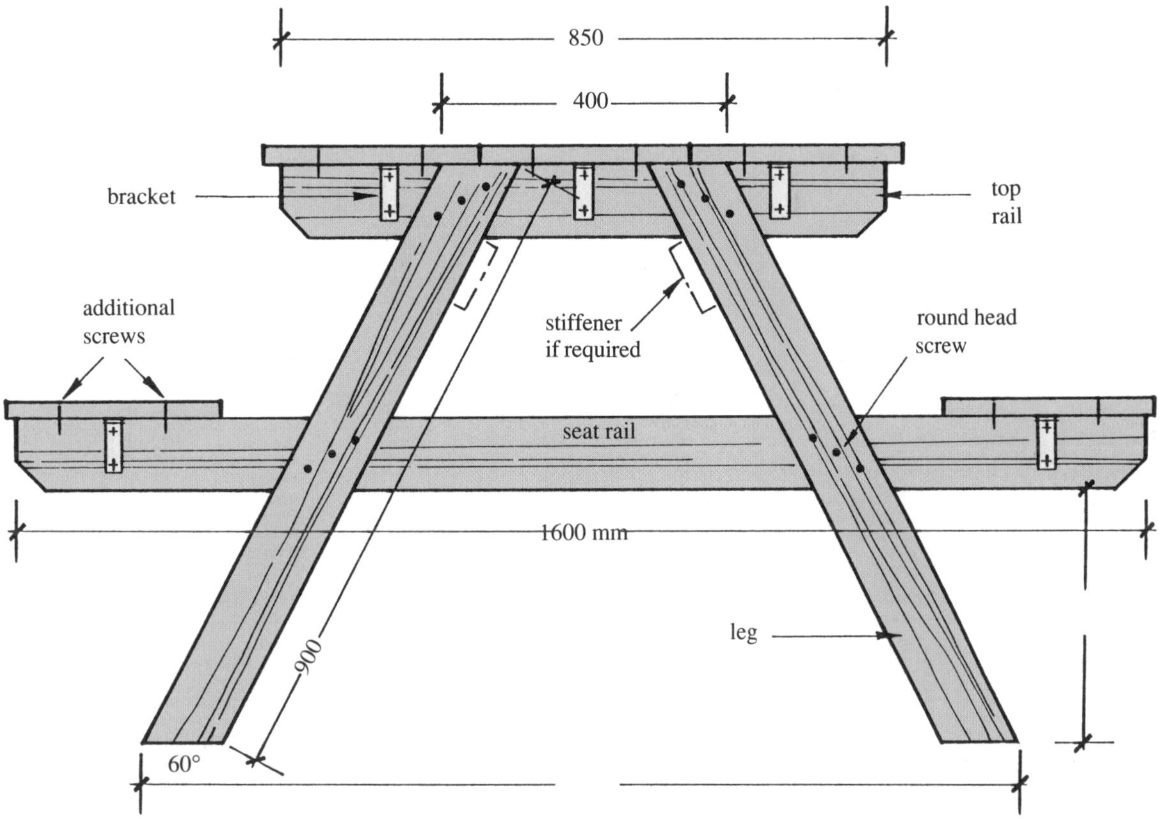

Diagram 38 End view of table

A Fixed Bench

As the photograph shows, the bench (shown with a matching table and seat) makes a handsome addition to any yard.

PROCEDURE

1 The construction is very simple as Diagram 40 shows. The four 125 x 50 mm hardwood bench posts, 1.100 metres long, are concreted into the ground using a 300 mm deep x 250 mm square footing. The gravel at the base assists drainage. Make sure you thoroughly creosote the post ends to deter white ants.

2 Once the posts are in place and the concrete has cured, cut them to length and shape the recess for the seat back. Then cut and shape the 100 x 50 mm hardwood seat supports (one 1.200 length will make a support and brace) and bolt them on using 125 mm bolts or (75 mm coach screws). Note that the top edge is slightly concave to provide a recess that more easily fits the average human posterior. This curve can be made with a plane.

3 After cutting the 100 x 50 mm braces, bolt them to the seat supports and then screw the other end to the posts with heavy gauge 100 mm brass screws. Drill a proper pilot hole for each screw or the screw may snap off as you're driving it.

4 To finish the bench, simply screw the back to the posts and the slats to the seat: 50 x 50 mm western red cedar is ideal for this. Keep them a couple of millimetres apart as they will shrink and this gap will hide any irregularity. Chamfering or slightly rounding the edges will lessen the possibility of splinters.

5 Note the detail which shows the screws sunk in about 10 mm. Your hardware store has a special bit for this purpose which will fit your electric drill. The holes are then plugged with a piece of dowel. Check on the dowel species to make sure it will not deteriorate. If necessary, you can get a plug cutter and make your own dowels out of a durable timber.

Alternatively, you could just countersink the screw heads and make a feature of them. In either case, draw a line to make sure the screws are in line. The effect is very pleasing.

6 The top rail is made from 150 x 50 mm while the front rail comes out of 100 x 75 mm. Both are from western red cedar. They are shaped with a plane, finished with sandpaper and screwed in place.

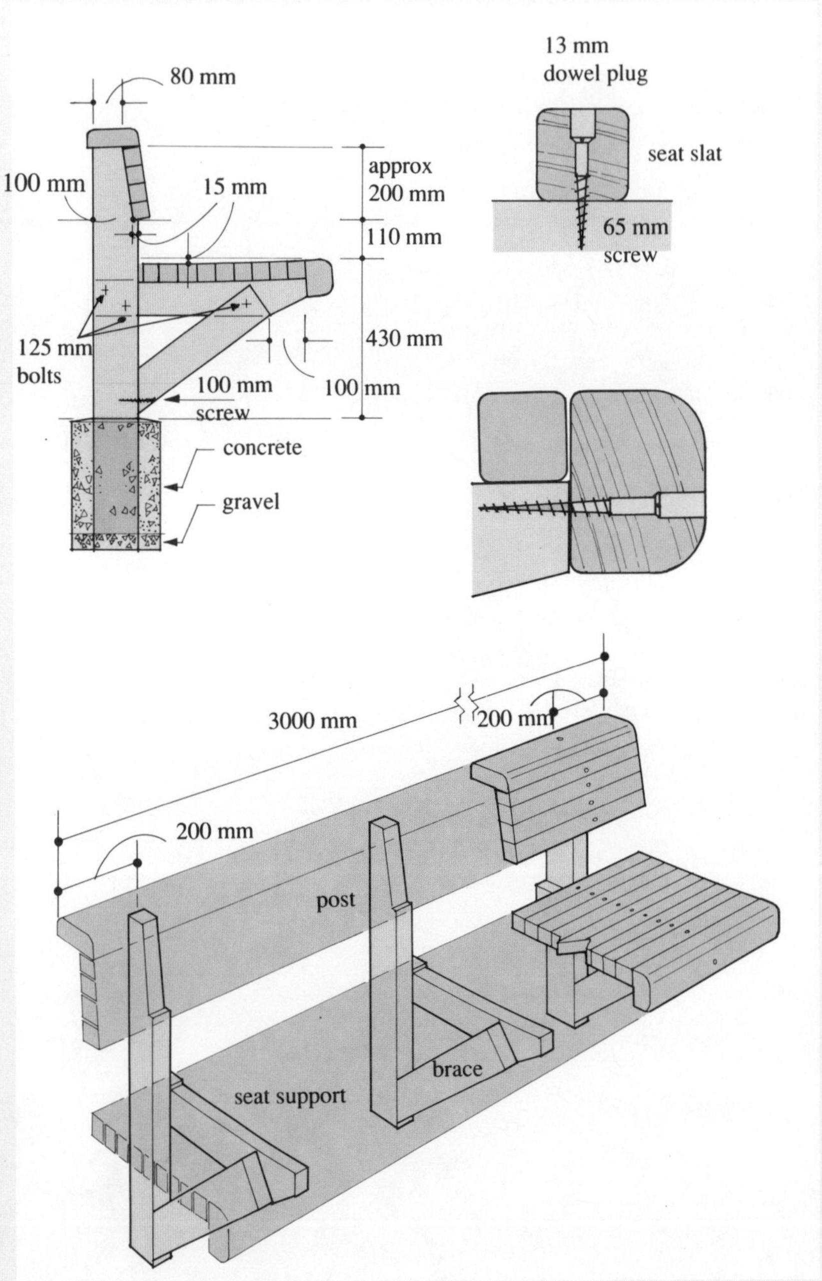

Diagram 40

The fixed bench, together with a matching table and seat would look good in any garden.

Seat Around a Tree

Building a garden seat around a tree will give your garden an attractive and intimate focal point. The seat can also double as a low table. Place the main seating area to take advantage of any view or favourable aspect. If the tree is deciduous and in the right location, the seat will get plenty of sun in winter yet be fully shaded in summer.

Diagram 41A shows the tree in one corner of the seat but you can, if you prefer it, put the tree in the centre. This requires only a slight modification of the structure and involves putting a cross-rail on either side of the tree.

MATERIALS

The best timber to use, considering the seat will be exposed to the elements, is one that requires no painting and will not rot. Treated pine is fairly good although painting will increase its longevity. Make sure the timber for the posts is treated to a standard suitable for being in contact with the ground. Sides and cross-rails, slats and edging can also be of treated pine. Other timbers to consider for this are western red cedar and tallow-wood.

The timber required to make a seat 1.8 metres square is shown in the table below. The recommended sizes may have to be adjusted to suit availability (always increase the dimensions). Note that on steeply sloping sites, the post lengths will have to be adjusted. Make the shortest one at least 900 mm.

You will also need galvanised nails (50 and 75 mm), four house bricks, and sufficient concrete to fill the holes around the posts.

TOOLS

Handsaw or circular saw, hammer, nail punch, tape, pencil, plane, square, spirit level, shovel or spade, hand drill or electric drill and drill bits to suit the nail diameters.

PROCEDURE

1 Accurately peg out the position of the four posts. Make sure they are at right angles by making a big, temporary square with some 50 x 25 mm battens (or use three slats) using the 3:4:5 rule illustrated in Diagram 41A. To make the square, temporarily nail the ends of two battens together at approximate right angles. Measure three units down one side, four units down the other and adjust them until the diagonal between the two marks is equal to five units.

When it's correct, nail a batten across to fix the position. The angle thus created is an exact right angle and, so long as the seat sides are parallel, all the other angles will also be right angles.

2 Dig the post holes 300 x 300 x 400 mm deep and place a house brick on the level bottom of each one. Make sure it is firm and level.

3 Cut the sides to length (1750 mm overall) mitring each one at 45°. The mitre joint ensures the end grain is not exposed to the sun or hot winds. This will greatly lessen the risk of splitting.

4 With the posts standing on top of each brick mark each one to the approximate height — cut them about 50 mm longer to allow for final adjustments. Use a spirit level and one of the frame sides as a straightedge and work from the shortest post to get the other lengths.

5 Stand the posts in position and, with the help of a friend, nail the frame sides to the posts, starting again from the lowest point. Check as you go to make sure the side pieces are level and the posts are vertical. When nailing is complete, check to see the frame is square using the 3:4:5 rule again. Nail a temporary brace across the frame to hold it in position.

6 Mix up the concrete with the required amount of water (too much water will seriously weaken the concrete) and place around the posts, tamping it well with a steel rod to get rid of any air bubbles. Leave for at least ten days to cure.

NO.	ITEM	LENGTH	WIDTH	THICKNESS
4	Sides	1800	200	50
4	Posts	1000	100	100
1	Cross-rail	1800	200	50
1	Trimmers	1800	200	50
27	Slats	1800	75	38
4	Edging	1800	75	25

All measurements are in millimetres.

Seat Around a Tree

7 Cut the posts level with the top of the frame, cut and nail the cross rails and trimmers in position. Leave at least 300 mm clearance from the tree to allow for the tree to add its annual rings. If you plan on leaning against the tree for support you may want to get a little closer than this. If so make provision to move the trimmers later.

8 Neatly cut the slats to length, chamfer the edges and fix in position with the 50 mm nails, two to each end. Flatten the point of each nail to lessen the chance of splitting the wood. A more foolproof method is to drill nail holes in the slat ends. The slats may be butted together though preferably they should be spaced 3 mm apart to allow for shrinkage. Use a spacer for this.

9 Nail the edge batten around the frame, again using mitre joints on the ends. This batten, shown in Diagram 41B, should be made flush with the top of the slats, thereby covering the end grain of the slats and providing an attractive finish. Chamfer the top edge to get rid of the sharp edge. Finish off the seat with a suitable timber finish.

The area around the seat may be left as lawn or paved. Red gravel makes good surround also as long as it is contained by timber edge strips.

To give the seat extra utility, some cushions could be scattered on it or a mattress could be laid along one edge. If the tree isn't comfortable for leaning against, a slatted back could be made and fixed by brass hinges at an angle that suits your posture.

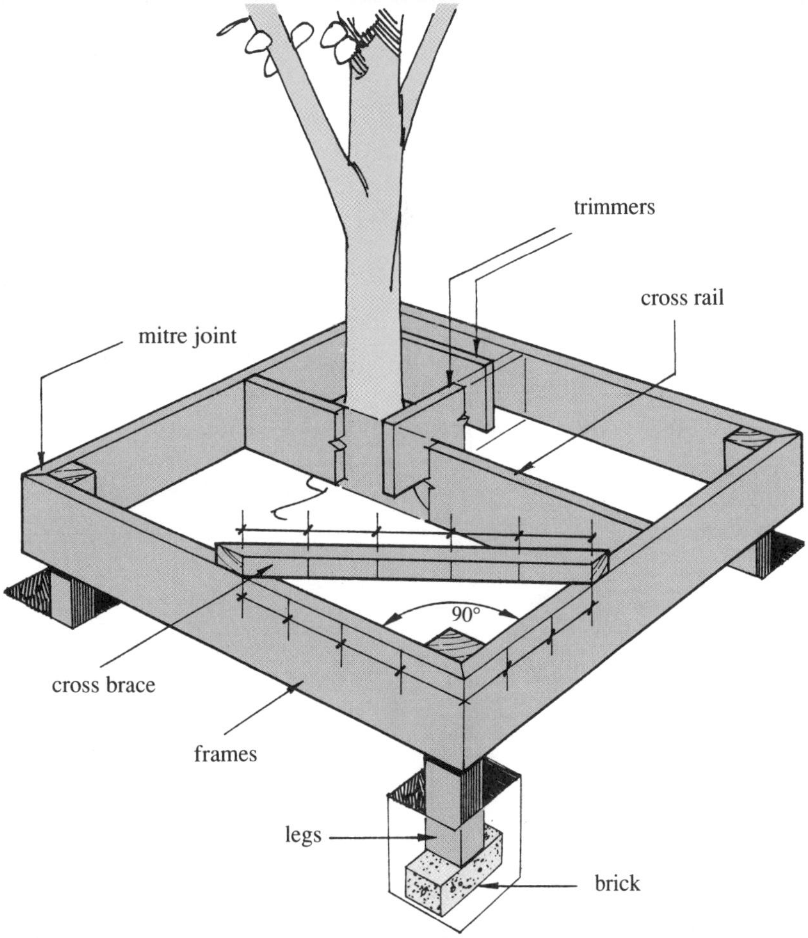

Diagram 41A

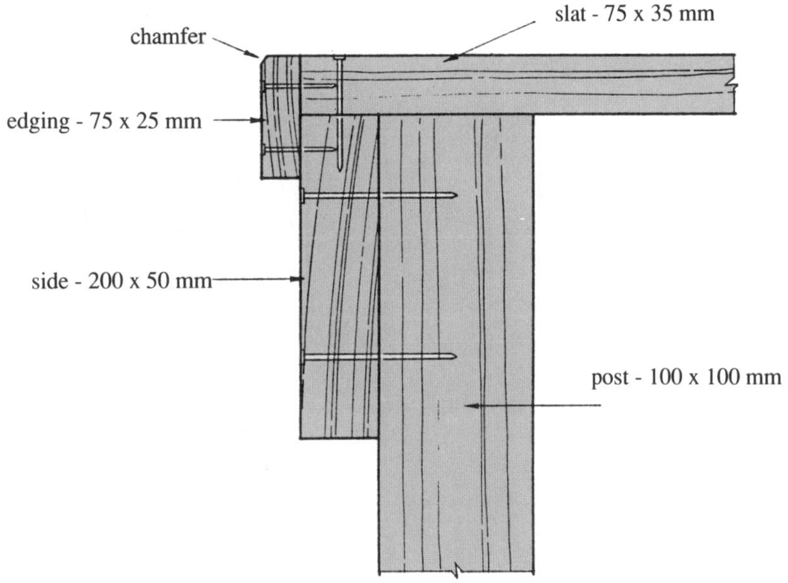

Diagram 41B

Bird Baths and Feeders

Once you begin planting trees, flowers and shrubs you'll probably attract some feathered friends. To encourage their quaint flutterings and assorted squawkings, why not put in a bird bath or two?

Bird baths provide busy birds with a place to drink, something which is rare in our wall-to-wall suburbs. Also, well positioned baths, as the name suggests, allow them to clean themselves without the fear of being attacked, tormented and then eaten by the friendly neighbourhood cat. Once they are sure of the location, they'll return again and again bringing their own unique music and colour.

The photograph shows a distinctive bath that any bird would be happy to use. Ideally the bath should be elevated to about a metre so that creeping felines can't get close. If you prefer a low or ground-level one, then it should be kept well clear of trees and shrubs — in the centre of a lawn is a good place. The cat would have to be green or have burrowing inclinations to approach unnoticed.

The style of bath should reflect your backyard theme. There is a bath for every taste, from classical simplicity in imitation store to metallic marvels. Make sure the bath has a rim for the newly bathed to preen themselves on. The water, which shouldn't be deeper than around 80 mm, must be kept clean or the fastidious birds will shun your well meant generosity. If a fountain is your style make sure it delivers a fine spray, one that will not almost drown your average bird.

Consider planting various native trees and flowers which tend to attract native birds. A feeder is also a good way to encourage birds in your backyard. The one shown in the photograph opposite is full of creature comforts. The gabled roop protects birds from sun and rain.

A distinctive bath that any bird would be happy to use.

Bird Feeder

The photograph and diagram 42 show the basic arrangement for a virtually indestructible feeder. The table gives the sizes and materials. The colour scheme is optional.

You will also need: 40 mm countersunk screws, 30 mm nails, glue, wood filler, sandpaper, 4 screw hooks, 2 m (or more) chain, split ring, primer/undercoat, gloss paint.

The triangular pieces that form the 'gables' are made by cutting the 150 x 150 mm piece from corner to corner. Bring them in 30 mm from the ends of the roof and screw them in place. The gap in the roof apex is filled by the quad, which should be glued in place with waterproof glue to ensure it doesn't leak. The pillar is screwed to the triangles. If you flatten the dowel a little where it butts against the triangle with a chisel it will stop it rolling. The tray corners are best cut with a coping saw and sanded or rasped smooth.

Make sure you thoroughly prime the feeder and then finish with a good quality acrylic paint. Alternatively, use a wood preserving stain.

Feed the birds with the right kind of food — no sugar.

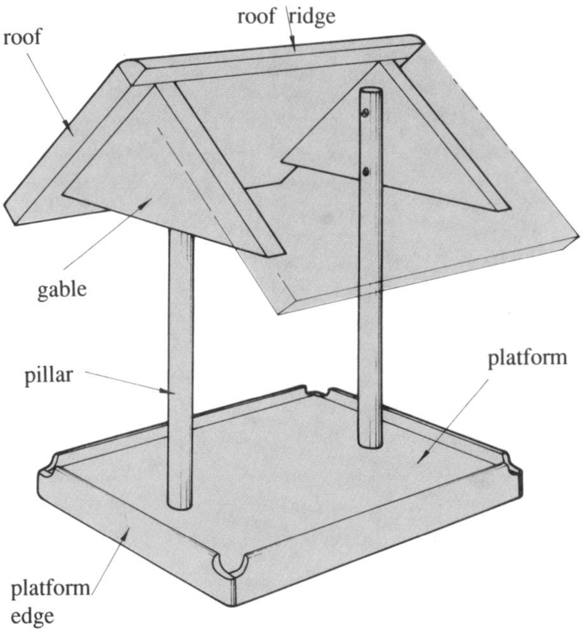

Diagram 42

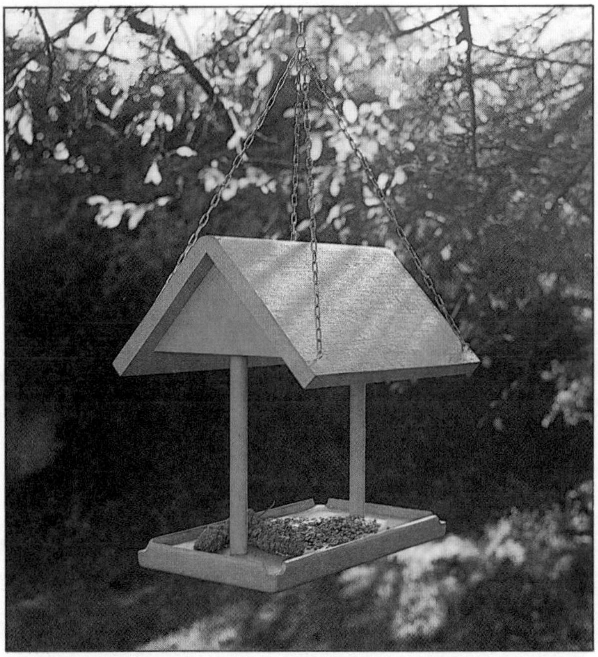

NO.	ITEM	MATERIALS	LENGTH
2	Roof	190 x 19 western red cedar	340
1	Platform	190 x 19 western red cedar	340
1 (halved)	Gable	150 x 19 western red cedar	150
1	Roof ridge	19 x 19 pine quad	340
2	Pillar	19 diameter dowel	300
1	Platform edge	30 x 6 cover strip	1200

All measurements are in millimetres.

You will also need: 40 mm countersunk screws, 30 mm nails, glue, wood filler, sandpaper, 4 screw hooks, 2 m (or more) chain, split ring, primer/undercoat, gloss paint.

Planters and Pots

As the name suggests, planters are receptacles that hold plants. They can be made from a variety of materials, although the most natural one that will blend in with any yard is timber.

Planters have no set pattern. They can be fashioned into a variety of shapes or made from unusual items. Imaginative people have turned old wheelbarrows and wine barrels into stunning planters. Handy backyarders have made their own. It's not hard and the satisfaction is immeasurable.

The pyramid planter shown in Diagram 43 is just waiting for someone with some real flair to build it.

Citrus trees grow well and look great in planters.

Diagram 43

The planters shown in the photograph and Diagram 44 are relatively easy to construct. A suggested size for the small one is 300 mm high with a 350 mm square opening at the top. The bottom is 120 mm smaller, which gives you the slope on the sides. The larger one could be 350 mm high with a 400 mm square opening at the top.

MATERIALS

Fixings and fasteners. 1.2 m x 10 mm-diameter dowel (24 x 50 mm pieces), 90 x 40 mm galvanised bullet-head nails, 40 x 25 mm galvanised fibrous cement sheet nails, 4 x 31 mm plate-fixing castors, 2m^2 black polythene sheet, suitable wood preservative.

Order quantities for timber. 1 piece x 2.1 m of 100 x 25 mm sawn durable timber; 1 piece x 3 m of 200 x 25 mm sawn durable timber; 1 piece x 1.8 m of 150 x 25 mm sawn durable timber; 1 piece x 0.9 m of 50 x 50 mm sawn durable timber.

PROCEDURE

1 The sides and bottom can be made up from a single width piece of timber (if you can get it), or by joining several narrower sections using dowels and waterproof glue. Western red cedar is an ideal choice as it doesn't rot. You can use either dressed or sawn timber.

2 Once you get the sides marked out (making sure they're in pairs), you must cut them with a circular saw inclined at 45°. With this method, no matter what the angle is on the face of the timber, you'll always get the correct edge angle. If you haven't got a saw, then borrow or hire one!

Simple Timber Planters

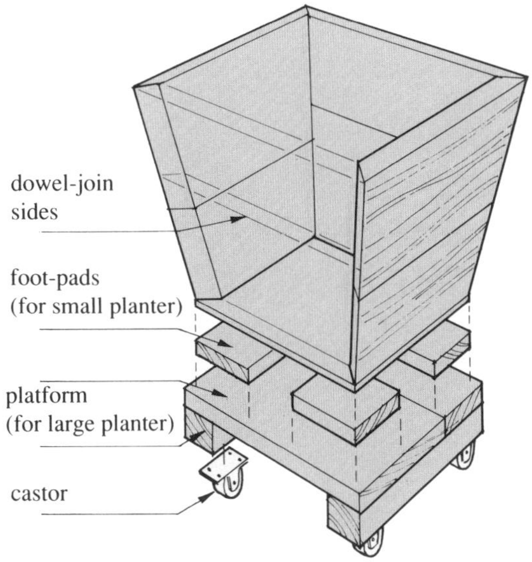

Diagram 44

3 Nail and glue the joints, affix the bottom (which should have a few holes bored in it to allow the water to drain away) and then the pads.

4 As Diagram 44 shows, the larger one is portable, which is great for moving it around the patio or into a sunny or shady spot. Simply add a suitable platform from the same timber, screw it to the 50 x 50 mm runners, affix the castors, which, like the nails, should be able to handle exterior weather, paint with a natural or solid-stain wood preservative, and put in the plants. Keep an eye on the timber in the planter. The sun will quickly strip off the preservative so it must be reapplied frequently. Any cracks should be filled with a waterproof glue like epoxy. In the event of hail, cover the planter.

NO. REQ'D	ITEM	MATERIALS	LENGTH OR SIZE IN MM
4	Small planter side	100 x 25 mm sawn durable timber	350
4	Foot-pads	100 x 25 mm sawn durable timber	100
1	Platform base	100 x 25 mm sawn durable timber	300
4	Small planter side	200 x 25 mm sawn durable timber	350
1	Platform base	200 x 25 mm sawn durable timber	300
4	Large planter side	200 x 25 mm sawn durable timber	400
4	Large planter side	150 x 25 mm sawn durable timber	400
2	Platform supports	50 x 50 mm sawn durable timber	300
1	Small planter bottom	Fibrous cement sheet	230 x 230
1	Large planter bottom	Fibrous cement sheet	280 x 280

A Large Planter

For a really large planter, one that could almost hold an oak tree, look at the photograph and Diagram 45. It's 1.1 metres square and once it's full of soil and plants, forget about moving it. The embellishments around the bottom and the top, made out of western red cedar battens and scotia, make the planter look a million dollars.

The sides are made from 17 mm waterproof ply which is covered with western red cedar shiplap or V-jointed lining boards. All the joints are simply butted and screwed. Inside the planter a 0.4 to 1 mm thick galvanised steel (or, if you've just won the lottery, copper) bin is created to hold the wet soil. A floor framework of 75 x 50 mm oregon joists strengthened by noggins and end supports holds the weight and keeps the planter square.

Four pads hold the planter up off the ground, an important point with oregon otherwise it will rot. If there is any possibility of the base coming into contact with the ground, use hardwood or treated pine instead.

For a simpler version of a great big planter, use railway sleepers or 100 x 100 mm treated pine sections, one on top of the other. The whole thing just sits on top of a level gravel bed which lies below ground level. The corners are made to interlock like brickwork and each layer steps in 25 mm. A bolt, metal rod or spike will secure the planter corners permanently. Just lay thick gauge polythene film over the ground and up the sides. Then fill with soil, being careful not to pierce the sides. Some holes in the bottom will assist drainage.

For a more formal garden or a city courtyard a great variety of pots, urns and troughs is available. These can be of terracotta or concrete made to look like stone. There are also plastic pots, some of which are very good imitations of urns in natural materials. Besides being relatively cheap, these pots have the advantage of being light and easy to move.

Hanging baskets are another kind of planter. They look very attractive with plants trailing down from them and are useful for brightening up corners where it isn't possible to grow plants in the ground. The baskets can be hung from hooks on a verandah or other structure, or from a post made specially for them. Whatever type you choose, planters bring colour and life to any backyard.

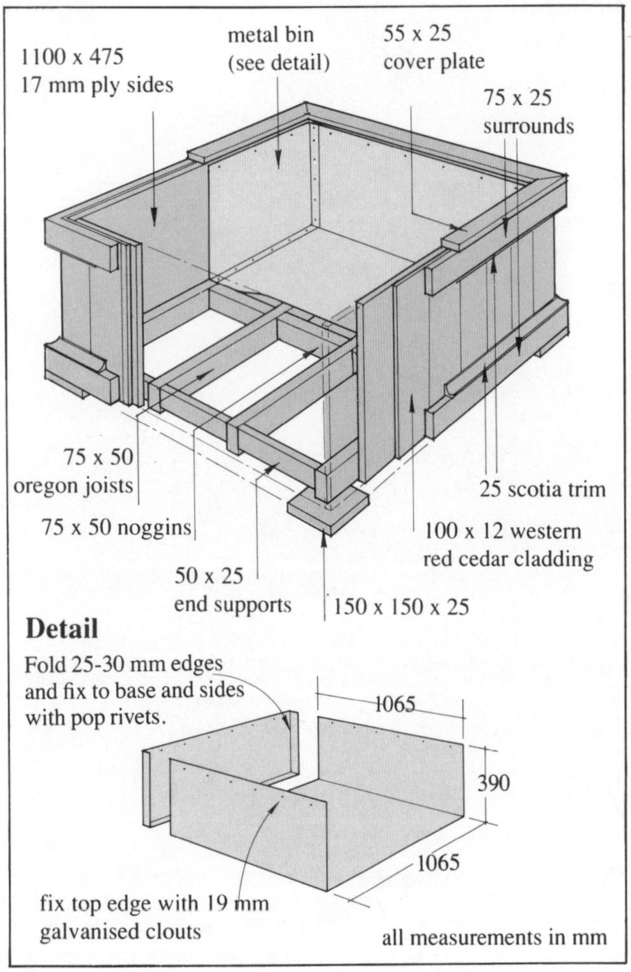

Diagram 45

A large planter, painted for protection.

A simple wooden window box filled with flowers brightens the inside as well as the outside of the house.

Children's Play Areas

There is nothing children like more than dabbling in acres of sand. Possibly your yard will not be big enough to accommodate all their wishes but a sandpit will surely stop them running away from home to seek out the Sahara.

To make a sandpit, simply excavate the available space 250 mm below ground level. Around the perimeter, put two layers of 200 x 150 mm treated pine. Hardwood can be used but it tends to splinter which can be a painful experience for both small children and big alike. Lap each layer so that the joints are not opposite and fix with galvanised spikes.

The pit can then be covered with thick plastic film to stop weeds growing through. Extend the film up the pit sides as well and tape any joins. Then fill with 150 mm of sand.

You could also incorporate a seat arrangement (see photograph). This is made by making a framework out of 75 x 38 mm timber which can be lapped and bolted and then attached directly to the pit sides. Space the frames at 400 mm centres. Use 50 x 25 mm slats to provide the back and seat supports.

A Play Gym

Your children will love you forever if you build them this simple gym (see Diagram next page). It consists of nothing more than a few 100 x 100 mm treated pine posts, which can be square or round, and some 40 mm galvanised pipe which is sunk into the posts 50 mm with a hole saw.

With the pipes in position, set the 3-metre posts in concrete one metre into the ground. As you can see the configurations are infinite and you can make up parallel bars, horizontal bars, ladders, etc. Chamfer all squared corners to reduce the risk of splinters. The twin layers of 19 mm exterior grade plywood in the bottom corner where the ladder is help to brace the structure. A sandpit at its base will soften a tumble and provide even more pleasure and fun for the kids.

A sandpit can incorporate a bench for the benefit of supervising adults.

Using Treated Pine

Treated pine is a boon to the backyarder. This versatile and long-lasting timber with its soft green hue defies attacks by rapacious white ants and fungi. This is because of the pressurised chemical impregnation which permanently saturates the fibres throughout the section. This is a far superior process to painting or dipping which only achieves surface penetration. Treated pine can therefore be used in contact with, or in, the ground (assuming you use the right grade — check with your supplier).

Fastening the timber is best achieved with nails, spikes or nail plates but make sure you choose ones that are hot-dipped galvanised. The treated pine can generally be painted or left to oxidise to a natural greyish toning. You can work it like ordinary timber though care should be taken not to inhale the dust created by sawing or sanding. Gloves should also be worn during erection. Offcuts should not be burnt because the smoke is toxic — bury them instead!

Apart from the play gym, some other items that you could make are: a child's swing, dividing fence between adjacent properties or a childproof fence for a pool, a compost bin, a mowing strip, a fern house (posts in combination with lattice and shade cloth), and an enclosed courtyard. Will that do for starters? — the list is almost inexhaustible!

Many treated pine stockists supply do-it-yourself brochures. Others have items in kit form. All you have to do is to fix bolts through pre-drilled holes and/or nail the unit together.

Treated pine will shrink of course, which may recessitate tightening of the fastenings. It may also crack, especially on the ends. Painting will help.

Ornaments and Sculptures

Ornaments and sculptures, providing they're not overdone, can bring a subtle quality to a backyard. Garden gnomes and Aboriginal statues are definitely passé (unless you are an enthusiast for kitsch) but an intriguing sculpture or unusual shape such as the Sphinx can add interest to a backyard nook.

Then also you could use a blacksmith's anvil, a sulky wheel, a disused plough — the list of things is endless. But don't be limited by manufactured items. A piece of driftwood, a tree root or a large clam shell could make an interesting feature in the garden picture that you are creating.

The main thing is not to overcrowd the scene. Add items slowly so that you have a chance to evaluate them. Try them in different places until each piece looks at if it belongs.

Sculptures can be used as a focal point in the backyard.

CHAPTER 10

GREENING AND GROWING

Now the building activity has almost ceased, you can begin the task of painting the area with flowers, lawns, shrubs and trees. In the planning stage, you considered a few, very basic aspects of plants. Now comes the time to add to the theory and put some of it into practice.

Given the scope of this book, I can only cover the bare bones of the species and the characteristics of the bewildering array of plants available. There are more detailed gardening books which will take you further but at least this introductory section will give you something to think about.

The Growth Cycle

Most parents have some idea of what makes children tick (though you sometimes wonder). Most animal owners make some effort to learn about the idiosyncrasies of their pets. Likewise, if you take a bit of time to try to understand the growth cycle of plants, it will help you to understand them better and to care for them properly. An examination of the growth cycle of a tree will provide a basis for your understanding of flora generally.

Basically, each tree consists of a root system and a trunk from which the crown, made up of branches and leaves, grows. (see Diagram 46) The roots forage in the soil for nutrients and water which they absorb through the root hairs by a process called osmosis. This mixture is transported, against gravity, up the trunk or stalk through the sapwood, which is a thick layer of softish spongy timber directly inside the bark.

It then goes out into the leaves where, using sunlight, it is made into a tree food through the action of photosynthesis. It's during this period the tree absorbs carbon dioxide and exudes not only life-giving oxygen but water vapour. For this reason most large trees need tonnes of water each day to survive.

The tree food then passes back down the tree through the inner bark (bast), the living layer directly under the dead outer bark. This is why if a tree is ringbarked it dies — it literally starves to death. The tree food is either used by the tree for its growth or stored in the dead heartwood, the dark, hard, strong core in the centre of the tree.

A tree grows by adding a new layer of cells each year. It takes place in the cambium layer, found directly under the bark. The cambium layer generates new sapwood and new inner bark each year (providing the seasons are good). This is why some varieties of trees have a series of concentric rings.

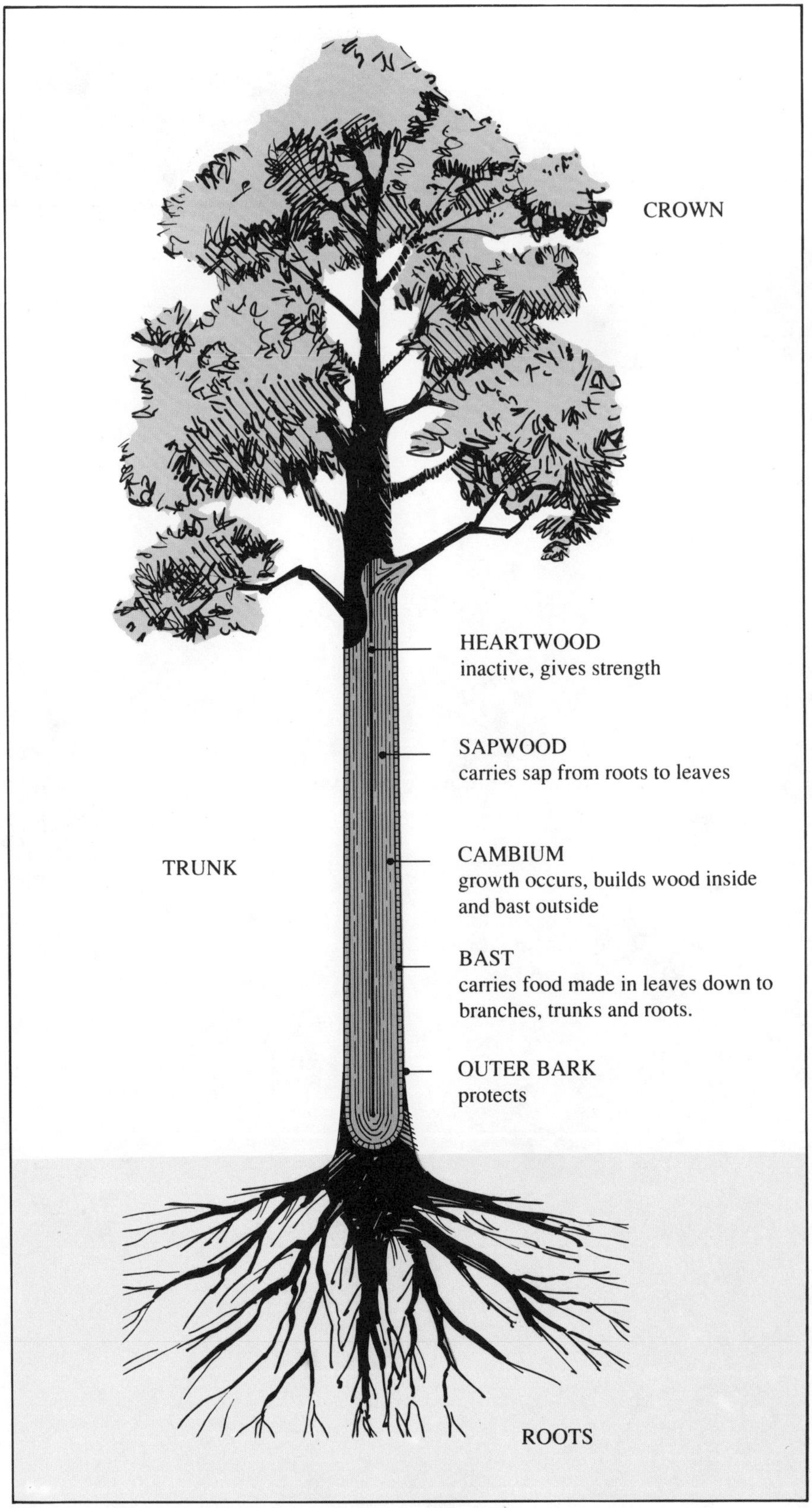

Diagram 46

In some species, these rings have two discernible sections: spring wood, a lightish broad section caused by rapid growth; and summer wood, a darker, thinner, more dense area that reflects the slower summer growth caused by the combination of greater heat and less water. In old trees, some up to 4000 years old, botanists, using the rings, can clearly trace the life history of the tree in terms of good and bad seasons, bushfires, etc.

As the tree expands it literally grows out of its skin each year! As the old bark peels off, the inner bark dies and becomes the new outer layer. As each new layer of sapwood is added, old inner layers die and become the supporting heartwood. It's a simple cycle, one which you can either assist or impede.

Armed with your simplified understanding of the ways plants grow, you now have to make a series of decisions about what to stock your backyard with. Proceed slowly. You have lots of time. Time spent in planning will pay off and reduce potential costly mistakes.

Choose plants suitable to your climate and conditions for optimum beauty.

Choosing Suitable Plants

If you were going to buy a car, you'd be unwise to buy the first thing you saw. You'd probably carefully investigate each model in your price range, take them for test drives, read motoring reports and ask around to ensure you got the best value for your money.

Though plants don't cost as much, they are not inexpensive and if you expect them to perform well and complement your personal paradise, there are some important questions to ask about them:

1. Is it a native or exotic species?
2. Does it grow well in your area?
3. How long will it live?
4. How big will it grow?
5. When does it flower?
6. Is it tender or hardy?
7. Does it prefer sunlight or shade?
8. Is it deciduous?

Apply these eight questions to any plant or tree and you'll soon establish if it's right for you or not. Each question is expanded upon below.

A shady corner can be an ideal place for reflection and contemplation.

1. Is it a native or exotic species?

Obviously a native species, one common to the country generally and your geographical area in particular, has a proven track record for survival whereas a newly introduced exotic species (one from another country) may or may not do well. Some exotics have of course been grown in other countries for hundreds of years and their colonial characteristics, warts and all, are well documented.

2. Does it grow well in your area?

Plants in the main do better in some environments than in others. This is primarily because of variations in climate, soil, and the intensity of the owner's gardening interest.

Each house has a distinctive climate which surrounds it. Features such as high elevation or salty sea air of course affect climate. The microclimate, the one contained within your boundary fences, varies also. For example, the climate in a south-facing backyard will be very different from that in a north-facing one.

Soils vary enormously as well. Basically, soil is a complex mixture of organic matter which comes from decomposed animals and plants, and minerals, which come from disintegrated rock. Mixed in with this is air and water plus numerous living organisms such as worms, insects, bacteria and fungi.

Soils, though seemingly inert, are not static. Their composition changes with the weather, the influence of various organisms and plants, and of course, interference by yourself. Taking the latter point, even turning the soil over will change its physical, chemical and biological properties.

Good soil provides plants with water, nutrients, oxygen and anchorage. Ideally soil should be: deep so that the plant's roots have plenty of room in which to grow; crumbly (known technically as friable) so that it can be worked easily and water can penetrate it; fertile, which means it is high in nutrients; well drained so that in periods of heavy rain it doesn't become boggy and actually drown the plant; and have a high organic content rather than being unduly sandy, clayey, etc. That's the ideal but few people are lucky enough to encounter it. However, if you know what your soil deficiencies are, you can take steps to improve it. The other solution is to choose plants that will grow in it.

The care of the gardener is another major factor which affects the ability of a plant to thrive. Perhaps, like many, you haven't got much spare time to spend on gardening. In that case, it would be foolish to choose finicky types of plants that needed constant devoted attention. If you're not a gardening enthusiast, go for hardy plants that will keep on growing cheerfully year after year. Keep in mind you can always grow lawn.

3. How long will it live?

Some plants are annuals and some are perennials. Like us, annuals have their brief moment of glory, then die. Then they must be pulled out and replaced. On the other hand, trees, shrubs and herbaceous perennials have a diversity of lifespans, a factor which has to be taken into account in planning the garden.

4. How big will it grow?

The answer to this simple question is often ignored by amateur gardeners. Within months, they are surrounded by plants that, like teenagers, just keep on growing. After some years, their house, along with the view, has disappeared inside a dark forest from which it (and they) may never emerge.

Remember in the planning section I stressed how important it was to create a height balance between plants, shrubs and trees, one that works for your backyard enjoyment, not against it. Check each plant's characteristics carefully.

Trees and shrubs not only grow upwards, but outwards. Some are slender and have only high branches with sparse foliage. Palms and eucalypts are examples. Grass and other plants can and do grow at their feet in spite of the enormous amount of water and nutrients they extract from the soil.

Other trees and shrubs will produce a dense foliage that begins almost at ground level and, in ever--widening circles, proceeds to overgrow anything that is planted near it. Conifers fall into this category. These trees, if their expansion is allowed for, are great for blocking out eyesores and, if densely planted, for blocking the wind. Again, you must plan well and get the right species in the right place.

Big plants have big root systems. Some roots are pervasive and invasive elements that love the moisture of drainage systems. They can also thicken to the stage where they crack unwary paths and innocent house footings. Select carefully and plant with care or expensive trouble will result.

5. When does it flower?

Flowers are fascinating things. Whether attached to herbaceous plants, shrubs or trees, their sometimes spectacular, sometimes understated, colours and scents give a special ambience to any backyard.

When planning your garden, try to have something in flower most of the year. Investigate the flowering cycles of each species and plan where they will show to best advantage. If you set up a rotating system, various areas of your yard will bloom at different times. That will draw the eye, pull family members into its orbit, and make sure that each area of your yard gets periodic attention.

6. Is it tender or hardy?

Some plants survive anything, while some keel over at the drop of a hat. Most fit somewhere in between and will respond to a bit of tender loving care. However, if you live in a difficult climate, or where the soil is poor, or where pests, domesticated animals and boisterous children proliferate, then choose wiry survivors. A look around the neighbourhood will generally confirm the winners.

Colour in your garden is a beautiful way to express your creativity.

Some plants can handle frosts whereas others respond very poorly if they are frozen, albeit for only a brief period. Unless you're new to an area, you'll know whether you get frosts never, occasionally or frequently. You'll also know how severe they are. If you live in a risk area, then choose accordingly.

If fragility attracts you, then you need to set up a special area for such species, one much like an intensive care ward where you can tend and succour to your heart's content. Your nursery may be able to advise on the survival characteristics of plant groups as a whole and the idiosyncrasies of each variety.

7. Does it prefer sunlight or shade?

Some plants have leaves that possess similar characteristics to human skin. They actually burn in the sun. Some will even shrivel and die. Other plants thrive in dawn to sunset exposure and will do poorly if grown in the shade.

Matching plants with their expected exposure is the name of the game. Keep in mind that the sun changes positions with the seasons so summer and winter light may differ dramatically. Some shrubs and trees are deciduous, which could overexpose diminutive shade lovers during the winter months.

8. Is it deciduous?

Some shrubs and trees shed their leaves annually and, after a glorious display of autumn magic, sit totally exposed, a mass of stark branches and twigs, until spring beckons the buds forth to soften and reclothe them. Maples, beeches, birches, ashes and oak are familiar deciduous trees.

This annual shedding has a negative side. It generates a lot of raking and creates the nefarious gutter-burners whose smouldering fires pollute many a good neighbourhood. If you have a pool, raking is not such a problem but endlessly cleaning the pool is.

On the plus side, the absence of leaves can let in warming winter sunshine as well as temporarily change the character and mood of your yard. To get the best results, check carefully what the leaf cycle of each plant and tree is before you buy it.

Trees

Trees provide shade, shelter, beauty and privacy while ungrudgingly attempting to clean the air which we humans continue to foul so stupidly. We need them for our survival!

Position

Having established the characteristics of your favourite trees keep in mind that generally they shouldn't be placed too close together. The reason for this is fairly obvious. Not only will they offer too much shade and potentially block out a view but, while maintaining their peaceful external demeanour, they will literally fight each other to the death as they compete for the available soil, light and water. This war can only result in stunted growth and shape for all the contenders and the demise of the weak. As a general rule, six to eight trees per average block (1000 square metres) is about the limit, depending on the species.

When choosing the positions for them, consider not only your own amenity, but that of your neighbours. Strangely, they probably enjoy a good view and sunlight as much as you do. Your foresting tendencies may be eminently praiseworthy but what of the rights of others? We can surely live in harmony with other forms of life, neither dominating nor being dominated!

Think carefully about services — the wires above, for example. Will the maturing tree foul them? Will their roots clog drainage lines? Will maintenance work to phone and gas lines be made difficult and cause irreparable damage to root systems?

As mentioned in the planning section, aspect is important. Plant only deciduous or low evergreens in the north-east to north-west sector to maximise winter sun. Never put evergreens in front of north-facing windows.

Energy authorities calculate that trees, properly placed, can lower the summer ground temperature substantially and, if close to the house walls (but not nearer than 3 metres unless they're palms), make the inside of your home noticeably cooler. In winter, wind-deflecting trees, properly placed, could reduce your heating bills by as much as 25 per cent.

Elephant's Foot Plant, an ideal small tree.

Shapes

Unless you're an artist, you could be forgiven for not having noticed that most trees fall into six rough shapes. When you're walking about, look at trees more closely. Imagine a string of lights joining their extremities and the outline they would make. It becomes glaringly obvious, doesn't it?

Trees can be roughly categorised into:

1. Rather blockish weeping shapes — willows, beeches and wilga form some of these.
2. Tall and narrow column shapes — conifers and poplars spring to mind.
3. Pyramid shaped trees — some of the oaks and liquidambars fall into this group.
4. Grecian vase shaped — broad on the top and narrowing down. Many eucalypts, plane trees and white cedar fit the bill.
5. Toffee apple or umbrella configurations — dates and some other palms feature here.
6. Beehive shapes — Cape chestnuts, robinias and hawthorns are candidates.

These categories will be modified by weather conditions (as with a stunted tree on an exposed headland). With the general outlines in mind, choose shapes that suit your particular needs and backyard preferences. Choose carefully, cutting down a tree that has become too large or is an inappropriate shape may be prohibited.

Shade Trees

To select correctly, keep in mind the relationship between the backyard, the sun's path and the potential shading effect of the tree given its shape, ultimate height, density of foliage, and whether it is deciduous or evergreen.

To shade a roof you need vase-shaped trees like eucalypts, brushbox, white cedars and plane trees that tower over the house. Leaves in the gutter may be the price you have to pay for such shelter, to say nothing of the possibility of a limb crashing through the tiles.

To shade walls, columnar trees like conifers and poplars are useful, especially if planted in a double row. They also act as a windbreak.

For human shade in summer, the pyramid-shaped African olive or the deciduous claret ash provide amenity and beauty, as do closely planted palms. In cold areas, the silver birch is a handsome survivor along with various conifers.

Whatever you choose remember to check its ultimate height and width or the bridge to the clouds in the Jack and the Beanstalk fairytale might become a nightmarish reality!

Small Trees

If your backyard is tiny and you want to maintain the scale by using smallish trees, there are many species to choose from. The first photograph shows the effect that can be created by planting an elephant's foot plant. It contrasts nicely with the golden conifer. Note the clever use of paving.

A Japanese-style garden effect can be created in a small space by the use of a sheared hedge, rhapis palms, and a carefully trained pine tree (*Pinus densiflora*). Boulders and mondo grass can be used to advantage, as can lawn and gravel.

Tree ferns and palms, though not strictly trees, are also good companions in courtyard-style backyards. The golden locust provides brilliant colour for a drab spot.

Some of these smaller trees can cope quite well in pots (providing they are large enough). When you place them, keep in mind that a cubic metre of soil weighs a tonne, so choose well! The containers, which may be of terracotta, concrete or wood (avoid plastic as it tends to fracture), should have a 75 mm layer of gravel on the bottom to assist drainage. Elevate the pot on bricks to stop the roots moving into the soil underneath.

The Japanese maple, varieties of citrus, the wilga tree and Hill's fig all provide the backyarder with enough variety of foliage and colour to complement any theme. The trees listed in the panel on page 107 give even more choice.

When placing the trees, keep them to one side so they don't dominate the open areas and don't be afraid to prune them. You, not they, should be in charge. However, when pruning, make sure you don't kill them.

Palms are an excellent choice for a courtyard garden, as long as they get some shade.

Planting Trees

Trees are generally sold as seedlings in a variety of stages of development but can be bought as half or even full-grown trees which have to be transported in a truck and placed by a crane. In the latter case their roots, those that are left, are enclosed in a large ball of earth.

Like babies, seedlings and root-balled trees and shrubs are rudely thrust into their new environment. If it isn't particularly favourable, then the tree, like a baby, will probably die unless it is properly cared for.

You can lessen the transplanting stress by observing the following points.

1 Don't plant in the middle of summer or winter unless the climate is moderate all year round. The reason for this is that root growth has to take place before the seedling is strong enough to survive any extreme temperature. Root growth is slowed by the dryness and fierce heat of summer and is almost negligible in the chilled soil of winter. Also the tree must properly implant itself in the soil so that the wind won't blow it over.

Spring and autumn are the ideal times to plant in most locations (unless they are especially well protected). If winter is is especially severe, always plant in spring.

2 Ideally, the soil surrounding the tree should be of good quality (fertile, deep and crumbly). If this isn't the case, at least make the area around the roots ideal to give the tree a chance. Dig a hole twice as wide and deep as the pot or root ball, bigger if possible, and, after checking it is well drained, get in enough good quality soil to fill it, making sure it is the best quality you can obtain.

3 Half-fill the hole, then sprinkle some blood and bone on the top and follow it with another 20 mm of soil. Take the tree out of its container and examine the roots. If they're visible but not tightly packed, place in the centre of the hole, making sure the top of the root ball is 20 mm higher than the surrounding ground level. This is to stop the newcomer sitting in a depression that will hold too much water if it rains for a prolonged period.

Slightly loosen the soil around the root ball to release some of the root tips. In the case of a hessian-wrapped root ball, make a few cuts in it and leave it as is. The hessian will quickly rot, releasing the roots. Plastic wraps must be removed.

If the roots are totally knotted, prise the soil away and gently try to untangle them. Like a surgeon work quickly and keep the roots moist. Cut away some roots if you have to. Keep in mind you are dealing with a living thing that could die if the operation is not done well.

If you remove twenty per cent of the roots, remove the same amount of foliage otherwise there'll be insufficient roots to support the current growth. Special root-promoting fertilisers should be used if exposing the plant to such excising stresses.

4 Then fill the hole, tamp down the soil and water well. Regular watering (fortnightly in spring and autumn, weekly in summer), not drowning, must be continued for at least six months. Thick mulching at the base of the tree, rather than lawn, will help to stop water evaporation.

Diagram 47A

Dig a hole at least twice as wide and deep as the pot in which the tree was bought and half refill with crumbly soil.

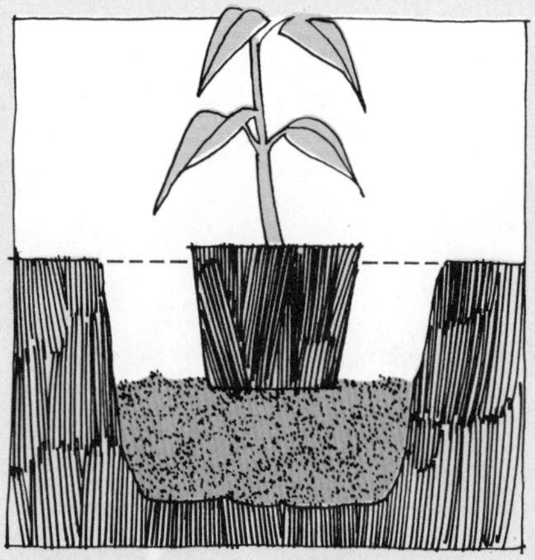

Diagram 47B

Place the tree so that the trunk will be a bit higher than it was in the pot.

Diagram 47C

Loosen roots, place on a mound in the hole and spread them down and out.

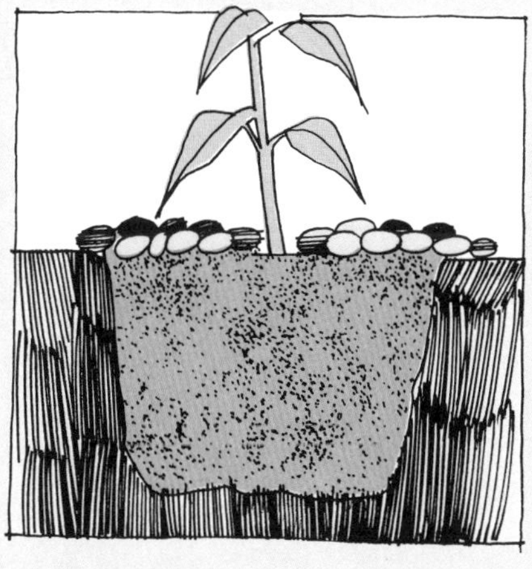

Diagram 47D

Fill the hole and firm down soil.

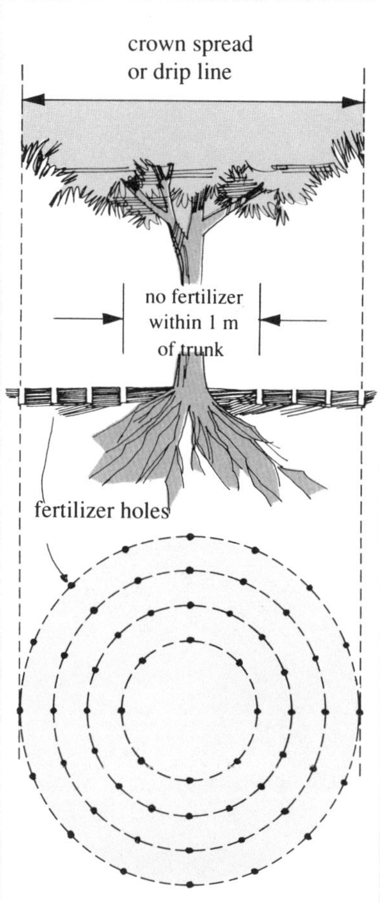

Drill holes 15-20 cm deep and 50 cm apart in rings around the trunk to ensure fertilizer reaches roots. Or use tree fertilizer spikes as directed on the pack.

Diagram 48

Lawn is not ideal as it usually ends up being patchy, it takes a lot of the moisture the tree needs and it tends to seal off the soil too much.

5 If the seedling is over 600 mm, it might pay to stake it to lessen the chance of it being blown over or having the roots damaged by excessive swaying. This involves either driving a single stake into the hole (to fit alongside the root ball) before planting the tree or driving three stakes around the perimeter of the hole in the twelve, four and eight o'clock positions. In both cases the tree should be tied with thick rope (or thin rope which runs through a piece of old hose) to avoid damaging the bark. Remember to loosen the knots periodically or the rope will cut into the bark, restricting the flow of food.

6 As you need to avoid a depression which may puddle and drown the tree, so also during its life you must avoid drowning it in soil. By this I mean that once the root system is established is established (around 600 mm below the surface), you can't fill in around the tree with more soil. As little as 100 mm (with some varieties) will mean that oxygen won't be able to get to the roots or it will be severely restricted. Either way the tree will probably die.

That's why planting must be left until the earthworks and other major projects are done, when the final levels are established.

Care taken in the planting will pay big dividends. Not only will the expensive seedlings survive, but they will grow into healthy trees. Should any yellowing of leaves occur, quickly contact your nursery.

Trees and Tree-like Plants for Courtyard Planting

Abutilon (flowering maple)
Acacia buxifolia (box leaf wattle)
Albizzia julibrissin (silk tree)
Bauhinia species (orchid trees)
Brassaia (octopus tree)
Caesalpinia (Barbadoes pride)
Camellia sasanqua
Caryota mitis (fishtail palm)
Cassia fistula (pudding pipe)
Clusea rosea (autograph tree)
Coffea arabica (coffee tree)
Cornus florida (dogwood)
  Cool climate only
Cordyline terminalis (ti plant)
Cyathea and Dicksonia (tree ferns)
Dizygotheca (finger aralia)
Dracaena fragrans (corn plant)
Dracaena marginata
Elaeocarpus (blueberry ash)
Fatsia (aralia)
Feijoa (pineapple guava)
Ficus diversifolia (mistletoe fig)
Ficus lyrata (fiddleleaf fig)
Grevillea 'Sandra Gordon'
Hibiscus rosa-sinensis
Jacaranda mimosifolia
Laburnum (golden chain)
Lagerstroemia indica (crepe myrtle)
Murraya paniculata (Mexican orange blossom)
Malus floribunda (Japanese crab)
Pandanus (screw palm)
Parrotia (Persian witchhazel)
Phoenix roebelinii (pigmy date palm)
Phyllostachys nigra (black bamboo)
Plumeria (frangipani)
Podocarpus macrophylla (yew pine)
Polyscias balfouriana (ming aralia)
Rhapis excelsa (lady palm)
Sapium (Chinese tallow tree)
Schefflera digitata
Syagrus weddeliana (palm)
Thevetia (yellow oleander)
Yucca aloifolia (Spanish bayonet)

Maintenance

If the planting has been properly done, all that most trees need is regular watering, occasional fertilisation, periodic pruning and perhaps attention to the occasional borer, white ant or troublesome insect.

Fertilising. Obviously the soil, however rich, has a limit to the feeding demands placed upon it. Farmers, of course, dig out or turn under a crop and leave the fields fallow (unused) for a period. They also plough in fertilisers that replace the lost elements. You haven't got this option.

But what about forest trees, you ask? They are left untouched. But consider the amount of rotting vegetation and the animal and bird droppings that replenish the soil. In a tidy backyard these things are removed and disposed of. Also forests hardly have the variety of things growing in them that might be considered normal in a suburban backyard.

The solution is simple. Introduce fertilisers. For surface-rooted things such as flowers and grasses, a liquid fertiliser is handy. Alternatively, use a powder type that is sprinkled around and hosed in. Pellets have a gradual release capacity which prolongs the fertilising.

For deep-rooted trees, make a series of 150–200 mm holes, 500 mm apart, with a crowbar. Start one metre out from the trunk and finish in line with the outer perimeter of the crown (see Diagram 48). These holes will bring air to the lower levels. Fill the holes with a suitable fertiliser and water well.

Fertiliser spikes are an alternative. You just hammer them in.

Pruning. I used to watch my father making mysterious cuts in roses and wonder why they were being so cruelly treated. Now I understand. For most living things, amputation, whether it concerns diseased or over-prolific limbs, destructive relationships, etc., is essential for survival and good health.

Trees are generally pruned or cut back to remove a split, diseased or unwanted branch, to get rid of suckers and water shoots, to train the tree to some desired shape or to reduce its size. Pruning of course takes away the leaves that make the food so don't be too savage.

Diagram 49 gives some idea of where to prune a tree. Cut as near to the trunk as possible. If branches overlock each other, remove the smaller one. If a tree is beginning to fork, remove one side. If you don't, later on the mature tree could split in half in a high wind.

First aid. In common with all living things, trees suffer from injury, disease and parasites. In their natural state new seedlings replace the victims. This is not the case in your garden so care has to be taken.

The first step is to be aware. An occasional examination of a tree

Palms and tree ferns will quickly hide an ugly fence or other eyesore.

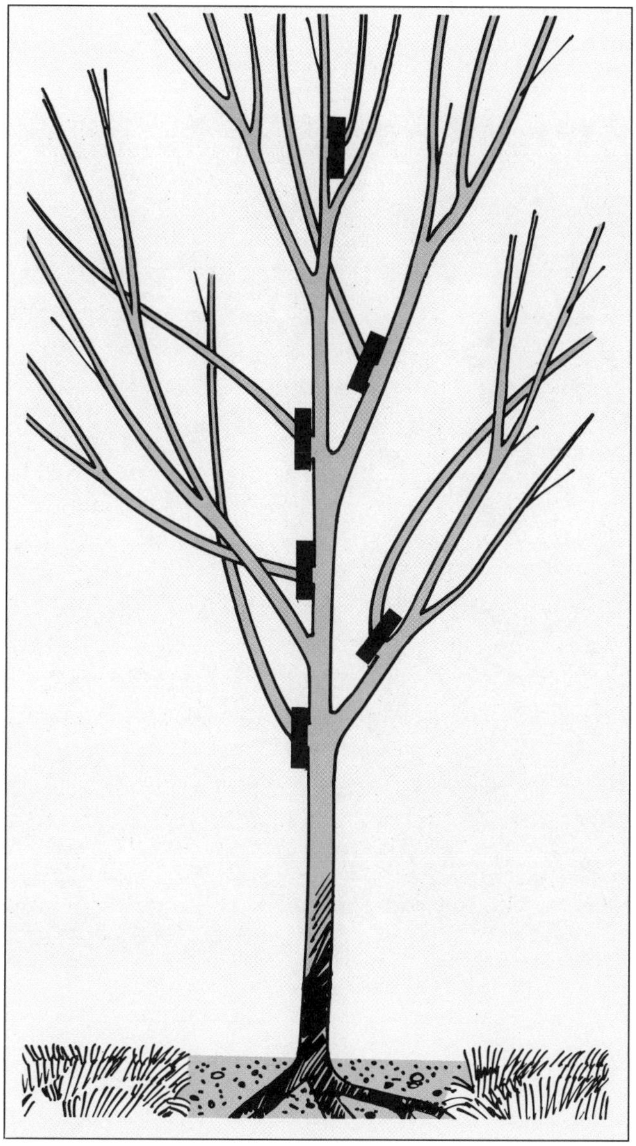

Diagram 49A How to prune a tree

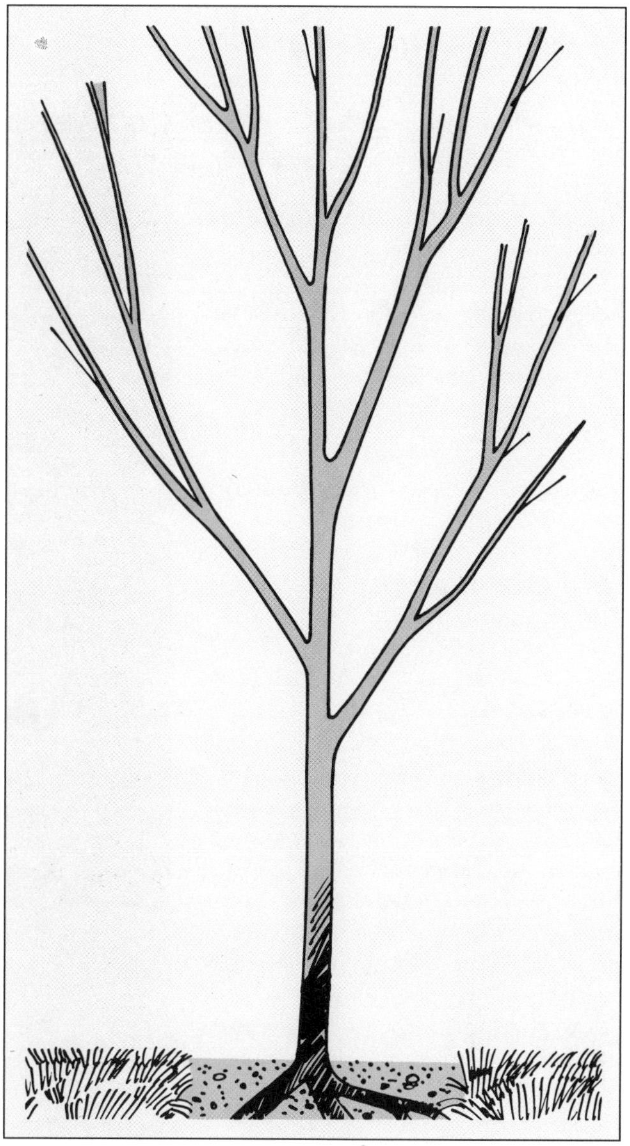

Diagram 49B The finished job

will reveal splits, borer holes, the beginning of white ant infestation, areas of rot caused by fungi, dying limbs, etc. Be especially watchful after violent storms.

The second step is to act quickly. A dead, fractured, broken or diseased branch should be removed. If it's large, cut it off in sections to lessen damage to other branches. As you approach the trunk, make a part cut 400 mm out from the trunk under the branch before cutting from the top. This will stop the bark tearing. The stump can then be removed completely and the wound treated with a suitable sealant which your nursery sells. Like a salve, it protects the trunk from fungus or other organisms. Reapply it in accordance with the directions.

If the bark is gashed, carefully chisel around it until the wound is circular or oval-shaped. This will, when combined with a wound sealer, help the healing.

If insect infestation becomes apparent — as evidenced by poor leaf quality or eaten leaves, by oozing gum, or sawdust in tree crotches and crevices — then action may be required. The best action of all is to have a healthy tree. For example, a healthy tree will exude gum to encase a sapwood-eating invader.

Should serious leaf attack occur, small trees can be sprayed. Larger trees require the services of a tree surgeon who will inject the tree with insecticide. Borers can't be dealt with as easily. If you're not squeamish, they can often be impaled on some fine wire if you can locate their holes. Otherwise you'll need to call in a pest control company.

If roots are disturbed or removed, prune the tree back by the same amount. Remember though, that if you cut a tree's roots too severely, there's a very good chance that it won't survive, despite your attempts at first aid.

Hedges and Bamboo

Hedge plants and bamboo provide the backyarder with an amazing range of screens and divisions. If high screening is required, bamboo will grow to enormous heights. If clipped screening is your fancy, a hedge can be trimmed to virtually any shape while its height can range from 600 mm upwards.

Hedges

A hedge, by definition, is a row of small trees or bushes planted closely together to form a barrier or boundary. By using such a centuries-old method, you provide an aesthetically pleasing barrier, one that also provides a habitat for small birds. The work involved in maintenance is not very hard.

Any dense shrub or small tree can be used. Azaleas can create a colourful hedge. Conifers, if closely planted, can provide an impenetrable high screen. The traditional hedge can be created from a bush such as *Photinia glabra* Rubens, providing you live in a climate cooler than the subtropics.

A good method which ensures even and vigorous growth is to dig a 600 mm wide by 450 mm deep trench along the full line of the pro posed hedge. If you fill the trench with top quality soil the result will be spectacular, providing you choose young bushes that suit your particular climate and soil.

When planting, space the shrubs at centres to suit the height required (see Diagram 50). If an immediate people or animal barrier is required, put a wire mesh fence alongside the small plants. As they grow they will gradually block it out.

Use holly and dark-leaved beech for a variegated effect. Pyracanthas, being thorny, are impenetrable. Their berries give colour. *Cordyline terminalis* is great for tropical areas. Though it looks untidy, it never needs trimming! An almost self-shaping hedge can be formed from Japanese oleaster, while the decidu-

The traditional *Photinia glabra* hedge.

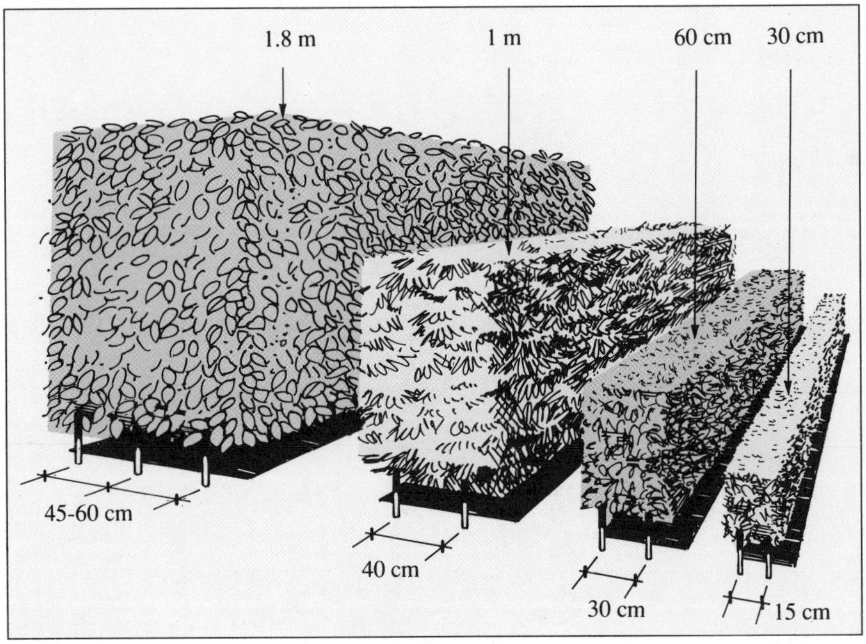

Diagram 50

ous hawthorn is great for colder climates. The photograph of an English garden shows what can be achieved in a formal garden in a cool climate.

Maintenance. Clip formal hedges three times a year (but not in frosty periods). This will keep new stems from exceeding 150 mm and create a dense growth. Use a string line on temporary posts to get the top straight. The sides of the hedge should slope a little so that the base of the hedge is wider than the top. Use hedge clippers for this job, either manual or electric.

An English hedge garden.

Plant camellias close together to form a spectacular informal hedge.

Bamboo

Bamboo is a form of grass which originates in places like China and Japan. Some types are fast-growing and can reach full height in one year. Mature plants can vary from 750 mm high to an incredible 24 metres, which is equivalent to an eight-storey building!

Contrary to popular belief, bamboo is controllable. It's all a matter of finding out whether it's a clumping or running variety. The former merely adds 20 or 30 mm to itself per annum. The latter is more adventurous and will send out underground rhizomes in all directions, including your neighbour's. To contain this itinerant activity, plant it in a bottomless drum (preferably one that won't corrode). Alternatively surround it with a continuous layer of corrugated iron which extends 450 mm below the surface. Should that not work, it can be poisoned very easily.

For best results, plant towards the end of winter.

The Chinese goddess bamboo shown in the photograph is a clumping type which grows well by a pond or fountain and creates a waterfall of fine foliage. The giant bamboo is suitable for blocking out tall eyesores. In contrast, the semi-dwarf *Sasa palmata* is more ornamental. Pygmy bamboo grows to 300 mm. Its slender stems and waxy green leaves make it great for groundcover. Most bamboos love water and warmth. Just make sure it doesn't get out of control.

Chinese goddess bamboo grows in clumps.

Vines

Vines, properly used, can be invaluable to the backyarder. Because they grow from one trunk they take up little ground space, a boon in small backyards, but the area they can cover is immense.

Judicious use of vines can not only bring brilliant colour and scents to your paradise but they uncomplainingly block out unsightly walls and fences and provide deep shade under trellises and pergolas. Spread across a wire framework, they can quickly create privacy and wind-deflecting screens.

Vines can be evergreen or deciduous. This is of great advantage for those who want summer shade and winter sun, Differing types of vines flower virtually in all seasons so theoretically the display, if you use differing varieties, can be almost continuous.

Sun, providing it is not too hot, is the key to the best displays. In tropical areas, some dappled shade could assist the longevity of the flowers. In colder areas, put vines in a position where they are sheltered and get winter sun. The soil should be top quality (full of rotted manure or compost) and well drained. It should be fertilised annually with manure or liquid plant food.

Watering depends on the amount of rainfall. Keep the soil moist at all times. Prune back to contain the growth otherwise your home may completely disappear! Deciduous summer-flowering vines can be pruned in winter. Evergreen types and deciduous spring bloomers should be done after the flowers are finished.

Take care that your vines don't grow into neighbouring properties. If they do, the neighbour has the right to trim them. As well, species like ivy can create problems with brick and stone work because the roots eat into the surface as they take hold.

Vines can turn an ordinary fence into a thing of beauty.

A flowering vine brings life to any backyard structure.

Flowers

The success of a good flower garden, like your whole backyard, depends on planning. This factor goes right through the process, from the setting up of the beds, to the decisions about whether to use perennials or annuals, what size plants to use, what mixture of colours to have, the flowering orchestration, whether they are to be cut for inside and so on.

Flowers can be grown in formal beds, or at the other extreme, planted seemingly haphazardly between shrubs, rocks and around trees. With beds, remember they have to be weeded so don't make them too wide unless you have extremely long arms. You can of course put stepping stones in a wider bed to allow access that won't damage the plants.

The range of flower colours is enormous and some care should be taken with their selection to ensure the best possible harmonies or contrast. A colour wheel will provide you with a simplified idea of how colours harmonise or contrast. Adjacent colours blend with each other whereas colours opposite on the wheel strongly contrast.

Keep in mind that it's the overall effect that should have some sort of balance, not individual groups of flowers. If you put strong colours near the front, then fade away into lighter shades, the result will be spectacular. The photographs show the type of effects that can be achieved.

It must be remembered that many flowers, both annual and perennial, are in bloom for a relatively short time. Each display, however brilliant, is shortlived. On the other hand, the leaves of perennials are there much longer – in many cases all year – so the foliage should receive some consideration in the planning process.

Leaves come in an infinite variety of shapes, colour and textures. Look at the amazing contrasts among the giant tree ferns, Rhapis palm, umbrella plant, New Zealand flax, philodendron and banana. At the other end of the scale the mother-in-law's tongue sits prettily among the baby's tears. Around a pond, why not try the giant rhubarb, New Zealand sago palm, golden-leafed hosta, European fan palm and yellow lilium interspersed with ferns.

Most flowers do best in sunlight so try to give them at least four hours per day, more in winter if possible. The soil should again be best quality, well turned to at least 250 mm and supplemented with humus. You can grow from seed or seedlings. The latter should be firmed in the soil to get rid of air pockets, then watered immediately. Fertilise regularly during the growing season.

Roses always look at their best when planted *en masse*.

A profusion of flowers borders this simple gravel path.

Water Plants

A pond can be a knockout as far as aquatic plants are concerned. If it's surrounded by other water-loving plants . . . well, the photograph speaks for itself. Not surprisingly water lilies are a traditional favourite when it comes to embellishing the surface of a pond with plant life. They are beautiful when they flower and some varieties have wondrous scents. They do of course demand full sunlight and will suffer if they don't get it.

They divide into two types: the tropical and the temperate. Tropical varieties grown in colder climes may have to be lifted out before winter and stored in cool, moist soil. Regardless of their climatic preference, they are voracious feeders and should be repotted in rich manured soil each spring.

The planting or repotting procedure for a water lily is shown in the sequence of photographs below. Note the hollowed-out planting hole that sets the base of the plant just above the soil level. After planting, cover with 20 mm of sand or fine gravel. This anchors the soil and stops it muddying the water. Place the pot in the water so the top is just submerged. Lower it gradually each week until it is 350 mm deep.

Other aquatic plants that you might consider include the native nardoo which, though it looks like the elusive four-leaf clover, is really a fern. If you plant it in shallow water, it'll soon pop up above the surface.

Should eastern religions be among your interests, you would be aware of the long history of the lotus. Its beauty has captivated countless generations. It is grown like a water lily but don't be deceived by the photographs — its blooms are the size of a dinner plate!

While we're floating about in history, what about some papyrus of Egyptian fame growing in one corner of your pond? It can reach three metres in height so make sure your pond is big enough.

Moving over to the other side of the world, we find the exotic Brazilian water poppy. It is a rapid grower and must be kept in check.

Some other types you might consider are the marsh marigold, water lettuce, thalia and parrot's feather.

1 Fill a large pot or heavy plastic bag with good soil, enriched with very well-rotted cow manure. Now hollow out a planting hole.

2 Set the water lily roots into the hole so that the crown or base of the plant is just above soil level. Plant as quickly as possible.

3 Hold the lily in position and bury the roots with extra soil. If the soil is not fertile, poke some slow-release fertiliser granules into it.

4 After planting, sprinkle 2 cm of sand or fine gravel onto the soil. This keeps the soil in place and prevents it discolouring the water.

5 Sink the lily into the water a little at a time, lowering it at weekly intervals over about six weeks to its ultimate depth of around 35 cm.

6 Blooms usually appear in less than six weeks. Cool-climate lilies come in white, pink, red, yellow and apricot. Tropical lilies include blues and violets.

Water lilies and water hyacinths grow well together.

The beautiful lotus.

Rockery Plants

The trick in a rockery is to effect a balance between the shape of the rock 'sculpture' and the plants which set it off. They should not dominate it either in profusion or height. Basically any low-growing plant will do.

In the rockery itself, create soil pockets of various sizes. In the small crevices tuck succulents and trailing plants. In deeper pockets the dwarf trees and shrubs will do well. Keep the pockets separate so that quick-growing varieties don't take over from their slower counterparts. Save a few areas for annuals and bulbs so things are happening whatever the season. Cacti, low-growing acacias, banksias and grevilleas, ferns, cycads and rock orchids are a few more varieties that could be considered. Methodical weeding should be done so that plant roots are not loosened.

Pansies, heartsease and forget-me-not will grow well in soil pockets of rockeries.

Shade Plants

Some plants have major difficulties with the sun. Their tissue burns if exposed to hot sunlight and leaves brown and die. As you realise from the growth cycle of trees, leaves are the food manufacturers so the burning effect on them is never good. It can easily be fatal.

When selecting plants for shady places keep in mind there are degrees of shade. Shade runs from a sun-dappled lightness to the deep, dark shade of a completely sunless spot. Partial shade means the plant gets both sun and shade at some part of the day. Of course these rough divisions have countless variations which are made even more complex because they vary from season to season as the sun's angle changes.

Sun in winter, shade in summer is the best for most plants. This can be achieved by planting under deciduous trees.

The trick is to match the shade intensity and amount with each plant's characteristics. Ferns generally require shade, especially in summer.

Shade-loving plants will thrive under a tree and provide a cool retreat in summer.

Groundcover

The term groundcover, though self-defining, is very broad. It includes any densely foliaged low plant or shrub that covers bare soil. It provides not only an aesthetically pleasing mantle which ranges from only a few millimetres high (like the Scleranthus) to a dense, knee-high cover (such as provided by the rampant Algerian ivy). If you let it go, don't stand still in the one place for too long.

Groundcover has a practical value in blocking out weeds, keeping the soil moist, stabilising a boggy spot, and stopping wind and water erosion. In the latter case, choose one that has a strong root system. Ivy, native violets, iceplants and lamium are good choices. Unfortunately groundcover isn't meant to be walked on although a few types will stand up to the occasional footfall.

When planting (not including vine types), follow these general step-by-step rules. First divide the well-watered clumps in autumn or spring. When separating plants, be especially careful of the root systems and try to avoid tearing them any more than necessary. Place them at 150 mm centres in well prepared and enriched soil. Keep the weeds away while the plants are growing and make sure they are kept watered.

The Japanese spurge makes a dense and attractive groundcover but it is slow-growing. Sun jewel makes up in summer for its unsightly winter display. Mixing groundcovers can give an interesting colour combination. The dark *Viola labradorica* mixed with yellow-leaved ivy and Tiarella gives a patterned effect, as do small ferns, goat's beard and buttercups.

Blue fescue, with its distinctive grassy leaves, provides an interesting clumping effect. Check with your local nursery for other species/types appropriate to your conditions.

When planting groundcovers, carefully divide the clumps so that their roots are not damaged.

Place them 150 mm apart in well prepared and enriched soil.

Lawns

Lawn, despite its heavy maintenance needs, is something that could, if the area is judged correctly, set off the rest of your garden. It provides an evenness that contrasts with undulating layers of flowers, shrubs and trees.

Whether it's in seed form, in runners or turf, it should not be walked on while it is getting established. While the lawn slowly grows, you can sit back and survey the results of your endeavours. Your paradise is nearly finished!

Situation and Preparation

Lawn grasses love sun. They need four hours per day to be healthy, although some varieties will do well in dappled shade.

When setting out the chosen area, try to avoid straight edges — long sweeping curves look best. Tight curves should be avoided as they are difficult to mow. If you lay a hose around the general shape it will give you some idea of the effect. Edging of some sort is a good idea because it frames the lawn and provides an easy to maintain border.

The soil should be well prepared and free from stones, weeds and rubbish. Spraying with a herbicide will get rid of unwanted plants, especially clover, onionweed and nutgrass. Several applications may be necessary. Check the drainage and put in an underground agricultural pipe system if necessary. This is because grass will not do well in soggy soil.

Rake the soil so that it is straight. Undulations are not a problem if

Some Lawn Grasses at a Glance

Where you live will determine the type of grass you should grow. Grasses that thrive in Darwin would only be seen dead in Dunedin and vice versa, so always seek the advice of a turf supplier before deciding on a particular grass.

TYPE OF GRASS	SUITABLE CLIMATE	AVAILABLE AS	ADVANTAGES	DISADVANTAGES
Couch	Subtropical, temperate	Turf, sprigs, runners	Soft, comfortable, quality fine-leaved appearance.	Can wear thin in high traffic areas, runners are very invasive of garden beds if not controlled, needs frequent mowing, goes brown after frost.
Kikuyu	Subtropical, temperate	Turf, runners	Hard-wearing, inexpensive as turf, soft, good around pools/spas as it resists chlorinated water.	Runners are invasive, fast growth necessitates frequent mowing, needs a lot of water and fertiliser, browns off after frost.
Buffalo	Subtropical, temperate	Turf, runners	Very hard-wearing, takes more shade than most other grasses, takes light frosts, needs less mowing.	Expensive, prickly and rough, fairly coarse looking.
Saltene	Subtropical, temperate	Turf, runners	Handsome fine leaves, soft, takes brackish water.	Looks unattractive through coldish winters.
Kentucky bluegrass/ ryegrass blends	Cool	Turf, seed	Stays green through cold winters, hard-wearing, attractive blue-green colour.	Demands a lot of feeding and watering in summer and very frequent mowing.
Bent	Cool	Turf, seed	Very luxurious looking, very soft and comfortable, stays green through cold winters.	Not hard wearing, needs frequent de-thatching and a lot of summer water, easily invaded by weeds.
Bahia grass	Tropical, subtropical	Runners, seed	Hard-wearing, fast-growing, takes some shade in the tropics, relatively inexpensive.	Rather coarse looking, needs a lot of dry-season water.
Zoysia	Tropical	Turf, runners, plugs	Very attractive luxurious looking lawn.	Slow-growing, easily invaded by weeds and expensive.

A well-maintained lawn takes time and care, but when it looks like this, it is worth the effort.

the area is large. If it has a slight fall, that will assist with surface water run-off which hopefully won't be excessive while the grass is getting established. Spread some lawn fertiliser over the whole area to promote quick growth.

Grass Types

The table shows some of the principal types of grass, their best climate, how they are sold and their advantages and disadvantages.

You have three options: to sow seeds, to plant runners or to turf. Obviously the last method creates an instantaneous effect while the other two will take up to a year before a proper cover is effected.

Seeds and Runners

Check which type of grass best suits your particular climate and area. Divide the lawn area into square metres with some string and temporary pegs. This will ensure you get a proper and even concentration of seeds. Sow the seeds (spring is a good time) preferably on a drizzly day and lightly rake them in. If rain is not imminent, water with a misty spray.

Birds could be a problem. A bird repellent or hawk kite could assist. Keep watering until germination has begun. Quickly reseed any bare areas. When the new grass is about 75 mm high, roll it. This will even the soil and firm it around the roots. A week later, attack it with a sharp-bladed mower, taking only 10 mm off. Let it continue to intensify, cutting it no shorter than 60 mm. Keep in mind it will take nearly a year to become strong and resilient.

Lay runners in rows, 100 mm apart. Keep moist until they've filled in, and then treat as for seeds.

Turf

Turf is like a grass carpet which is sold in rolls. The grass, which comes in various species, is grown in commercial areas, then peeled off in layers which include the roots and a few centimetres of earth. You simply unroll it, firm it down and your lawn is finished!

Setting Up a Low-care Garden

I use the word low-care because there is no such thing as a no maintenance garden. In fact no maintenance really means jungle-like confusion in which weeds prosper.

However, with some judicious planning and a fair amount of hard work at the onset, you can achieve a beautiful low-care garden which will continue to look good with the minimum of effort. The main factors that lead to such a desirable situation are outlined as follows.

- Get rid of all weeds before you begin. A good herbicide, a sprayer, and your personage clad in gumboots, overalls, gloves and face mask (to lessen the risk of poisoning yourself) and you're half-way there. Several doses may be necessary before the weeds are eradicated. If their concentration is sparse, you could of course pull or dig them out. If so, don't let any oxalis, onionweed or nutgrass survive.
- Improve the soil. Poor, infertile, dry or badly drained soil won't support healthy plants and will thwart all your efforts. Good drainage, which we discussed earlier, is also essential for good soil.

  Mulching is useful, too. Fifty-millimetre layers of rotting grass, straw, etc. spread over the soil helps to keep moisture in and provides new organic material.
- Avoid or minimise lawns. This is because they need constant mowing, edging, weeding, watering and fertilising which absorb great amounts of time and energy, especially during summer. Instead use groundcover where possible. In high traffic areas use paving or stepping stones.
- Avoid masses of annuals. These plants may be spectacuar but, from the planting out of the seedlings to the end of their cycle when you have to dig them out and enrich the soil ready for the next batch, they mean work.

Once the area is prepared (loosened, fertilised and levelled), simply lay the rolls side by side. Cut them with a sharp spade to fit against curved edging. Stagger any end joints and keep the joints tightly together to ensure they interlock as the grass becomes established. Tamp them lightly as you go and avoid walking on them any more than is necessary (a plank is handy for this).

When you're finished, roll with a lightweight roller to ensure the roots are pressed down into the soil and any irregularities are evened out. Water well but not to excess or you may erode the underlying soil. Mow lightly after a few weeks.

Maintenance

Watering of any lawn is important. Do it daily in the heat of summer, weekly in winter, assuming there is no rainfall. Six to ten millimetres is a goodly amount. You can work this out by putting a few empty lids of that depth under the sprinkler. When they're full, the watering is done!

Fertilising is important because grass, like other plants, once it exhausts the soil nutrients, will not get any more unless you apply more. There are several lawn foods on the market and a full application in November and April followed by a lesser dose in December and

February, will assist greatly. Distributing it in a light shower may seem strange but it is an ideal time.

Fertilising will also attract weeds so pull them out should they appear. If they're too far advanced, spray with a herbicide that won't damage the grass.

Mowing frequency and height depends on the season. In spring, short grass is good. Longer grass in summer helps to conserve moisture and keep the soil cool — in winter it helps the grass to survive the lack of sunlight and the chance of frosts. Don't let the grass stay too long for extended periods, however, as it tends to go spongy.

A beautiful lawn, once established, is a constant delight.

Relaxation at Last

Now that you've transformed your backyard and set up a low-care garden, all you have to do is to lie back and relax, perhaps in a hammock slung between two of your loveliest trees. The hammock is a convenient item to finish this book with. It symbolises the relaxing retreat you've created for yourself. While the rest of the family or friends enjoy the pool, or play on the lawns, or wander through the nooks and crannies you've sculptured out of the expanse of land once enclosed by a paling fence and inhabited only by a clothes hoist, you've earned the right to climb into the hammock with a good book plus perhaps a glass of chablis, and, in the shade of the grape-vined pergola, a palm, or a whispering conifer, truly relax.

You are in your very own Garden of Eden. Only this time around, there should be nothing to spoil it! But, to be sure, have some insect repellent to hand.

Your backyard is complete and it's time to relax.

THE HOME WORKSHOP

CHAPTER 11

TOOLS AND MATERIALS

This chapter is included because, if you are to become a successful do-it-yourselfer, you need to have a little knowledge about the materials and tools you will be using.

I know, I know! You're already saying, 'Isn't a *little* knowledge dangerous?' In some instances, I suppose, that's true. I have therefore tried to include all the *essential* facts, those which I judge to be necessary for your safety and success, given the space constraints of this book. If you want further information, besides standard textbooks on these subjects, many of the manufacturers or their associations supply, free of charge, printed information in the form of booklets and brochures on their products.

They also employ experienced technical staff to answer questions about particular problems. Use them! They love to show off their knowledge. They, like me, want to see you succeed.

Basic Hand Tools

Doing projects and minor maintenance jobs around your home requires some tools. This section describes some of the basic hand tools you should acquire with hints on their selection, maintenance and use. (The use of chisels, planes and saws, because of their complexity, is done in the relevant maintenance topics.) The sharpening of chisels and plane irons is included in this section.

Check with your closest *builder's* hardware shop to get advice on particular brands. I've stressed *builder's* because too often the person serving you in supermarket type stores knows little or nothing about practical things. Experience is a great teacher!

A nail punch is a useful tool for driving nails below the surface of timber before puttying and painting.

Hammer

A hammer is used for driving in nails and pulling them out. Be careful to select one that isn't too heavy. Try swinging it at an imaginary nail. If you can't control it buy a lighter one. Look for quality. Poor quality hammers eventually suffer from broken claws, chipped faces and snapped handles.

Clean the face with sandpaper occasionally to keep it from slipping off the nails and painting your fingernails blue! When extracting nails, put a scrap piece of timber under the hammer head so you don't mark the timber.

If you keep missing the nails, get a scrap piece of hardboard and bore a small hole in it (see picture on right). Start the nail, then put the hardboard over the nail. Then if you miss, you'll hit the hardboard, not the timber. If the timber is hard, rub candle wax on the nail to make driving easier. Or you can drill a hole, one slightly smaller than the nail thickness.

Use a hardboard nail foil to avoid damaging the timber you are working on.

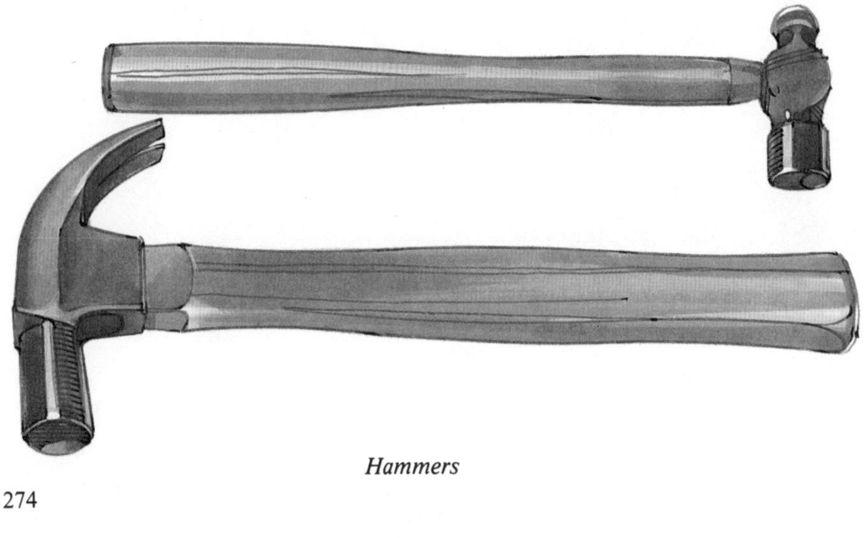

Hammers

Nail Punch

A nail punch is a useful tool for driving nails below the surface before puttying and painting. Get two different sized ones (a fine and medium) to suit different gauge nails. Don't use a fine punch on a large nail or you'll ruin the end. Punches are also handy when used for making pilot holes to drive small screws into.

Pliers
Pliers work like your dentist's extraction pincers and can cut wire, grip nails, and, if you don't have spanners, provide a crude method of loosening nuts and bolts.

Tape
A tape is an accurate, easily stored measuring device. Get one that extends to at least five metres so you can measure long lengths. Buy one with clear numbering and divisions and, whatever you do, don't bend it or it may crack. Try not to get it wet but if you do, carefully dry it before storing otherwise it will rust.

Pencil
A carpenter's pencil, with its thick lead, will not wear out as quickly as an ordinary lead pencil. You can get various grades of hardness. Pencil lines can be more easily cleaned off than pen. For accurate work pencils should always be sharp. A chisel point stays sharper longer.

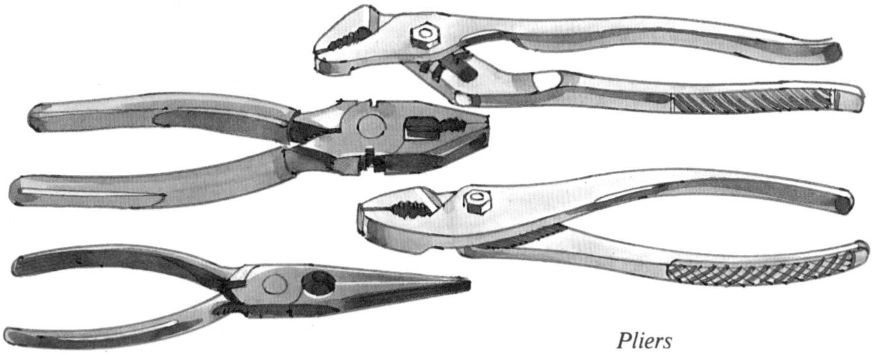

Pliers

Spirit Level
A spirit level is essential for accurate levelling (making things like bench tops, door heads, etc., exactly horizontal) and vertical truing of window and door stiles, etc. The longer it is the better. A 900 mm one is ideal.

Spanner
A spanner is used for loosening or tightening nuts. One that opens out to 25 mm will do most jobs.

Square
A square is a very useful tool for marking lines square to each other. Possibly the best one for the handyperson is a combination square. This useful tool can be used for making right angles, marking 45° lines (for mitring), and, with the blade slid back into the handle, for gauging pencil lines parallel to one edge.

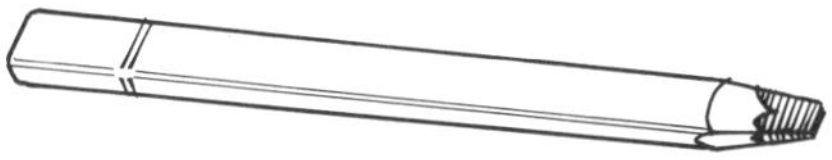

An adjustable spanner is an indispensable tool for loosening or tightening nuts.

Plane

A plane is used for reducing timber to size or making it smooth. There are many types and qualities. I'd recommend you get a jack or a smoothing plane. Again hold the plane before purchasing and pretend you're planing. If your arms feel as though they want to fall off, get a smaller one that you can control.

There are many brands on the market. Some of the cheaper ones may break, which means they are no longer cheap. It's a question of relating cost to potential use.

The parts of the plane are shown in the drawing below. When you've finished with it, wind the blade back in and store the plane in its box. A light rub of oil helps to prevent rust.

A smoothing plane should be comfortable to hold. Check carefully before you buy.

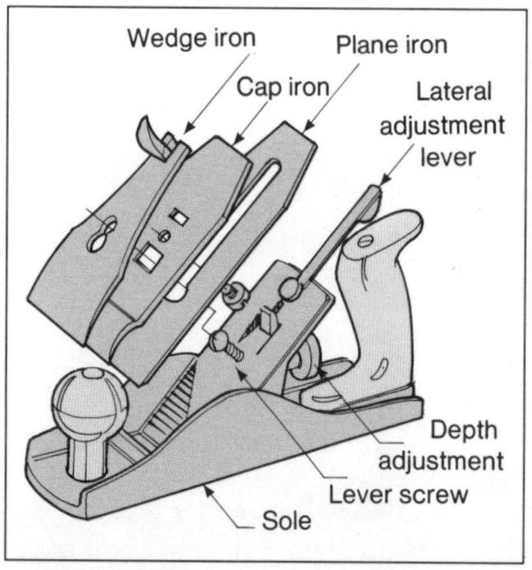

The parts of a plane

Check the adjustment of the blade of the plane.

Sharpening Planes and Chisels

You'll need your oilstone and some light machine oil mixed with turps or kerosene. The oil floats away the metal particles while the solvent cleans the stone.

To sharpen a plane iron (or chisel), first coat the stone with a layer of the lubricant. This layer, which should be re-applied throughout the sharpening operation, will keep the stone cutting.

1 First extract the plane iron. This involves taking off the lever cap iron (see drawing on this page) and removing the double iron. Undo the screw and swivel the backing iron at right angles, and then slide it down until the screw head comes out of the hole in the plane iron. Examine the plane iron carefully. If it's gapped or if the bevel is rounded, get the plane iron reground at a knife-sharpening outlet or hardware store.

2 Lay the plane iron (or chisel), bevel down on the stone and then lift it up until the oil squeezes out. This means the grinding angle is against the stone.

3 Lift the end of the tool a further 10 mm and, locking your wrists, begin to rub the plane iron along the full length of the stone. Use the whole width of the stone (see page 280).

4 Lift the plane iron up and feel the flat side for a burr. If there isn't one or it's only part way across, repeat the process. Once the burr is full length turn the plane iron over, lay it on the stone and, being careful not to lift it (or you'll make a bevel on the flat side making it impossible to sharpen), take off the burr.

5 Repeat the procedure several times, pressing more lightly and with fewer strokes each time. On the final one make only one stroke on each side. If you've followed the procedure correctly you should have a sharp tool. To check if it's sharp, run your finger *lightly* along the edge from the flat side. It should, if sharp, slightly nick your skin.

When putting the plane iron back in, be careful you don't let the sharp edge touch the backing iron (which must be set 1 mm back) or any other metal surface.

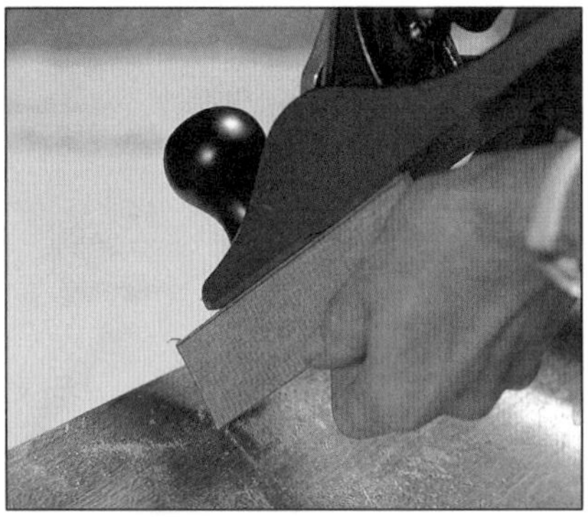

Planing a small block

File and Rasp

A long, flat file and a rasp with both a curved and a flat surface are useful for many jobs when it's hard to plane or saw.

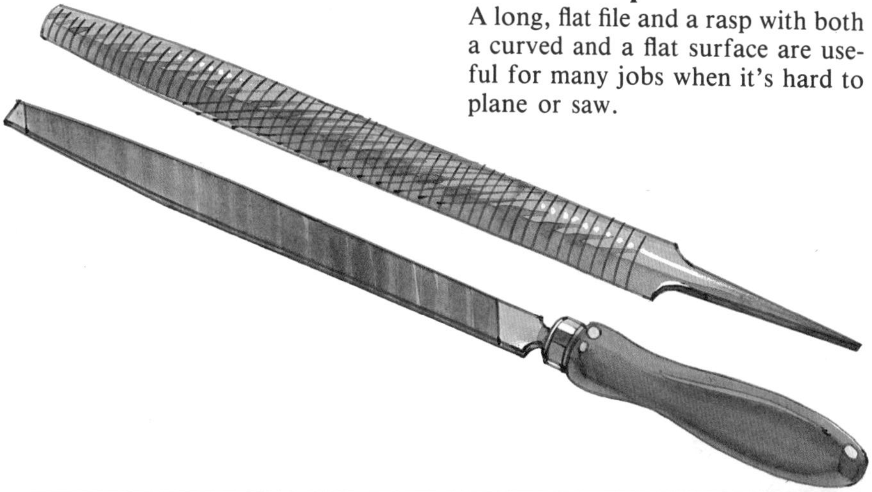

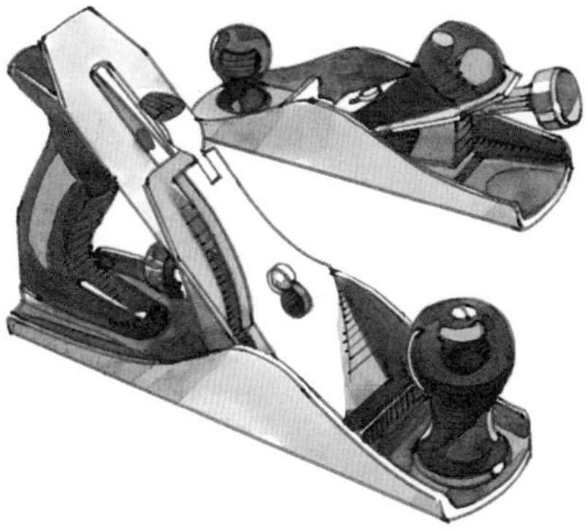

A block plane (above) and a bench plane (below).

Chisels

Chisels are used for chopping holes in, or paring away, timber. There are many types of chisels. Buy two for starters: say a 10 mm and a 25 mm firmer chisel with either a plastic or a steel-ferruled wooden handle. These chisels are good for general work and will stand up to rigorous hammering or levering.

When not in use, put your chisels in a cardboard box so the edges can't touch any metal or children. And remember NEVER put your hands in front of the blade while chopping or paring.

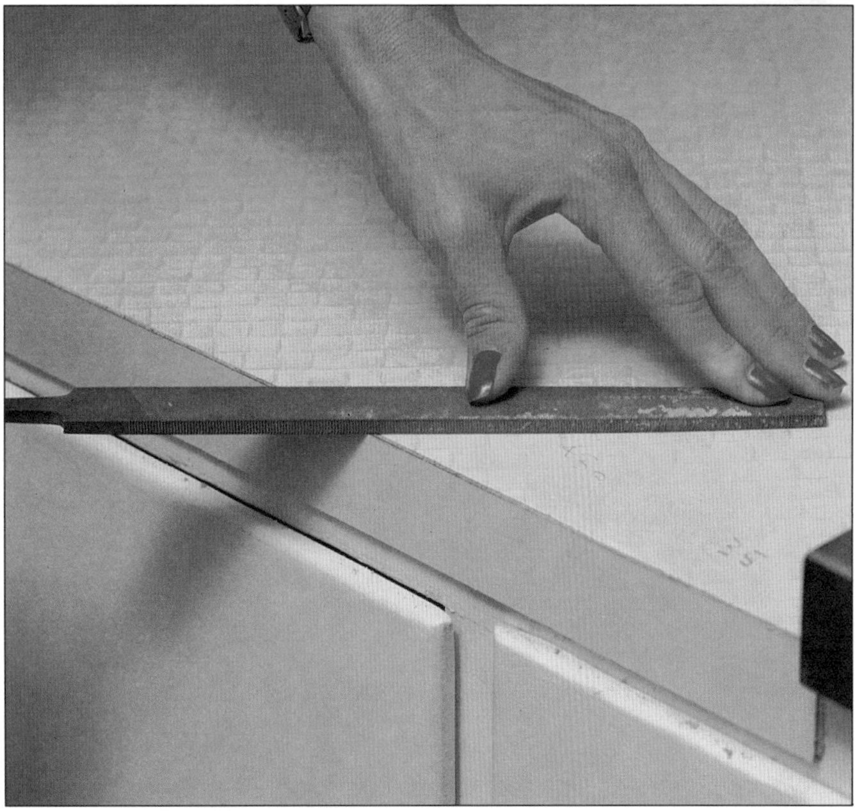

A file can be used to finish off the edges of a variety of surfaces and materials.

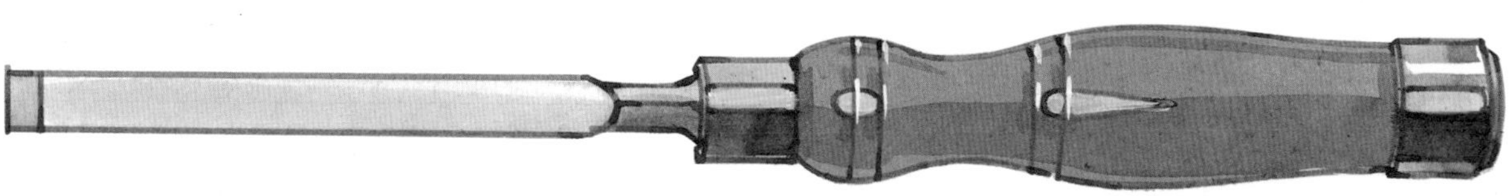

Chisels

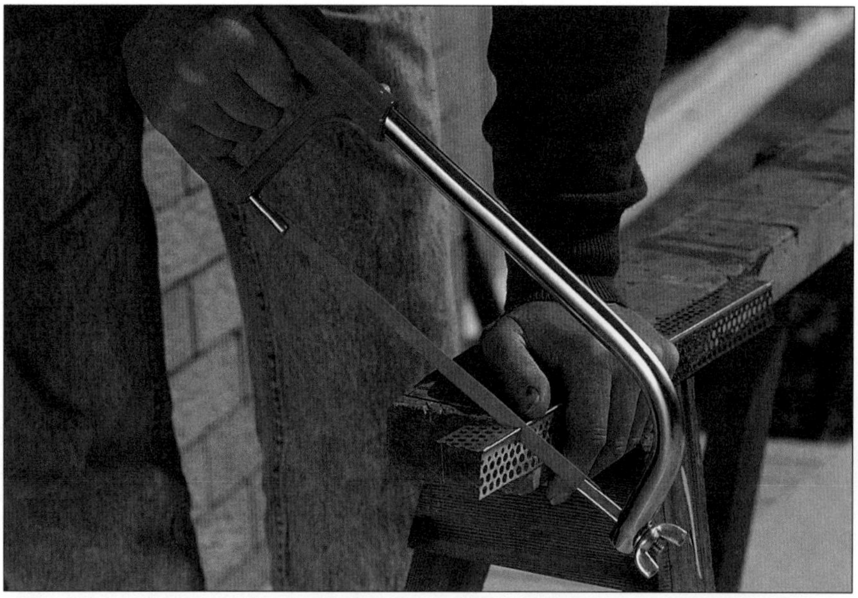

Use a hacksaw for cutting metal and plastic. There are different blades available to suit various materials and kinds of metal.

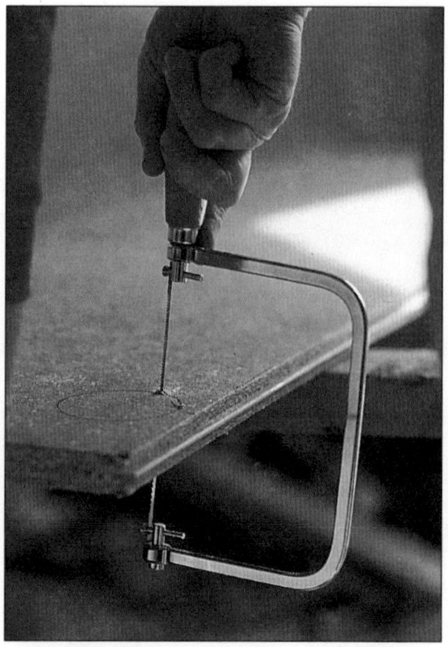

A coping saw is used to make circular cuts. Drill a hole to start.

Saws

Saws are used for cutting things to length. For fine joinery work a tenon saw is useful. For more ambitious projects which involve larger timber sections you can add a panel or handsaw. The tenon saw, with its rigid back, has very small teeth. Don't be deceived — they cut wood or flesh with ease so keep your hands away from the cutting edge.

An inexpensive but handy saw is the coping saw. It is used for scribing or making circular cuts.

A hacksaw is used for cutting metal and plastic. There are many different blades available to suit various metals.

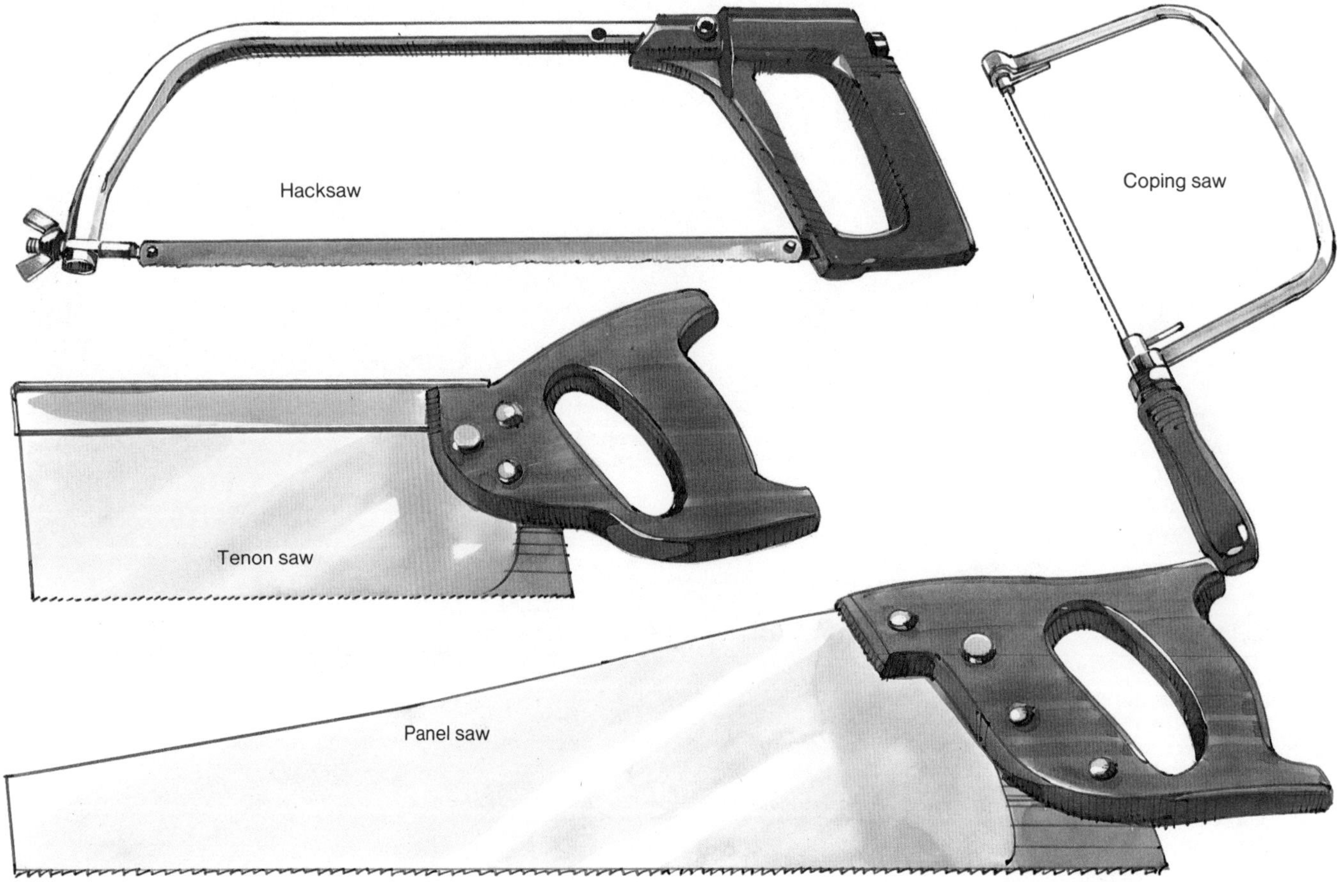

Hand Drill

A hand drill is a useful tool which, in combination with various drill bits, is handy for drilling holes for plugs or screws. It works on the same principle as your hand eggbeater.

The turning handle spins the chuck which holds the drill bit (a touch of oil on the drive wheel will lubricate the turning action). To put in a bit, hold the turning handle still and unwind the chuck until the bit slips into the jaws. Then simply tighten the chuck with one hand while immobilising the turning handle.

As an alternative to buying a hand drill, you can hire electric drills (see Electric Drills on page 282).

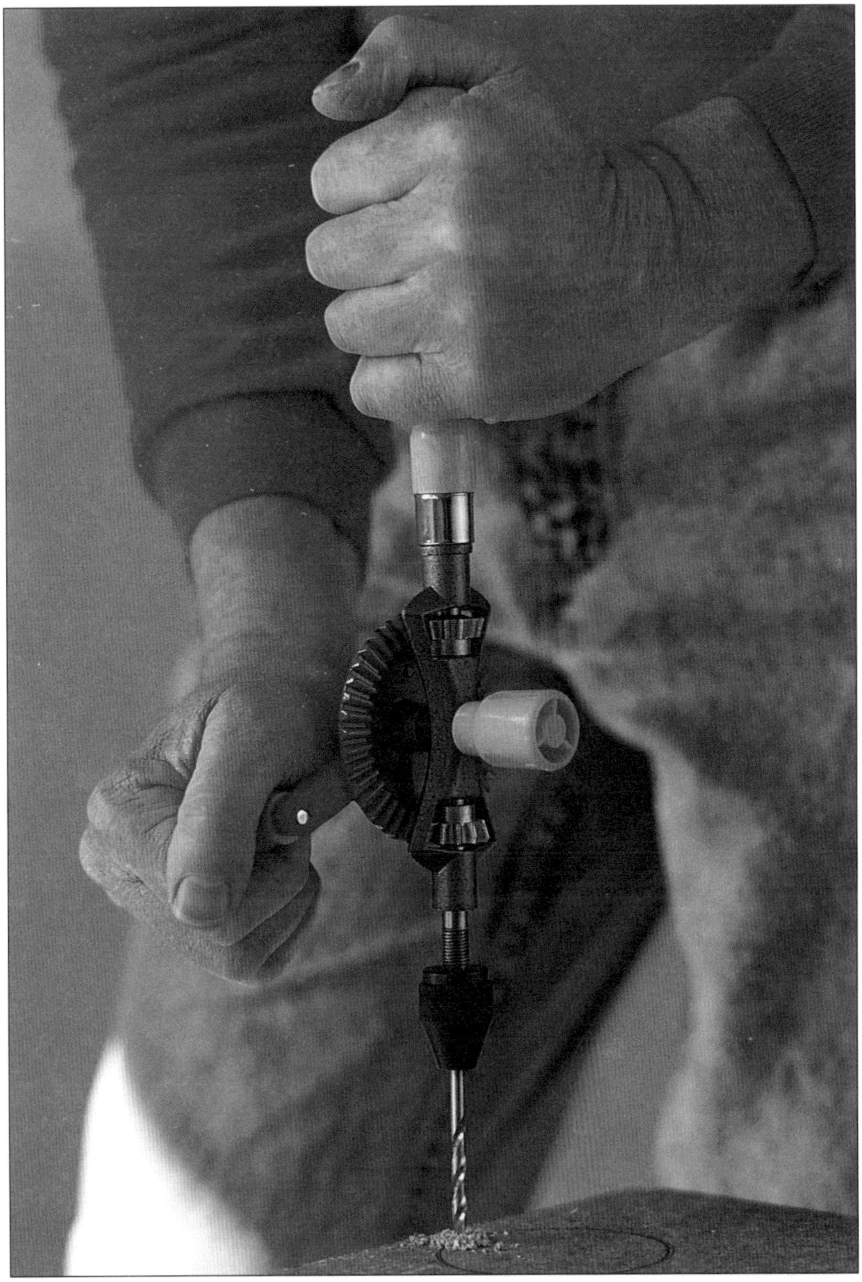

A hand drill is cheap and is a very useful tool for tight situations or fine work where the electric drill is not needed.

Drill Bits

Get a set of drill bits to suit home use. Your hardware store will advise you on quality but they should range between 2 mm and 10 mm. A 6 mm masonry bit is handy if you have brick walls.

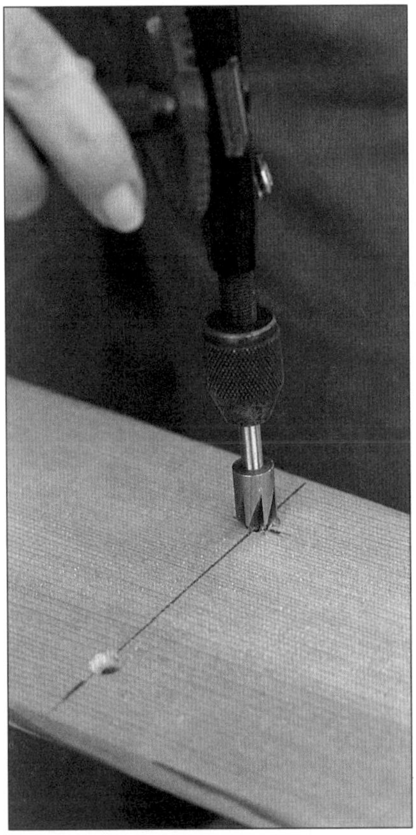

A countersinker is used in a drill to produce a neat finish for screws.

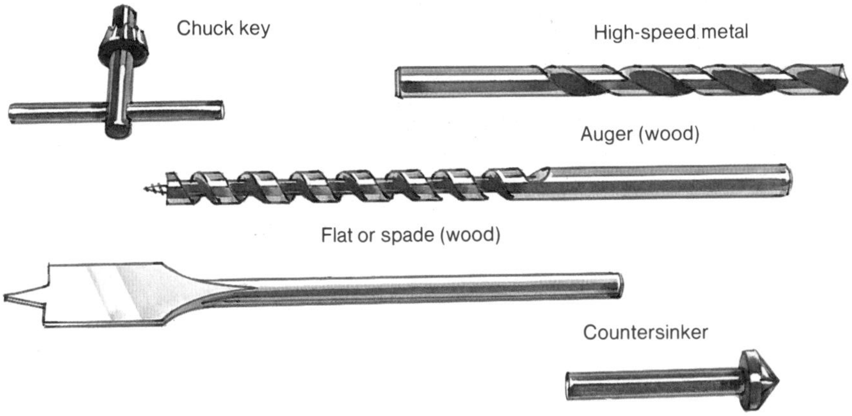

Screwdrivers

Screwdrivers are for driving in or removing screws. The tips of screwdrivers are shaped to suit various profiles and sizes of screw heads (slot head, Phillips head, etc.).

The important thing is to select the right-sized screwdriver to fit the screw. One wider than the screw head will damage the timber and one too small will ruin the slot of the screw, making it impossible to get it in or out. Keep in mind that a screwdriver with a large handle is easier to get both purchase and weight on than a small one. A ratchet screwdriver allows you to turn the screw without having to move your grip with each turn. It can be adjusted for driving or removing as well as being fixed.

Buy a small set of mixed screwdrivers to begin with and perhaps one with a ratchet. You can add special types as the need arises.

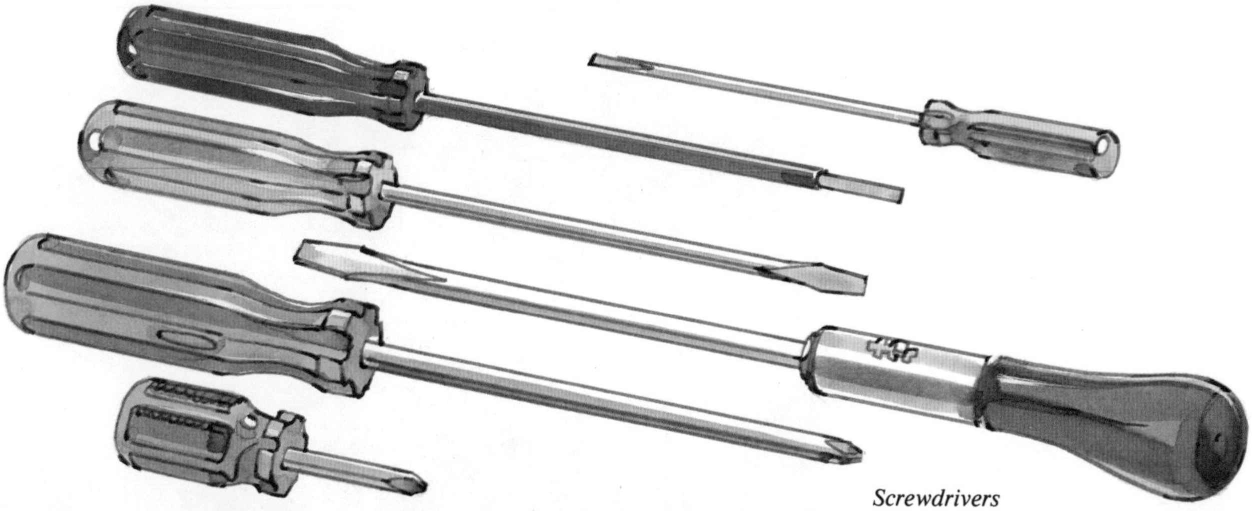

Screwdrivers

Use a well-oiled stone to keep tools like chisels and plane blades sharp and working efficiently.

Oilstone

Natural stones are the best but the most expensive. For the do-it-yourselfer, a synthetic stone is adequate. Your stone, kept in its box, should last for years. Left on a bench it will soon get chipped or cracked.

Trimming Knife

With its renewable and retractable blade, a trimming knife is handy for cutting plasterboard, vinyl tiles, plastic, etc.

G–Cramp

A couple of G–cramps are handy if you are doing some single-handed jobs or gluing. Always use two scraps of timber underneath the jaws to avoid damaging the timber of the job you are working on.

Obviously there are many more tools you can acquire but for most of the jobs described in this book, these ones will suffice.

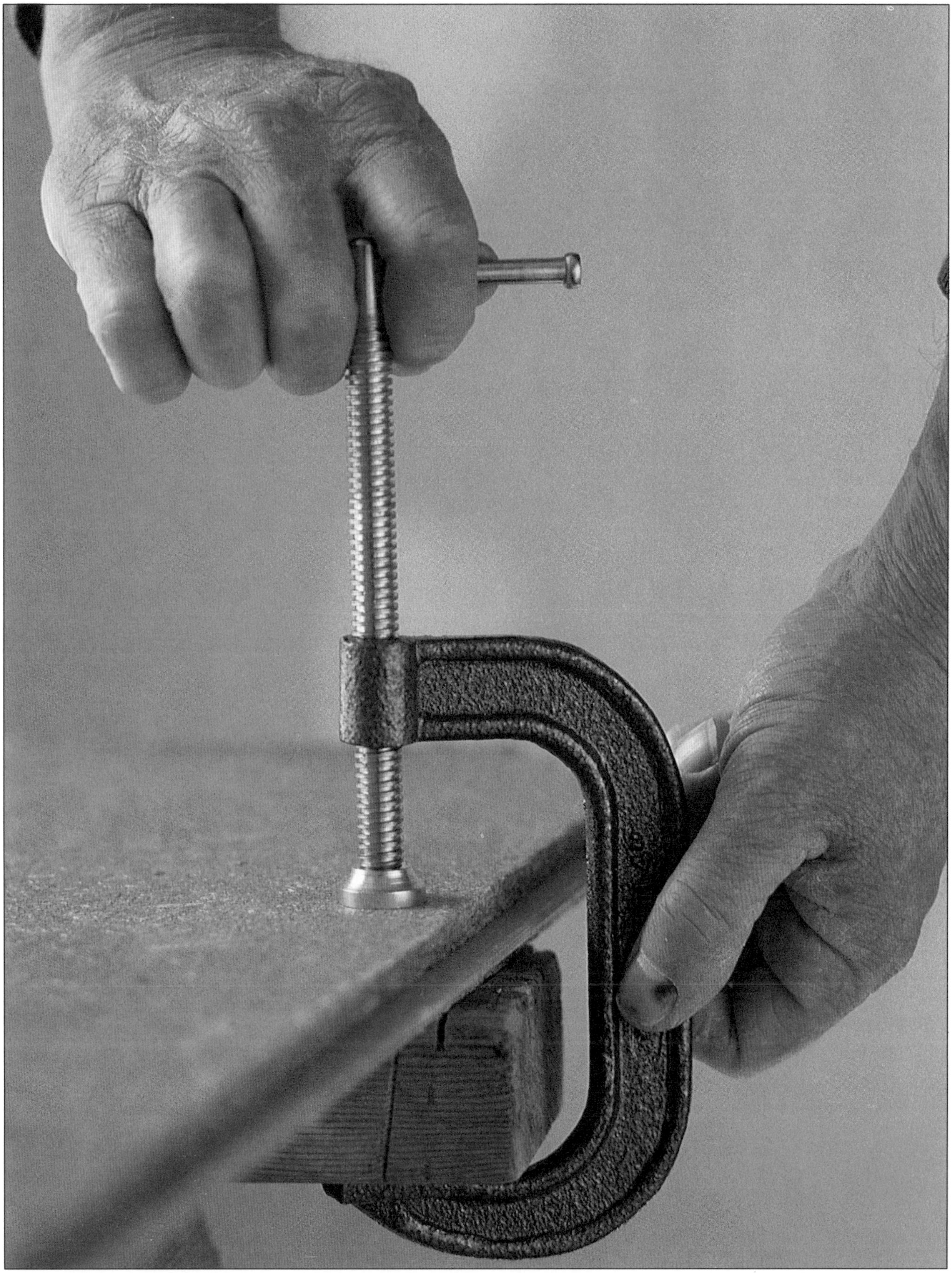

A G-cramp is very useful if you are doing some single-handed jobs or gluing. Always use a scrap of timber under each jaw to avoid damaging your timber.

Basic Electric Tools

There are many electric tools available, many of which take the drudgery and hard work out of home maintenance. The three that are generally the most useful are the electric drill, the circular saw and the sander. As with hand tools, quality is important — that and adequate power (not too little, not too much). Before you select, keep in mind the old adage: you usually only get what you pay for!

When buying a tool, check whether it is designed for a tradesperson or a handyperson. A tool for the handyperson is too often poorly made, or underpowered, or both. Such a tool may soon burn out or spend much of its life at the repairers. Go to where the local builders buy their tools and ask for advice.

An electric drill is a boon, and a necessity if you have masonry walls.

Electric Drills

Although most drilling can be done with a hand drill, an electric drill is a boon. If you have a home that has masonry or rendered walls it is a must. A popular size is one with a 6 mm chuck. It will hold most standard drill bits and, if it's good quality, usually has sufficient power to cope with boring into the occasional hard brick. Of course, if you have the money, a drill with a 10 mm chuck, especially if it has a hammer facility, will give you years of effortless service.

The question of whether it's better to buy a cordless drill or one with the conventional 240 volts is a hot issue. I admit I'm suspicious of battery-powered electrics, but then having to run extension leads everywhere can be a nuisance and sometimes, in wet weather, dangerous. Cordless drills generally cost a bit more, have the same warranty, but have a limited use capacity (two to three hours) whereas you can drill all day with a standard one. But then there is no chance of electrocution and, if you only use it for small jobs, it is very convenient.

Prices range from one hundred and twenty to three hundred dollars plus. A 10 mm, conventionally powered 7.2 volt unit with a hammer action (they come in 4.8, 7.2 and 9.6 volt capacity) is the one I'd probably buy for myself but then old habits die hard.

To complement your drill, you'll need a set of drill bits (2–10 mm). A 6 mm and a 10 mm masonry bit are handy for drilling into brick or stone. A set of speed borers makes drilling large holes in timber a breeze.

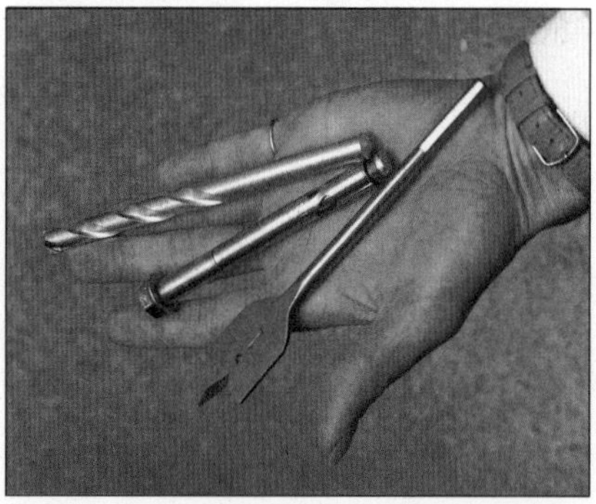

A masonry drill bit, a masonry bolt and a speed drill for timber.

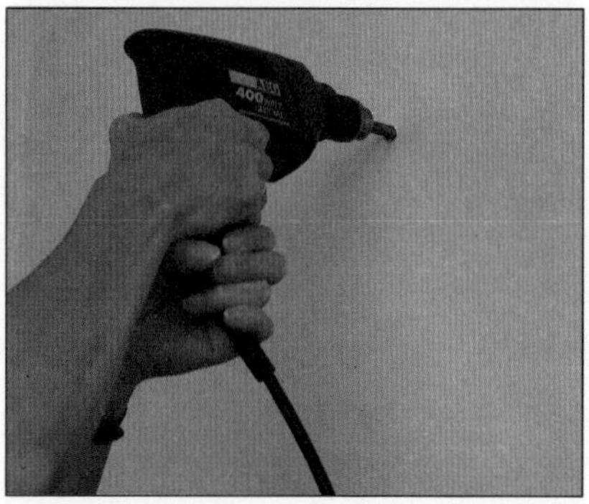

An electric drill makes short work of boring a hole in masonry walls.

SAFETY POINTS WHEN DRILLING

- Turn off the power when putting in the bit.
- Make sure the drill is tight by using the chuck key.
- Properly secure the work to be drilled.
- Make sure no loose clothing or hair can get wrapped around the chuck (unless you want to be naked or bald).
- Turn on the drill and check the bit is in the centre.
- Make an indentation in the work (with a punch or nail) so the drill stays in the centre of the hole.
- When drilling deep holes, withdraw the drill several times to clear it.
- Don't stand in water while drilling or let the lead dangle into a puddle.
- Wear rubber-soled shoes for added safety.

Circular Saw

Few electric tools have the popularity of the circular saw. Yet it is possibly one of the most misused and therefore potentially dangerous tools on the market. Every year it severely lacerates or lops off numerous fingers and thumbs, to say nothing of fatalities.

Like the electric drill, its work can be done, albeit much more slowly and laboriously, using a hand tool such as a panel or tenon saw. Again the choice is one of considering the high cost against the ease, quickness, and of course, the likely amount of use.

Circular saws come in a variety of blade sizes with the 185 mm (7¼ inches) being the most useful one for the average do-it-yourselfer. Of course, the larger the blade, the more robust and heavy the saw will be but keep in mind it will also be more difficult to control.

Again go for quality. It will be reflected in the solidity of the base frame, the design of depth and tilt adjustments, and, most importantly, the efficiency of the telescoping guard (which keeps the blade isolated from your precious fingers).

Although it's expensive, buy a tungsten-tipped blade for your saw. You'll rarely have to have it sharpened (unless you continually cut through nails) and the cut it makes looks as if it has been planed.

A circular saw is a most useful tool, but care is needed when using it.

SAFETY POINTS WHEN SAWING

The work should be held tightly with clamps or temporary nails so that you can keep *two hands on the saw and two feet on the ground* at all times.

- Unplug the saw if adjusting it.
- Set the saw depth to cut a fraction (say 3 mm) more than the timber thickness.
- Support the work in such a way that it won't close in on and jam the saw blade.
- Never stand behind the saw when cutting in case it throws back at you.
- Keep the work area clean so there is nothing to trip on.
- Make sure the lead is well clear of the blade at all times.
- Most importantly, never immobilise, hold back, or remove the telescoping guard (unless you would like to be permanently short-handed!). It's against the law for starters and incredibly dangerous.

Orbital Sander

Although more expensive belt sanders are available, they are probably too difficult for the beginning do-it-yourselfer to use successfully. The orbital sander has a place if you are predisposed towards electric tools and saving energy. However, for the best finish to timber, nothing really beats careful planing and a final rub with a cork block and abrasive paper.

An orbital sander gives a smooth finish with little effort. The model in the picture has a dust bag.

The orbital sander is primarily a finishing tool, one that is used after scraping and planing. It cuts very slowly so it won't flush off badly fitting joints or sand smooth sawn timber but then neither will it ruin the job. Go for a large capacity one otherwise the cutting action will be so minimal as to be useless.

It is a safe tool to use, so no particular safety aspects, other than the general ones that apply to all electric tools, need be considered. Use different grades of abrasive paper to achieve a good result (a coarse one to start with and a fine one to finish).

Hint. Alternately holding the sheet at diagonally opposite corners, run the smooth side of the abrasive paper sheet over the sharp edge of a table. This will make the backing sheet more flexible and less inclined to crack.

Timber

Timber is one of the most versatile yet easily worked materials available for home and furniture construction. It is relatively light, strong, flexible, and has a natural appearance which, when covered with a clear finish, gives a warmth and variety that few synthetic materials possess.

There are many species, each one of which has advantages and disadvantages. Timber comes in an amazing variety of sizes, profiles, and combinations (plywood for example). Timber also forms the basis for many manufactured building products such as particle board, hardboard, etc.

Popular Types and Uses

While the indigenous Australian species are mainly hardwoods, some exotic types are now grown commercially while many more are imported. The result is a bewildering array of choices for you, the do-it-yourselfer. Because space does not permit a full coverage of every species, I have included only the major ones that you should consider using.

Before you select a particular species, ask yourself the following questions.

- Is it to be used internally or is it partly or completely exposed to the weather (the sun being most destructive)?
- Is strength important?
- Is appearance important?
- Should it be termite and fungus resistant?

Answers to these four questions will narrow the range of choices considerably.

Western red cedar This attractive Canadian timber typically ranges from light straw or a pale reddish colour through to a deep brown. It has a high resistance to termites and fungi, stands up to the elements well, has limited strength and is, relatively speaking, inexpensive. (Californian redwood, which has similar characteristics, is much more expensive.)

Though soft and easily damaged, it is used extensively for windows, external doors and door frames, and outdoor furniture. It is also sawn into weatherboards for cladding, and milled into a variety of shiplap and lining boards for use in feature walls or as a lining for bathrooms. It takes paints, stains, oils or waxes with equal enthusiasm.

Oregon (Douglas fir) This pine, mainly imported from the USA and Canada, is widely used as a structural and joinery timber and is easily sawn, nailed and planed. Its lightness, strength, flexibility, attractive yellow colour, and relatively good weather resistance (if painted) are its strengths. On the down side, it has little termite resistance, has a tendency to have seeping gum pockets, splinters easily, and the ends will split badly if not sealed.

It comes in various grades depending, amongst other things, on the number and size of the knots. You should clearly outline what you want it for so your supplier will give you the correct grade. (The price goes up in quantum leaps with each improvement!)

Radiata pine This straw-coloured Californian timber which, grown locally, makes up 20% of all sawn timber, is widely used for framing, joinery, furniture, benchtops and panelling. Its cheapness and easy workability assist its popularity.

In its natural form it is not durable in exterior situations (Cypress pine is better), but when treated with a copper chrome arsenate solution under pressure, it becomes durable and is widely used for decks, wall cladding, lattice, etc. Sold as logs, the treated pine is used for playground structures, log cabins and pole houses.

Australian hardwoods Varying in colour from straw to pinkish brown to dark red, these heavy, hardwearing, close-grained timbers are used in many structural (posts, joists, bearers, wall and roof framing), joinery (flooring, window sills, etc.), and furniture applications.

For in-ground contact use dur-

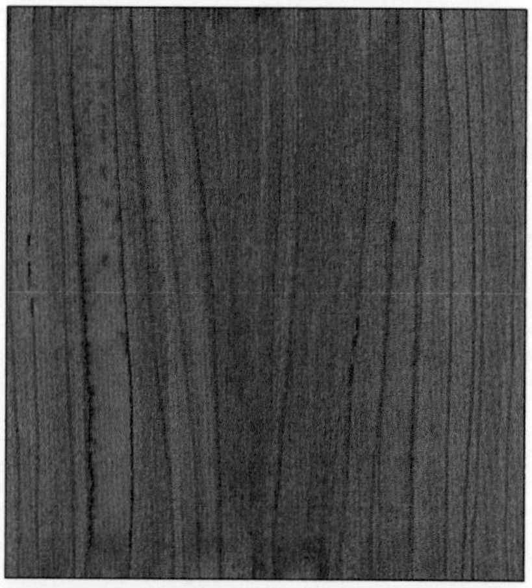

Western red cedar

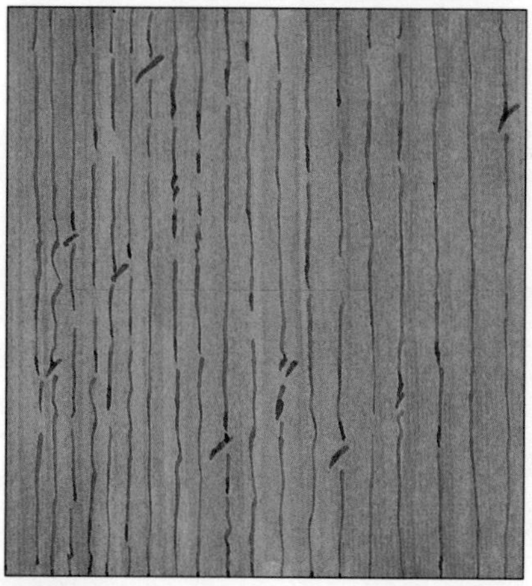

Oregon

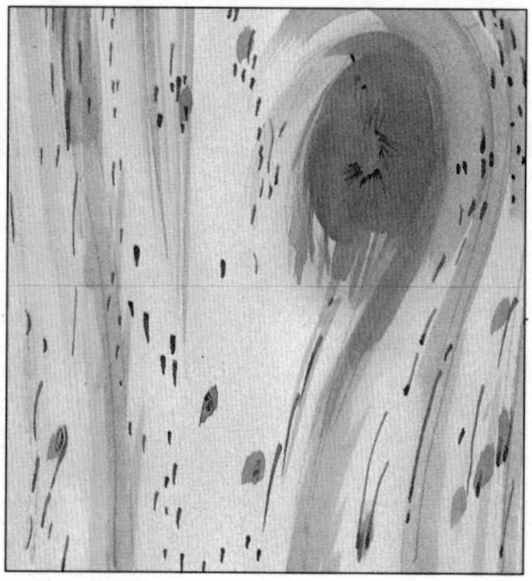

Radiata pine

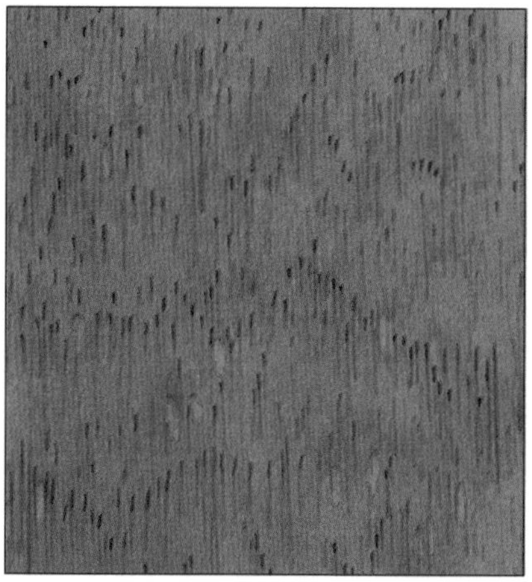

Australian hardwood

able species such as tallowwood or red gum (treated hardwoods are also available). These two can be used above ground together with blackbutt, turpentine, brushbox, etc. Well known decorative hardwoods include silver ash, coachwood, Tasmanian oak, red mahogany and karri.

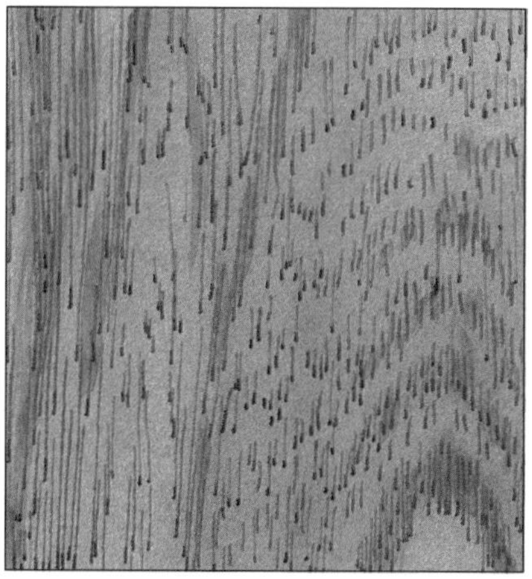

Pacific maple

Many of these hardwoods, over time, achieve a rocklike hardness and have been known to bow somewhat dramatically. Many carpenters shudder when confronted with a hardwood frame because of the weight but once it's there, white ants permitting, it should last forever!

Pacific maple (Meranti) This popular, easily worked joinery timber, which comes from exotic places like Malaysia, Indonesia and the Philippines, is used extensively in Australian home construction for jambs, architraves, skirtings, shelving, doors and plywood. It is not considered suitable for external use.

Though its strength varies (usually the darker it is the stronger), it saws, planes and sands easily and, like cedar, readily takes most timber finishes. Because of its abundant supply it is fairly cheap.

Timber Profiles and Sections

If you go into a large timber yard you will find a bewildering array of timber sections (round, square and rectangular shapes) and profiles (irregular shapes). For general home maintenance you will only need to be acquainted with the ones described below.

These timbers are sold either

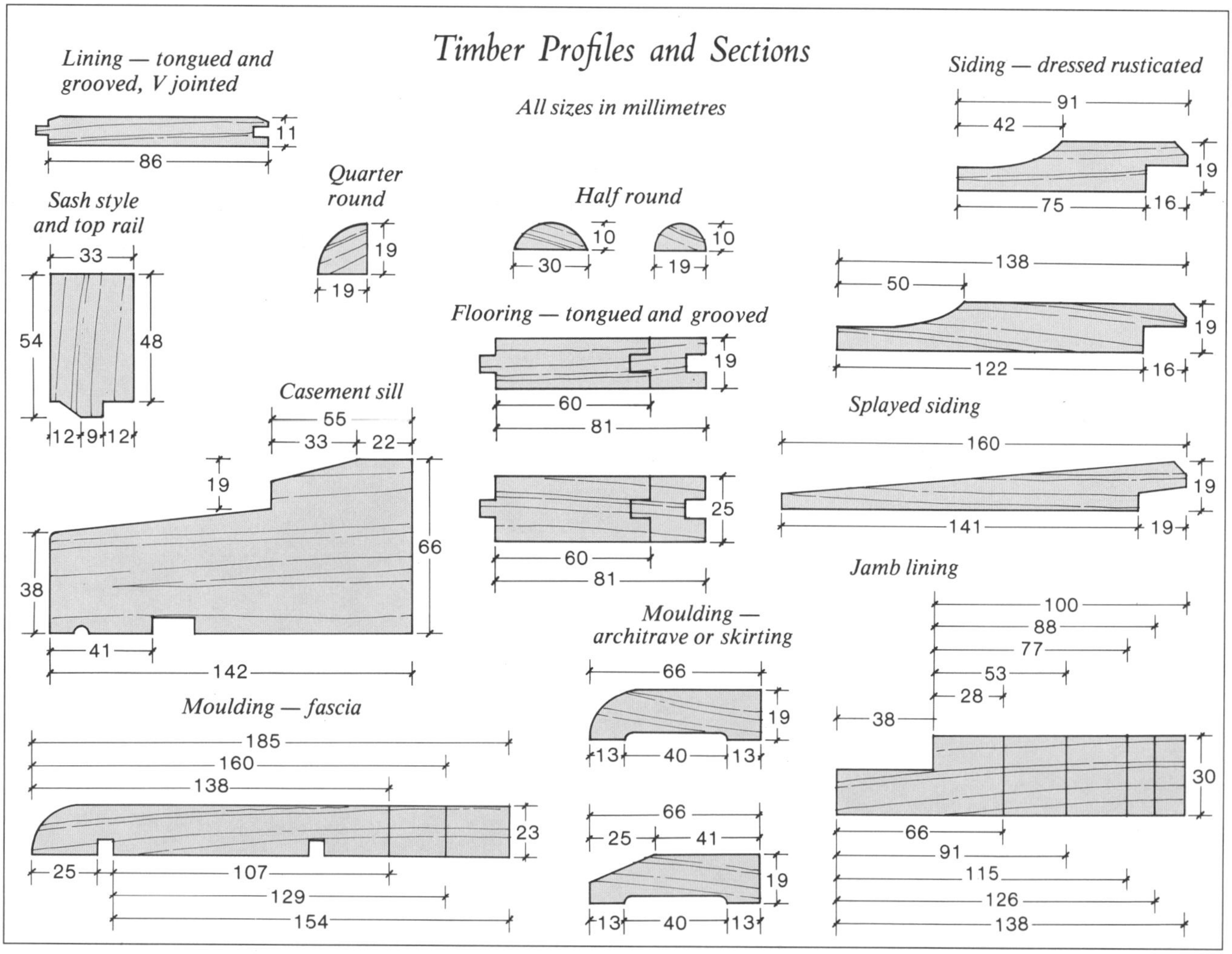

sawn, that is, straight off the saw (which gives a rough but even finish) or dressed (that is, fed through a thicknesser so the wood is smooth and usually only requires some sandpapering before applying a finish). Dressed timber is more expensive than sawn not only because of the extra work involved but also because dressed timber is usually better seasoned (has a lower moisture content to lessen the potential shrinkage).

Common sections

Battens range from 25 mm × 25 mm (1 × 1) through the popular 50 mm × 25 mm (2 × 1) up to 75 mm × 38 mm (3 × 1½). In a sawn state they are often used for roofing, and when dressed, for supporting shelves.

Scantlings typically range from 75 × 50 mm up to 300 × 75 mm and in a sawn form make up the bulk of structural timbers such as joists, bearers, plates, studs, noggings, ceiling joists, rafters, etc. When dressed they are used for posts, handrails, etc.

Common profiles

Jamb. The frame a door hangs in is made from jamb material. It has milled into its surface a single or double rebate (which can also be formed by nailing on a stop). Entry doors usually have heavier jamb sections than internal ones.

Architraves are trims that fit around doors and windows and provide an attractive finish.

Skirting hides the joint between the flooring and the internal walls. It is usually wider than the architrave and should have the same profile.

Quarter round (quad) is a useful mould, which ranges from 50 mm (2 inches) down to 13 mm (½ inch), finishes off a variety of right angle corners.

Flooring. The tongued and grooved joint hides shrinkage and seals out draughts and dampness. Widths range from 75 mm (3 inches) up to 150 mm (six inches). It comes in both hardwoods and softwoods.

Sill is found at the bottom of a window and is often made from tallowwood. This profile is milled to suit the type of window (box frame, casement, etc) and the type of wall frame (brick veneer, timber frame, etc). The slope helps to shed water while the small groove underneath it forms a drip which stops the water from running underneath.

Window head and stile. Rebated like a jamb, this profile is used for the side and top members of timber window frames (not box frames, which are made up from a number of different profiles).

Sash stock is used to make the frame that the glass fits in. It comes in a variety of sizes and mould shapes depending on the size of the window. Typically the lowest member (the bottom rail) is wider than the sides (the stiles) and the top rail.

Linings. Thinner than flooring but having the same tongued and grooved joints (unless it's shiplap), linings come in a variety of timber species and are used for feature walls and ceilings. The edges are often veed so that shrinkage gaps are less obvious.

Fascias. Nailed to the ends of the rafters, these dressed and often bullnosed (quarter round) profiles are grooved at the back to take the eave lining (which is usually fibrous cement).

Sidings. Often known as weatherboards, they are available in a variety of profiles (splayed, rusticated, log cabin) and widths. Splayed ones are usually sawn.

Few materials possess the warmth and variety of timber, here used for kitchen cupboards.

Ordering Timber

For small orders, timber is usually sold in linear metres which run in increments of 0.3 of a metre, with the shortest length available being 1.8 m. This means that the sizes will run: 1.8 m, 2.1 m, 2.4 m, 2.7 m, 3.0 m, etc. However, this practice varies with each timber yard and they will often take orders in imperial sizes and sell lengths shorter than 1.8 m.

To check whether you have an orderable length, simply divide the length you want by 3. Say you need a 4.3 m length, 4.3 divided by 3 is uneven so take it up to a measurement that divides exactly by 3: 4.4 doesn't work but 4.5 does. So the length you will have to order and pay for is 4.5 m (this is not really such a waste because the ends of the timber may well have splits and having the bit extra assists you to cut them out).

Keep in mind also that when you order, say, a length 100 x 50 mm, sawn it will end up around 95 mm x 46 mm and, when dressed, 91 mm x 41 mm. You pay for the wastage! Such is life.

Bricks

Used for 7000 years, few products have as much diversity and application as bricks. Ranging from the many-coloured and multi-textured face bricks to common bricks suitable for rendering and use in unseen locations and thence to the ubiquitous pavers, masonry is used extensively in residential construction for structural and feature walls.

Because the basic ingredient is clay, bricks are relatively cheap (although professional laying is not) and supply, except for building boom times, is usually good. Clay, with a little help from other additives, yields an amazing range of colours from white and yellow, through all the pinks, reds and light to dark browns to the clinkers, which are almost black.

Baked in kilns at extremely high temperatures, bricks are a virtually indestructible building material, except where exposed to high salt-water inundation, say near coastlines and swimming pools. Specially made bricks should be used in those situations.

Brickwork, assuming it has been properly manufactured, relies for its strength on four things:

- A good underlying foundation, one that is consistent throughout and, ideally, stable (clay, for example, is often a problem).
- A good concrete footing, one that is of adequate dimensions and properly reinforced.
- High quality laying using a properly proportioned and well-mixed mortar.
- Room to expand (bricks grow over time as each bone-dry unit gradually absorbs moisture).

Brickwork requires little or no maintenance and, if the colour or texture becomes dated, it can be successfully stuccoed, rendered and painted, or merely painted.

Ordering Bricks

There are approximately 48 bricks per square metre in standard single skin, stretcher bond brickwork (assuming a 10 mm joint). It is wise to allow for at least 10% wastage to allow for chips and breakages (simply multiply the total by 1.1 if you want to add 10%). This means if you have a wall 5 × 2 m, the number of bricks required will be:

5 × 2 = 10 square metres.
10 times 48 = 480 bricks.
480 times 1.1 = 528 bricks.

If the fence is double thickness (230 mm thick) or cavity brick simply double the number (1056).

A corner in stretcher bond

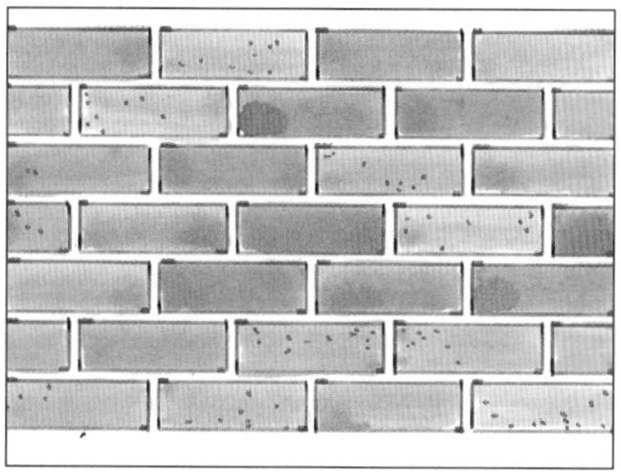

Stretcher bond

Fine brickwork in the wall of a home

Bricks used for paving

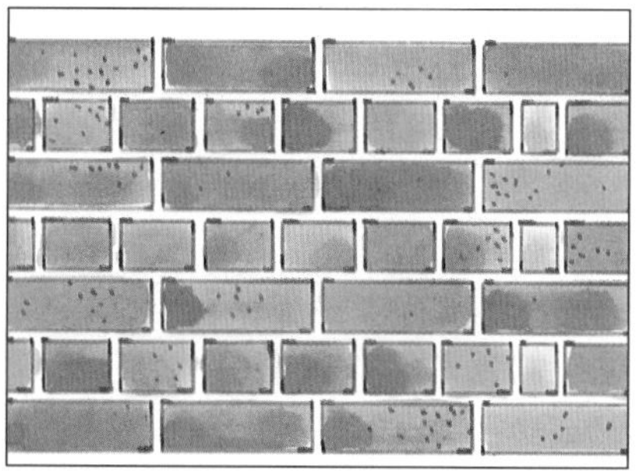

English bond

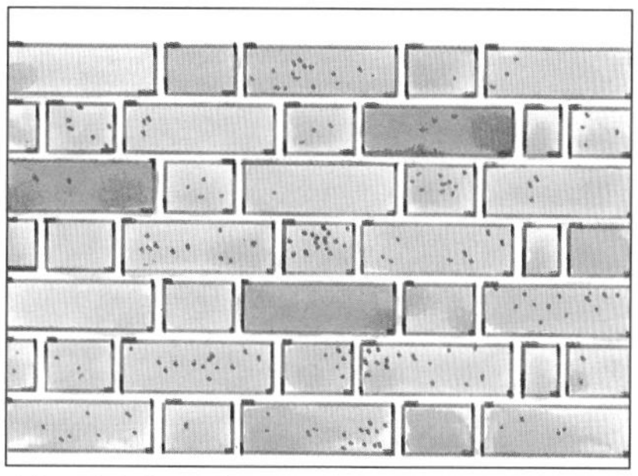

Flemish bond

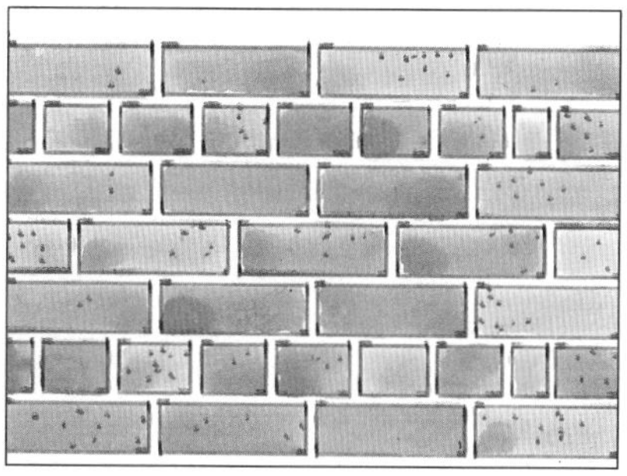

Colonial bond

Building Boards

Building boards, which come in sheets, are made from organic materials combined with various mineral or synthetic ingredients. They are used extensively in home construction for a variety of claddings (the material covering the outside of your house) and linings (materials covering the inside). The products used to make sheet materials are also used to make a variety of tiles, panels, planks, weatherboards, etc.

Because of their diversity, only the main ones will be mentioned and they are presented in terms of softness through to hardness.

Softboard

Once known as Cane-ite because the fibre used was sugar cane, this cheap, low-density building board (now made from radiata pine fibres to which have been added waterproofing agents and binders) has been used for many years as wall and ceiling linings because of its good thermal and fair sound insulating qualities. Another common use is for notice boards. Its soft, pin-absorbing quality comes in part from the light pressing it receives.

It is typically available in sheets of varying thickness (9.5 mm, 12.7 mm, 19.1 mm) and widths (915 mm and 1220 mm). Lengths range from 610 mm up to 3660 mm. It is also manufactured as acoustic tiles and panels.

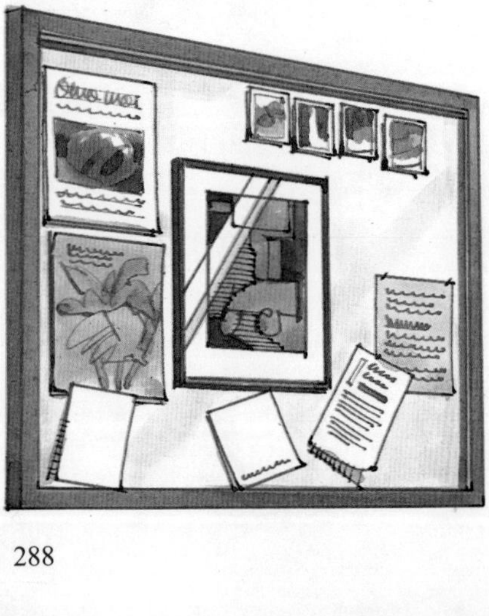

It should not be used in areas of dampness or where it could be subjected to possible damage (such as children's rooms — there steel plate is best!). It can't be flush-jointed successfully (a batten finish is best but don't forget to leave a 2 mm gap between the sheets to allow for expansion) and won't take wallpaper, but it can be painted or covered with fabrics. Termites love it, but then they also like many other timber products too. Its flammability, unfortunately, is high.

Fixing is achieved by nailing, screwing, stapling or gluing. This should only be done after leaving the sheet exposed to the air for a minimum of 24 hours to allow it to absorb moisture. If gluing, shellac the back of the sheet beforehand to ensure adhesion.

Plywood

This medium-density board, made from thin veneers of timber which are peeled or sliced from logs, then dried and glued together under pressure, is a marvellous material which imparts a warm, natural, non-manufactured look. This contrasts well with the flood of plastic and synthetic products that daily threatens to engulf us.

Because the veneers are laid at right angles to each other, great strength is achieved. The fact that cheaper timbers can be used in the core and/or as a backing, keeps the price down while retaining the expensive timber look (even if the appearance is only skin deep).

Because plywood is, in essence, solid timber, it has good insulating qualities and can be easily worked, fixed and finished with clear or opaque coatings. It is typically available from 3 to 25 mm thick, in widths from 900 to 7500 mm, and lengths from 1800 to 2100 mm. The glue used largely determines where it can be used. Interior quality means just that — don't let water near it! If you are putting ply outside use exterior or marine quality.

Particle Board

This product, which comes in many forms, is basically made from myriad flakes of radiata pine which are glued together with resin, then pressed to make a homogeneous, semi-hard, buff-coloured building board. The flakes near the surface are finer than in the centre, giving a smooth finish.

Particle board, in standard form, is not, I repeat, is *not* waterproof and should never be used where there is any likelihood of it getting wet or damp (say under a kitchen bench or in a bathroom). It absorbs water like blotting paper and then bulges alarmingly while it falls apart.

There are on the market other types of particle board which have varying degrees of moisture resistance. Your supplier, if you describe the situation, will make sure you get the product you need.

Like timber, particle board can be planed, sanded, nailed or screwed, and glued. Unlike timber, it is grainless, which lessens the possibility of splitting and it is equally strong in both directions. But it also means that the edges, being rough textured, are difficult to finish. If exposed, they should preferably be edge-stripped with timber. Particle board shelving can be bought already edge-stripped. Alternatively, you can buy particle board shelving already covered on both faces and one edge with a thin layer of laminated plastic.

Sheet sizes typically range from 1500 × 900 mm up to a whopping 3600 × 1200. Thicknesses start at 10 mm, then move to 13 mm, 16 mm, 18 mm, 25 mm, 33 mm and finish at 43 mm.

There is on the market a better quality particle board (Customwood) which, because the wood chips are reduced into individual fibres before the resins and emulsions are added, yields a more finely textured and easily worked panel board with no edge problems. Mouldings such as skirting and architraves are also made from this excellent product.

An effective use of painted wallboard with a timber profile.

Gypsum Plaster

This versatile lining board has largely replaced the old fibrous plaster of yesteryear. Made from a hard core of calcined gypsum which is faced on both sides with a layer of paper, it gives a relatively strong, non-combustible, sound reducing, vermin-proof lining which can be used for walls, ceilings, etc.

Its flexibility allows it to be curved and the surface, if properly prepared, will take most decorative finishes. For wet or humid areas such as bathrooms and laundries, a special water-resistant type of gypsum plasterboard has been developed. This plasterboard can be successfully tiled over.

Gypsum plaster is typically sold in sheets 1200 mm and 1350 mm wide and either 10 mm or 13 mm thick. Standard lengths range from 2400 mm up to 6000 mm. It is important to select the right edge finish. Order recessed edges if you want an invisible joint. The slightly tapered edge makes room for the jointing material and reinforcement, hence disguising the unsightly bulge.

Square edge, usually applied vertically, requires a moulding finish whereas bevelled edge permanently shows a vee-joint. Both of these types are mainly used in commercial work. You can also get a foil-backed version which provides extra insulation as well as creating a vapour barrier (stops water vapour from penetrating into the wall cavity).

Fixing of gypsum plaster sheets is usually achieved either by galvanised clouts, or adhesive, or a combination thereof. Screws are also used and are considered a superior fastener to nails.

Fibre Cement

Using cellulose fibres to replace the extremely hazardous asbestos fibre, this product, known colloquially as 'fibro', has many applications. It comes in sheet form as a lining for water-prone areas, in thick, dense sheets for flooring to wet areas (compressed fibre cement), and in a variety of weatherboard and planked profiles for cladding. Because of the cement content, it has many of the qualities of concrete (hard, durable, fire resistant, termite proof), but, because of the cellulose reinforcing, it is flexible and light in weight.

It is normally nailed to the framing with galvanised flat-head nails (see Fasteners) which are lightly punched and then filled.

Hardboard

High-density wood fibre board, commonly known as hardboard, has many internal lining and external cladding applications around your home. It is made from Australian hardwood which has been reduced to a fine fibre-like consistency. It is impregnated with synthetic resins before being subjected to high heat and pressure.

It is this high heat that, like bricks, dries the product out completely. Twenty-four hours before use, therefore, the back of the sheets should be thoroughly wet so that the initial expansion can take place. If this isn't done, the sheet will gradually absorb moisture from the air and expand on the wall causing buckling or even popping. A gap of nearly 2 mm should be left between sheets and 6 mm between where the sheet meets the floor, walls or ceilings to allow for further expansion.

It comes in sheets (both standard and the more water-resistant and harder 'tempered' type) which have a variety of surface finishes (smooth, timber-grained, sawn, etc.). Sheet sizes, a standard 4.8 mm thick, range from 1220 mm and 1372 mm wide and from 1830 mm up to 3600 mm long. It is also available in weatherboard profiles and as flooring underlay.

Hardboard can be sawn, planed, sandpapered and nailed like normal timber. Joints can be veed, battened or moulded (using PVC or aluminium moulds). Recommended nails should be cadmium-plated and have slightly flattened heads which may be punched and filled.

If painting, seal with approved wallboard sealer first, and then finish with two coats of paint.

Laminates

Plastic laminates are wonderful products that have many uses. They are made from special papers that have been impregnated with resins, then covered with either a melamine-impregnated colour or a printed design paper with a facing of melamine, before being subjected to high heat and pressure.

They come in an amazing variety of colours, textures and patterns. By varying the core and the thickness of the melamine-impregnated surface, the sheets can be used for thin facings or on curved surfaces (0.8 mm), or for hard-wearing bench tops (1.2 mm), or, if 3 mm thick, for unbacked panels which can be used in bathrooms instead of traditional ceramic tiling. By varying the composition solid colours can be achieved, which means that scratches won't show or can be polished out. Changing the chemicals used can also yield surfaces that are static, burn and chemical resistant.

Plastic laminate used to great effect in a kitchen

Laminates come in sheets, panels, or in edging strips. The latter are useful for the do-it-yourselfer who is involved in laminating new work or re-laminating (covering old bench tops and doors with new, up-to-date laminate). Regardless of the form it comes in, it should be carefully handled to avoid cracking or scratching.

Laminates can be cut with a fine, sharp saw or heavily scored with a tungsten-tipped laminate cutter and then laid over a straight edge and bent away from the cut. The edges can be finished with a plane (or file) although for a large job an electric laminate trimmer is handy.

Plastic laminate is usually fixed by gluing with contact glue (the most popular because it grips immediately and pulls the laminate flat) or PVA (which requires a weight to be applied for several hours). The subsurface is most often particle board (use a moisture-resistant one if water or steam is present) or medium-density fibre board.

Plastic laminate should never be cleaned with powder cleaners.

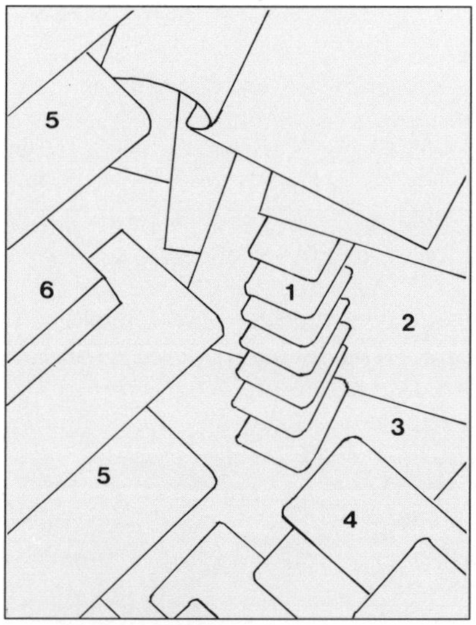

Plastic laminates
1. *Textures and colours imitating natural materials*
2. *and 3. Leathergrain textures*
4. *Printed designs*
5. *Curved edge profiles*
6. *Square edge profile*

Glass

For more than 5000 years, people have known how to make glass. The Egyptians were among the first to make an industry out of it. Though the basic materials haven't changed much, the manufacturing processes have been greatly improved and refined.

The main ingredient is silica which surprisingly is just sand! Other additives include limestone, soda ash and sodium sulphate. Heating the sand mixture up to around 1500°C causes it to melt. In this state it can be blown, spun, drawn, rolled or floated (in a tank of molten tin). The last is now the most common method for making flat glass.

Regardless of the process, the result is a transparent, hard-surfaced, glossy, semi-solid liquid. (Did you know that a pane of glass in time becomes thicker at the bottom than the top?)

The important thing is to get the right glass in the intended position. For example, in high wind areas, glass must be a certain thickness otherwise it may implode (explode inwardly). For access doors, or where a window may be mistaken for an access door, it must by law be laminated safety glass (in case someone runs into it).

Distortion-free glass used in large picture windows should be float (this has largely replaced polished glass). Bathroom and toilet windows should be glazed in patterned or rolled glass which lets in light but not prying eyes. Items such as glass shower screens should be wired or laminated for safety. In areas subject to severe sunlight, heat-absorbent or light and heat reflecting glass can be of great benefit assuming the increased cost can be justified.

If you're going to do some reglazing, the supplier will know what is required assuming you tell him or her where the glass is to be used. When dealing with glass be careful. It's a semi-liquid that cuts!

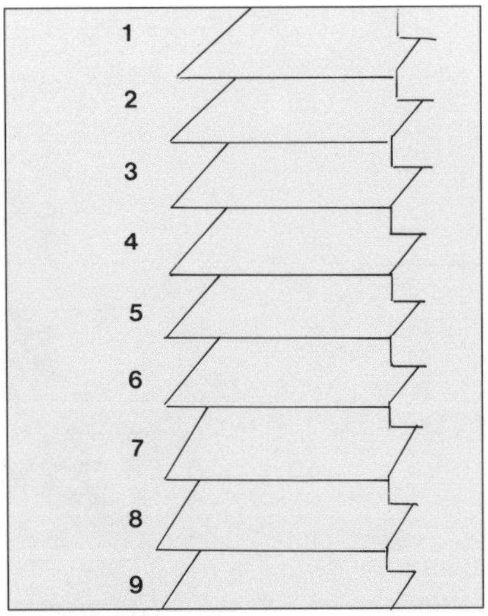

Patterned and wired glass, 3 and 5 mm
1. Clear ribbed
2. Smoked ribbed
3. Square wired, clear
4. Smoked textured
5. Clear textured
6. Rough-textured clear
7. Smoked dimpled
8. Irregularly textured clear
9. Flecked smoked

Concrete

Next to masonry, concrete is one of the oldest building materials, having first been used by the Romans, who used crushed shells (lime) as a binder. Its modern form consists of three basic components: coarse aggregate (gravel), fine aggregate (sand) and a binding agent (cement). When mixed with water, the binding agent generates a chemical reaction which turns it into a powerful 'mineral glue', one which bonds the aggregates together. Concrete, once it has set, continues to gain in strength throughout its life. Its main strength is obtained in 28 days.

The secret to achieving good, strong concrete involves three things.

1. Clean, well-shaped and proportioned aggregates.

A well-shaped aggregate is one with sharp edges (say from crushed material like gravel). Sand should have a mixture of both fine and coarse particles to help fill up the voids between the gravel, hence avoiding thick concentrations of the cement glue which otherwise tends to shrink and crack.

2. Proper measuring and mixing of the dry materials.

Like a cake, maintaining the correct balance of ingredients is essential for good results. For small jobs, bags of pre-mixed concrete are available. For larger jobs, say to 2 cubic metres (over this it is better to order ready-mix), use a volume measure such as a cut-down drum or steel bucket. Mix on a surface that is impervious. A wheelbarrow or concrete mixer is ideal.

If you are mixing it yourself keep in mind that a 1:2½:4 mix (which is ideal for paths and driveways) needs 8 bags of cement, ½ cubic metre of sand and 1 cubic metre of metal to make 1 cubic metre of wet concrete.

3. Clean water.

If you can't drink it, don't use it! The water should be added gradually. Use just enough to make the mix workable. Too much severely weakens the concrete.

Once the concrete is mixed, transport it to the required location, taking care not to shake it too much (because the coarse aggregate may separate from the fine). Place it in position slowly and work it well with a shovel and straight edge. This will bring the bubbles to the surface and compact the mix, thus avoiding honeycombing (a series of interconnected holes). As it begins to harden, a steel (for a smooth finish) or wooden (for a gritty one) float should be used.

If you use reinforcing steel, make sure that you maintain 50 mm minimum clearance from the surface of the concrete to the rods, otherwise the steel may rust and explode the concrete.

Don't allow the concrete to dry out too quickly or it may crack. Once the surface has hardened, periodically hose it during daylight hours or cover it with damp cloth, tarpaulins, or plastic for several days, especially in hot weather.

Pour clean water into well in the middle of concrete mix. Use just enough to make the mix workable.

Wheel the concrete mix carefully and pour it slowly from the wheelbarrow.

Paints

A paint has a twofold purpose: to decorate and protect. Since the advent of the do-it-yourselfer, great progress has been made in producing paints that are easy to apply, long-lasting, and available in a great variety of colours and finishes. The relative cheapness of paint and the startling effect that a new coat of paint can create make it a product that is a boon to the homemaker.

While there is a great deal of information available about paint technology, I'm sure you don't really want to know more than which paint to use on what surface and how to put it on correctly so it will stay there. Later sections tell you how to go about painting a room and rejuvenating the outside of your property.

There are three major types of surface coatings.

Resin-based

Commonly called plastic paints, resin-based paints are made from vinyl, acrylic or polyvinyl acetate (PVA) resins. These paints are water soluble, quick drying, easy to apply, have little odour, and are long lasting. Unlike oil-based paints, they tend to go powdery with age rather than dry out and crack which makes recoating much easier (you don't have to burn or scrape off the old surface as you do with badly deteriorated oil-based paints).

Oil-based

These solvent-borne paints are thinned with mineral turpentine and dry to a hard 'enamel' finish. While the finish is very durable inside a house, unless an exterior surface is frequently recoated the oil can dry out, which can result in blistering, cracking and peeling paint. They are in the main harder to put on, have strong fumes, and cleaning brushes is more difficult.

Polyurethanes

These tough paints are synthetic (a polymer of urethane for the inquisitive), easy to apply and long-lasting.

Before you select a paint, keep in mind where it is going. As a general rule use exterior-type paints wherever the situation is exposed to sun and weather or where extremes of moisture and steam exist (bathrooms, etc.). Elsewhere use the cheaper interior quality paint.

Achieving Good Results

The stability of the home you live in depends to a large extent on having a good foundation. Similarly, the final success of painting depends on the foundation surface, its careful preparation, and the underlying layers of paint supporting the finishing coats. These layers (primers, sealers and undercoats) are often made from the same basic ingredients listed above in paint types but are specially formulated to provide a sound base.

Primers. Oil-based primers penetrate porous surfaces such as are found in timber and other wood products, thereby providing a good key for subsequent layers. Special primers are used for metals.

Sealers. They are used on porous surfaces such as brick, gypsum board and render and are usually plastic-based. They penetrate and seal off the surface.

Undercoats. They are the bridging medium between the primer or sealer and the finish coat. With some plastic paints, the undercoat and final coat are the same.

Finish coats. As the name implies, these are the final coats which impart the colour, surface texture, and sheen (flat, matt, low sheen, semi-gloss and gloss).

Typical Combinations (or Systems)

- Fascias:
  one coat of oil-based primer
  one coat of undercoat (oil-based)
  two coats of enamel.

Or better still

- Fascias:
  one coat of oil-based primer
  two coats of acrylic (semi-gloss or gloss)
- Gypsum Board:
  one coat of sealer (resin-based)
  one coat of undercoat
  one finish coat.

There are many combinations. Make sure when you choose your paint brand and type you read carefully the directions on the can regarding the correct surface preparation and compatible base layers for that product.

Information on surface preparation, painting equipment and techniques is provided in the section on Painting a Room.

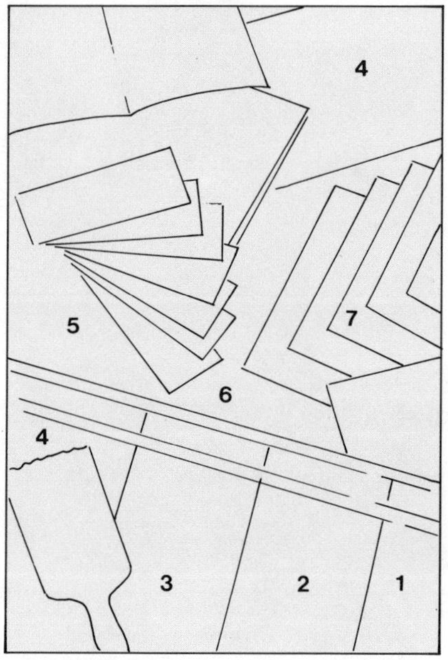

Paint and fabric
1. Raw timber 2. Pink primer
3. Undercoat 4. Enamel gloss finish
5. Semi-gloss enamel 6. Flat acrylic
7. Co-ordinated upholstery fabrics

Fasteners

There is a bewildering array of fasteners on the market. For you, the home handyperson, they may be categorised into three broad groups:

- nails, which are driven with a hammer.
- screws, which are turned with a screwdriver.
- bolts, which usually require a spanner.

Sometimes bolts (and occasionally screws) are used in combination with expanding sleeves, gravity or spring activated toggles and anchors when fixing to masonry or hollow walls.

Keep in mind that for exterior work, hot-dip galvanised fasteners should be used to stop rusting.

Nails

Nails are sold by weight and to order them you should know the length (which must ensure adequate penetration and holding power), the gauge or thickness (to ensure strength), and the head shape (to make sure that the object being nailed is retained).

There are also nails available with special shanks (square, serrated or twisted) to increase their holding power.

For general home maintenance the following types are most commonly used.

Jolt-head. Ranging in length from 15 mm to 150 mm, these general purpose nails can either be left flush with the surface or punched below it and filled.

Flat-head. These come in a variety of head diameters and are used when fixing a softish product (such as fibre boards and plaster) to timber. The bigger head gives better holding power than the jolt-head but cannot be punched as easily or neatly. Common ones are clouts (12 mm to 50 mm), flat-head nails (15 mm to 150 mm) with a serrated head for easy nailing), wallboard nails (15 mm to 25 mm), and fibre cement nails (which have a blunt point to lessen the possibility of splitting).

Panel pin. This fine gauge nail (12 mm to 50 mm) with a small head is excellent for fine joinery and lessens the chance of splitting the timber, especially if nailing near the ends. A hardboard nail is similar to a panel pin but has a diamond-shaped head for an invisible finish.

Screws

Screws, properly installed, have greater holding power than nails but their greatest advantage is that they are easily removed.

Disadvantages are they are more visible, take longer to install, and are more expensive (that's why they are sold by number, not weight).

The major parts of a screw are the head, the shank and the slightly tapered thread. The thread bites into the timber, anchoring itself. Sometimes, for extra strength or for use with metal, the thread is extended right up to the head (e.g. particle board screws and self-tappers).

Screws, like nails, have different heads which relate to the finish required and the material to be fastened. They are recessed to suit the driving system (slot or Phillips head), and are available in a variety of gauges (expressed in numbers) and lengths.

Most screws are made from mild steel (either natural, galvanised, or plated with nickel, zinc, etc.), but, like some nails, are also made in copper, brass, and silicon bronze.

Common types are:

Countersunk. The head of this screw, if the work is recessed with a special bit, can be made flush with the surface.

Raised and round head. A feature is made of this screw head by allowing it to project from the work.

Coach screw. This heavy-gauge screw (25 mm to 200 mm) has a hexagonal head which is turned by a spanner. It is used for heavy jobs like decks and pergolas where strength, not appearance, is the most important factor.

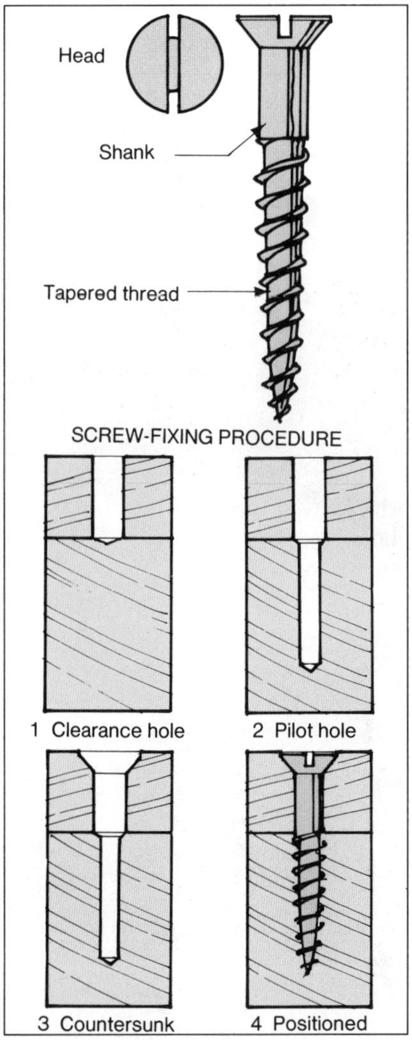

Bolts

Unlike screws, bolts do not cut a thread in the timber or metal but usually project through it and tie into a nut or other threaded material. Unlike screws, the centre core is cylindrical, not tapering, and the threads are much finer. The holding power of bolts in timber can be increased by using suitable washers. The most commonly used types of bolts are:

Hexagon bolts. Available in diameters of 6 to 20 mm and lengths from 20 to 600 mm, hexagon bolts are mainly used for securing heavy timber sections.

Cup bolts. A variation is the round-headed, square-collared cup bolt, which, if the collar grips properly, can be tightened by just turning the nut (no need to hold the head with a spanner). It also gives a slightly neater finish.

Miscellaneous Fasteners

Anchor bolt. A metal or plastic sleeve on the end of the bolt expands to grip concrete, brick or stone around the pre-drilled hole. Diameters range from 6 to 25 mm and lengths from 50 to 300 mm.

Toggles. Using bolts which fit into a threaded toggle, these handy little devices can be poked through a hole in a hollow wall where gravity or springs expand the toggle. Tightening the bolt locks the arms against the back of the hollow material.

Anchors. Using basically the same principle as toggles, they employ a plastic or nylon sleeve to lock the bolt or screw.

Screw hooks and eyes. Used for hanging pictures, etc., these multi-shaped, screw-threaded items can be screwed into timber framing or, in masonry walls, plugs.

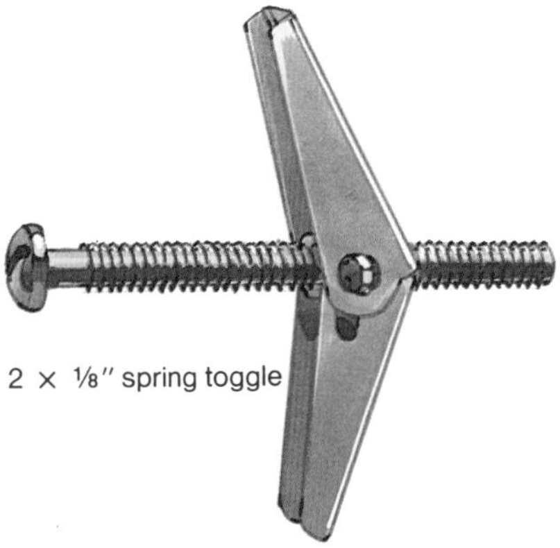

2 × 1/8″ spring toggle

Screw hooks and eye

1 1/2″ flat-head nail

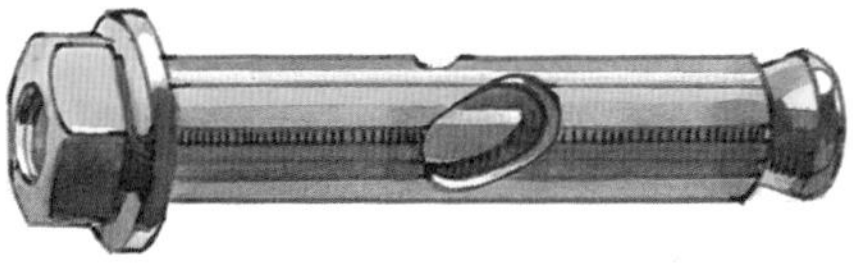

2″ masonry bolt

1 1/2″ jolt-head nail

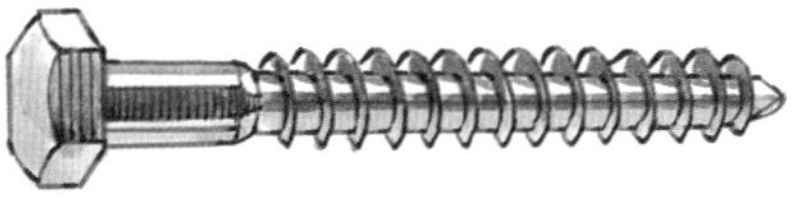

2 × 1/4″ coach screw

1″ panel pin

2 × 1/4″ cut-head bolt

1 × 3/16″ round head screw

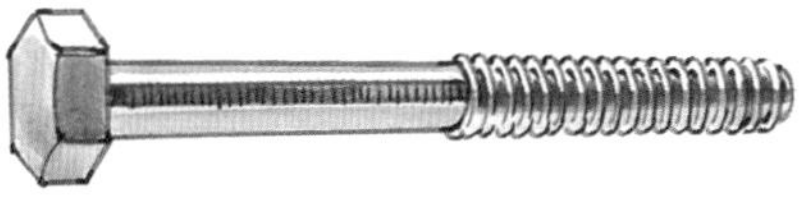

2 × 1/4″ hexagon-headed bolt

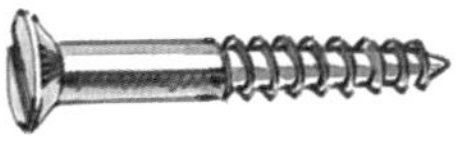

1 1/4″ countersunk woodscrew

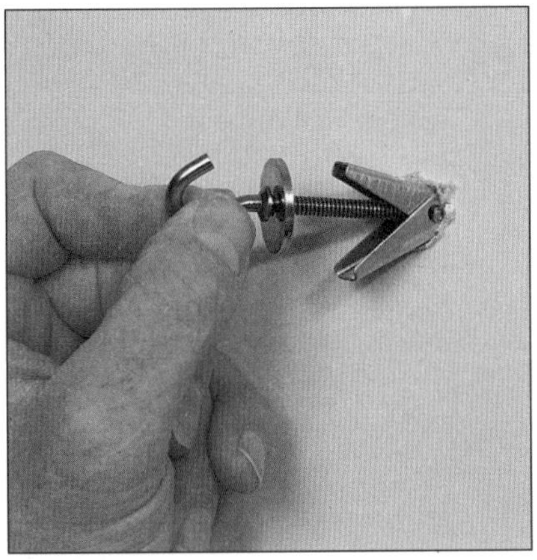

A hook with a spring toggle for use in a hollow wall.

A bolt projects through the timber it is in and ties into a nut.

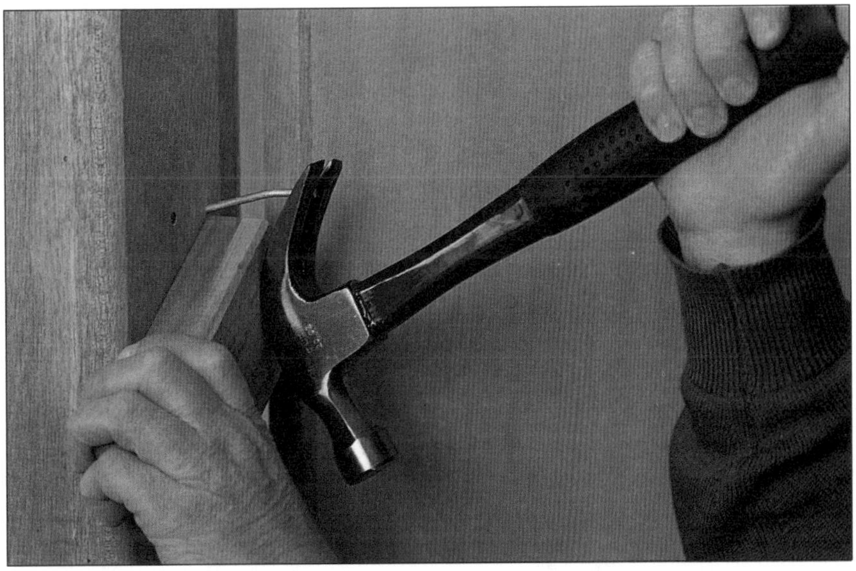

To pull out a nail use the claw end of a hammer and protect the surface with an odd scrap of wood.

Glues

Glues are products that, used properly, can save you a small fortune by restoring broken and faulty household items to a close replica of their former glory.

Unlike the old days of messy glue pots containing boiled down animal hides, etc., there are now on the market a large number of easily mixed and applied types. I will discuss the three most useful ones (and one minor one) for the home and how they should be used. Remember that they are much cheaper if bought in large amounts.

The rules for preparing any surface for gluing are simple. The surface must be totally clean, dry, and, for best results, roughened slightly with a suitable abrasive paper.

Epoxy Resin

This is the glue with the greatest universal application. Unfortunately, it is also the most expensive. This two-part adhesive can be bought in tubes for small jobs or tins for larger applications. When mixed properly, it sets to a hard finish which is tremendously strong, water-resistant, non-staining, gap-filling, heat-resistant and it sticks to virtually everything (excluding thermoplastics). It is excellent for mending glassware, china, metal, wood, etc. as well as for exterior applications.

It sets quickly (in about one hour depending on the temperature) but for special jobs which don't require great strength you can get one that sets in five minutes (although the strength suffers). However, full strength is not achieved for 24 hours.

When using epoxy, care must be taken to mix equal quantities of each part on an impervious (waterproof) surface. A plastic, glass or ceramic lid is ideal but select one that can be thrown away. After you've squeezed out a line of equal length from each tube (or equal scoops from tins), watch you don't get the container tops mixed or you'll never get them off! Use a paddle-pop stick as a stirrer and mix thoroughly.

Smear the adhesive thinly on both surfaces making sure you don't get the glue on your skin (it can cause dermatitis) or inhale the vapours (they're toxic). Use plastic gloves if it's an awkward job. Compress the surfaces together if possible, using a clamp, or put them between newspapers under a pile of books. Rounded items like the pieces of a teapot or coffee mug can be temporarily held in place with masking tape.

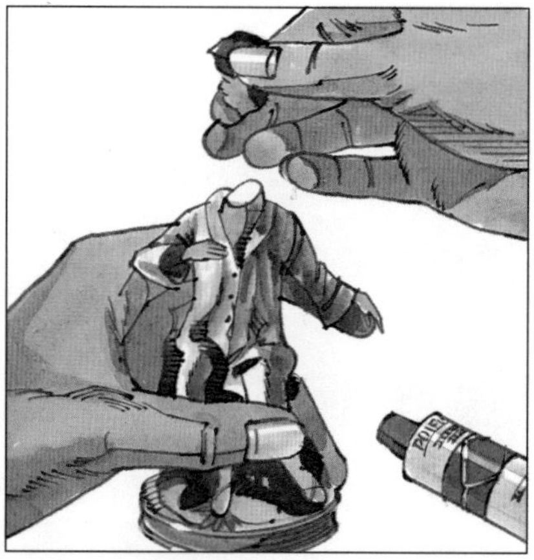

PVA Adhesives

This multi-purpose, non-toxic, one-part, medium strength white glue is cheap and very useful for sticking wood, some plastics (polyvinyls), and paper. It's also easy to wipe off. It's not recommended for use where moisture can get into a joint or where timber staining could be a problem. It's good for fixing wooden toys and for positions where you need a glue to run into a joint (such as in a wobbly table or chair leg). Apply glue liberally to one surface only and clamp surfaces while drying for 12 hours. Wipe off excess glue immediately.

Unlike epoxy, this product does not pose any health hazards.

Contact Glue

This one-part glue is useful for a large number of jobs, but is not ideal for timber joints, glass or ceramics. Its major advantage is that it is self-cramping — once it grips it won't let go! Cheaper than epoxy, it can be used to glue many things (it is especially good for sticking plastic laminate). It lacks the strength of epoxy and is not gap-filling but it remains flexible so it can be used on substances like rubber, leather and textiles.

It is brushed or spread on both surfaces (porous surfaces require two coats) and left until it is touch dry (no longer sticky). Then carefully align the two surfaces and place them together. Bingo! They're stuck. If you're unsure of the alignment, use some plastic or wooden spacers to help you line it up, then gradually withdraw them. Light pressure can assist the bond.

Acrylic Glue

This product, often called Liquid Nails (trade name), is available in tubes or, for large jobs, a cartridge. It can be used for a variety of jobs which involve bonding porous and even damp materials such as timber, plaster, fibrous cement, ceramics, masonry, etc., to each other. Made from acrylic, and looking like brown toothpaste, this adhesive is squeezed on in dobs or beads. The materials to be glued should then be held with temporary fasteners until the adhesive dries. It's handy to have a tube of this versatile product around.

With these glues you can confidently attack most household repairs. For special jobs check with your hardware store or contact the adhesive manufacturers. They happily supply technical information free of charge.

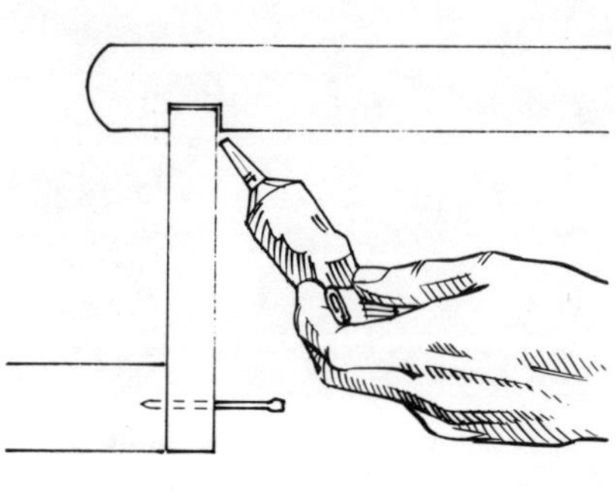

Fillers and Caulkers

Fillers are products that, as the name implies, fill cracks, holes and dents in building materials. Sealants, just as obviously, stop the ingress or egress of water, draughts, odours, etc.

Fillers typically fall into two major categories: oil-moistened and water-moistened. The most common oil-moistened filler is putty. Made from whiting and linseed oil, this useful product can be used to fill smallish holes in timber. It forms a skin on the top that will take paint but will remain soft underneath and won't crack because the oil stops it being totally dried out by the timber. Interestingly, when putty is used for glazing, it becomes a sealant as well as a filler.

Exterior and interior quality water-moistened fillers are often made from cellulose (the main constituent of wood), PVA, acrylic or cement. Mixed to a putty or paste-like consistency (or bought ready-mixed), when applied to cracks in render, plaster, wood etc., they dry to a hard, non-shrinking finish which can be nailed or screwed into and sanded smooth. Large patches should be primed with an oil-based undercoat or sealer.

One of the most useful sealant/caulkers on the market today is made from silicone. It remains flexible, allowing differential movement without cracking. With various additives, it can be applied to most surfaces where it forms a skin in 10 minutes, cures in 24 hours, but shouldn't dry out or crack for two decades! It comes in a translucent colour for a virtually invisible joint as well as grey (for concrete), white (for around baths) and bronze (for brown aluminium windows). Special types can be painted over. Other common sealants have bitumen or butyl rubber bases.

Surfaces to be sealed should be clean, sound (no rust or flaking), fully cured and dry. Silicone joints should ideally be no more than 6 to 12 mm in cross-section.

Here a hardening wood filler is being used to fill a hole in floorboards. If a hole is too large, glue in a block.

Index

Page numbers in italics refer to illustrations

This edition published by Murdoch Books® and distributed by
The Book Company International Pty Ltd
9/9-13 Winbourne Road
Brookvale, Sydney, NSW, Australia 2100

Published September 1994

Published by Murdoch Books®, a division of Murdoch Magazines Pty Ltd,
213 Miller Street, North Sydney NSW 2060

Designers: Leong Chan, Dawn Daly, Warren Penney
Editor: Lynn R. Humphries
Photographs: Better Homes and Gardens® Picture Library, Geoffrey Burnie,
Steve Clementson, Per Dalsgard, Per Ericson, Tony Fragar, R. Goard,
Ray Joyce, Stirling Macoboy, Andrew Payne, D. Ralph, R. Hyett Stubbings,
Hyett Trethewan, Rodney Weidland
Illustrations: David Stokan, Diane Bradley

Publisher: Anne Wilson
Publishing Manager: Mark Newman
Managing Editor: Susan Tomnay
Art Director: Lena Lowe
Production Manager: Catie Ziller
Marketing Manager: Mark Smith
National Sales Manager: Keith Watson
Photo Librarian: Dianne Bedford

National Library of Australia
Cataloguing-in-Publication Data
Smith, Dennis M. (Dennis Maxwell), 1939–
The essential do-it-yourself manual: a complete guide for the home handyman.
Includes index.
ISBN 0 86411 436 2.
1. Garden structures – Design and construction. 2. Dwellings – Maintenance and repair – Amateurs' manuals. I. Smith, Dennis M. (Dennis Maxwell), 1939– . Backyard project book. II. Smith, Dennis M. (Dennis Maxwell), 1939– . Home repairs and maintenance. III. Smith, Dennis M. (Dennis Maxwell), 1939– . Easy home projects. IV. Title. V. Title: Backyard project book. VI. Title: Home repairs and maintenance. VII. Title: Easy home projects.
643.7

Produced by Mandarin Offset, Hong Kong
Printed in China